KARL BARTH AND
PENTECOSTAL THEOLOGY

T&T Clark Systematic Pentecostal and Charismatic Theology

Series editors

Wolfgang Vondey
Daniela C. Augustine

KARL BARTH AND PENTECOSTAL THEOLOGY

A Convergence of the Word and the Spirit

Edited by
Frank D. Macchia, Terry L. Cross,
and Andrew K. Gabriel

t&tclark
LONDON • NEW YORK • OXFORD • NEW DELHI • SYDNEY

T&T CLARK

Bloomsbury Publishing Plc, 50 Bedford Square, London, WC1B 3DP, UK
Bloomsbury Publishing Inc, 1359 Broadway, New York, NY 10018, USA
Bloomsbury Publishing Ireland, 29 Earlsfort Terrace, Dublin 2, D02 AY28, Ireland

BLOOMSBURY, T&T CLARK and the T&T Clark logo are trademarks of Bloomsbury Publishing Plc

First published in Great Britain 2024
Paperback edition published 2025

Copyright © Frank D. Macchia, Terry L. Cross, Andrew K. Gabriel, and Contributors, 2024

Frank D. Macchia, Terry L. Cross, Andrew K. Gabriel, and Contributors have asserted their rights under the Copyright, Designs and Patents Act, 1988, to be identified as Authors of this work.

Cover design by Anna Berzovan
Cover image © naqiewei / GettyImages

All rights reserved. No part of this publication may be: i) reproduced or transmitted in any form, electronic or mechanical, including photocopying, recording or by means of any information storage or retrieval system without prior permission in writing from the publishers; or ii) used or reproduced in any way for the training, development or operation of artificial intelligence (AI) technologies, including generative AI technologies. The rights holders expressly reserve this publication from the text and data mining exception as per Article 4(3) of the Digital Single Market Directive (EU) 2019/790.

Bloomsbury Publishing Plc does not have any control over, or responsibility for, any thirdparty websites referred to or in this book. All internet addresses given in this book were correct at the time of going to press. The author and publisher regret any inconvenience caused if addresses have changed or sites have ceased to exist, but can accept no responsibility for any such changes.

A catalogue record for this book is available from the British Library.

Library of Congress Cataloging-in-Publication Data
Names: Cross, Terry L., editor. | Gabriel, Andrew K., editor. | Macchia, Frank D., 1952-editor.
Title: Karl Barth and Pentecostal theology : a convergence of the world and the spirit / edited by Frank D. Macchia, Terry L. Cross, and Andrew K. Gabriel.
Description: London ; New York : T&T Clark, 2024. | Series: T&t clark systematic pentecostal and charismatic theology | Includes bibliographical references and index.
Identifiers: LCCN 2023038571 (print) | LCCN 2023038572 (ebook) | ISBN 9780567686008 (hardback) | ISBN 9780567714657 (paperback) | ISBN 9780567686015 (pdf) | ISBN 9780567686022 (epub)
Subjects: LCSH: Barth, Karl, 1886-1968. | Political theology.
Classification: LCC BX4827.B3 K337 2024 (print) | LCC BX4827.B3 (ebook) | DDC 269/.4–dc23/eng/20231226
LC record available at https://lccn.loc.gov/2023038571
LC ebook record available at https://lccn.loc.gov/2023038572

ISBN: HB: 978-0-5676-8600-8
PB: 978-0-5677-1465-7
ePDF: 978-0-5676-8601-5
ePUB: 978-0-5676-8602-2

Series: T&T Clark Systematic Pentecostal and Charismatic Theology

Typeset by Deanta Global Publishing Services, Chennai, India

For product safety related questions contact productsafety@bloomsbury.com.

To find out more about our authors and books visit www.bloomsbury.com and sign up for our newsletters.

CONTENTS

Chapter 1
A CONVERGENCE OF THE WORD AND THE SPIRIT: AN INTRODUCTION   1
   Frank D. Macchia, Terry L. Cross, and Andrew K. Gabriel

Part One
THEOLOGY AND REVELATION

Chapter 2
THEOLOGY AS A POINTING FINGER: BARTH AND PENTECOSTALISM
ON THE NATURE OF THEOLOGY   9
   Todd Pokrifka

Chapter 3
REVELATION AS ENCOUNTER: KARL BARTH, PNEUMATOLOGICAL
REALISM, AND THE PENTECOSTAL NOTION OF *PROPHETIC* PREACHING   29
   Gary Tyra

Part Two
GOD AND CREATION

Chapter 4
ONENESS PENTECOSTALS AND KARL BARTH: THEOLOGICAL
COUSINS WHO NEVER MET?   47
   David A. Reed

Chapter 5
BARTH AND PENTECOSTALS ON THE DIVINE PERFECTIONS OF
(IM)MUTABILITY AND (IM)PASSIBILITY: CHRIST, THE SPIRIT, AND
THE DIVINE ATTRIBUTES   63
   Andrew K. Gabriel

Chapter 6
BARTH, ELECTION, AND THE SPIRIT   78
   William Atkinson

Chapter 7
EMPOWERED BY THE SPIRIT: A PNEUMATOLOGICAL REVISION OF
KARL BARTH'S THEOLOGICAL ANTHROPOLOGY   91
   Lisa P. Stephenson

Part Three
CHRIST AND SALVATION

Chapter 8
JESUS THE SPIRIT BAPTIZER: A PENTECOSTAL REVISION OF KARL BARTH'S SPIRIT CHRISTOLOGY — 107
  Frank D. Macchia

Chapter 9
GIVING THE DEVIL (NO MORE THAN) HIS DUE: KARL BARTH, PENTECOSTALISM, AND THE DEMONIC — 124
  Michael J. McClymond

Chapter 10
SUBJECTS AND PREDICATES: BARTHIAN GRAMMAR AND PENTECOSTAL SOTERIOLOGY — 143
  David J. Courey

Chapter 11
SLAMMING THE DOOR AND CRACKING A WINDOW? PNEUMATOLOGICAL INVESTIGATIONS FOR POSSIBLE OPENINGS IN KARL BARTH'S GENERALLY CLOSED THEOLOGY OF RELIGIONS — 160
  Tony Richie

Chapter 12
BARTH, PENTECOSTALISM, AND THE ESCHATOLOGICAL CRY FOR THE KINGDOM — 176
  Christian T. Collins Winn

Part Four
HOLY SPIRIT AND THE CHURCH

Chapter 13
SPIRIT, LOVE, AND CHARISMA: PNEUMATOLOGY IN THE THEOLOGY OF KARL BARTH AND PENTECOSTALISM — 199
  Peter Althouse

Chapter 14
LET THE CHURCH BE THE CHURCH: BARTH AND PENTECOSTALS ON ECCLESIOLOGY — 213
  Terry L. Cross

Chapter 15
YOU WONDER WHERE THE REAL PRESENCE WENT: THE SACRAMENTS AND THE PENTECOSTAL EXPERIENCE OF GOD — 232
  Chris E. W. Green

List of Contributors — 247
Index — 249

Chapter 1

A CONVERGENCE OF THE WORD AND THE SPIRIT

AN INTRODUCTION

Frank D. Macchia, Terry L. Cross, and Andrew K. Gabriel

This volume brings Pentecostal scholarship into conversation with Karl Barth's theology. It is long overdue, for Karl Barth (1886–1968) is recognized as one of the most influential Christian theologians of the twentieth century. And, similarly, there is no doubt that Pentecostalism has had a significant impact on contemporary Christianity. Over the last century the movement has grown from consisting of a small number of revivals to representing over a quarter of the world's Christians.

Barth and Pentecostals share some important common theological interests. Barth's mature theology has a decidedly christological emphasis. Likewise, historically Pentecostals have often spoken of a "full gospel" with an emphasis on Christ as savior, healer, baptizer (in the Spirit), and soon-and-coming King, with some Pentecostal traditions also adding a fifth emphasis on Christ the sanctifier.

With respect to the Holy Spirit, Barth was open to the Pentecostal experience of Spirit baptism, including glossolalia.[1] However, in his only published remarks on Pentecostalism (in response to a question from a group of Mennonites in 1967), Barth was ambivalent about the movement. He said, "we cannot have enough Pentecost, right?"[2] Barth then mentions meeting an American Pentecostal (probably David du Plessis). Barth elaborated on the spread of Pentecostalism in South America: "It is quite necessary that someone draws attention to the fact that we all need the Holy Spirit. When ones does that, and then something from Pentecost becomes visible again, how can we say something against it? There is nothing to be said against it." As long as these visible signs of Pentecost are judged as justifiable, Barth noted that "we want to praise and thank God that there is a Pentecostal movement." Barth also mentions reading du Plessis's newsletters,

---

1. As reported by David du Plessis in "Agora Talks to David du Plessis," *Agora* 2, no. 1 (Summer 1978): 11.

2. Karl Barth, "Conversation with Mennonites: December 13, 1967," in *Barth in Conversation: Volume 3, 1964–1968*, ed. Eberhard Busch, Darrell L. Guder, Matthias Gockel, trans. The Translation Fellows of the Center for Barth Studies, Princeton Theological Seminary (Louisville: Westminster John Knox Press, 2019), 288.

which talk about the numbers of conversions and the numbers of people who came to meetings. "The language is like that of an accountant," remarked Barth. In this accounting for meetings, it no longer "tastes like the Holy Spirit," but rather "like circus or cinema."[3] Yet concluding this exchange, Barth admits that he knows too little about the Pentecostal movement. Reflecting the wisdom of Gamaliel in the book of Acts, he notes that the church should not be afraid of these Pentecostals. If Pentecostals emphasize that we need the Holy Spirit in our churches, then "there is nothing to say against it; everything speaks for it. If it is aboveboard, then we want to praise and thank God that there is a Pentecostal movement. But one would have to see it up close, how things are done there."[4]

Near the end of his life, Barth anticipated

> the possibility of a theology of the third article, a theology where the Holy Spirit would dominate and be decisive. Everything that one believes, reflects, and says about God the Father and God the Son in understanding the first and second articles would be demonstrated and clarified basically through God the Holy Spirit. . . . I give only indications of what I occasionally dream of regarding the future of theology.[5]

The realization of Barth's dream is no doubt coming to pass in part through the development of Pentecostal theology in as much as pneumatological theology (exploring how pneumatology affects, supplements, and might reform other doctrines) is one emerging paradigm for Pentecostal theology.

The chapters in this volume evaluate and build on Barth's theology from the perspective of Pentecostal theology and, thereby, contribute to constructive Pentecostal systematic theology by using Barth as a valuable dialogue partner. This volume will aid those in the wider theological community in their own constructive efforts as they seek a convergence of the Word and the Spirit in theology. In saying this, we do not mean to imply that Barth is providing the "Word" and Pentecostals are providing "the Spirit." Rather, our sense is that both Barth and Pentecostals have something to contribute when seeking a convergence of the Word and the Spirit. Similarly, Pentecostal ecumenist David du Plessis remarked, "For Barth, the truth in Jesus Christ liberates us from defending ourselves, and the truth of the Word of God continues to unfold to us through the Holy Spirit as we go all the

---

3. Ibid., 288–9.

4. Ibid., 289. See further Frank D. Macchia, "Karl Barth Meets David du Plessis: A New Pentecost or a Theater of the Absurd?" *Pneuma* 23, no. 1 (Spring 2001): 5–8.

5. Karl Barth, "Nachwort," in *Schleiermacher-Auswahl mit einem Nachwort von Karl Barth*, ed. Heinz Bolli (Munich: Siebenstern-Taschenbuch, 1968), 311, as translated in Kilian McDonnell, *The Other Hand of God: The Holy Spirit as the Universal Touch and Goal* (Collegeville: Liturgical Press, 2003), 209.

way toward the full stature of Jesus Christ. That's the best message a pentecostal can discover!"[6]

Scholars of Pentecostalism do not always agree on how to define "Pentecostal." Some emphasize historical ties to the Azusa Street Revival, some emphasize doctrine, others certain experiences of the Spirit. Given this, some use the term Pentecostal to refer to those who identify with and worship within the historic or "classical" Pentecostal denominations, while others use the term Pentecostal to refer to the wider charismatic–Pentecostal movement as a whole. As far as the authors of the chapters in this specific volume, the majority of authors worship within classical Pentecostal denominations and, in many cases, are ordained ministers within their respective denominations. This includes the editors of this book, Frank Macchia, Terry Cross, and Andrew Gabriel, and many of the contributors: Peter Althouse, William Atkinson, David Courey, Tony Richie, Lisa Stephenson, and Gary Tyra. Some of the authors in this book are Pentecostal in the broader sense of the term, in as much as they are not currently members of churches within classical Pentecostal denominations (although some were previously), even though they value and participate in typical Pentecostal experiences of the Spirit. This includes Chris Green (Anglican), Michael McClymond (Anglican), David Reed (Anglican), Todd Pokrifka (nondenominational church), and Christian Collins Winn (Baptist).

In Part One ("Theology and Revelation"), several authors take on an important theme for both Barth and Pentecostals, namely, the doctrine of revelation. In Chapter 2, Todd Pokrifka demonstrates some interesting convergences between Barth and Pentecostals on the nature of theology—in particular as their views relate to Scripture. Utilizing the imagery of the "pointing finger" in the portrait of John the Baptist and the crucifixion by Matthias Grünewald, which was a favorite of Barth's for describing the role of preaching or theology in the church, Pokrifka notes how Pentecostals also stand with a finger pointing to God as a testimony to Christ's work. Looking at Barth's theological method through the fourfold lens of the so-called Wesleyan Quadrilateral, Pokrifka underscores the differences between Barth's method and Pentecostalism. Pokrifka concludes that Pentecostals can help Barth appreciate the role that experience plays in theological method while Barth can help Pentecostals maintain a focus on Christ.

In Chapter 3, Gary Tyra offers a comparison of Barth's pneumatological realism with the Pentecostal concept of "prophetic preaching." Arguing that the Spirit is crucial to Barth's theological realism, Tyra proceeds to describe a pneumatological realism that infuses his theological enterprise. Added to this, Barth's understanding of preaching as a dynamic event of the Spirit who brings an encounter of revelation through the Word becomes a fertile ground for building Pentecostal prophetic preaching.

In Part Two, several authors consider various themes related to God and creation. In Chapter 4, David Reed develops a fruitful, creative dialogue between

---

6. "Agora Talks to David du Plessis," 11.

Barth and Oneness Pentecostals, suggesting that they may be "theological cousins who never met." Their convergence suggests to Reed that they are both "theological particularists," in that they both are committed to the divine initiative in revelation and the demand that humans cannot truly understand God. Scripture, then, becomes the anchor for their theological conceptualizations. While Barth is not a Oneness Christian, Reed thinks his approach to the Trinity would allow for some open space for Oneness Pentecostals to go in their thinking about God.

In Chapter 5, Andrew Gabriel follows Barth's lead by engaging the divine perfections (or divine "attributes") from a trinitarian perspective while challenging Barth and those who follow him to develop a more robustly trinitarian doctrine of the divine perfections by integrating *both* christological and pneumatological insights into this doctrine. Focusing on the doctrines of (im)passibility and (im)mutability, he argues that in Jesus Christ and the Holy Spirit, God suffers impassibly and is immutably constant in every change.

In Chapter 6, William Atkinson provides a clear exposition of Barth's doctrine of election—a doctrine for which Pentecostals usually have some antipathy. Atkinson wonders what adding a consideration of the Spirit for Barth's doctrine of election might have done to enrich it. He plays with these pneumatological "if's" in a creative and insightful way, providing an appreciative assessment of Barth's theology while nudging it toward a fuller conclusion through pneumatological considerations.

In Chapter 7, Lisa Stephenson focuses on Barth's anthropology with an eye toward how one might elaborate on it from a Pentecostal perspective, one that prioritizes the Spirit that brings about a just sharing of life in God. To accomplish this task, Stephenson draws from the Synoptics and especially from Luke–Acts to find in Christ the man of the Spirit who, as Lord, passes the Spirit onto us. The Spirit belongs to Christ uniquely, since Christ is the divine Son on whom the Spirit rested in eternity. Receiving the Spirit upon his human flesh, Christ then bestows the Spirit onto us in grace as pure gift. Humanity, made for a mutual I–Thou encounter that comes from life in the Spirit, finds fulfillment in the gift of new life that Christ provides at Pentecost.

Part Three focuses on Christ and salvation. Frank Macchia seeks to detect implications in Barth's massive treatment of Christology for a Spirit Christology. Significantly, Barth grants the Spirit material significance for Christology. In the person of the God-Man (Christ), God turns in the freedom of the Spirit (the freedom of divine love) to sinful humanity, and humanity is enabled to reach back. More specifically, the Son of God descends at the incarnation and the cross for us into suffering and death (his baptism in fire) so that as the Son of Man he could be exalted for us to communion (baptized in the Spirit). Macchia elaborates on Christ's baptism in fire and Spirit to develop Barth's Spirit Christology, granting in the process Christ's reception of the Spirit at the Jordan, the resurrection, and Pentecost greater material significance in Christ's messianic mission than Barth explicitly allowed.

In Chapter 9, Michael McClymond finds in Barth's demonology a penetrating mystery, the riddle of evil. Rather than viewing Satan as a fallen angel (or anything created), Barth finds in Satan that which God rejects or negates in election as well as in creation and its redemption. Rather than accusing Barth's demonology of granting the divine negation too much explanatory power, McClymond uses the metaphor of a black hole to probe its richer meaning. The demonic in Barth is to be viewed according to McClymond as analogous to black holes, which are formless and destructive of all form, especially in the spiritual lives of humans.

In Chapter 10, David Courey explores the issue of integrating divine initiative and human agency in salvation in Barth's theology. The problem that Courey addresses is whether or not Barth opens adequate space for human agency in salvation. Courey explores this issue in the context of Barth's Spirit Christology, assuming that this issue of agency is for Barth both christologically and pneumatologically determined. One finds in Barth's Spirit Christology, according to Courey, potential for a soteriology that is determined primarily by divine initiative but also, secondarily but still significantly, determined by the contribution of a responsible human response.

Tony Richie tackles the problem of Barth's implicit contrast between revelation and religion in Chapter 11. Is religion opposed to God's self-disclosure in Christ and through the Spirit? Richie notes that the issue is complex. Though Barth, in Richie's reading, does seem at first to slam the door on religion as a witness to divine revelation, Barth seems later to crack open a window to this possibility. Though religion for Barth is to be placed under the criticism of natural theology, Barth implies that by the Spirit religion may yet be used to bear witness to Christ. It is thus pneumatology that holds the most promise for Richie for developing Barth's open window to religion as a positive witness to revelation.

In Chapter 12, Christian Collins Winn engages eschatology through a comparison of Barth's and Pentecostals' theologies of prayer. Given their unique emphases and shared expectation of the coming kingdom of God, Winn presents prayer as an ecstasy of revolt that leads to prophetic and life-giving action.

While pneumatology receives attention throughout the volume, Part Four gives focused attention to the Holy Spirit and the church. In Chapter 13, Peter Althouse draws on Barth's theology of the self-giving Spirit of divine love and Pentecostal theologies of speaking in tongues as an embodied sigh. He presents the gifts of the Spirit as acts of love that promote hope and freedom but also as expressions of lament.

In Chapter 14, Terry Cross engages Barth's theology in an area which is often overlooked, namely, his understanding of the nature and mission of the church. Whereas Pentecostals have tended to limit their approach to ecclesiology to the *mission* of the church, Barth offers them something to consider in his discussion of the *nature* of the church. Basing his view of the church on the doctrine of the triune God, Barth speaks clearly of the relational God who is bent toward the "other." Cross argues that this nature of God is the basis for the mission of God, which in turn should also be the basis for the mission of the church. Conversely, Pentecostals could provide Barth's ecclesiology with a broader appreciation for the encounter with God and the Spirit, who transforms the people of God into the likeness of Christ.

In the book's final chapter, Chris Green observes that Barth's theology of the sacraments in *CD* IV/4, which is in opposition to traditional sacramental theology, might seem to cohere with Pentecostal theology, with its focus on obedience. At the same time, Green draws on aspects of Barth's theology and Pentecostal experience that can lead Pentecostals to recognize the live-giving work of Christ and the incarnational work of God's grace in the Holy Spirit at work in the sacraments.

Our hope is that this whole volume will aid those seeking a convergence of the Word and the Spirit.

Part One

THEOLOGY AND REVELATION

Chapter 2

THEOLOGY AS A POINTING FINGER

BARTH AND PENTECOSTALISM ON THE NATURE OF THEOLOGY

Todd Pokrifka

Introduction

What happens when one brings Barth's approach to the nature of theology into dialogue with Pentecostalism's approach? What are Barth's and Pentecostalism's conceptions of the nature of theology, including its goals, limits, and methods? Where do they converge with and diverge from each other? These questions carry great significance for the practice of theology in the world today. Barth is seen by many to be the leading Protestant Theologian of the twentieth century. Pentecostalism is one of the largest and fastest growing Christian movements of our time. To explore how Barth and Pentecostalism might come together in theological dialogue is therefore one of the important questions facing contemporary theology.

Any attempt to answer these questions must navigate two related problems. First, there is the challenge of apparent incommensurability. Barth is a single theologian and Pentecostalism is a massive global movement. How can we reasonably compare and relate the two? Second, there is the related problem of a unified definition for Pentecostal theology. With all the varied "Pentecostalisms" and theologians that can claim to be Pentecostal, how can we speak of a singular Pentecostal theology?

A provisional solution to these two problems is found in the fact that Pentecostalism, including charismatic and renewalist groups,[1] while not united

---

1. I will use the terms "Pentecostal" and "Pentecostalism" in a way that includes charismatics, "Third-wave" Christians and independents, not merely classical, denominational Pentecostals. My use of the upper case refers to a distinct Christian theological tradition.

in its theological conclusions,[2] is relatively unified in its approach to theology. It is united, I propose with Keith Warrington, in being a "theology of encounter" that is appropriately "experiential" in its sources, methods, and goals.[3] Encounter and experience are loaded terms that I will unpack more fully below, both for Barth and Pentecostalism. For now, it suffices to say that Pentecostal theology in practice possesses certain typical characteristics that mark it as a theological tradition, not least in its approach to the realities of divine encounter and experience. These characteristics enable a comparative study between a broadly Pentecostal approach to theology and Barth's approach to theology.[4]

The seeming incomparability of Barth and Pentecostalism is further reduced by their shared tendency to regard theology as a "pointing finger"—a finger or hand that points or witnesses, not to ourselves, but to God and God's works.[5] That said, the ways in which Barth and Pentecostalism point or testify are distinct and complementary. Barth's approach points primarily to the objective revealing and saving work of Christ attested in Scripture. The Pentecostal approach, in some contrast, testifies in multiple ways to the supernatural, experientially accessible works of Christ and the Spirit.

After I compare Barth's and Pentecostalism's approaches to theology, I will bring them into a dialogue with one another to illuminate their similarities, differences, and complementary contributions. While both point to the breaking in of the triune God as fundamental for theology, Barth points singularly to faith-based knowledge of the objective past revelation of Christ while Pentecostals point beyond this to the prospect of ongoing encounter with God through Jesus and the Spirit.

---

2. Warrington, *Pentecostal Theology: A Theology of Encounter* (New York: T&T Clark, 2008), 18–20.

3. Ibid., 15–16, 20–7, and 48–51. Wolfgang Vondey's *Pentecostal Theology: Living the Full Gospel* (New York: T&T Clark, 2017) represents a similar approach to Warrington's in several ways. He also sees Pentecostal theology as united, not by a set of doctrines, but by an encounter-oriented approach defined by the specific, symbolic event of Pentecost and the "theological narrative" of "the full gospel" (1).

4. For Pentecostalism to be a distinct theological tradition does not require that it has a formal academic style, including explicit methodology or prolegomena.

5. Besides his frequent use of the concept of "witness," Barth uses the metaphor of "pointing" in his 1920 sermon on "Biblical Questions, Insights and Vistas," in Karl Barth, *The Word of God and Theology*, trans. Amy Marga (New York: Bloomsbury/T&T Clark, 2011), 71–100. Douglas Horton originally translated the relevant phrase in 1928 as a "pointing hand," but the recent English translator Amy Marga calls it a "pointing finger" at times and a "pointing hand" at other times. As Terry Cross indicated to me, this is likely because in English we do not really speak of a hand "pointing," but only of the finger that points. The more typical Pentecostal language for this act of pointing or witness to God is the language of testimony.

Describing Barth on the Nature of Theology

Dogmatics, the Word of God, and Dogmatic Criteria

Barth unfolds his view of the nature of theology within his "prolegomena" to *Church Dogmatics* (*CD*) in part-volumes I/1 and I/2,[6] his Doctrine of the Word of God. While this introduction of his indicates how he conceives of theology and its method, it allows him much methodological freedom.[7]

Barth's focus among the theological disciplines was on dogmatic theology or dogmatics.[8] Dogmatics is "the scientific self-examination of the Christian church with respect to the content of its distinctive talk about God."[9] The church conducts this self-examination in the light of the threefold Word of God. Much like the Trinity, there is one Word of God, but it exists in three interrelated and interpenetrating modes or forms.[10] These are the incarnate Word or revelation of Jesus Christ, the written word of Holy Scripture, and the proclaimed Word of the church.[11] When there is agreement between God's Word and human proclamation, there is "dogma." Dogma supplies content for dogmatics, yet dogmatics is also the practice of ongoing critical enquiry into dogma.[12]

In his critical response to natural theology, which Barth regards as different in subject and method from proper dogmatics,[13] Barth offers two criteria for dogmatics. First, Barth's concern for the proper subject or content of theology results in what we could call its *material criterion*. Theology must have "the revelation of Jesus Christ" as its fundamental content. Christian speech about God must always be "tested by its conformity to Christ."[14] Second, Barth's *methodological criterion* is that dogmatics should be fundamentally the "exposition of Holy Scripture."[15] This scriptural method is related to the first, material criterion, since he regards the

---

6. I will use the following conventions to refer to the "paragraphs" and subparagraphs into which Barth divided his *Church Dogmatics* (*CD*): for example, §1, §§1–2, or §1.1.

7. Todd B. Pokrifka, *Redescribing God: The Roles of Scripture, Tradition and Reason in Karl Barth's Doctrines of Divine Unity, Constancy and Eternity* (Eugene: Pickwick Publications, 2010), 47–8.

8. *CD* I/1, 3–44 (§§1–2).

9. Ibid., 3.

10. Ibid., 121 ff. The threefold Word is unfolded in *CD* I/1, 47–292 (§§3–7).

11. *CD* I/1, 88–120.

12. Ibid., 265.

13. Karl Barth and Emil Brunner, *Natural Theology: Comprising "Nature and Grace" by Professor Dr. Emil Brunner and the Reply "No" by Dr. Karl Barth*, trans. Peter Fraenkel (London: Centenary, 1946), 74 ff.

14. *CD* I/1, 13.

15. Barth and Brunner, *Natural Theology*, 74 ff.

scriptural text as the only reliable witness to Jesus Christ. As exposition, theology must avoid "eisegesis," a subtle handmaid of natural theology.[16]

The material criterion keeps the methodological criterion from turning dogmatics into a disparate, disorderly set of comments on various biblical passages. Conversely, the methodological criterion keeps the material criterion from turning dogmatics into a static christological system, because the various parts and authors of Scripture witness to Christ in diverse ways. Further, despite the ordered, interconnected character of Barth's dogmatics, it is not a system because Barth does wish to allow a principle to replace Jesus Christ himself as the dynamic, living center of dogmatics and also because Barth opposes the speculative epistemological assumptions that systems tend to require.[17]

Because theologians can never claim to possess or control the threefold Word of God nor the Spirit, dogmatics is a provisional and reverent human work. Dogmatics cannot proceed "by building with confidence on the foundation of . . . results already achieved," but must always "beginning once again at the beginning."[18] Barth eschews all forms of a priori speculation to engage in reverent, a posteriori reflection on God's actual speech and action.

The Hearing and Proclamation of the Church and of Dogmatics

Barth regards dogmatics as a function of both the "hearing church" (*CD* §23) and the "teaching Church" (*CD* §24).[19] Responding well to God's normative Word first involves hearing it well as it is "mediated" through various sources:[20]

> Dogmatics must be marked by three "attitudes" of hearing: (1) a *biblical attitude*, in which it listens to and follows the example of the biblical witnesses;[21] (2) a *confessional attitude*, in which it reverently listens to the creeds and confessions of the church's tradition, both ecumenical and specifically Evangelical or Reformed;[22] and (3) a *churchly attitude*, in which it listens to the church of today and its situation.[23]

---

16. The theologian must "allow even the detailed words of the text to speak exactly as they stand" (*CD* I/2, 726).

17. *CD* I/2, 861; cf. *CD* I/2, 861 ff; Karl Barth, *Evangelical Theology: An Introduction*, 1st ed. (New York: Holt, Rinehart and Winston, 1963), 180 f, cf. 165; Pokrifka, *Redescribing God*, 50–1, 170–9.

18. Barth, *Evangelical Theology*, 165.

19. *CD* I/2, 797–884.

20. The quote that follows comes from Pokrifka, *Redescribing God*, 48.

21. *CD* I/2, 816–22.

22. Ibid., 822–39. This relates directly to the role of tradition in Barth's method; see below.

23. *CD* I/2, 339–43.

Barth implies that the theologian, as "hearer," should be preoccupied with a set of consistent practices: the respectful, attentive reading of Scripture and traditional theological sources and engagement with the contemporary church.

Then, taking up the task of teaching after (and while) hearing, dogmatics finds its own method (CD §24.2).[24] Dogmatic method or thinking is marked by a dialectical tension between constraint and freedom. It cannot take up just any method, since Jesus Christ "prescribes its way and method."[25] Yet dogmatic method, in its details, is freely chosen, a matter of "arbitrary"[26] yet responsible obedience to revelation. Dogmatics must remain open to the critical and constructive capacity of God's ongoing acts of revelation. Although the Word is known in rational, verbal expression, it also has a personalistic, actualistic character that resists conceptual closure.[27]

Reflection on the Barth's Method as Revealed in His Theological Practice

I have explained how Barth spoke of the nature of the theological task, but how does his actual practice shed light on his approach to theology? One helpful way of uncovering Barth's theological method is to examine his theology through the lens of his usage of four traditional theological sources.[28] How do Scripture, tradition, reason, and experience function and interrelate in Barth's theology? In summary, *Scripture functions as the authoritative source and basis for theology, with tradition, reason, and experience being functionally subordinate to Scripture. Barth employs both direct and indirect ways of relating Scripture and theological proposals, with the indirect ways allowing tradition, reason, and experience to play important mediatory roles in the relationship between Scripture and doctrinal conclusions.*[29] I will explain the roles or functions of each of the four sources in turn.

First, what is the role of Scripture in Barth's theology? Scripture is the authoritative source and basis of Barth's theological work, yet in a way that upholds the ultimate authority of Jesus Christ himself, the Revealed Word. The primary concrete locus in which humans come into contact with Christ is through the words of Scripture. As attesting witness to christocentric revelation, Scripture is God's Word.[30] Accordingly, Scripture has a unique, nonreciprocal capacity to "correct" other sources like tradition, reason, or experience. These sources or

---

24. Ibid., 853–84.
25. Ibid., 856.
26. Ibid., 860 f; Pokrifka, *Redescribing God*, 49, 151–3.
27. For example, *CD* I/2, 862, 872.
28. These four sources are sometimes known as the "Wesleyan Quadrilateral" due to their use in the theology of John Wesley. However, my use of the four sources does not require knowledge of their place in Wesley or his followers.
29. This statement in italics modifies the thesis of my book on Barth, expanding its scope (see Pokrifka, *Redescribing God*, 41–2 and 294).
30. See *CD* I/2, 532.

norms do not function with independent, non-hermeneutical authority. Barth's "principle of subordination" to Scripture[31] applies even in areas of doctrine in which Scripture can only be indirectly applied.[32] Although Barth does not adhere to typical doctrines of the inerrancy or infallibility of Scripture,[33] he works hard to bend his conceptuality and methods into conformity with the biblical witness. In addition to the "christocentric concentration" of his work, there is a "Scriptural concentration" whereby Scripture consistently authorizes his theological proposals.[34]

The four hermeneutical factors of author, referent, text, and readers help us to understand better the use of Scripture in Barth's theology.[35] Without denying their historical situatedness, Barth sees the human *authors* of Scripture as the primary witnesses of God's self-revelation. They point away from themselves to God's christocentric self-revelation as the unifying *referent* or "object" of all they say. Yet the *text* itself is crucial because it is God's chosen means of access to his self-revelation in Christ.[36] *Readers* need to be vivified and illuminated by the Spirit to receive the revelation to which the text points.

Second, what is the role of tradition for Barth? Church tradition has either a positive or a negative role to play, depending on its degree of perceived conformity to the Scripture-attested, Spirit-illumined Word of God.[37] Positively, traditions like the early ecumenical creeds or Reformed confessions function as a guide for Barth's dogmatics, reinforcing the christological and soteriological realities to which Scripture points. Negatively, tradition sometimes acts as an example of ways the church has failed to hear the Word of God. For example, in CD II/1, Barth offers extended critiques of *analogia entis*, natural theology, and the anthropocentrism of neo-Protestantism. Barth regards the theologian's relationship with tradition as similar to one's relationship with one's natural parents: honor, but without slavish obedience.[38]

---

31. CD I/2, 722; Pokrifka, *Redescribing God*, 59–62.

32. Pokrifka, *Redescribing God*, 65–8, 295 ff.

33. Following Bruce McCormack, Barth may hold to Scripture's "dynamic infallibilism." See Frank D. Macchia, "God Says What the Text Says: Another Look at Karl Barth's View of Scripture," in *Karl Barth and the Future of Evangelical Theology*, ed. Christian T. Collins Winn and John L. Drury (Eugene: Wipf and Stock, 2014), 202.

34. Pokrifka, *Redescribing God*, 296–8.

35. See Todd Pokrifka, "The Role of the Spirit in Interpretation: An Ecumenical and Comparative Discussion of Karl Barth and Kenneth Archer" (Unpublished paper, 2014), 4–37. For a helpful summary of Barth's hermeneutics, see Stanley E. Porter and Jason C. Robinson, *Hermeneutics: An Introduction to Interpretative Theory* (Grand Rapids: Eerdmans, 2011), 214–26, especially 220–3.

36. Macchia, "God Says What the Text Says," 195–5.

37. Pokrifka, *Redescribing God*, 72–87.

38. Karl Barth, CD I/2, 585 ff.

Third, what is the role of reason?[39] Barth is committed to faithful reasoning as an expression of our obedient witness to God's revelation. God is known and thus can be known,[40] which allows for rational dogmatic talk about God. Yet, because the knowability of God is based on the actuality of God's miraculous self-revelation,[41] reason must conform to revelatory "speech" that takes place "in the mystery of God."[42] God's Word is "impossible" for unaided human capacities.[43] Reason becomes reconciled and obedient to God only through faith. Yet faith rightly seeks rational understanding. Faithful reason has both critical and constructive functions that ensure that our theological concepts and proposals rightly point to God's revelation rather than obscuring it.[44] Dogmatics is not a matter of "parroting" the words of the scriptural witness, but of absorbing their inner logic and then thinking and talking freely in accord with it.[45]

Lastly, what is the role of experience for Barth—a question of particular importance for comparing him with Pentecostal theology? While Barth is generally reticent about ascribing a significant role to experience in theology, there are several ways in which he directly or indirectly acknowledges its place, so long as that experience is governed by revelation. In his treatment of "The Word of God and Experience,"[46] Barth says: "If knowledge of God's Word is possible, this must mean that an experience of God's Word is possible."[47] Such experiences of God's Word involve God's "determination" of humanity,[48] particularly through awakening our knowledge or acknowledgment.[49] The Spirit, as "subjective reality" and "possibility" of revelation,[50] works within people, implying and legitimizing certain experiences. Barth leaves room for God-shaped experiences to which theology should witness, but is keen to deny a role for independent or immediate experience in theology.

First, true experience of God's Word is *not independent* or the product of unaided human capacities. He critiques liberal modern Protestantism for exalting humanity and human religious experience even above the transcendent God and his revelation. Because "experience" was often used by them to refer to the product of independent, universal human capacities, Barth is ambivalent about whether an

---

39. See Pokrifka, *Redescribing God*, 88–105.
40. See *CD* II/1, §§25–6.
41. John E. Colwell, *Actuality and Provisionality: Eternity and Election in the Theology of Karl Barth* (Edinburgh: Rutherford House Books, 1989), 181–7.
42. *CD* I/1, 125.
43. See the summary on *CD* I/1, 147.
44. Pokrifka, *Redescribing God*, 90–2.
45. *CD* I/2, 718; Pokrifka, *Redescribing God*, 60–4.
46. *CD* 198–227 (§6.3).
47. *CD* I/1, 198.
48. Ibid., 200.
49. Ibid., 203.
50. *CD* I/2, 203–79.

authentic human encounter (*Begegnung*) with God should be called an experience. In one place he says an encounter is "more than experience" because it is dependent on God's miraculous work.[51] He also says, "the presence of the Word of God is *not* an experience" but "the divine decision concerning us."[52] He explains, "God Himself decides our past and future, defining our recollection as thankfulness and our expectation as hope."[53] By speaking of thankfulness and hope he clearly refers to human experiences, albeit ones that are dependent on God's initiative. Elsewhere he says as much: "[t]he real experience of the man addressed by God's Word is the very thing that decides and proves that what makes it possible lies *beyond itself*."[54] In the end, Barth affirms the God-dependent experience involved in a faith-based knowledge of Christ and calls theology to testify to God's work in such experiences.[55]

Second, theologically valuable experience is *not immediate* encounter with God, but is mediated by veiled, mysterious self-revelation. God's speech is marked by "secularity,"[56] for it always occurs in and through this-worldly events and media and is only discernable as God's Word by the Spirit's enablement. The mediated nature of revelation leads Barth to a method that resists certain mystical claims of direct encounter with God.[57] Authentic revelation, with its necessary "indirectness," is met by the knowledge of faith[58] that is interpreted by the Word attested in Scripture. Faith-based experience goes against ordinary or universal experience, for "the Word must be believed against all sight and feeling of the understanding."[59] Again, Barth refrains from speaking of the realities of faith, revelation, and salvation in concrete "experiential" terms to avoid the dangers of anthropocentrism.

What Is the Goal of Theology? Theology as a Pointing Finger

Besides Scripture as the supreme witness to revelation, the church and its theologians are also witnesses—secondary witnesses who point to the glorious triune God. This call to witness or testimony defines the overall goal of dogmatic theology. Theology is to be a "pointing finger" or "pointing hand."[60] From his earliest theological beginnings, Barth had hung above his desk Matthias Grünewald's

---

51. *CD* I/1, 208.
52. *CD* I/2, 532.
53. Ibid., 533.
54. *CD* I/1, 221.
55. Ibid., 206.
56. Ibid., 165; cf. 165–74.
57. Ibid., 168, 178, 212, 222, 323 and *CD* II/1, 9 ff, 57, 192 ff.
58. *CD* II/1, 57.
59. *CD* I/1, 221.
60. Eberhard Busch, *The Great Passion: An Introduction to Barth's Theology* (Grand Rapids: Eerdmans, 2004), 6–9.

painting of the crucifixion, the Isenheim Altarpiece of 1516, which included the hand of John the Baptist in its right-hand side pointing to the crucified Christ. Eberhard Busch comments, "All proper theology in his view must be like this hand, with which a person does not point to oneself nor at some idea or program but towards the God who for his part completely turns to that person."[61] Barth believed that he must "carry out the ministry of this pointing hand."[62] The goal of pure doctrine is to "point beyond itself" so as to instruct people "in hearing the Word of God."[63] Without this "service of witness,"[64] even our valuable tools and methods—the exposition of Scripture and other sources of theology—become speculative or idolatrous. This requires intellectually and spiritually demanding work to bring a constant extrinsic focus on God, casting off laziness of thought and self-reliant prayerlessness.[65] As a witness, the theologian is rightly empowered and guided by the Spirit who inspired the biblical witnesses—for the Spirit's purpose is to testify to and glorify Christ (Jn 16:14).

The Role of the Spirit in Theology

Although Barth says little about the Spirit's work in experiential terms, he strongly affirms the necessity of the Spirit for theology. The Spirit is the divine witness to Christ, the "subjective reality" and "possibility" of revelation,[66] who awakens minds to God's objective work in Christ.

Barth's chapter on the "The Spirit" in his late work *Evangelical Theology* draws together key aspects of his understanding of the role of the Spirit for theology. He affirms the Spirit as the "true" or "real" power behind all theological assertions,[67] who remains "hidden" and "totally superior to theology itself."[68] Theologians must depend on the Spirit for theology to be "pneumatic, spiritual theology."[69] "Unspiritual theology . . . would be one of the most terrible of all terrible occurrences."[70] Barth, therefore, warns against the failure of theology to "submit itself fearlessly and unreservedly" to the Spirit's work.[71] He also warns against undue "familiarity" with the Spirit that would fail to "acknowledge the vitality and sovereignty of this power which defies all domestication"[72] and would deal with the Spirit as though it "hired

61. Ibid., 6.
62. Ibid.
63. *CD* I/2, 763.
64. Busch, *The Great Passion*, 12.
65. Ibid., 13.
66. *CD* I/2, 203–79.
67. Barth, *Evangelical Theology*, 50–1.
68. Ibid., 51.
69. Ibid., 55.
70. Ibid., 56.
71. Ibid.
72. Ibid., 57.

him or even attained possession of him."[73] As remedy for these temptations toward "unspiritual theology," Barth urges theologians to be continually desperate for the fresh work of the Spirit. In a turn of phrase that coincides with Pentecostalism's call to "tarry" for the Spirit, Barth says: "Only where the Spirit is sighed, cried and prayed for does he become present and newly active."[74]

Describing Pentecostalism on the Nature of Theology

As indicated in the introduction, Pentecostal theology is distinguished from other forms of theology not only by its specific doctrinal conclusions (its views of the gifts of the Spirit, etc.), but by its *approach* to theology, a set of methods and assumptions that expects biblically grounded, transformational encounters with God.

I will examine the nature of Pentecostal theological practice to discern its method, although making some references along the way to relevant theoretical comments about theology made by Pentecostal theologians. As I did with part of my treatment of Barth above, I will refer to how Pentecostals use the four sources of Scripture, tradition, reason and experience. In summary, *for Pentecostals (as for Barth), Scripture functions as the authoritative source and basis of theology, with tradition, reason, and experience being functionally subordinate to Scripture. In some contrast to Barth, experience plays a particularly significant role in the mediation of Scripture and doctrinal conclusions, although tradition and reason are also potentially involved in this mediation.*

Scripture in Pentecostal Theological Practice

As a whole, Pentecostals believe the Bible is the Word of God and ascribe to its unique theological authority.[75] The specific authoritative role of the Bible in theology varies according to the form of Pentecostal theology, yet Pentecostal theologians tend to interpret and use Scripture in three distinct ways.

First, Pentecostal biblical interpretation and theology, especially in its classical Pentecostal forms, is guided by a full gospel narrative.[76] The fullness is often

---

73. Ibid., 58.
74. Ibid.
75. Stephen Land, *Pentecostal Spirituality: A Passion for the Kingdom* (Sheffield: Sheffield Academic Press, 1993), 163. Pentecostal denominations and institutions have generally subscribed to either inerrancy, infallibility, or both (Warrington, *Pentecostal Theology*, 182 ff).
76. Vondey, *Pentecostal Theology*, 21–4; Kenneth J. Archer, *A Pentecostal Hermeneutic: Spirit, Scripture, and Community* (Cleveland: CPT Press 2009), 160–1 (This book was previously published by Continuum in 2005 in the Journal of Pentecostal Theology Supplement Series (no. 28)); Kenneth J. Archer, "A Pentecostal Way of Doing Theology: Method and Manner," *International Journal of Systematic Theology* 9/3 (July 2007): 301–14.

expressed in either the four or fivefold gospel, depending on whether sanctification is included as a distinct expression of the gospel. In the full gospel, Jesus is the central figure. He is not only the savior/sanctifier and coming King (emphases of Barth and most Christians), but also baptizer and healer. The christocentrism of this narrative is complemented, but not contradicted, by a strong emphasis on pneumatology, for it is by the Spirit that the risen Christ is present and active. Whether or not the full gospel pattern is seen as a sufficient guide for Pentecostal theological method in general,[77] it is crucial for understanding Pentecostals' use of Scripture.

Second, Pentecostal theology's use of Scripture is marked by a Spirit-enabled "contemporaneity" between biblical and current events and experiences. In a sense, Pentecost can happen again. "The goal of the full gospel . . . is to preserve the availability of the experiences of Pentecost . . . and their perpetuation."[78] Thus, Pentecostal sermons and liturgies often focus on "reexperiencing" the text through facilitating God-encounters or testimonies of them.[79] Even as Peter linked the words of Joel to what was happening on the Day of Pentecost, saying that "this is that," so contemporary Pentecostal preachers and theologians link their time with past biblical events. The Spirit is the "bridge" between the ancient authors and present interpreters.[80]

Third, Pentecostal theological hermeneutics focus on the practical application of the Scriptures. The still-unfolding story of the full gospel is "a narrative for a way of living."[81] Personal or corporate application is often seen as the main purpose of the Bible.[82] The Bible leads to sound doctrine, but this is not an end in itself. The goal is a transformative encounter with the divine realities to which Scripture testifies, which leads to an obedient and missional response. For Wolfgang Vondey, "theology *cannot* proceed without being practiced but *can* proceed without being articulated as doctrine."[83] One could say that doctrinal norms are often implicit in Pentecostal practices of worship and action, sometimes without (or before) those norms becoming explicit or formal doctrine.

Tradition and Reason in Pentecostal Theological Practice

How does tradition function in Pentecostal theology? Generally, Pentecostals and Pentecostal theologians have emphasized the value of their own traditions, but have not placed much emphasis on the value of traditions drawn from the majority

---

77. Archer, "A Pentecostal Way of Doing Theology," sees the fivefold gospel as such a guide.
78. Vondey, *Pentecostal Theology*, 21.
79. Archer, *A Pentecostal Hermeneutic*, 167 ff.
80. Ibid., 196, affirming French Arrington's view.
81. Vondey, *Pentecostal Theology*, 22.
82. Warrington, *Pentecostal Theology*, 188 ff.
83. Vondey, *Pentecostal Theology*, 28; cf. 28–30.

of church history. Pentecostalism has often viewed tradition with suspicion as a "man-made" departure from Scripture and the way of the Spirit.[84] A common primitivist, restorationist reading of history in Pentecostalism greatly restricts the scope of positive church traditions.[85] However, there is a growing minority of Pentecostal leaders and theologians who are making efforts to strengthen Pentecostalism and its theology through connection to the "Great Tradition" of the early church and to other Christian traditions.[86]

Whether tradition has a narrower (Pentecostal) or broader scope, it can, as in Barth's theology, function either positively as a guide or negatively as an example of failure to follow God's Word and Spirit. Tradition is seen as accountable to Scripture, yet in practice it can guide and limit Pentecostal use of Scripture, including which parts of Scripture are heard and followed.

Reason has not been given a significant, explicit focus by most Pentecostal theologians. While some might ascribe this to a lingering anti-intellectualism among Pentecostals,[87] it may have more to do with a general lack of explicit accounts of theological methodology in Pentecostalism. Yet Pentecostal theology employs reason, as human intellectual activity must, and does so in accord with its particular tradition or style of rationality. James Smith speaks of a "Pentecostal philosophy" arising out of a Pentecostal spirituality and worldview.[88] By "making explicit what is implied in Pentecostal spirituality and worship,"[89] as Smith does, I wish to make three observations about Pentecostal theology's use of reason. First, Pentecostalism's use of reason transcends typical limits for rationality and is marked by a "liminality"[90] that can offer an advantageous imaginativeness for the conceptual tasks involved in theology. Second, Pentecostal use of reason tends to be resistant to rationalism and open to mystery. For example, "critical reflection" upon informal testimonies[91] is careful not to diminish the transcendent dynamics of the Spirit. Third, Pentecostal theological rationality is marked by a "grounded-ness" in human life and experience that enables it to bridge the worlds of experience, informal spiritual-practical reflection, and academic reasoning and communication.

---

84. See Peter D. Neumann, *Pentecostal Experience: An Ecumenical Encounter* (Eugene: Wipf and Stock/Pickwick, 2012), 133 ff.
85. Archer, *A Pentecostal Hermeneutic*, 136–61.
86. See, for example, the works of Simon Chan and Chris E. W. Green.
87. Warrington, *Pentecostal Theology*, 194–5.
88. James K. A. Smith, *Thinking in Tongues: Pentecostal Contributions to Christian Philosophy* (Grand Rapids: Eerdmans, 2010), esp. xvii–xix.
89. Ibid., xix.
90. Ibid., xx–xxii.
91. Vondey, *Pentecostal Theology*, 33.

The Role of Experience in Pentecostal Theological Practice

Finally, what is the role of experience in a Pentecostal approach to theology? Pentecostal theology is clearly more "experience oriented" than many other forms of theology, including Barth's, being open to and oriented to experiences of God. Pentecostal theology is concerned with pointing to God-encounters of various kinds, encounters that are "ecstatic" because they take a person beyond herself.[92] Yet to testify to such ecstatic experiences of God in theology requires the tasks of reflection, interpretation, and discernment—tasks in which other theological sources (e.g., Scripture, tradition, and reason) are engaged and integrated.[93] Whether or not one can have an entirely unmediated experience of God, as claimed by many mystics and some Pentecostals, is a significant philosophical and theological question in itself, with Terry Cross regarding encounters with God as involving a "mediated immediacy."[94] Whatever a given Pentecostal theologian's precise conclusions on whether or how encounters with God might lead to specific knowledge of God,[95] God-encounters cannot have meaningful theological force in the community unless they are conveyed in thought and language. While the language of testimony or story is often most fitting as a way of communicating a God-encounter, this is still theological in nature. Pentecostal language for pre-reflective experience is shaped by the theological biases of the Pentecostal community.[96]

Layperson Lucy M. Leatherman interprets an ecstatic experience in Pentecostal terms in this testimony of it, recorded in an early issue of William Seymour's *Apostolic Faith* magazine:

> While seeking the baptism with the Holy Ghost [seeking a Pentecostal experience] in Los Angeles . . . I praised and praised and saw my Savior in the heavens. . . . By and by I swept into the wound in His side . . . and there found

---

92. Land, in *Pentecostal Spirituality*, sees Pentecostalism as concerned with an ecstatic lifestyle (my term) that includes particular ecstatic moments: "The ecstasy of Pentecostals . . . is a relinquishment of control in a trust that believes that the kingdom . . . is a gift of God that has nothing to do with self-willed and technique-manipulated progress" (177). This kind of ecstatic experience avoids the problems with experience that Barth was concerned about: that is, self-will, self-reliance, or straying from revelation.

93. This case is made at length by Neumann, *Pentecostal Experience*. Neumann understands theological mediation of the experience of the Spirit to be evidence of a maturation process that is unfolding in Pentecostalism. He identifies mediation through the Word/Scripture with the work of Frank Macchia, mediation through tradition with Simon Chan, and mediation through reason with Amos Yong, devoting a chapter to each.

94. Terry L. Cross, *The People of God's Presence: An Introduction to Ecclesiology* (Grand Rapids: Baker Academic, 2019), 93–161, esp. 126–36.

95. Cross appears to affirm that they can while Yong appears to deny this (Cross, *The People of God's Presence*, 132–5, 147 ff).

96. Vondey, *Pentecostal Theology*, 19.

that rest that passeth all understanding [an allusion to Philippians 2:7, with "peace" interpreted as "rest"], and He said to me that you are in the bosom of the Father. He said I was . . . in the secret place of the Most High [a personal word from God, using biblical allusions from John 1 and Psalm 91]. But I said, Father, I want the gift of the Holy Ghost, and the heavens opened and I was overshadowed, and such power came upon me and went through me. . . . I was passive in His hands, and by the eye of faith I saw angel hands working on my vocal chords, and I realized they were loosing me. I began to praise Him in an unknown tongue [as in Acts and in Paul's writings]. . . . Anywhere with Jesus I will gladly go [a readiness for mission].[97]

As my bracketed comments highlight, sister Leatherman's testimony includes basic theologizing. Her experience is ecstatic, pointing to God and not her own capacities. Her inner experience is real but leads to a transformed life of surrender and mission.[98] Such God-encounters and testimonies about them form communal ways of thinking and interpreting Scripture and are thus a vital part of Pentecostal theology.

How do these observations about Pentecostalism's use of theological sources relate to Pentecostalism's characteristic theological convictions? All Pentecostals, including charismatics and neo-Pentecostals, subscribe to a couple of general claims: (1) the gospel is a "full gospel," more than a gospel of eternal, future salvation; and (2) all, or nearly all, of the New Testament gifts of the Spirit continue, against cessationism. There may be much variety and division over the proper doctrinal interpretation of these two experience-rooted claims, but Pentecostals share a conviction that God's work can be experienced and that theology rightly reflects on those experiences. The functional interrelation of Scripture and experience is central for Pentecostalism, with some Pentecostal theologians also giving explicit "supporting roles" for tradition and reason.

The Role of Community in Theology and Hermeneutics

A Pentecostal approach to theology has another notable feature, namely, the importance of Christian community.[99] The community, with an important but not exclusive emphasis on local Pentecostal churches and fellowships, plays a formative role in theology.

First, the role of Scripture in Pentecostal theology is deeply rooted in the community. The Pentecostal theologian does not simply do theological interpretation in isolation, but in dialogue with the local congregation and,

---

97. Lucy Leatherman, as cited in Archer, *A Pentecostal Hermeneutic*, 37–8.

98. Land notes that this Lucy Leatherman went to serve as a missionary in Beirut, following a later encounter (*Pentecostal Spirituality*, 160; cf. 177).

99. See the extensive treatment given to community by theologians Kenneth Archer (e.g., *A Pentecostal Hermeneutic*) and Amos Yong (e.g., *Spirit-Word-Community*).

potentially, the global church. The intersubjective Body of Scripture-readers offers helpful checks and balances for individual theologians.

Second, the role of tradition in Pentecostal theology is clearly related to both past communities and to the current community in its process of tradition-formation or traditioning.[100] The theologian is united with and indebted to both the global church of the present and the riches of the church of the past.

Third, the role of reason in Pentecostal theology is also inescapably communal. The social location of Pentecostal theologians, both in church subcultures and in wider societies, includes being informed by one or more communal traditions of rationality. Such traditions inform social and theological judgments about which experiences are authentic, which Bible passages are most decisive, and what are the most ethical decisions.

Lastly, the community is always involved in the role of experience in Pentecostal theology. Even when an individual's experience is in view, the community offers the language through which the individual's experience is interpreted or discerned. Furthermore, varied communal practices of worship and ministry, including laying on of hands or "tarrying" in prayer, often become the contexts in which encounter with the presence of God takes place. Although the Spirit's voice can sometimes come directly to an individual, the Spirit's voice is more often heard "in and through" the community, especially the local and global Pentecostal community.[101]

Dialogue between Barth and Pentecostals on the Nature of Theology

Now that I have treated the nature and methods of theology according to Karl Barth and Pentecostalism, I am prepared to bring them into dialogue with one another.

Convergences and Similarities

First, in contrast to many modern and postmodern theologies, Barth and most Pentecostals offer biblically oriented approaches to theology. This is reflected in the predominance of biblical language and references in their theologies, as well as their frequent appeals to Scripture as theologically authoritative. Barth and Pentecostals often lay a particular emphasis on scriptural narratives, with Barth focusing especially on the four gospel's portrayal of the incarnate Jesus[102] and with Pentecostals giving special emphasis to the stories of Acts.

---

100. Vondey, *Pentecostal Theology*, 30–4 and Amos Yong, *Spirit-Word-Community: Theological Hermeneutics in Trinitarian Perspective* (Eugene: Wipf and Stock, 2006), 269 ff.

101. Archer, *A Pentecostal Hermeneutics*, 248–1 and Cross, *The People of God's Presence*, 159–61.

102. David F. Ford, *Barth and God's Story: Biblical Narrative and the Theological Method of Karl Barth in the* Church Dogmatics (Eugene: Wipf and Stock, 1985). See Pokrifka, *Redescribing God*, 15–17, 56.

Second, both Barth and Pentecostals manifest christocentric theologies. Barth and most Pentecostals (with the exception of Oneness Pentecostals) are christocentric in a way that is also trinitarian, with Jesus seen as the revelation of the triune God.[103] They also use christocentrism to emphasize the contemporaneity of today's believers with Christ and Christ with them. They manifest this "hermeneutics of simultaneity" in different ways. While Pentecostals claim that "this is that"—that what we now experience is that to which Scripture testifies[104]—Barth emphasizes that the contemporary Christian reader is united to Christ's story in the gospels.[105] In their distinct forms of christocentrism, Barth and Pentecostals share a tendency to interpret all of Scripture in ways that point to Christ and the christocentric gospel.

Third, both Barth and Pentecostals are open to what we might call the "indirect authorization" of doctrine in Scripture.[106] Barth and most Pentecostals often allow for the authority of Scripture to bear on theology in indirect and mediated forms.[107] The relationship between Scripture and contemporary application is mediated, under the Spirit's guidance, by secondary authorities like tradition, reason, experience, or the community of faith.

Fourth, Barth and Pentecostals embrace mystery in theology, resisting rationalism. Barth's view that all God's acts of self-revelation are marked by "hiddenness" or "veiling" means that theology manifests dialectical tensions.[108] Pentecostal theologians often make similar claims, as when Yong states "God is . . . always both disclosed and hidden."[109] Pentecostals aim to make room for the liminal and miraculous in both life and theology.[110] Barth is less likely to testify to experiences of miracles, but affirms that the divine works of reconciliation and revelation are miracles that transcend and even contradict the fallen created order.[111]

---

103. For Barth's rejection of "Christomonism," see *CD* IV/4, 19–30. Frank Macchia has expressed concerns about Christomonism in Pentecostalism, not least in some uses of the fivefold gospel, a concern that Ken Archer finds largely misplaced (Archer, "A Pentecostal Way of Doing Theology," 314).

104. See Vondey, *Pentecostal Theology*, 17 and Cross, *The People of God's Presence*, 156–7.

105. *CD* IV/4, 20–1.

106. Pokrifka, *Redescribing God*, 65–7.

107. A Pentecostal exception to this indirect approach, at least in intention, would be the "Bible Doctrines" approach. See Christopher A. Stephenson, *Types of Pentecostal Theology: Method, System, Spirit* (Oxford: Oxford University Press, 2013), 11–27.

108. Pokrifka, *Redescribing God*, 94, 170–9; George Hunsinger, *How to Read Karl Barth: The Shape of His Theology* (New York: Oxford University Press, 1991), 32–5 (on "particularism") and 281–2 (on "hermeneutical adequacy" over coherence).

109. Yong, *Spirit-Word-Community*, 210.

110. Ibid., 211, 283.

111. Hunsinger, *How to Read Karl Barth*, 30–2. In *Evangelical Theology*, Barth says, "theology is necessarily the logic of wonders" that are "incompatible and unassimilable to the norm of common experience" (66).

Divergences: Opportunities for a More Adequate Conception of Theology

Yet important differences remain between Barth and Pentecostalism on the nature of theology. The differences on which I wish to focus are so closely related that they could be seen as one main difference with several aspects. Expressed in a dense, unitary form, the multifaceted contrast is this: *Barth calls theology to focus on Spirit-based knowledge of Christ's objective, realized accomplishments, while Pentecostals call theology to focus on a Spirit-based subjective encounter with Christ's present work.* This generalized claim involves three facets: (1) differing eschatological interpretations of God's work in the present age, (2) differing construals of the mode of reception of God's work and revelation, and (3) differing views of the proper focus of faith and theology. I will treat these three contrasts in turn.

First, Barth and Pentecostal theology offer differing accounts of God's work in the present age. Barth and Pentecostals share a biblical eschatology that is broadly realistic and inaugurated by Christ but differ in how they conceive of it. The main, relevant difference concerns the "already-not yet" time between the incarnation and the return of Jesus, not the final consummation. In Barth's christocentric view of history, Jesus Christ establishes God's kingdom on earth in his first coming, rendering all future events as further unveilings of what has already been accomplished and revealed by his incarnation and resurrection.[112] Independent of contemporary empirical "evidence" of their transformation or salvation, then, faith affirms that God's people are included or incorporated in the life history of Jesus Christ.[113] This is Barth's christocentric "soteriological objectivism."[114] Barth's view contrasts somewhat with Pentecostal approaches to eschatology, which testify to the experiential, transformative presence of the Spirit, who mediates the risen Christ. This work of the Spirit can be understood as "pneumatological realism."[115] While Barth affirms the real work of the Spirit in our time, he understands the Spirit's work almost exclusively as opening our minds to Christ's already-realized, objective work of salvation.[116] Barth is reticent to make concrete claims about the Spirit's work beyond this role, in contrast to Pentecostals. Within a Pentecostal view, Christ's work is often dramatically evident in Christian experience, as when he baptizes and heals by the Spirit.

Second, and relatedly, Barth's and Pentecostal theology's different understandings of God's work in the present age lead to and are correlated with different views of how humans subjectively receive God's present work. This involves distinct construals of faith. For Barth, genuine faith, which is possible only by the Spirit, enables humans to receive God's revelation of the objective work of Christ. The

---

112. Colwell, *Actuality and Provisionality*, 155 ff.
113. Ford, *Barth and God's Story*, 165 f, 168 ff.
114. This is contrasted to what Hunsinger calls "soteriological existentialism" (*How to Read Karl Barth*, 105 ff).
115. See Gary Tyra's use of this terminology in the next chapter.
116. Colwell, *Actuality and Provisionality*, 264–308.

Spirit illumines our minds to the reality that "His history is . . . our true history."[117] Although for Barth the Word of God, attested in Scripture-based theological language, addresses the whole human person in some sense,[118] he repeatedly gives precedence to the cognitive elements of the Spirit's subjective/internal work in us[119] and deemphasizes possible trans-cognitive dimensions or effects of the Spirit's work related to emotion or experience.[120] Pentecostals, by contrast, embrace both cognitive and trans-cognitive elements of the Spirit's work in us as either part of faith or as faith's fitting accompaniment. This broader Pentecostal conception of the human mode of reception of God's work matches the Pentecostal teaching that the works of God in our time are themselves much more diverse than the revelation of accomplished salvation. When a person receives something like the tongues-speech or a physical healing, they experience "something more" than a faith-based knowledge.

Third, Barth's and Pentecostal theology's different views of God's work in our time and of the nature of faith and experience lead to different views of the proper, primary focus of theology. Barth calls theology to focus on God's objective, realized saving–revealing work in Christ, understood in our minds through faith-seeking-understanding. Pentecostal theology tends to focus on diverse, experientially accessible, dimensions of the present work of Christ and the Spirit. That is, Barth's approach to theology calls contemporary believers to *look back with faith-ordered minds* on the objective realities of the life, death, and resurrection of Jesus. Barth does not deny that Christians should also "look around" or perhaps even "look within" at the ongoing work of God through the risen Christ in the Spirit. But Barth tends to regard these other possible foci as secondary to the proper and foundational focus on the past accomplishments of God in Christ. By contrast, a Pentecostal approach to theology calls contemporary believers to *look around (in the community and even the world) and even to look within, with our whole person (not just mind), at the present works of the Spirit*. Instead of exclusively looking back to the Christ of the Scriptures, although this is certainly a necessary component in our theologies, the eschatological reality of the kingdom that Jesus inaugurated can be known and experienced now, at least in part. Such "looking" and "participation" require the active engagement of the whole person, including the "heart" and the "hands," beyond the primarily noetic (head) focus of Barth.[121]

---

117. CD IV/1, 548, IV/2, 483. See Ford, *Barth and God's Story*, 165–6 and Hunsinger, *How to Read Karl Barth*, 120–1.

118. Hunsinger, *How to Read Karl Barth*, 44–5.

119. Ibid., 163 (cf. 180 ff): "conversion, for all its concomitant existential and ethical implications, is presented primarily in noetic terms." See *CD* IV/3, 519.

120. Hunsinger, *How to Read Karl Barth*, 121 ff.

121. Barth gives more attention to whole person engagement in his later work, especially in his account of the Baptism with the Holy Spirit (as an aspect of conversion–initiation) in *CD* IV/4, 22–5. See Terry L. Cross, "Christ in Us: The Hope of Glory or the Sentimentality of a Bohemian Private Enterprise? Barth, Pietists and Pentecostals," in *Karl Barth and the*

Barth resists such an emphasis as "a supposed 'pneumatic actuality' in the sphere of experience," associating it with deceptive self-reliance.[122] In contrast, Pentecostals seek and testify to the presence and work of the Spirit, precisely as a way to get beyond reliance on themselves. Through his presence and gifts, the Spirit not only brings Pentecostals into saving knowledge of Christ, but propels them into witness until the final coming of the King.

These three related areas of difference between Barth and Pentecostals imply certain largely complementary emphases in their theological approaches. These emphases can be combined to reach a better view of the nature of theology than each offers on its own.

Barth's approach to theology can address various problems associated with the role of experience in Pentecostalism. To begin, Barth can rightly emphasize the need to interpret experience rightly, in light of God's manifold Word. Further, as some Pentecostal theologians have noted, Barth's theology can provide a helpful reminder of the objective grounding of the Christian life and experience of God.[123] Accordingly, Barth's approach helps resist experience-seeking or sensationalism,[124] "religious emotionalism" or experiential individualism,[125] or a general lack of adequate discernment. Barth can also remind Pentecostals of those aspects of their own tradition that urge faith in the biblical or prophetic word even against or without "sight" or experience. Barth's emphasis on "faith not sight" (2 Cor. 5:7) has the advantage of enabling believers to stand strong even when there is no subjective "encounter." Barth's perspective on faith should form an essential part of theological endeavors, yet without denying the Pentecostal openness to encounters with God. Barth's grounding of faith in the Word of Christ can help keep all Christians from allowing powerful emotions and deceptive experiences to become co-opted by "culture Christianity" that is derailed from revelation, as happened in Barth's day with Hitler's "German Christians." Barth helps Pentecostal theology to avoid becoming "unspiritual" through a supposed "familiarity" with the Spirit who "defies all domestication."[126]

Conversely, Pentecostals can help followers of Barth's approach to overcome unfounded fears that experience will necessarily take them away from a proper focus on the self-revealing God. Pentecostals can emphasize that such encounters with God are often precisely of the kind that point people to God—being of an

---

Future of Evangelical Theology, ed. Christian T. Collins Winn and John L. Drury (Eugene: Wipf and Stock, 2014), 85–6.

122. Hunsinger, *How to Read Karl Barth*, 123, from his own revised translation of Barth's *CD* II/2, 775–6.

123. Cross, "Christ in Us," 69–90, esp. 86–7. Cross sees Barth as more open to the subjective, inner workings of the Spirit than many readers see him to be, yet without neglecting Barth's welcome emphasis on the objectivity of revelation.

124. Warrington, *Pentecostal Theology*, 26–7.

125. Cross, "Christ in Us," 80, 86.

126. Barth, *Evangelical Theology*, 57.

ecstatic or extrinsic character—rather than, as Barth feared, pointing them back to self-centered reliance on human capacities. Theological reflection on such experiences, beginning with narrative or testimony, can be another legitimate way for theology to be "a pointing finger" to the triune God. By acknowledging and testifying to experiential, active reception of the Spirit's work in our time, Pentecostal theology integrates helpful biblical emphases on orthopathos and orthopraxis with the orthodoxy or orthopistis that Barth emphasized.[127] Against Barth's general lack of expectation concerning the Spirit's trans-cognitive work, Pentecostals can testify to the contrary from the spiritual experiences of God's people in Scripture, history, and the contemporary church. Furthermore, Pentecostals can stress that the Spirit integrates and makes possible crucial aspects of theological work that Barth valued. The Spirit is the one who enables Scripture's right interpretation and use and guides God's people to adopt what is salutary from tradition, reason, and experience, avoiding stale orthodoxy, reductionistic cultural rationality, or undiscerning and anthropocentric experientialism.

Barth and Pentecostalism represent approaches to theology that have enough in common to be theological allies in the common cause of Christ in the world, in contrast to certain liberal and fundamentalist extremes. They converge in their christocentrism, their biblical orientation, and in their common determination that theology should be fully reliant on God's work rather than in unaided human reason and experience. Yet they present ways of doing theology that are sufficiently distinct to offer complementary ways of being more faithful to God. When brought together, they present a stronger, more complete approach to the nature of theology that has a greater potential to testify to God and God's kingdom.

---

127. See Archer, "A Pentecostal Way of Doing Theology," 309–11.

Chapter 3

REVELATION AS ENCOUNTER

KARL BARTH, PNEUMATOLOGICAL REALISM, AND THE PENTECOSTAL NOTION OF *PROPHETIC* PREACHING

Gary Tyra

Introduction

My conversion and initial formation as a Christian occurred in a Pentecostal, essentially fundamentalist, ecclesial environment. I had never even heard of Karl Barth before reading him in seminary. However, what I discovered in that reading greatly impacted my spiritual and ministry journey.

As a young pastor-seminarian, I was immediately struck by the importance Barth placed on preaching. But Barth did more than enhance my already passionate commitment to the preaching task. He provided the categories (or constructs) which enabled me to form a more nuanced, theologically informed understanding of something we Pentecostals refer to as "anointed" preaching. It was Barth who helped me see that *Spirit-empowered* preaching is not about how loud and animated the preacher is. Truly anointed sermons are *prophetic* in that they help people sense that Jesus himself has, through his Spirit, been there with them, speaking to them, caring, confronting, and calling them as only he can.[1]

---

1. Perhaps a word of clarification is in order from the outset. Old Testament scholar Walter Brueggemann has made the following assertion: "The task of prophetic ministry is to nurture, nourish, and evoke a consciousness and perception alternative to the consciousness and perception of the dominant culture around us." (Walter Brueggemann, *The Prophetic Imagination*, 2nd ed. [Minneapolis: Fortress Press, 2001], 3, emphasis original.) Put simply, Brueggemann's widely embraced understanding of prophetic seems to center in the dynamic of confrontation: the role of the prophet is to challenge the enculturation of the faith community and steer it toward a greater faithfulness vis-à-vis its tradition. While I am certainly able to endorse this type of prophetic ministry, I am suggesting that it is possible, from a Pentecostal perspective, to broaden our understanding of prophetic preaching. Given Paul's reference to prophetic speech in 1 Corinthians 14:3, I contend that any sermon which enables its auditors to sense that the risen Christ has encountered them in an especially personal, powerful, transformational manner can be

In his book, *Reading Karl Barth*, Kurt Anders Richardson suggests that "Barth wanted his readers to focus on the active revelation of God's Word, which God is constantly accomplishing through Scripture, and the preaching of Scripture by the power of the Holy Spirit."[2] This observation refers to three of Barth's distinctive doctrines: revelation, Word of God, and proclamation as the Word of God. As well, the phrase "by the power of the Holy Spirit" suggests that Barth possessed a rather dynamic rather than merely conceptual understanding of the Spirit. The question at the heart of this essay is: *What might happen were we to consider all these themes in tandem?* My thesis is that when we combine the *pneumatological realism* implicit in Barth's theology with his encounter-oriented understanding of revelation, Word of God, and Christian proclamation, we find some *implicit* theological support for the Pentecostal notion of *prophetic* preaching—sermons, which not only convey biblical truths, but also evoke a sense of *encounter* with the risen Christ.[3] To be clear, I am not suggesting that prophetic preaching presents hearers with "new revelation" on par with Scripture. Neither am I insinuating that Barth was a Pentecostal. I am simply drawing attention to the fact that there is such a thing as "anointed" preaching which, as we will see, bears the earmarks Barth attributed to the "true proclamation" of the Word of God.[4]

Barth's Pneumatological Realism

I have written elsewhere of the need for a more robust, fully trinitarian, *realist rather than non-realist* doctrine of the Holy Spirit.[5] As I conceive of it, a realist doctrine of the Spirit acknowledges the Spirit's divine personhood, agency, and the crucial role he plays in enabling human beings not only to *know* the Father through the Son, but also to *experience* what both are about. In other words, a *pneumatological realism* insists that, rather than conceive of the Holy Spirit as a philosophical concept or impersonal force that is simply presumed to be at work in believers' lives, he can and should be known and interacted with in ways

---

considered prophetic, whether the message is provocative/confrontational or not. I believe I find in Barth some implicit, even if unintended, theological support for this broadened understanding of anointed, Spirit-empowered, prophetic preaching.

2. Kurt Anders Richardson, *Reading Karl Barth: New Directions for American Theology* (Grand Rapids: Baker Academic, 2004), 106.

3. Elements of this chapter have been adapted from an essay titled "From Sola Scriptura to the Sacramental Sermon: Karl Barth and the Phenomenon of Prophetic Preaching" included in Gary Tyra, *Getting Real: Pneumatological Realism and the Spiritual, Moral, and Ministry Formation of Contemporary Christians* (Eugene: Cascade, 2018), 141–81, used by permission of Wipf and Stock Publishers (www.wipfandstock.com).

4. These earmarks will be elaborated upon in final section of this chapter.

5. Tyra, *Getting Real*, ix, 3–4, 7, 10, 15, 21–5, 54–5, 57, 85, 87, 99, 103, 106, 108, 118, 122, 124–5, 128, n. 11, 129–30, n. 15, 135–7, 139–40, 145, 158, 160–1, 172, 174, 178, n. 106, 181.

that are personal, phenomenal, and life-story shaping. Thus, a pneumatological realism produces among church members an important sense of *pneumatological expectancy* rather than *presumption* (or even *indifference*). While this emphasis upon pneumatological expectancy is something with which Pentecostals will readily resonate, I am convinced that a realist understanding of the Holy Spirit is crucial to the spiritual, moral, and ministry formation of all Christians, whether they self-identify as Pentecostal–charismatic or not.

As it happens, a growing number of scholars (not all of whom are Pentecostal) have acknowledged a "pneumatological deficit" observable in some Protestant, post-Reformation theologies.[6] Interestingly, some have argued that Barth, due to his pronounced christocentrism, was himself complicit in this marginalizing of the Spirit, guilty of reducing the Holy Spirit to "a function or 'power' of the Son."[7] Anyone concerned about impoverished pneumatologies that put forward truncated, depersonalized, overly conceptualized depictions of the Holy Spirit must take this critique seriously. And yet, my own reading of Barth, informed by the commentary provided by some experts on Barth's pneumatology, has caused me to conclude that just the opposite was true.

What I am suggesting is that behind Barth's theologizing is a "metaphysics rooted in divine reality"[8] in which *both* Christ and the Holy Spirit play vital, indispensable roles. Indeed, so crucial is the Holy Spirit to Barth's widely acknowledged theological realism[9] that a pneumatological realism can be inferred as well. Moreover, as we

---

6. For example, see Timothy Tennent, *Invitation to World Missions: A Trinitarian Missiology for the Twenty-First Century* (Grand Rapids: Kregel Academic, 2010), 94; Roger Olson, *The Story of Christian Theology* (Downers Grove: IVP Academic, 1999), 521, 523; and Veli-Matti Kärkkäinen, *Pneumatology: The Holy Spirit in Ecumenical, International, and Contextual Perspective* (Grand Rapids: Baker Academic, 2002), 17–18. Moreover, Jürgen Moltmann provides not only a nuanced discussion of the reason for the "reserve in the doctrine of the Holy Spirit" within the established churches in Europe during the modern era, but also an eloquent critique of the tendency among some Evangelicals to conflate Word and Spirit, and to conceive of the Spirit only in an intellectual manner. See Jürgen Moltmann, *The Spirit of Life: A Universal Affirmation* (Minneapolis: Fortress, 1992), 2–3.

7. For example, see Robert W. Jenson, "You Wonder Where the Spirit Went," *Pro Ecclesia: A Journal of Catholic and Evangelical Theology* 2 (1993): 296–304. The quote in this paragraph is from Eugene Rogers, *The Holy Spirit: Classic and Contemporary Readings* (Hoboken: Wiley-Blackwell, 2009), 9. See also Eugene Rogers, *After the Spirit: A Constructive Pneumatology from Sources Outside the Modern West* (Grand Rapids: Eerdmans, 2005), 19–23.

8. This phrase in quotes is from Philip J. Rosato, *The Spirit as Lord: The Pneumatology of Karl Barth* (Edinburgh: T&T Clark, 1981), 72.

9. For example, see Alister McGrath, *A Scientific Theology: Volume 2: Reality* (Grand Rapids: Eerdmans, 2002), 257–64. See also Katherine Sonderegger, "Barth and Feminism," in *The Cambridge Companion to Karl Barth*, ed. John Webster (Cambridge: Cambridge University Press, 2000), 258–73, here 264; Graham Ward, "Barth, Modernity, and

will soon see, Barth's dynamic view of Christian preaching, while immediately grounded in his doctrine of the threefold Word of God, ultimately derives from his notion of revelation as encounter. I contend that, while Barth was no Pentecostal, all three of these critical doctrines and their interplay become even more coherent when we take his latent pneumatological realism into account.

I am encouraged by the fact that my thesis regarding Barth's latent pneumatological realism is buttressed by the fact that we see something very similar in the theology of Scottish theologian T. F. Torrance, another notable proponent of *theological realism*. Both Barth and Torrance famously insisted that because of the incarnation of Christ, a real, trustworthy knowledge of our trinitarian God is possible.[10] This mutually held conviction was grounded on this christological tenet: "what God is antecedently and eternally in himself he really is toward us in the concrete embodiment of his Truth in Jesus Christ the word made flesh."[11] Obviously, this theological precept possesses huge epistemological significance. But Torrance and Barth also spoke of the dramatic, critical importance of the *indwelling of the Holy Spirit* to the process of divine self-revelation. For instance, in a passage underscoring the need for orthodox understandings of *both* Christ and the Spirit, Torrance wrote:

> Everything hinges on the *reality* of God's *self*-communication to us in Jesus Christ, in whom there has become incarnate, not some created intermediary between God and the world, but the very Word who eternally inheres in the Being of God and is God, so that for us to know God in Jesus Christ is really to know him as he is in himself. *It is with the same force that attention is directed upon the Holy Spirit*, whom the Father sends through the Son to dwell with us, and who, like the Son, is no mere cosmic power intermediate between God and the world, but is the Spirit of God who eternally dwells in him and in whom God knows himself, so that for us to know God in his Spirit is to know him in the hidden depths of his divine Being.[12]

Postmodernity," in *The Cambridge Companion to Karl Barth*, ed. John Webster (Cambridge: Cambridge University Press, 2000), 274–95, here 281; George Hunsinger, *How to Read Karl Barth: The Shape of His Theology* (New York: Oxford University Press, 1991), 4–5. Even though "realism" is the label Hunsinger attaches to one of six Barthian motifs, I will offer that the theological/pneumatological realism I have in mind, and see in Barth's work, comprises elements of all six of the motifs to which Hunsinger refers. See Hunsinger's survey of the motifs in ibid., 27–64.

10. See Thomas F. Torrance, *Reality & Evangelical Theology* (Downers Grove: InterVarsity Press, 1999), 23. A very concise comparison of the ways in which the theological realisms of Barth and Torrance compare can be found in McGrath, *A Scientific Theology: Volume 2: Reality*, 265.

11. Torrance, *Reality & Evangelical Theology*, 141. See also Karl Barth, *Church Dogmatics* I/1, ed. Thomas F. Torrance and G. W. Bromiley, trans. G. W. Bromiley (Peabody: Hendrickson, 2010), 466.

12. Torrance, *Reality & Evangelical Theology*, 23, emphasis added.

Torrance held that it's *both* the *incarnation of Christ* and the *indwelling of his Spirit* that makes a theological realism—a real, trustworthy knowledge of our trinitarian God—possible. Thus, my contention that, even though Torrance never used the term "pneumatological realism" in his writings, given the importance of the Spirit to his theological realism, the presence of a pneumatological realism can be inferred. As the succeeding paragraphs will demonstrate, I am convinced that the very same thing can be said of Barth!

For instance, here are several quotes from the mature Barth which indicate the critical importance he attached to the Holy Spirit for Christian theology:

> It is clear that evangelical theology itself can only be pneumatic, spiritual theology. Only in the realm of the power of the Spirit can theology be realized as a humble, free, critical, and happy science of the God of the Gospel.[13]

> Only the Spirit himself can rescue theology! He, the Holy One, the Lord, the Giver of Life, waits and waits to be received anew by theology as by the community. He waits to receive from theology his due of adoration and glorification. He expects from theology that it submit itself to the repentance, renewal, and reformation he effects. He waits to vivify and illuminate its affirmations which, however right they may be, are dead without the Spirit.[14]

These quotes certainly seem to indicate that Barth fully understood how important the Spirit is to a biblically grounded, evangelical theology. Indeed, late in his career Barth famously referred to the possibility of a "theology of the Third Article."[15] However, what he meant by this remark is the subject of much debate. In the light of the quotes presented above, I want to pose the question: When Barth referred to the possibility of a theology of the Third Article, did he have in mind an entirely new theological paradigm (per Schleiermacher), or simply one that, while still christocentric, is also informed by what I am referring to as a pneumatological realism? In other words, perhaps what Barth had in mind was a Spirit Christology, but one informed by Nicea/Chalcedon, and which avoids "the ambiguities of either an overly philosophical, overly-institutional or overly-personal [immanentist] understanding of the Holy Spirit."[16]

---

13. Karl Barth, *Evangelical Theology: An Introduction* (Grand Rapids: Eerdmans, 1963), 55.
14. Ibid., 57.
15. See Karl Barth, "Nachwort," in *Schleiermacher-Auswahl: mit einem Nachwort von Karl Barth* (Gütersloh: Gütersloher Verlagshaus Mohn, 1980), 310–11, as cited in Aaron T. Smith, *A Theology of the Third Article: Karl Barth and the Spirit of the Word* (Minneapolis: Fortress Press, 2014), 51.
16. The quote is from Rosato, *The Spirit as Lord*, 63. Eugene Rogers suggests that some inconsistency in the way Barth spoke of the Spirit had been in reaction to Schleiermacher's immanentist pneumatology. (Rogers, *After the Spirit*, 34–5.) See also Veli-Matti Kärkkäinen, *Spirit and Salvation: A Constructive Christian Theology for the Pluralistic World, Volume 4* (Grand Rapids: Eerdmans, 2016), 13–15.

Some tacit support for this supposition may be found in Aaron T. Smith's *A Theology of the Third Article: Karl Barth and the Spirit of the Word*. In this work, Smith not only provides a "summary defense of Barth" against the charge that his christocentrism had left him "little room for thinking and speaking of the Holy Spirit,"[17] he also argues forcefully against the notion that Barth's famous "Third Article" remark meant that he "was thinking of a theology which, unlike his own, was not written from the dominant perspective of Christology but from pneumatology."[18] Smith's contention seems to be that inherent in Barth's dogmatic work are the seeds of a theology of the third article, his christocentrism notwithstanding.[19] This explains why Smith's book is filled with passages which evidence Barth's latent pneumatological realism.[20]

Additional support for the proposition that a pneumatological realism is crucial to Barth's theological project can be found in Philip J. Rosato's *The Spirit as Lord: The Pneumatology of Karl Barth*. In this work, Rosato indicates not only the profound *epistemological significance* that Barth attributed to the work of the Holy Spirit,[21] but the *existential significance* he associated with the Spirit as well.[22] It is hard to read Rosato and not be convinced that Barth's pneumatology was realist rather than non-realist in nature. Moreover, presented below is a quote from Barth himself which seems to underwrite Rosato's commentary. Barth speaks here of a *freedom* the Spirit imparts to Christian disciples that has implications for just about every aspect of the Christian life:

> To receive the Spirit, to have the Spirit, to live in the Spirit *means being set free and being permitted to live in freedom*. . . . To have inner ears for the Word of Christ, to become thankful for His work and at the same time responsible for the message about Him and, lastly, to take confidence in men for Christ's sake—*that is the freedom which we obtain, when Christ breathes on us, when He sends us His Holy Spirit*. If He no longer lives in a historical or heavenly, a theological or ecclesiastical remoteness from me, *if He approaches me and takes possession of me*, the result will be that I hear, that I am thankful and responsible and that finally I may hope for myself and for all others; in other words, that *I may live in a Christian way*. It is a tremendously big thing and by no means a matter of course, to obtain this *freedom*. We must therefore every day and every hour pray

---

17. Smith, *A Theology of the Third Article*, 2.
18. Ibid., 19, 50–1.
19. This contention that a biblically informed pneumatological realism will necessarily be Christ-honoring also finds support in George Hunsinger's essay titled "The Mediator of Communion: Karl Barth's Doctrine of the Holy Spirit," in *The Cambridge Companion to Karl Barth*, ed. John Webster (Cambridge: Cambridge University Press, 2000), 177–94, here 181–2.
20. For example, see Smith, *A Theology of the Third Article*, 18–19, 19, n. 10, 52–3.
21. For example, see Rosato, *The Spirit as Lord*, 55, 57, 72.
22. See ibid., 60–5, 71.

Veni Creator Spiritus [Come, Creator Spirit] in listening to the word of Christ and in thankfulness. That is a closed circle. We do not "have" this freedom; it is again and again given to us by God.[23]

This is one of many passages from Barth's hand which, I believe, indicates a realist rather than non-realist understanding of the Holy Spirit—one which possesses both an *epistemological* and *existential* significance. It is difficult for me to read Barth (and those more familiar with his theology than I am) and not be convinced that his theological project was and is, as it were, "pregnant" with the sense of expectancy I associate with a pneumatological realism.

At the same time, I acknowledge that any amount of evidence for the importance Barth placed on the Holy Spirit does not by itself constitute compelling support for the Pentecostal notion of prophetic preaching. To be clear, my thesis holds that such support is discerned when we go on to add to Barth's realist understanding of the Spirit the emphasis on *encounter*, which earmarked his doctrines of revelation, Word of God, and Christian proclamation.

Barth's Distinctive Views of Revelation, Word of God, and Proclamation

More than one scholar has observed that Barth's doctrine of revelation "is of central importance to his theological system as a whole."[24] However, I believe there is good reason to begin with a brief discussion of Barth's *prophetic* understanding of *Christian proclamation* before grounding it in his doctrines of revelation and the Word of God.

As a young pastor-seminarian, I was intrigued to learn that it was a crisis in his preaching ministry which compelled Barth to eventually abandon his liberal training and move in a new direction in his theology.[25] Bernard Ramm explains that the Enlightenment-driven liberal Christianity Barth had been trained in had "reduced preaching to a purely human performance," its theological presuppositions preventing it from "rising above the level of human discourse."[26] But Barth became convinced that preaching not only *could* be more than merely

---

23. Karl Barth, *Dogmatics in Outline* (New York: Harper & Row, 1959), 138–9, emphasis added.

24. See Sven Ensminger, *Karl Barth's Theology as a Resource for a Christian Theology of Religions* (New York: Bloomsbury T&T Clark, 2014), 9.

25. See Eberhard Busch, *Karl Barth: His Life from Letters and Autobiographical Texts*, trans. John Bowden (Philadelphia: Fortress Press, 1976), 61. See also John Webster, "Introducing Barth," in *The Cambridge Companion to Karl Barth*, ed. John Webster (Cambridge: Cambridge University Press, 2000), 1–16, here 3; Gregory G. Bolich, *Karl Barth & Evangelicalism* (Downers Grove: InterVarsity Press, 1980), 108.

26. Bernard Ramm, *After Fundamentalism: The Future of Evangelical Theology* (San Francisco: Harper & Row, 1983), 51.

human discourse, it *must* be! In other words, I am suggesting that, as a young pastor, Barth came to understand the need for preaching that is *prophetic* in nature—not simply because the sermon focuses on the end times, or is confrontive in nature, or is based on writings of the Old Testament prophets, or even because it encourages social change, but in the sense that it creates the possibility of a personal *encounter* between the sermon's hearers and a speaking God. Barth wrote:

> Proclamation is human speech in and by which God Himself speaks like a king through the mouth of his herald, and which is meant to be heard and accepted as speech in and by which God Himself speaks and therefore heard and accepted in faith as divine decision concerning life and death, as divine judgment and pardon, eternal Law and eternal Gospel both together.[27]

Barth seems to have been in touch with the fact that the Scriptures describe the *prophetic phenomenon* as occurring in two stages, both of which rely on the activity of God's Spirit. The first stage involves *discernment*—the Spirit enabling the prophet to somehow "hear" from God so as to receive a message and/or ministry assignment from him. The second stage involves *deployment*—the Spirit empowering the prophet to speak and/or act into the lives of people on God's behalf.[28] For sure, Barth insisted that because the preacher lacks the power or authority to speak for God, to attempt to do so would be "blasphemous rebellion."[29] Still, the passage presented above seems to indicate that he also believed that preaching, when it is *true proclamation*, will possess a Spirit-enabled, prophetic quality.

This leads then to a tandem discussion of Barth's theologically (and pneumatologically) real understanding of *revelation as encounter* and *Word of God as event*. Trevor Hart explains that "when the word 'revelation' occurs in Barth's writings, we are being referred to a reality which is essentially dynamic rather than static, and always under God's control. Revelation, as Barth never tires of reminding his readers, is an event; it is something which happens, something which God does, and something in which we are actively involved."[30] The notion of revelation as event (Greek: *ereignis*) connotes the realism at work in Barth's theology as a whole. Pentecostals, who see Luke portraying Spirit in-filling as an *event* (e.g., Acts 2:4; 4:31; 10:41-46) and Paul teaching that the reception of the Spirit is an *experience* so palpable that it provides assurance with respect to a changed status before God (e.g., Rom. 8:15-16; Gal. 4:6), cannot help but believe that a biblically

---

27. Barth, *CD* I/1, 52.

28. For more on this pneumatocentric understanding of prophetic activity, including the biblical support for it, see Gary Tyra, *The Holy Spirit in Mission: Prophetic Speech and Action in Christian Witness* (Downers Grove: IVP Academic, 2011).

29. Barth, *CD* I/1, 52-3. See also Karl Barth, *Homiletics* (Louisville: Westminster John Knox Press, 1991), 48-9.

30. Trevor Hart, "Revelation," in *The Cambridge Companion to Karl Barth*, ed. John Webster (Cambridge: Cambridge University Press, 2000), 37–56, here 45.

informed theological realism infers a pneumatological realism as well. Moreover, Barth's personal, experiential understanding of revelation as an event that is always under God's control would seem to warrant the pneumatological expectancy and prayerful waiting on God that are at the heart of Pentecostal experience.

In addition, we Pentecostals also resonate with the relational aspect of Barth's view of revelation as event. When God, in his freedom, graciously speaks in a self-revelatory manner to his creatures, this results not simply in instruction—cognitive knowledge—but *encounter*—relational knowledge, a "personal knowing of God."[31] Pentecostals hear this and immediately think of 1 Corinthians 2:10-16 and the suggestion presented there by Paul that the Holy Spirit wants to help Christ's followers gain his own understanding of who God is and what he's about.

And Barth used similar language when speaking of the Word of God. He did not understand Word of God in a nominal, static, merely propositional sense. For Barth, the Word of God, too, is an event—that is, God's speaking. Says Barth: "Church proclamation is talk, speech. So is Holy Scripture. So is even revelation in itself as such. . . . God's Word means that God speaks."[32]

Furthermore, as is well known, Barth understood God's speaking as taking place in three forms: the Word of God *revealed* (Jesus Christ), the Word of God *written* (the Scriptures), and the Word of God *proclaimed* (Proclamation).[33] Barth maintained that while there is a processional flow at work in this threefold expression of the Word of God, all three forms are the Word of God and none should be considered inferior to the other two.[34] That said, it would seem that when Barth states that "[p]roclamation must ever and again become proclamation,"[35] and that

---

31. Ibid., 42. Barth, himself, wrote: "The personalizing of the concept of the Word of God, which we cannot avoid when we remember that Jesus Christ is the Word of God, does not mean its deverbalising. But it (naturally) means awareness of the fact it is person rather than thing or object even if and in so far as it is word, word of Scripture and word of preaching. . . . In its form neither as proclamation, Holy Scripture, nor revelation do we know God's Word as an entity that exists or could exist merely in and for itself. We know it only as a Word that is directed to us and applies to us. . . . God need not speak to us. What He says by Himself and to Himself from eternity to eternity would really be said just as well and even better without our being there. . . . Only when we are clear about this can we estimate what it means that God has actually, though not necessarily, created a world and us, that His love actually, though not necessarily, applies to us, that His Word has actually, though not necessarily, been spoken to us." Barth, *CD* I/1, 138–40.

32. Barth, *CD* I/1, 132.

33. For more on this, see ibid., 88–124.

34. See Karl Barth, *Göttingen Dogmatics: Instruction in the Christian Religion*, ed. Hannelotte Reifen, trans. Geoffrey W. Bromiley (Grand Rapids: Eerdmans, 1990), 15, as cited in David Guretzki, *Karl Barth on the Filioque* (New York: Taylor and Francis, 2016), 86.

35. Barth, *CD* I/1, 88.

"[t]he presupposition of this event is the Word of God,"[36] he was also suggesting that a crucial contingency is at work in Christian preaching if it is to be what Barth keeps referring to as "real proclamation."[37] While true (or real) proclamation is contingent upon both the Word of God written (the Scriptures) and Word of God revealed (Christ), it is ultimately contingent on (or only a possibility because of) the dynamic of "God's speaking." In other words, as a Pent-evangelical biblical and practical theologian, I am suggesting that we find in Barth's doctrine of the Word of God some implicit support for the notion that true proclamation will not only be biblical and Christ centered, but *prophetic* as well. *Real proclamation is a possibility precisely because of the reality of the Word of God—God's speaking—and humanity's Spirit-endowed ability to hear/receive it.*[38] God deigning to speak in a self-revealing, encounter-facilitating manner, and humans enabled by his Spirit to experience it: this dynamic is at the heart of the prophetic phenomenon as portrayed in Scripture.

Barth's Understanding of the Earmarks of True (Prophetic) Proclamation

All that is left for us to consider are some of the distinctive features which Barth seemed to associate with Christian preaching done right. Barth insisted that the key to effective Christian preaching is prayer. He wrote: "it is prayer that puts us in rapport with God and permits us to collaborate with him."[39] *Could it be that the earmarks presented below are what we Pentecostals hope to experience when we pray for God's anointing upon our preaching?*[40]

Barth's "Incarnational" Understanding of Christian Proclamation

According to Barth, a foundational feature of true proclamation is its capacity to facilitate for hearers a genuine encounter with *divinity*—the *humanity* of the preacher and sermon notwithstanding.[41] Barth was never reticent in his insistence that true proclamation is a miracle.[42] However, he was also very careful to specify that the miraculous is not merely the divinization of human utterance, nor the humanization of the divine. Instead, true proclamation involves something akin to

---

36. Ibid., 89.
37. Ibid., 89–93.
38. Barth, *Göttingen Dogmatics*, 89.
39. Karl Barth, *Prayer* (Louisville: Westminster John Knox Press, 2002), 20, as cited in Thomas Christian Currie, *The Only Sacrament Left to Us: The Threefold Word of God in the Theology and Ecclesiology of Karl Barth* (Eugene: Pickwick Publications, 2015), 113.
40. For a discussion of the role of "pneumatologically real prayer" in a "pneumatologically real approach to the preaching task," see Tyra, *Getting Real*, 173–80.
41. Barth, *CD* I/1, 93–4.
42. Ibid.

the phenomenon of *incarnation*.[43] Barth's reasoning seems to have been thus: just as the Word of God revealed (Christ) involved the assumption of human flesh, and just as the Word of God written (the Scriptures) involved the pen and intellect of human authors,[44] even so, the Word of God proclaimed (Proclamation) involves the full involvement of fallible, imperfect human heralds. Barth writes:

> The miracle of real proclamation does not consist in the fact that the willing and doing of proclaiming man with all its conditioning and in all its problems is set aside, that in some way a disappearance takes place and a gap arises in the reality of nature, and that in some way there steps into this gap naked divine reality scarcely concealed by a mere remaining appearance of human reality.[45]

Though Barth did not view the Scriptures or proclamation as incarnational in an *ontological* sense (as in Christ's incarnation), he did seem to be open to them being *incarnational* in a *functional* sense.[46] Thus, while avoiding a direct correlation with the Chalcedonian definition, Barth did seem to steer away from a docetic understanding of the miracle of proclamation toward one that is more incarnational (or wholistic) in nature. At the very least, his language is certainly evocative of the incarnation when he writes:

> The willing and doing of proclaiming man, however, is not in any sense set aside in real proclamation. As Christ became true man and remains true man to all eternity, real proclamation becomes an event on the level of all other human events. . . . But as Christ is not just true man, so it is not just the willing and doing of proclaiming man. It is also and indeed it is primarily and decisively the divine willing and doing. Precisely for this reason the human element is not set aside. What seems to be the burning question of the nature of the co-existence and co-operation of the two factors is a highly irrelevant question. God and the human element are not two co-existing and co-operating factors. The human element is what God created. Only in the state of disobedience is it a factor standing over against God. In the state of obedience it is service of God. Service of God does not have to be removed in order that God Himself may be honoured in it.[47]

---

43. Ibid., 94.
44. I refer to the possibility and missional utility of an incarnational model of biblical inspiration in my book, Gary Tyra, *A Missional Orthodoxy: Theology and Ministry in a Post-Christian Context* (Downers Grove: IVP Academic, 2013), 134–8.
45. Barth, *CD* I/1, 94.
46. See Angela Dienhart Hancock, *Karl Barth's Emergency Homiletic, 1932–1933: A Summons to Prophetic Witness at the Dawn of the Third Reich* (Grand Rapids: Eerdmans, 2013), 12.
47. Barth, *CD* I/1, 94.

Again, to be clear, neither Barth nor I are suggesting that the Scriptures, or the preaching of them, are divine in the sense that Jesus is. I am simply drawing attention to the fact that Barth used language that is roughly, imperfectly analogous to Christ's incarnation when speaking of the "miracle of real proclamation."

At the same time, I am suggesting that the work of the Spirit in the Word of God written and Word of God proclaimed is what makes a genuine, life-story shaping encounter with the divine possible by means of them. Some support for the assertion can be found in Aaron Smith's book, *A Theology of the Third Article*. Following Barth, he emphasizes the full divinity, personhood, and agency of the Spirit,[48] while referring often to a dynamic he calls "inverberation."[49] For instance, Smith writes:

> I argue that the Spirit of God is God a third time, subsisting in ontological unity with the Father and Son, yet distinctly his own Person in that he is the contemporaneity of the revelation event in which God has his existence.... The Spirit is contemporary instantiation of the Incarnation, or, the parallel life-act of *Inverberation*.[50]

The term *inverberation* is intended to connote three ideas: *incarnation*, *verba* (words), and the dynamic of *verberation* (resounding). According to Smith, the concept of inverberation best describes the contemporaneous, ongoing manner in which the Holy Spirit, himself incarnate in the reading and preaching of sacred Scripture, functions as a fresh, contemporaneous incarnation of the prophetic and apostolic witness to Christ presented in it.[51]

The significance of *inverberation* for the type of prophetic preaching I am advocating for should be apparent. Though the notion of the Spirit himself becoming incarnate can seem to be at odds with the Spirit's mission to ever reveal the risen Christ (cf. Jn 16:12-15), I find in Smith's Barth-informed construct some tacit support for what I am proposing: the possibility of biblically grounded, Christ-honoring sermons that are incarnational in the sense that Christ's Spirit is actually speaking through the preacher in a genuinely prophetic manner for the strengthening, encouragement, and comfort of the sermon's auditors (1 Cor. 14:3).

---

48. Smith, *A Theology of the Third Article*, 2, 7, 194, 241, 249.
49. Ibid., 7, 12, 20, 22, 35, 44, 58, 60, 82, 83, 92, 108, 110, 114, 120, 121, 127, 156, 169, 189, 200, 253.
50. Ibid., 7.
51. Ibid. Likewise, Thomas Christian Currie implies that an incarnational dynamic is at work in Christian preaching when he asserts that, for Barth, "the Holy Spirit is the bond of union between the divine voice and the human voice in the event of the Word of God." Currie, *The Only Sacrament Left to Us*, 31.

Barth's "Sacramental" Understanding of Christian Proclamation

In his book, *Scripture as Real Presence: Sacramental Exegesis in the Early Church*, Hans Boersma acknowledges the significant influence of Barth on what he refers to as "a remarkable and growing interest in theological interpretation of Scripture."[52] According to Boersma, a theological interpretation of Scripture makes possible not only a sacramental reading of God's Word[53] but a sacramental preaching of it as well.[54] Thus, if only indirectly, Boersma points to Barth's work as a major cause of the recent upsurge of interest in the notion of sacramental preaching.[55]

Early in his career, Barth opined: "The best preaching is as such an equivalent to the kerygma that the Roman Catholic church offers every day in the form of the sacrament of the altar."[56] Aaron Smith clarifies Barth's meaning thusly: "Whereas for Rome, the presence of God is mediated in the Eucharist, *that presence is encountered in Reformation theology in the event of the sermon.*"[57]

A book-length treatment of this topic is provided by Thomas Christian Currie in *The Only Sacrament Left to Us: The Threefold Word of God in the Theology and Ecclesiology of Karl Barth*. Of special note is the way Currie emphasizes *Christ's ongoing presence made possible through the work of the Spirit* as he describes Barth's understanding of the sacramental nature of Christian proclamation:

---

52. Hans Boersma, *Scripture as Real Presence: Sacramental Exegesis in the Early Church* (Grand Rapids: Baker Academic, 2017), xi.

53. Ibid., 2.

54. Hans Boersma, *Sacramental Preaching: Sermons on the Hidden Presence of Christ* (Grand Rapids: Baker Academic, 2016), xvii–xxiii.

55. I should briefly note how Boersma's conception of sacramental preaching differs from mine. Boersma advocates for sermons that "move from the surface level of the text . . . to the deeper, contemplative level"—that is, preaching that, following the practice of the early church fathers, points hearers to "Christ as the sacramental mystery present in the text" (Boersma, *Sacramental Preaching*, xxii). My understanding of the "sacramental sermon" is a bit more pneumatologically explicit, dependent, and immediate. The focus moves beyond the spiritual/theological *exegesis* that's presented to the congregation, to the existentially impactful *encounter* with the risen Christ that results when the Holy Spirit prompts and enables the preacher to speak to the congregation in a prophetic, Christ-honoring manner. In other words, while both Boersma and I agree that there is such a thing as sacramental preaching, I suspect we may disagree somewhat as to whether an engagement in what he refers to as "sacramental exegesis" is, by itself, capable of producing sermons that function sacramentally. It is my contention that an anointing of the Spirit upon the preparation and presentation of the sermon is also required—prophetic prompting and enablement by the Spirit of Christ that the preacher can and must prayerfully cooperate with for the sacramental encounter between congregants and the risen Christ to occur.

56. Barth, *Göttingen Dogmatics*, 31, as cited in Smith, *A Theology of the Third Article*, 85.

57. Smith, *A Theology of the Third Article*, 85, emphasis added. See also Richardson, *Reading Karl Barth*, 114–15.

Barth describes this proclamation event in . . . *sacramental* language. Any reference to sacrament does not begin with the Lord's supper or baptism, Barth maintains, but begins with *Jesus Christ and his ongoing presence* in the life of the Christian community *through the work of the Spirit*. This broader view of sacramental presence, not only includes Scripture and preaching, but renders baptism and the Lord's Supper dependent on the gospel, on the proclaimed and heard Word of God. This sacramental understanding of Scripture and preaching in the church's life is why Barth maintains that *preaching grounded on the witness of Scripture*, "is the only sacrament left to us."[58]

To be sure, we must keep in mind how Barth's understanding of this topic evolved over time. To their credit, both Smith and Currie acknowledge this fact.[59] Thus, I want to make clear that I am not contending that the mature Barth explicitly affirmed the kind of sacramental preaching I, as a Pentecostal, have mind; only that Barth's theological project has room in it for the possibility of prophetic sermons that, while not grace conferring, are nevertheless encounter facilitating in their effect (cf. 1 Cor. 14:25).

Barth's "Transformational" Understanding of Christian Proclamation

What is the sign of prophetic preaching? How will we as preachers know that it is occurring or has occurred? Such preaching occurs within the church, I will suggest, when: the theme of the sermon is due to a special prompting of the Spirit; when the study of the pertinent biblical text(s) seems to possess an unusually insightful quality; when the dynamic of serendipity occurs during the acquisition of illustrative material; and when the Holy Spirit seems to "speak through" the preacher during the preaching event, sometimes even articulating sermonic content the preacher had no intention nor natural capacity to deliver. And yet, the ultimate indication that prophetic preaching has occurred, I propose, is when we find that the Spirit has impressed the message delivered upon the minds and hearts of those listening in an especially powerful manner. In other words, *genuine transformation occurs*.

Proclamation is true, said Barth, when it is "talk which has to be listened to and which rightly demands obedience."[60] Barth's assumption seems to have been that, when God speaks, those with "ears to hear" (Ezek. 12:2; Mk 4:23) know it (cf.

---

58. Currie, *The Only Sacrament Left to Us*, 20. Quotation is from Karl Barth, "The Need and Promise of Christian Preaching," in *The Word of God and the Word of Man* (New York: Harper & Row, 1957), 114, emphasis added.

59. For example, see the chapter titled "What Happens to the Threefold Word of God: Revision or Rejection," in Currie, *The Only Sacrament Left to Us: The Threefold Word of God in the Theology and Ecclesiology of Karl Barth* (Eugene: Pickwick Publications, 2015), 89–137.

60. Barth, *CD* I/1, 93.

Jer. 23:29; Isa. 55:10-11).[61] Put differently, Barth seems to have had in mind the possibility of encounter-facilitating preaching that leaves a mark!

This notion of an existentially impactful, paradigm-shifting, faithfulness-producing encounter with a holy God is implicit in this description of Barth's high view of the Sunday sermon. Citing Barth, Aaron Smith writes:

> The sermon is instructive for Barth because of its existential poignancy. "On Sunday morning when the bells ring to call the congregation and minister to church, there is in the air an *expectancy* that something great, crucial, and even momentous is to *happen*." It is not, of course, that everyone feels or is equally conscious of this anticipation, but that does not alter the fact that "*expectancy* is inherent in the whole situation."
>
> The sermon is wreathed in *readiness*. For what? Not merely for edification, entertainment, or instruction, Barth says, but to hear and confess that "God *is* present."[62]

Barth seems to suggest that it is a sermon-enabled experience of the divine presence that is to take place each Sunday—an existentially poignant audience with God that cannot help but be existentially impactful as well. Indeed, when I think of the ecclesial encounter Barth seems to have had in mind, I cannot help but think of Isaiah 6:1-8. If Isaiah's experience in the temple is any indication, the appropriate response to the manifest presence of God is a sincere turning away from sin toward an eager engagement in the *missio Dei*. Some tacit support for this association is provided by Thomas Currie when he writes:

> It is in the church's attempt to proclaim and hear the gospel, that the risen Christ comes and comes again, speaking the Word of God through broken human words, *freeing* the Christian community to *get up and follow in discipleship*, and *sending* the Christian community to *engage the world* in correspondence to the life and activity of Jesus Christ at work in their midst.[63]

To be sure, we Pentecostals believe that the Holy Spirit is at work in prophetic preaching to awaken Christian faith, but he is also graciously drawing those who have ears to hear deeper into the reality of an intimate, interactive, existentially impactful, ministry-engendering relationship with the risen Christ. Indeed, it has been my experience that, at times, he may even provide—for specific disciples or the community as a whole—some Christ-honoring spiritual, moral, or ministry guidance that is amazingly timely and specific (Jn 16:12-15)![64]

---

61. Ibid., 92–3.
62. Smith, *A Theology of the Third Article*, 39. The quotations are from Barth, "The Need and Promise of Christian Preaching," 104, emphasis original.
63. Currie, *The Only Sacrament Left to Us*, xiii, emphasis added.
64. For more on the dynamic of *prophetic* spiritual, moral, and ministry guidance, see *Getting Real*, 61–118.

Conclusion

I have endeavored in this chapter to briefly expound upon several Barthian constructs which, when considered together, seem to suggest that it is possible to find in his theologizing some implicit support for the phenomenon of Spirit-empowered sermons that facilitate prophetic encounters with the risen Christ.

Critical to the experience of this phenomenon, however, is the way the preacher approaches the biblical text. In the foreword he provided for Barth's published lectures on homiletics, David Buttrick writes:

> Those who preach the scriptures will not be pontificating clerics or detached visionaries or merely dull. For, again and again, the scriptures will speak God's *new* word. "The proper attitude of preachers," Barth says, "does not depend on whether they hold on to the doctrine of inspiration but on whether or not they expect God to speak to them. . . ." Barth calls ministers to "active expectation" and "ongoing submission" in their study of the Bible.[65]

I am convinced that the type of anointed proclamation referred to in this chapter is already occurring much more often than many congregation members and preachers realize (and not just in Pent-evangelical churches). That said, what would happen, I wonder, if more evangelical and pent-evangelical preachers, taking Barth's pneumatological realism and encounter-oriented understanding of revelation, Word of God, and Christian proclamation seriously, were to approach the preaching task with the deliberate, prayerful sense of expectation and submission Barth prescribed?[66] Perhaps the answer to that question is *even more prophetic preaching*. May it be so!

---

65. David G. Buttrick, "Foreword," in Barth, *Homiletics*, 9.

66. For more on the missional import of "prophetic preaching" and the need for even Pentecostal–charismatic preachers to avoid a "routinization of charisma," see Tyra, *The Holy Spirit in Mission*, 130, n. 2, 156–7.

Part Two

GOD AND CREATION

Chapter 4

ONENESS PENTECOSTALS AND KARL BARTH

THEOLOGICAL COUSINS WHO NEVER MET?

David A. Reed

Introduction

Karl Barth was my evangelist!

I found Barth in the pages of Claude Welch's *In This Name: The Doctrine of the Trinity in Contemporary Theology*.[1] I was a young, naïve student embarking on a new venture in theological studies at a small Christian college. One day, curiously scanning book titles in the library stacks, my eyes locked onto the words *"In This Name"*—emblazoned it seemed—on the book's cover. I immediately found a chair, began to read as best I could understand, and soon discovered one scholar whose views seemed surprisingly similar to my own Oneness views. Like me, he didn't like the word "persons" to describe "Father, Son and Holy Spirit." He preferred "modes of being," a concept I could only hunch at the time. After a few visits to that book, I began to grasp the argument that these three somehow belong together within God's being, not just God's revelation in history. By this time, Karl Barth was dismantling my theological defenses and giving me a compelling reason to embrace the trinitarian faith—the One who is revealed must be the One who is! Months later I thought, "I can be a Trinitarian." My own surprise at such a conclusion which tumbled so effortlessly out of my thoughts was that I had entered theological studies with absolutely no intention of changing direction, only to teach in a Oneness Bible school. It was not the various baits of wider acceptance, potentially better teaching opportunities, or the ladder of success. It was simply the force of a weightier understanding of the God whom I knew I had been following from my childhood.

It would generally be considered impossible or frivolous at best to attempt to bring into conversation two of the most unlikely representatives of the Christian faith: the frequently assailed heterodox Oneness Pentecostals (OPs) and the undisputed leading Protestant Theologian of the twentieth century, Karl Barth.

---

1. Claude Welch, *In This Name: The Doctrine of the Trinity in Contemporary Theology* (New York: Charles Scribner's Sons, 1952).

OPs originated as part of the raucous Pentecostal Revival during the early decades of the twentieth century. They outright, and with not a little enthusiasm, did battle with proponents of the doctrine of the Trinity. For this they paid dearly. In 1916, they were isolated from their spiritual home, the newly formed Assemblies of God (AG), over its adoption of a strongly worded trinitarian Statement of Faith. That same year, a young Swiss Reformed pastor and product of European intellectual tradition by the name of Karl Barth took pen in hand to write *The Epistle to the Romans*.[2] This was to be his first theological shot across the bow of the Liberal theology that dominated European Protestantism.

OPs and Barth would have been strangers in every way—culturally, linguistically, theologically. An appeal to their common Christian faith would pass for very little among these restorationist Pentecostals for whom Barth represented the worst of the dead church—which in their mind had long since been abandoned by the living God. What could these two Christian representatives possibly discover together that would reveal their deepest theological conviction and release their most cherished doxological dedication? If there is an answer, it would be the person of Jesus Christ—as revelation and theological method. Both parties have a cohering theological interest in this Jesus. And if this be the case, certainly the least we can say is that OPs and Karl Barth are theological cousins who never met.

This chapter will be an opportunity for OPs and Barth to meet. The first section provides a brief historico-theological overview of the Oneness movement, highlighting theological themes intended to catch the eye of Barth the theologian. The second section introduces Barth's own interested thoughts on these themes. The aim of this dialogue is to accomplish two things: (1) create an appreciation for the theological challenge that Oneness theology brings to the table, though often buried in its sometimes polemical and exclusive presentation, and (2) offer insight into how Barth might be helpful in affirming, challenging, enriching, and enlarging foundational Oneness doctrines.

OP Theology—A Historical Sketch

The Birth of a Theological Movement

Oneness Pentecostalism was an enigma. The Pentecostal Revival had already produced its share of shock to sacred and secular alike. The interracial Azusa Street Revival of 1906 was a religious and cultural jolt. In 1910, the Pentecostals suffered their first schism at the hands of William Durham (1873–1912), controversial evangelist from Chicago. But given time these early Pentecostals would overcome their differences and find ways to express *koinonia* with one another and the wider Christian church.

---

2. Karl Barth, *The Epistle to the Romans* (German: *Der Römerbrief*, 1st ed., 1919).

The Oneness movement was different. After two turbulent years within the AG fellowship, the OPs were set adrift because they had chosen to abandon the doctrine of the Trinity, a fundamental tenet affirmed by the vast majority of Christian bodies.³ Admittedly, fellowship is known to occur at personal and local levels. But here's the enigma. Although denial of such a fundamental orthodox Christian doctrine is prima facie severe, the intuition of many trinitarians is that these unorthodox Pentecostals are truly sisters and brothers in the faith. Some may speculate that they could be a bit muddled, uninformed, or saying the same thing in another way, yet they are nevertheless sincere believers worthy of fellowship. But due to near universal commitment to the creedal affirmation of the Trinity in denominational Statements of Faith, formal open fellowship is more difficult and fraught with political landmines on both sides. It is this enigma—the un-sureness about what is beneath each other's theology and praxis—which constitutes the potential for a fruitful dialogue with Barth.

The event which set the trajectory for the emergence of OP occurred in 1913 during an advertised Worldwide Camp Meeting in Arroyo Seco on the outskirts of Los Angeles. Invitations were issued primarily to the followers of Durham who brought with them teachings that reached back to their evangelical roots.

Two events at the Camp Meeting set the trajectory for the emergence of OP. The first was a baptismal sermon delivered by Canadian evangelist, Robert E. McAlister (1880–1953), in which he noted in passing the apparent inconsistency in the baptismal name between Jesus' triune invocation in Matthew 28:19 and the variants of "Lord Jesus Christ" recorded in the Acts of the apostles. The two passages, he proposed, were intended to be harmonized christocentrically, with the names, "Lord Jesus Christ," which correlated with the triune name, "Father, Son, Holy Spirit."⁴ The second event introduced the role of revelation into McAlister's speculation. In the early hours of the morning following McAlister's sermon, John B. Schaepe (1870–1939)—a little known Pentecostal follower—ran through the camp shouting that God had revealed to him the truth of baptism in the name of Jesus Christ and the Oneness of the Godhead.⁵ Schaepe left no written account, but the oral testimony of his "revelation" became embedded in the Oneness narrative

---

3. The New Issue unfolded with less rancor in Canada due to at least three factors: many ministers were sympathetic, some had already been rebaptized, and the leadership was concerned to avoid the divisions occurring south of the border. See David A. Reed, "Oneness Seed on Canadian Soil: Early Developments of Oneness Pentecostalism," [agree]*Winds from the North: Canadian Contributions to the Pentecostal Movement*, ed. Michael Wilkinson and Peter Althouse (Boston: Brill, 2010).

4. Frank J. Ewart, *The Phenomenon of Pentecost—"A History of the Latter Rain"* (St. Louis: Pentecostal Publishing House, 1947), 76-7.

5. Fred J. Foster, *A History of the Oneness Movement* (St. Louis: Pentecostal Publishing House, 1965), 52.

through the account given by Harry Morse, a young Pentecostal convert who was present and heard Schaepe expound his views.[6]

It was Australian evangelist Frank J. Ewart (1876–1947), however, who would eventually formulate the new doctrine. Friend and colleague of McAlister, he heard McAlister's sermon and later engaged in study and ongoing conversations with him. By the spring of 1914, he was persuaded of not only the new baptismal name, but more crucially, a radical reformulation of the nature of the Trinity. He would later mark McAlister's sermon as the catalyst which was "destined to resound throughout all Christendom."[7] In April, Ewart launched his campaign in Belvedere on the outskirts of Los Angeles. With the help of Glenn Cook, an evangelistic colleague, they pitched a tent and installed a baptismal tank. Ewart's message was simple: the singular invocational name "Jesus" in baptism, supported by a confession of an undifferentiated God in divine essence and threefold in historical manifestation. Ewart's prophetic key was Zechariah 14:9: "In that day shall there be one LORD, and his name one" (KJV).[8]

While Ewart's revival was gaining in both momentum and disturbance, his fellow Durham disciples were organizing their fellowship under the name, AG. The conflict was inevitable as Ewart's revival became a movement within AG, soon to be labeled the New Issue. By 1915, it had won over two key leaders who themselves would become theological architects of OP—Garfield T. Haywood from Indianapolis and Franklin Small from Winnipeg, Canada. Haywood, an African American pastor from Indianapolis, introduced the teaching that the threefold elements set forth in Acts 2:38—repentance, baptism in the name of Jesus Christ, and the gift of the Holy Spirit—represent the new birth as promised by Jesus to Nicodemus in John 3:5. As a Canadian, Small's influence was less prominent in the United States. He, however, held the distinction among all of Durham's followers to have understood most clearly and embraced most thoroughly the Finished Work of Calvary teaching.

The fourth theological architect was Andrew Urshan (1884–1967), a Persian American missionary and evangelist. By his own account, he had been baptizing in the name of Jesus since 1910 and continued to do so after he affiliated with AG. This combined with his refusal to disfellowship the new Oneness churches after the 1916 schism within AG led to his dismissal and eventual realignment with the new Oneness organization, the Pentecostal Assemblies of the World (PAW). His understanding of the Trinity was unique: while he opposed what he called a

---

6. Harry Morse, an early convert to the Oneness movement, was present and heard Schaepe's ideas, which in 1943 he recounted as "new ideas on water baptism in Jesus' name, and the oneness of the Godhead"; quoted in Arthur L. Clanton, *United We Stand—A History of Oneness Organizations* (St. Louis Pentecostal Publishing House, 1970), 16.

7. Ewart, *Phenomenon of Pentecost*, 77.

8. Ewart, *The Revelation of Jesus Christ* (St. Louis: Pentecostal Publishing House, n.d.), 33.

Trinity of "three separate and distinct persons," he consistently affirmed the great divine mystery with terms like "triune," "Tri-one," and "three-one."[9]

By 1919, OP finally emerged with its own institutional identity as the PAW. For many, the New Issue had seemed to appear out of nowhere. But, like all social movements, it had a history. As British sociologist Bryan Wilson points out, a sect is "a unique combination of variations, few of which in themselves are wholly distinctive of that sect alone."[10] OP was no exception.

Early Evangelical Resources

Evangelicals had been battling for the soul of orthodox biblical faith for more than a quarter century before OP appeared. Their mission was to defend the full deity of Christ against an encroaching modernist theology of the "sweet and gentle Jesus." Three influences in particular helped shape Oneness Christology. The first was an expression of what is best described as an orthodox version of Jesus-piety, a legacy of German Pietism. Hymns, poems, and devotion were often directed to Jesus in which even the name "Jesus" would carry more spiritual weight than the tepid titles of "Christ" and "Lord." The second was their devotional exaltation of the *name* of Jesus. Echoing the ancient Jewish belief that one's personality resides in the name, praise to the name of God was an act of devotion to the Person of God. When they mined the Old Testament (OT) for the various names and titles for God, their devotion frequently culminated with the name, Jesus.[11]

The third and most significant for Oneness theology was the *apologetic* appeal to the name, especially by representatives of the growing premillennial theology and Keswick Holiness movement. Their purpose was to defend the unadulterated deity of Christ and safeguard his atoning work. But unlike the Fundamentalists of the next generation who focused on the virgin birth to defend Christ's deity and protect the theology of substitutionary atonement, these early Evangelicals directed their attention to a biblical study of the names and titles of God in the OT to demonstrate that Jesus fulfilled all the qualifications as fully as did Yahweh. Put simply, the Yahweh of the OT is the Jesus of the New.[12]

---

9. Daniel L. Segraves, *Andrew D. Urshan: A Theological Biography* (Lexington: Emeth Press, 2017).

10. Bryan R. Wilson, *Sects and Society, A Sociological Study of the Elim Tabernacle, Christian Science, and Christadelphianism* (Berkeley: University of California Press, 1961), 7.

11. These roots can be traced to German Pietism, and later influence on Revivalism and late-nineteenth-century evangelical leaders such as Albert B. Simpson, Essek W. Kenyon, and Arno C. Gaebelein; see F. Ernest Stoeffler, *The Rise of Evangelical Pietism*, Studies in the History of Religions 9 (Leiden: E.J. Brill, 1965), and Dale Brown, *Understanding Pietism* (Grand Rapids: Eerdmans, 1978). See also chapter 2, David A. Reed, *"In Jesus' Name": The History and Beliefs of Oneness Pentecostals* (Blandford Forum: Deo Publishing, 2008), ch. 2.

12. Numerous examples are reviewed in chapter 3, Reed, *IJN*.

Finally, it is worth speculating on the future significance of this particular effort to defend the deity of Christ. The fourth-century christological debates focused on the ontological distinctions between the Father and the Son. In contrast, the burden of late-nineteenth-century Evangelicals was to defend the divine identity, the *oneness*, of the Father and Jesus. This evangelical movement may well have set the stage for a more radical theology to come, Oneness Modalism.

OP and Evangelical Meet

In 1913, the year of the Worldwide Camp Meeting, another significant event occurred. William Phillips Hall published a thin volume, "*What Is the Name*"? Or "*The Mystery of God Revealed.*"[13] Hall was a successful businessman and lay evangelist from New York who was encouraged by friend and prominent Dispensational Fundamentalist, Arno C. Gaebelein, to embark on a study of the name of God in Scripture. The embattled Evangelicals were witnessing a dead and powerless church being gutted by modernist theology. Hall and Gaebelein believed the key to restoring the church's spiritual power would be found in discovering the true identity of Jesus through a study of the biblical name of God. And it would begin with a Hebrew understanding of "name" in the OT.[14] The expectation was that a recovery of the *name* would bring people into life-changing contact with the *Person* of God: "'the Name' of God is . . . in a very true sense, the very Essence, or Essential Personality, of God Himself."[15]

The critical act in which the power of the name of God would be restored to the church was the moment of that name being invoked over the candidate in the waters of baptism. Hall, however, faced the exegetical challenge of determining precisely what name was to be invoked. He was aware of an apparent discrepancy between Jesus' commission to baptize in "the name of the Father, and of the Son and of the Holy Spirit" (Mt. 28:19) and the apostolic practice of baptizing in some variation of "Lord Jesus Christ" as recorded in the Acts of the Apostles—and paradigmatically stated in Acts 2:38.

Hall resolved the discrepancy by claiming the names in Matthew were "relationship" names, not personal names, and thereby were disqualified as a proper New Covenant name of God. He concluded that Jesus spoke those words parabolically, since the hearers—except his inner circle—would be unable to grasp what was to come. Only on the Day of Pentecost were the apostles released to declare the full name of "Lord Jesus Christ" as the covenantal name of the triune

---

13. William Phillips Hall, "*What Is the Name*"? Or "*The Mystery of God Revealed*" (Greenwich: By the Author, 1913).

14. Gaebelein and Hall were both strong advocates of the Jewish People as the People of the Covenant. This explains Hall's statement in the beginning of his book, that it is being addressed first to "God's ancient and beloved people the Jews; who, according to the flesh, are the children of Abraham," in *What Is the Name?*

15. Hall, "*What Is the Name*"? 15.

God, the One through whom we have access to the Father and the Spirit, the name which encompasses the whole enterprise of salvation.[16] Since Jesus was made both "Lord and Christ" (Acts 2:36), the baptismal name must be the same; or in Hall's words, "The true baptismal 'Name' is the saving 'Name of the Lord Jesus Christ.'"[17]

For Hall, the name "Lord Jesus Christ" perfectly embodies the name of the Trinity. As Yahweh is called Lord (Jer. 16:21), now Jesus claims to come in his *Father's* name (Jn 5:43; 10:25).[18] Jesus is the personal name of the incarnate *Son* of God, not merely the human name of a man from Nazareth.[19] The name of the *Holy Spirit* is the name of "Christ," since the Spirit "is of, incarnate in, and proceeds from" the incarnate Son of God. The Holy Spirit is one with the Spirit of the Father and the Son. More importantly here, the Pauline language of "Christ in you" is another way which Scripture expresses the indwelling Holy Spirit.[20] Hall was not unaware that his proposal to adopt the christocentric name would be a radical break with the church's tradition. But the reason cannot be overstated: a spiritually powerless church was desperate for the one thing that would restore that power: the strong name of the Lord Jesus Christ.[21]

Hall's account brings us full circle to McAlister's sermon. Both sermon and book occurred in 1913, and McAlister's explanation given to Ewart some months later represents precisely Hall's interpretation:

> Lord, Jesus, Christ, being the counterpart of Father, Son, and Holy Ghost, . . . made Jesus' words in Matt. 28:19, *one of those parabolic statements* [emphasis mine] of truth, which was interpreted in Acts 2:38 and other scriptures.[22]

McAlister later gave credit for the insight to George Studd, fellow Pentecostal pioneer working in the Los Angeles area.[23] Hall's little book likely came at some point into his possession.

---

16. One of Hall's favorite and paradigmatic texts is Colossians 2:9, "For in him dwelleth all the fulness of the Godhead bodily."

17. Hall, *"What Is the Name"?* 70.

18. See Jn 5:43, 10:25, and others, Hall, *"What Is the Name"?* 87–98.

19. See Lk. 1:31-32; Mt. 3:16-17, 16:13-17; 1 Jn 5:5; and others, Hall, *"What Is the Name"?* 99–103.

20. See Jn 14:26; Gal. 2:20; Col. 1:27; Rom. 8:9-11; and others, Hall, *"What Is the Name"?* 105–15.

21. Hall opens the Preface of his book with these words: "In publishing this book the writer is fully aware of the fact that he is presenting an interpretation of 'the Name' and 'Personality' of the Triune God that cannot be considered otherwise than as revolutionary in itself and in its prospective influence upon the teachings and practice of the Christian Church in all lands," *"What Is the Name"?* 21.

22. Quoted in Ewart, *Phenomenon of Pentecost*, 77.

23. McAlister, "Is the 'New Thing' New?" *Truth Advocate* 1, no. 2 (1949): 16; quoted in Thomas Fudge, *Christianity without the Cross: A History of Salvation in Oneness Pentecostalism* (Parkland: Universal Publishers, 2003), 46, n. 16.

Summary

The following two accounts are unmistakably similar: Hall's "remarkable biblical discovery" and Schaepe's Camp Meeting "revelation." Both believers were clearly biblicist in nature. Neither appealed to an extra-biblical authority. Neither was speculative. Both believed they had unearthed truth hidden for centuries within the pages of the Bible. Both read the Bible through a common restorationist lens. But one was Evangelical, the other a primordial Pentecostal. Such common ground might not be sufficient for visible unity, but certainly adequate for respectful dialogue. And so it might be with Karl Barth.

OP Theology and Karl Barth: A Conversation

Here we bring Karl Barth into conversation with Oneness theologians. We focus on three theological themes that offer a basis for such dialogue. These are (1) revelation, (2) the name of God in revelation and baptism, and (3) the nature of God as Trinity.

Revelation

The theme of revelation does not appear in the Oneness narrative in a systematic way as a fundamental doctrine. Its appeal to authority is primarily apologetic. Since Schaepe's early morning "revelation" in 1913, it has persisted on the edge of OP discourse. Ewart based the revelation upon Paul's christological statements regarding the "revealed mystery" of Christ's identity, namely, that the Father is revealed *in* the Son.[24] More specifically, the revelation of the name of God cannot be rationally deduced: "Mere intellect cannot open the treasury of the Name of God. God speaks to the heart. If the heart is dead, the Name is sealed."[25] Haywood likewise regarded the Oneness and name of Jesus as a "mystery" hidden from the "wise and prudent" but revealed to "babes," the humble children of God.[26]

It is clear from the writings of OP leaders that the revelation was not an extra-biblical revelation or "soulish mysticism," as AG antagonist, Carl Brumback, charged.[27] Rather, it was rooted in the experiential faith of Pietism and Wesley,

---

24. Ewart, *The Revelation of Jesus Christ*, 10–13.
25. Frank J. Ewart, *The Name and the Book* (Chicago: Daniel Ryerson, 1936), 85.
26. G. T. Haywood, *The Victim of the Flaming Sword* (Indianapolis: Christ Temple, n.d.), 46.
27. Carl Brumback, *Suddenly from Heaven – A History of the Assemblies of God* (Springfield: Gospel Publishing House, 1961), 203.

in which "experience was emphasized as a receptive medium rather than the productive source of revelation."[28]

In current OP scholarly discourse, this apologetic appeal to "revelation" plays no substantive role. It was addressed, however, in the Final Report of the five-year Oneness-Trinitarian Pentecostal Dialogue (2002–7), commissioned by the Society for Pentecostal Studies. There it appears as a bipartisan affirmation which denounced any revelation that would conflict with the authority of Scripture:

> Despite differences of biblical interpretation, we also affirm together that all revelation must pass the test of harmony with Scripture. No private or new revelation can contradict or supersede Scriptural teaching. . . . This affirmation was valued and shared by both sides, in part, to dispel the idea that the Oneness/Trinitarian division had to do with a "new revelation" by the Oneness intentionally proposed as an insight beyond the teaching of Scripture.[29]

Appeal to revelation also does not appear in what is probably the most scholarly theological work by a Oneness scholar, David Norris's *I AM: A Oneness Pentecostal Theology*.[30] This may be due to Norris's specialty in biblical theology. Yet the appeal was prominent in the early years and still lingers, hanging there to be plucked for conversation. Enter Karl Barth.

Barth and OPs have this in common: they are both theological particularists. That is, both are committed to the premise that without divine initiative, whatever revelation means, it is utterly unattainable by an autonomous human mind. Both OPs and Barth understand there is no universal human capacity to truly "know" God. And for both, Scripture is the unrivaled touchstone of authority.

OPs came by their revelation as End Times Restorationists; that is, it did not come primarily through a dispassionate rational study of hermetically sealed inerrant texts. The experiences suggest something deeper—that same hunger for a more compelling vision of Jesus Christ which had begun three years earlier with Durham's message of the Finished Work of Calvary. It was God, not they, who was restoring the true apostolic church in these Last Days.

Barth arrived at his particularist view of revelation in reaction to the prevailing optimism in European Protestant theology, that humans have the innate capacity for knowing God. For Barth, knowing God through revelation is a purely divine act that "will remain a miracle to all eternity of completed redemption,"[31] a claim he elsewhere describes as "the tearing of an untearably thick veil, i.e., His

---

28. Dale Brown, "The Wesleyan Revival from a Pietist Perspective," *Wesleyan Theological Journal* 24, no. 1 (Spring 1989): 6–16. See also Part I in Reed, *IJN*.

29. "Oneness-Trinitarian Pentecostal Final Report, 2002–2007," *Pneuma* 30 (2008): 206.

30. David Norris, *I AM: A Oneness Pentecostal Theology* (Hazelwood: Word Aflame Press, 2009).

31. *CD* I/2, 245. Cited in Trevor Hart, "Revelation," in *The Cambridge Companion to Karl Barth*, ed. John B. Webster (Cambridge: Cambridge University Press, 2000), 42. Hart

mystery."³² Though far apart culturally and theologically, Barth and OPs share the conviction of the utter incapability of unaided humans to know God. Thus, the need for revelation that would be initiated and enacted by God alone.

One aspect of revelation in which OPs and Barth diverge significantly regards the status of doctrine in relation to revelation. As confessional biblicists, OPs tend to conflate—directly or indirectly—their construal of the revelation of Jesus Christ with the miraculous event itself. When the early OP leaders came to believe that the narrative they produced was in and of itself revelation, their confessional statements in effect took on the authority of divinely given "revelation." Unfortunately, one consequence of this direction can be a hardening of the doctrine which permits little room for self-critique and renewal.

Barth, however, may well have a word of both comfort and counsel in this regard. For comfort, he would agree that revelation is the dynamic power of the living Word of God, an encounter with the living God, an event, not merely a set of facts. Along with OPs, he would regard the authentic Christian life to be the *experience* of being addressed by God, "the very thing that decides and proves that what makes it possible lies beyond itself."³³ When Jesus Christ is proclaimed and received, it is an encounter.

For counsel, Barth would warn against any human effort to assert control over the things of God. For OPs, by way of example, the "precious truth" of the name of Jesus is bound when the revelation becomes fixed in its formulation. All theological talk, including Oneness theology, is second-order discourse, not small deposits of revelation. As necessary as theological discourse is, Barth warns against the idolatrous "word-bound ego" which attempts to wrest ownership from what rightfully belongs to God.³⁴ Barth might say at this point: "Let the main thing be the main thing."

The Name

The theological centerpiece of OP theology is the name of God, not a dispute over baptismal formulas. It is the revelation of God's New Covenant name, Jesus, that will restore apostolic identity and, when invoked in baptism, enact the moment of the great covenantal transfer. As Norris puts it: "When the first Jewish members of the audience were plunged into baptismal waters and the name of Jesus was invoked over them, what happened was nothing less than the birth of Christianity, for it was not Yahweh who was the covenant partner, but it was Jesus Christ."³⁵

---

helpfully traces the influences that led to Barth's theological Particularism and theology of revelation, beginning with Ritschl.

32. *CD* I/1, 168.

33. Ibid., 221. Barth devotes a whole section to experiencing God in *CD* I/1, "The Word of God and Experience," 198–227.

34. *CD* I/1, 220.

35. Norris, *I AM*, 143.

Biblically, God's identity and character are revealed in the OT through names and titles, particularly God's covenantal name, Yahweh. OPs find their authorization for claiming Jesus as God's covenantal name in the angel's instruction to Joseph: "She [Mary] will bear a son, and you are to name him Jesus, for he will save his people from their sins" (Mt. 1:21, NRSV).[36] Other names and titles, especially LORD (e.g., Phil. 2:11) reinforce the Oneness dictum, "The Yahweh of the Old is the Jesus of the New."[37] Drawing its theology primarily from biblical sources, OP is free to develop Jewish rather than Hellenistic categories to interpret the identity and mission of Jesus. This has at least the potential—though not necessity—for constructing a theology outside a post-apostolic Greek philosophy. A theology of the name of God is one example. As a theologian of the particularity of revelation, Karl Barth travels the same terrain.

Barth begins his study of the OT roots of Christology with the name of God, in much the same manner as OPs. For him, the name, simply put, is: "Knowing God a second time in another way." Stated similarly, Barth wants to emphasize that the name is not a mere attachment to God, an external representation or anthropomorphism for God. The name is itself intrinsic to Yahweh, even a hypostasis of God. The name is the hidden God in revelation. Yet God had planned from the beginning to be revealed under this name of Jesus Christ, so that the revelation of this name might be, "the epitome of the expectation of Israel and the recollection of the Church . . . also in Holy Scripture the epitome of the reality of God's mercy."[38] So, as if to remind us, Barth underscores the point that the OT "knows only one God."[39] It is difficult to consider anything here that would be outside the broad parameters of OP theology of the name. For that we need to turn to Barth's treatment of the name in baptism.

First, OP dialogue partners need to know that Barth approves of baptism in the name of Jesus Christ! The reason is by now clear: following Paul in Romans 6:3f and Galatians 3:27, he can say that "the goal of baptism is now Jesus Christ concretely in the fulfillment of His work for all on the cross." This christocentric pattern is also consistent with baptismal accounts in Acts. In a way, Barth's christocentric hermeneutic calls for such acknowledgment. But it does come with two qualifications. One is that such early accounts do not warrant the conclusion that they embodied a fixed baptismal formula with "binding validity" throughout the apostolic church. The other is that the trinitarian name in Matthew 28:19 should be allowed without emendation, since it is consistent *in its meaning* with the christocentric form. Specifically for Barth, "Father, Son and Holy Ghost is to be regarded as the enumeration of the dimensions of the one name of God, i.e., of His

---

36. David K. Bernard, *In the Name of Jesus* (Hazelwood: Word Aflame Press, 1992), 29–34.
37. See also chapter 11, "Theology of the Name," in Reed, *IJN*.
38. *CD* II/1, 373.
39. *CD* I/1, 317, 319.

one work and word, of His one act of salvation and revelation."⁴⁰ The traditional OP interpretation, in contrast, requires the exclusive use of the christocentric formula, precisely because "Jesus" is the revealed and proper name of the "Son," while "Lord" and "Christ" are distinguishing titles.⁴¹

Barth continues his reflection on the continued use of the two formulas. He makes clear that, while the trinitarian formula has become normalized throughout Christendom, it does not belong to revelation but to the dogma of the church, and hence is relativized in its authority for the church. For this reason Barth concludes that, while the christocentric formula is theologically valid and should be recognized as such, the trinitarian form is "a custom that should be observed *for the sake of ecumenical peace* even though its exegetical, dogmatic and theological necessity cannot be demonstrated" (emphasis mine). In the end, Barth's indispensable minimum for the baptismal formula is that it secures for the sake of "into the name" "its teleological character as a reference to the goal of baptism."⁴²

In this section, the Restitutionist OPs and ecumenist Karl Barth discover a common interest in the revelational name of God. If that interest is to expand, a pivotal question is asked by Hall, "What is the Name?"⁴³ Is it to be "Jesus," which is based on a customary human name? Or, as Barth proposes, will it be common words and titles that eventually transition into proper names, for example, Lord Jesus Christ? Barth does show preference for "LORD" precisely because it is the New Covenantal "name" of the OT covenantal name, YHWH.⁴⁴ But other NT names are rightly recognized because "in this name" represents the core *intrinsic* reality upon which all "names" given to Jesus gain their ontological significance.

God—One and Three

Historically, the christological shift that began with Durham's Finished Work of Calvary finally rested in the New Issue's radical christocentrism which was accompanied by a rejection of the doctrine of the Trinity. The sole motivation to exalt Jesus as "Absolute Deity" reveals that the doctrine of the Trinity was not its prime target. Based upon a popular misunderstanding of the meaning of "persons" in the Godhead, any suggestion that the deity in Jesus was merely a "second" Person was a diminishment too far and an indignity too great. It was, therefore, a logical move to conclude that the doctrine of the Trinity is fundamentally "three separate and distinct" persons.⁴⁵ Therefore, the solution was to consign the three to

---

40. *CD* IV/4, 91–2, 96.
41. See chapter 6, Bernard, *In the Name of Jesus*, and Norris, *I AM*.
42. *CD* IV/4, 92.
43. See above at n. 13.
44. Barth, *The Epistle to the Philippians* (Richmond: John Knox Press, 1962), 67–8.
45. This phrase, and especially the word "separate," frequently appeared in Andrew Urshan and continues in other Oneness writers, including Bernard; for example, *The Oneness of God* (Hazelwood: Word Aflame Press, 1983), 134.

the temporal realm and rename them "manifestations" (1 Tim. 3:16).[46] Similarities with the ancient heresy of Sabellianism, or more generally Modalism, eventually caused the schism within the AG.[47]

It is of interest, however, that by mid-century there were a few attempts to explore what preexistent threeness might look like. There could be no eternal Son, since the word itself is a personal and relational term. But Kenneth Reeves (1921-2005), United Pentecostal Church minister and writer, spoke of two "aspects" within God: transcendence (Spirit) and expression (Word).[48] Andrew Urshan (1884-1967) reflected throughout his life how God can be "Tri-One" without being "three separate persons."[49] Canadian Oneness writer, John Paterson (1898-1998), proposed a distinct status within the Godhead depicting the Word as "the embodiment of the invisible God."[50] This "embodiment" exists *within* the pre-incarnate state, similar to a hypostatic distinction, but in a way that does not threaten the one nature of God. Paterson gleaned his insights from the "us" passages, Genesis 1:26 and 3:22. For these authors, God's being cannot be simply an undifferentiated unity. In contrast to these explorations, there is a strand within OP—a weak one—which views Father, Son, and Spirit as nonexclusive attributes, roles, or manifestations of God, alongside holiness, omnipotence, and so on. Jesus is *simpliciter*, the incarnation of the Father, Yahweh.[51]

Surprisingly, there is much in OPs that Barth shares, in sentiment and substance. Both believe that the OT is the proper grounding and starting point for Christian monotheism. Both reflect a methodological option for Jesus Christ. Barth makes the striking claim that the Bible is not equally interested in the Father, Son, and Spirit, but rather is focused primarily on God's revelation in Jesus Christ. And historically, the doctrine of the Trinity emerged from the christological debates. Barth sees this priority echoed in Paul's triune blessing, beginning with "the grace of our Lord Jesus Christ" (2 Cor. 13:14).[52] Both OPs and Barth are convinced that the language of "persons" to represent the Trinity is misleading and, as Barth complains, achieves only "fresh confusion."[53] Even Barth's more nuanced term, "Triunity," appears as a nod in the Oneness direction.[54] Furthermore, he insists that the name of God cannot be parsed as plural; God's name is a single name. Finally,

---

46. Reed, *IJN*, 257-3.

47. See Reed, *IJN*, 176-82, ch. 12, 246-73. Norris rejects the broad label of Modalism in favor of the Modalism of the early Monarchians, Praxeas in particular, *I AM*, 4, 156, 175-8.

48. Kenneth Reeves, *The Godhead* (Granite City: By the Author, 1971), 10, 14, 20-1, 24.

49. For a detailed account of Urshan's theological view, see Chapter 7, "The Mystery of the Godhead," in Daniel L. Segraves, *Andrew D. Urshan: A Theological Biography* (Lexington: Emeth Press, 2017).

50. John Paterson, *God in Christ Jesus* (Montreal: By the Author, 1964), 39.

51. Bernard, *Oneness*, 144.

52. *CD* I/1, 315.

53. Ibid., 355.

54. "Triunity" is a chapter heading in *CD* I/1, 348.

Barth makes clear that the doctrine of the Trinity belongs to the church's dogma, not revelation. So, although OPs regard their doctrine as biblical revelation and the teaching of the Trinity the product of a wayward church, they at least hear in Barth that the doctrine of the Trinity belongs to a lesser authority than the Bible—an insight which might furnish common ground, if not yet common cause.[55]

Barth's distinctive account of the nature of the triune God sheds light on OP theology in at least two ways. The first is his attack on Modalism. Reflecting the fourth-century debates, he states the problem with Modalism: if the threeness exists only in revelation, there is no bridge leading to knowledge of the unveiled God. Assuming the context of the dualistic world of ancient Platonism, Barth concludes that humans will be inquiring "about a God that doesn't exist."[56] While early OP writers seemed unaware of this lacuna, I have argued that OP theology does not reflect the Hellenistic worldview, but is closer to the Semitic world of the OT in which the "name" carries weight similar to Greek notions of "substance." It is therefore plausible that, given a credible claim that the name is *intrinsic* to God's being and remains so in the act of revelation, OP theologians have reason to mount a persuasive argument that their doctrine of the name does bridge the gap between the hidden and revealed God.[57]

Furthermore, current OP scholars are putting forward a more nuanced interpretation of their Christology. For instance, biblical theologian David Norris concludes that Oneness theology resembles more closely third-century Praxean Modalism than Sabellianism (a pejorative label dating from the 1916 schism) since Praxeas enjoyed broad popular appeal among the Christian churches, did not engage in neo-Platonic philosophical debate, and represented a more faithful biblical theology.[58] Descriptively, theologian David K. Bernard notes that while OP "bears affinity to modalistic thought," it is unique in this sense: the Father, Son, and Holy Spirit are "simultaneous, not sequential manifestations of God, and . . . God's essence is not hidden behind changing masks but is revealed in Christ."[59] While the implications are still forthcoming, the traditional charge of Modalism, especially if considered a heresy, will require a more nuanced response in the future.

Second, distinctions within the Godhead reflect the unique character of Christian monotheism in two ways. The divine One is not a monad but a differentiated unity. Barth insists that Scripture does not permit any attempt to dismantle the dual truth of what he calls an "unimpaired distinction" within an "unimpaired unity" of the Godhead. He does require, however, that this unity-

---

55. *CD* I/1, 308.

56. Ibid., 382; see also 310, 351, 353.

57. See ch 11, Reed, *IJN*. Also explored in Norris, *I AM*.

58. Norris, *I AM*, 175–81.

59. David K. Bernard, *The Glory of God in the Face of Jesus Christ: Deification of Jesus in Early Christian Discourse*, Journal of Pentecostal Theology Supplement Series, 45 (Blandford Forum, Dorset: Deo Publishing, 2016), 48. See also Reed, *IJN*, 267.

with-distinctions be affirmed in such a way, and only in this way, that it does not threaten or confuse Christian monotheism with suggestions of three centers of consciousness or individualities.[60] Christologically, this means for Barth that the deity in Jesus is at once the revelation of the eternal Son and of the One God without compartmentalization: "thrice single voice of the Father, the Son, and the Spirit," "one God in threefold repetition," "thrice of the one Divine I."[61]

As OP theologians reflect upon their own priorities in light of Barth's thinking, one might ask whether and to what degree Barth addresses their deepest concerns in these two areas: (1) prioritizing the oneness of God by refusing to apply the term "persons," and thereby providing protective boundaries around the oneness of God, and (2) acknowledging that the name of God in revelation belongs to the one who is named "Jesus." Here Barth enfolds this name in the sweep of redemptive history, noting that God who bears the name "Lord" or YHWH in the OT is none other than Jesus Christ. Commenting on Matthew 1:21 and Philippians 2:9, he states: "He is called Jesus because in His history the history of the deliverance and salvation of all men takes place."[62] Elsewhere he writes, "The purpose of God's grace in giving Jesus the name 'Lord' is, that through him his people may be gathered, his Church constituted, that in *this name*, in *this* Lord, under *his* law, within *his* order, God may be worshipped by every creature."[63]

Conclusion

The theological and institutional distance between OPs and Karl Barth is perceptibly far. OPs are "separated brethren" from both Christian groups and fellow Pentecostals. Their restorationist roots have defined their boundaries. Their language of faith has been rooted in an oral culture characterized more by narrative than abstract logical categories and worship more than intellectual discourse. Yet, there is an uncanny familiarity between Barth and OP—on the naming of the name, baptizing in that name, and reimagining the distinctively Christian vision of monotheism as revealed in that name. As a fellow christocentric theologian, Barth can model for OPs that the centrality of Christ—his "supreme" and "absolute" deity—need not be compromised by embracing the triune nature of God. As a fellow theologian of the name, Barth can claim that the very name of Jesus Christ bears all the power and authority of the "fullness of God." As a member of the church universal, Barth can defend the legitimacy—indeed, the equivalency—of baptism in the name of Jesus Christ.

---

60. *CD* I/1, 295, 358.
61. Ibid., 347, 350, 351.
62. *CD* IV/4, 93.
63. Barth, *Epistle*, 68.

Progress in mutual understanding has been hampered by binary orthodoxy–heresy modalities. But there are resources for a different kind of dialogue.[64] So it is not that the way has disappeared. We sometimes simply lose our vocational calling. Barth reminds us from whence this calling comes: "It is with the biblical witness to God's revelation, as we have felt we must understand it, that knowledge [of theological concepts] is imposed on us as at least the task of dogmatics."[65] And with this calling comes patience, trusting that, as historian Lewis Ayres wisely points out, mutual understanding is indeed the fruit of "slow and subtle modifications."[66]

---

64. As an example, see the brief introduction to Walter Hollenweger's proposal for a theological understanding of what he calls "responsible syncretism," a hermeneutic for engaging the Pentecostal "other," in Allan H. Anderson, "The Intercultural Theology of Walter J. Hollenweger," *Journal of the European Pentecostal Theological Association* 41, no. 1 (May 2021): 35–51.

65. *CD* I/1, 428.

66. Lewis Ayres, *Nicaea and Its Legacy: An Approach to Fourth-Century Trinitarian Theology* (New York: Oxford University Press, 2004), 70.

Chapter 5

BARTH AND PENTECOSTALS ON THE DIVINE PERFECTIONS OF (IM)MUTABILITY AND (IM)PASSIBILITY

CHRIST, THE SPIRIT, AND THE DIVINE ATTRIBUTES

Andrew K. Gabriel

Karl Barth challenges Pentecostals to think about the divine perfections (Barth's preferred term for "attributes") from a trinitarian perspective. And, yet, Barth tends to have a specifically christological emphasis in this doctrine. Pentecostal theology shares with Barth an emphasis on the place of Jesus Christ in theology, while giving more focus to the Holy Spirit, thereby fulfilling a trajectory which Barth began to reach toward later in his life. Contemporary Pentecostal theology, then, in turn, challenges Barth and those who follow him to develop a more robustly trinitarian doctrine of the divine perfections by integrating *both* christological and pneumatological insights into this doctrine. As a case study, this chapter focuses on engaging Barth's proposals regarding divine (im)passibility and (im)mutability and argues that in Jesus Christ and the Holy Spirit, God suffers impassibly and is immutably constant in every change. This chapter thereby demonstrates the fruitfulness of a Pentecostal and robustly trinitarian approach to the divine perfections in order to adequately articulate both the immanence and transcendence of God.

I focus on the attributes of impassibility and immutability for three main reasons. First, Barth reformulates each of these attributes. Second, these are two of the more debated attributes in contemporary scholarship, including even in Barth studies. Third, when discussing the divine attributes, recent Pentecostal scholarship has given the most attention to impassibility, first, and immutability, second. These three reasons show the current relevance of these two attributes for Barth studies and Pentecostal theology along with wider discussions regarding the doctrine of God.

Barth's Trinitarian Approach to the Doctrine of God

Christopher Holmes notes that in contrast to many theologians who came before Barth, within the *Church Dogmatics* Barth does not want to describe the divine attributes apart from faith "by the traditional ways of negativity, eminence, and causality . . . because he does not want *the world* to function as a negative and positive witness to the perfections of the Creator" in place of understanding God "on the *basis of himself*."¹ As a result, Barth takes a trinitarian approach to formulating his doctrine of the divine perfections. His approach is trinitarian not simply because, in contrast to many of his theological forerunners, he develops his doctrine of the Trinity in *CD* I/1, before his doctrine of the divine perfections in *CD* II/1, but more importantly because, first, Barth makes clear that he has no intention of speaking of "God's being in general" but specifically as the God who reveals Godself as Father, Son, and Holy Spirit.² He writes, "In a dogmatics of the Christian church we cannot speak correctly of God's nature and attributes unless it is presupposed that our reference is to God the Father, the Son and the Holy Spirit."³ A second feature of Barth's doctrine of God that makes it trinitarian is that Barth aims to show that the divine perfections are true of God's eternal triune being, rather than only in relationship to creation.⁴ In doing this, Barth's concern is to affirm that God's being eternally exists in the same manner in which God reveals Godself, and supremely so in Jesus Christ. So, for example, Barth notes how God is omnipresent not only because God is present to all of creation, but also because God is three eternal persons who are present to one another in eternity.⁵

While Barth's discussion of the divine perfections is trinitarian in nature, in many respects he takes a christological approach, more specifically, in that he consistently presents christological insights throughout his doctrine of God. For example, when beginning to discuss God's grace and holiness, Barth explicitly claims that knowledge "of God is grounded in his revelation in Jesus Christ and remains bound up with it, [so] we cannot begin elsewhere."⁶ In light of similar comments throughout Barth's doctrine of God, Don Schweitzer rightly observes

---

1. Christopher R. J. Holmes, *Revisiting the Doctrine of the Divine Attributes: In Dialogue with Karl Barth, Eberhard Jüngel, and Wolf Krötke*, Issues in Systematic Theology, 15 (New York: Peter Lang), 64 (emphasis added). On Barth's more immediate and inherited Protestant Orthodox context, see 12–21. On Barth's treatment of the divine attributes in his earlier Göttingen lectures (1924–6), see 65–71 and Robert B. Price, *Letters of the Divine Word: The Perfections of God in Karl Barth's Church Dogmatics*, T&T Clark Studies in Systematic Theology, 9 (London: Bloomsbury, 2011), 3. On p. 195 Price notes that among Barth scholars, the verdict it still out regarding the extent to which Barth's doctrine of the divine perfections continued to mature after he wrote *CD* II/1.

2. Barth, *CD* II/1, 348.

3. Barth, *CD* I/1, 312.

4. Regarding the second point, see *CD* II/1, 260, 323–4, 327, 344–5 and at various places as he discusses specific attributes.

5. *CD* II/1, 463.

6. Ibid., 351. It must be noted, then, that the reason that Barth focuses on Christ is because he wishes to ground his theology, and the doctrine of God specifically, in the knowledge of God from God's act of revelation rather than in the logic of philosophy and a general understanding of "perfection." Terry L. Cross, *Dialectic in Karl Barth's Doctrine of God*, Issues in Systematic Theology, 7 (New York: Peter Lang, 2001), 179–80, 188, and 193.

that Barth has a "christologically focused Trinitarian doctrine of God" and Christopher Holmes speaks of its "Christological concentration."[7] The influence of Barth on those trinitarian theologians who follow him—such as Wolfe Krötke, Eberhard Jüngel, and Jürgen Moltmann—clearly shows in their similar christological emphases as well.[8]

Pentecostal Approaches to the Doctrine of God

Pentecostals have certainly shown concern for the doctrine of God, but on account of the historical division between Oneness Pentecostals and their trinitarian Pentecostal counterparts, their discussion of the doctrine of God has focused specifically on the doctrine of the Trinity.[9] Pentecostals have not been forced to think about the doctrine of the divine attributes in the same way. As an illustration of this reality, though written as recently as 2008, Keith Warrington's 102-page chapter on "God" in his *Pentecostal Theology* includes less than two pages on the divine attributes. Terry Cross is certainly correct to observe, "Pentecostals have been deficient in crafting a doctrine of God."[10]

When Pentecostals have written on the doctrine of God, like the remainder of Evangelicals, they have been more concerned with being "biblical" than with offering much attention to the theological and trinitarian implications of the biblical text. In this, Pentecostals have exhibited what John Franke calls a "'concordance' conception of theology,"[11] which is exhibited in their efforts to write books on

---

7. Don Schweitzer, "Karl Barth's Critique of Classical Theism," *Toronto Journal of Theology* 18 (2002): 241 and Holmes, *Revisiting the Doctrine of the Divine Attributes*, 53 (cf. 55). Similarly, Dolf te Velde, *The Doctrine of God in Reformed Orthodoxy, Karl Barth, and the Utrecht School: A Study in Method and Content*, Studied in Reformed Theology, 25 (Leiden: Brill, 2013), 338.

8. Wolfe Krötke, *Gottes Klarheiten: Eine Neuinterpretation der Gottes "Eigenschaften"* (Tübingen: Mohr Siebeck, 2001); Eberhard Jüngel, *God as the Mystery of the World: On the Foundation of the Theology of the Crucified One in the Dispute between Theism and Atheism*, trans. Darrell L. Guder (Grand Rapids: Eerdmans, 1983); Jürgen Moltmann, *The Crucified God: The Cross of Christ as the Foundation and Criticism of Christian Theology*, trans. A. Wilson and John Bowden (London: SCM Press, 1974). For an evaluation of some theologians Barth has influenced, see Andrew K. Gabriel, *The Lord is the Spirit: The Holy Spirit and the Divine Attributes* (Eugene: Pickwick, 2011), 81–7.

9. For example, see chapter three, "Beyond Doctrine: Trinity, Oneness, and the Crisis of the Creed," in Wolfgang Vondey, *Beyond Pentecostalism: The Crisis of Global Christianity and the Renewal of the Theological Agenda*, Pentecostal Manifestos (Grand Rapids: Eerdmans, 2010).

10. Terry L. Cross, "The Rich Feast of Theology: Can Pentecostals Bring the Main Course or Only the Relish?" *Journal of Pentecostal Theology* 16 (2000): 46.

11. John R. Franke, *The Character of Theology: An Introduction to Its Nature, Task, and Purpose* (Grand Rapids: Baker Academic, 2005), 88.

"Bible Doctrine," rather than dogmatics or systematic theology.[12] That is, for many years Pentecostals typically viewed theology as an attempt to arrange scriptural statements in an orderly and systematic fashion. Following this concordance model of theology, when outlining a doctrine of the divine attributes, Pentecostals tend to focus their attention on verses in the Bible which refer to "God" or "the Lord" when discussing the divine attributes. Even though the majority of Pentecostals do affirm that God is triune,[13] this approach to theology has inhibited Pentecostals from adequately integrating this confession into their doctrine of God's attributes.[14]

Within Pentecostalism there is, nevertheless, promise for developing a trinitarian doctrine of God. Aside from some of the recent trinitarian insights of Pentecostal theologians, which I will draw on below, pneumatological theology appears to be one emerging paradigm for Pentecostal theology in general.[15] And, as Ralph Del Colle remarks, "to be more thoroughly trinitarian is to be more thoroughly pneumatological."[16] There are many intuitions within Pentecostal theology that have implications for the doctrine of the divine attributes, and in this chapter I will continue to develop my previous work by exploring some of these christological and pneumatological emphases in conversation with Karl Barth.[17] Barth himself anticipated the latter approach to theology when he wrote near the end of his life that he dreamed of "the possibility of a theology of the third article."[18]

---

12. For example, William W. Menzies and Stanley M. Horton, *Bible Doctrines: A Pentecostal Perspective* (Springfield: Gospel Publishing House, 1993). On this issue and the growth of critical theological reflection by Pentecostals, see Frank D. Macchia, "The Struggle for Global Witness: Shifting Paradigms in Pentecostal Theology," in *The Globalization of Pentecostalism: A Religion Made to Travel*, ed. Murray Dempster, Byron D. Klaus, and Douglas Petersen (Oxford: Regnum, 1999), esp. 8–13.

13. Even though Oneness Pentecostals do not affirm the historic doctrine of the Trinity, they still affirm the divinity of the Father, the Son, and the Holy Spirit.

14. Andrew K. Gabriel, "This Spirit is God: A Pentecostal Perspective on the Doctrine of the Divine Attributes," in *Defining Issues in Pentecostalism: Classical and Emergent*, ed. Steven M. Studebaker, McMaster Theological Studies Series (Eugene: Pickwick, 2008), 71–6.

15. See, for example, Amos Yong, *The Spirit Poured Out on All Flesh: World Pentecostalism and the Possibility of Global Theology* (Grand Rapids: Baker Academic, 2005) and Frank D. Macchia, *Baptized in the Spirit: A Global Pentecostal Theology* (Grand Rapids: Zondervan, 2006).

16. Ralph Del Colle, "A Response to Jürgen Moltmann and David Coffey," in *Advents of the Spirit: An Introduction to the Current Study of Pneumatology*, ed. Bradford E. Hinze and D. Lyle Dabney, Marquette Studies in Theology, 30 (Milwaukee: Marquette University Press, 2001), 339.

17. For earlier attempts, see Gabriel, *The Lord is the Spirit* and Andrew K. Gabriel, "Pneumatological Insights for the Attributes of the Divine Loving," in *Third Article Theology: A Pneumatological Dogmatics*, ed. Myk Habets (Minneapolis: Fortress, 2016), 39–53.

18. Karl Barth, "Nachwort," in *Schleiermacher-Auswahl*, ed. Heinz Bolli (Munich: Siebenstern-Taschenbuch, 1968), 311.

(Im)passibility

In his doctrine of God, Barth's discussion of divine impassibility appears in his discussion of God's mercy. Mercy includes God's compassion, which is a disposition of the heart. "The mercy of God," he writes, "lies in His readiness to share in sympathy the distress of another."[19] As Barth continues, he explicitly rejects the doctrine of impassibility as he understands it: "God has a heart. He can feel, sense, be affected. He is not impassible. He cannot be moved from outside by an extraneous power. But this does not mean that He is not capable of moving Himself."[20] This quote might appear contradictory where Barth states that "He cannot be moved from outside." But Barth's intent is simply to state that nothing causes God to suffer unless God wills or allows it. But God does suffer "pain because of our sin and guilt."[21] Barth proposes further that God's mercy includes pity for the sinner, and, therefore, God's sorrow is greater than ours.[22] Most importantly, for Barth, God's mercy impels God to take the initiative to be gracious toward us.

In *CD* II/1, Barth's brief christological reflection on this doctrine comes along with a likewise brief pneumatological observation. Barth observes that it is due to "the power of the divine mercy" that we receive "a living hope through the resurrection of Jesus Christ from the dead" (1 Pet. 1:3) and that "according to His mercy" God has saved us "by the washing of regeneration and renewing by the Holy Spirit" (Tit. 3:5).[23]

In later sections of the *Church Dogmatics*, Barth further reflects on the suffering of Christ and the implications this has regarding divine suffering. Bruce McCormack summarizes Barth's Christology in *CD* IV/1–3:

> There can be only one Subject of the human sufferings of Jesus, and this Subject is the Logos. . . . If the Logos is the Subject of the human sufferings of Jesus, then suffering is an event which takes place *within the divine life*—which also means that the divine 'nature' cannot be rightly defined in abstraction from this event.[24]

---

19. *CD* II/1, 369.
20. Ibid., 370. I say Barth rejects the doctrine of impassibility *as he understands it* because, like many contemporary theologians, Barth seems to confuse impassibility with divine apathy. This was not the case in patristic theology. See Paul Gavrilyuk, *The Suffering of the Impassible God: The Dialectics of Patristic Thought*, Oxford Early Christian Studies (Oxford: Oxford University Press, 2004) and Daniel Castelo, *The Apathetic God: Exploring the Contemporary Relevance of Divine Impassibility*, Paternoster Theological Monographs (Milton Keynes: Paternoster, 2009).
21. *CD* II/1, 373.
22. Ibid., 374.
23. Ibid., 373.
24. Bruce L. McCormack, "The Actuality of God: Karl Barth in Conversation with Open Theism," in *Engaging the Doctrine of God: Contemporary Protestant Perspectives*, ed.

Today, such claims seem almost banal given the significant influence that Barth's conclusions have had on contemporary doctrines of the divine attributes.

Barth's influence extends to Pentecostal theology via Jürgen Moltmann, a theologian who many Pentecostals have found to be a fruitful dialogue partner. And like Barth and Moltmann, Pentecostal reflection on divine impassibility has come with christological focus, often in connection with reflections on human suffering. Chris Green, for example, observes that "Spirit-empowerment finds its epitome in Jesus' shameful death," in order to remind Pentecostals that "people of the Spirit are by definition the suffering people of the suffering God."[25]

In their spirituality, Pentecostals are just as concerned, or perhaps even more concerned, with their present-day experience of Christ as with reflecting on his suffering and death in the past. Pentecostals believe in Jesus as the one who still heals *today*. Wolfgang Vondey observes, "The believer's experience of Jesus as healer passes through Jesus's experience of victory over suffering."[26] In other words, the Son of God suffered, but with "the goal of redemption" and the "end of all suffering (see Rev. 21:4)."[27] In this sense, the Pentecostal expectation of healing, or a theology of glory, points back to a theology of the cross and to a theology of the suffering of God.

Pneumatology can provide another means for Pentecostals to reformulate the doctrine of impassibility and confirms for trinitarian theology what has already been argued christologically. In fact, the suffering of the Spirit is a common theme in contemporary pneumatology. Moreover, in pneumatology theologians are not faced with the question of whether Christ suffered only in his humanity, since the Spirit has no hypostatic union to complicate the question of divine suffering.

Pneumatology confirms Barth's insight that God's mercy includes suffering. In God's mercy, the Holy Spirit grieves from human sin. Isaiah reports that the Israelites "rebelled and grieved his Holy Spirit" (Isa. 63:10), and Paul warns the Ephesians that they should not "grieve the Holy Spirit of God" by how they treat one another (Eph. 4:30). While this "grief" may be, in some sense, metaphorical, these texts do nevertheless state that at times humanity causes the Holy Spirit to suffer with grief.

The Spirit also suffers in all of creation. This is a widespread recognition in contemporary pneumatologies.[28] Though not incarnate in creation, the Spirit

---

Bruce L. McCormack (Grand Rapids: Baker Academic, 2008), 222. See also *CD* II/2, 163–5; IV/1, 244–56, 485; IV/2, 225–6, 357–8; IV/3.1, 396–8, 411–13.

25. Chris E. Green, "The Crucified God and the Groaning Spirit: Toward a Pentecostal *Theologia Crucis* in Conversation with Jürgen Moltmann," *Journal of Pentecostal Theology* 19 (2010): 134, 142.

26. Wolfgang Vondey, *Pentecostal Theology: Living the Full Gospel*, Systematic Pentecostal and Charismatic Theology (London: Bloomsbury T&T Clark, 2017), 273.

27. Ibid., 275.

28. For example, Sigurd Bergmann, *Creation Set Free: The Spirit as Liberator of Nature*, trans. Douglas Stott (Grand Rapids: Eerdmans, 2005), 296; Jürgen Moltmann, *The Spirit of*

empathetically participates in the travail and suffering of creation. Like the Spirit groans within Jesus as Jesus cries (like believers following him) "Abba, Father" (Mk. 14:36; Rom. 8:15; Gal. 4:6), the Spirit groans within the groaning of creation (Rom. 8:22) as the Spirit anticipates the day, and draws creation toward the day, when "the creation itself will be liberated from its bondage to decay" (Rom. 8:21).

An awareness of the "Spirit's sigh" may be one of the key characteristics of Pentecostal spirituality, and especially as it relates to the practice of speaking in tongues.[29] Pentecostals observe that when the Spirit was poured out at Pentecost, all the people present "were filled with the Holy Spirit and began to speak in other tongues as the Spirit enabled them" (Acts 2:4). Today, Pentecostals speak in tongues for various reasons, sometimes during celebration and praise, sometimes during turmoil. With respect to the latter, Pentecostals find a correlation between their personal groaning and the groaning of the Spirit. As they pray in tongues, they believe "the Spirit himself intercedes . . . with groans that words cannot express" (Romans 8.26).[30] Edmund Rybarczyk confirms, "Indeed, to hear Pentecostal prayer warriors, the Spirit's travail can be an overwhelming burden that drains a person's energy."[31] In such times of prayer, Pentecostals sense the passion of the Spirit which supports a doctrine of divine passibility.

Pentecostal and pneumatological theology supports the conclusion that God suffers in Christ's death and in the Spirit's relationship with creation. Nevertheless, this does not necessitate a wholesale rejection of the doctrine of divine impassibility. Moreover, Pentecostals have reason to develop an apophatic side to their theology, and with respect to the question of divine impassibility in particular. In contrast to a frequent desire of Pentecostals to express themselves with many, sometimes loud, words, Pentecostals also have quiet moments during worship services when they sense the presence of God. These moments are what Daniel Castelo refers to as "the holy silence that occasionally emanates from the Spirit's hushing."[32] This is an apophatic practice of Pentecostal spirituality. The practice of speaking in tongues is another Pentecostal apophatic practice, in as much as speaking in tongues implies a recognition of the limits of human language.[33] Speaking in tongues, then, may be

---

Life: A Universal Affirmation, trans. Margaret Kohl (Minneapolis: Fortress, 1992), 51; Denis Edwards, *Breath of Life: A Theology of the Creator Spirit* (Maryknoll: Orbis, 2004), 141–2.

29. Eldin Villafañe, *The Liberating Spirit: Toward an Hispanic American Pentecostal Social Ethic* (Lanham: University Press of America, 1992), 123.

30. For example, Anthony D. Palma, *The Holy Spirit: A Pentecostal Perspective* (Springfield: Logion, 2001), 169, 245.

31. Edmund J. Rybarczyk, "Reframing Tongues: Apophaticism and Postmodernism," *Pneuma* 27 (2005): 101.

32. Daniel Castelo, "An Apologia for Divine Impassibility: Toward Pentecostal Prolegomena," *Journal of Pentecostal Theology* 19 (2010): 126.

33. Daniel Castelo, "Toward Pentecostal Prolegomena II: A Rejoinder to Andrew Gabriel," *Journal of Pentecostal Theology* 21 (2012): 179; and, Rybarczyk, "Reframing Tongues," 90–6.

considered a form of apophatic speech or prayer, where, according to the apostle Paul, a person's "spirit prays" even though their "mind is unfruitful" (1 Cor. 14:14). The apophatic practices of Pentecostalism lend support to the use of the doctrine of impassibility as an apophatic qualifier—that is, as a means of qualifying one's recognition of divine suffering with a recognition of divine transcendence and the limits of our knowledge of God.

To utilize the concept of impassibility as an apophatic qualifier is to acknowledge that God's passions differ from human passions and that God does not have morally problematic emotions. As an apophatic qualifier, impassibility also reinforces the fact that God suffers voluntarily and is not inhibited by his suffering—God is not ruled by his passions and, therefore, God remains in control of his actions as God works toward redemption.[34]

In Barth's rejection of the doctrine of divine impassibility in *CD* II/1, he did not adequately recognize how impassibility has served well historically as an apophatic qualifier. Barth scholars disagree on whether Barth made room for a doctrine of divine impassibility in later parts of the *Church Dogmatics*.[35] Certainly, on the face of it, it appears that he did. In his doctrine of reconciliation, for example, Barth maintains that God "is absolute, infinite, exalted, active, *impassible*, transcendent, but in all this He is the One who loves in freedom."[36] Regardless of the nature of Barth's later theology, even in *CD* II/1, Barth offers reasons that one might affirm a doctrine of impassibility. Specifically, when Barth explains why he prefers to speak the divine "perfections" instead of "attributes," he emphasizes that all of the attributes of God belong to God in a unique way.[37] As an example of this, even as Barth explicitly rejects the concept of impassibility, he cautions, "God is moved and stirred, yet not like ourselves in powerlessness, but in power."[38] The uniqueness of the divine perfections means that whenever we speak of God's attributes, our language is not univocal, and, therefore, one might say that there needs to be an apophatic element in our speech about God.[39] Both Pentecostals and those who

---

34. Gavrilyuk, *The Suffering of the Impassible God*, 16, 51; Castelo, *The Apathetic God*, 2, 128; Castelo, "Toward Pentecostal Prolegomena II," 174–5.

35. Bruce L. McCormack states, "Barth's later Christology leaves no remaining room for *any* doctrine of divine impassibility," in his essay "Divine Impassibility or Simply Divine Constancy?: Implications of Karl Barth's Later Christology for Debates over Impassibility," in *Divine Impassibility and the Mystery of Human Suffering*, ed. James Keating and Thomas Joseph White (Grand Rapids: Eerdmans, 2009), 184. In contrast, see Paul D. Molnar, *Faith, Freedom and the Spirit: The Economic Trinity in Barth, Torrance and Contemporary Theology* (Downers Grove: IVP Academic, 2015), 250.

36. Barth, *CD* IV/1, 187 (emphasis added).

37. *CD* II/1, 322–3.

38. Ibid., 370.

39. Granted, Barth's preference would be to use dialectic "as a *limiter* of human speech about God." Cross, *Dialectic in Karl Barth's Doctrine of God*, 155. On Barth's use of dialectic within his discussion of the divine perfections, see 178–93.

follow Barth might say that God suffers impassibly. Price even suggests that in *CD* II/1, Barth himself "preserves the core concern of the traditional affirmation of divine impassibility while avoiding what he considers its errors."[40]

Immutability

Any revision to the doctrine of the impassibility of God generally implies a reformulation of the doctrine of immutability, and both Barth's theology and Pentecostal theology do turn in this direction. In *CD* II/1, Barth does not completely reject the term "immutability," though he does prefer to employ the unique and uncommon term divine "constancy" since "immutability" is a "suspiciously negative word."[41] The word "constancy," in contrast, serves Barth's goal of emphasizing that God is not immobile, but the living God who, in freedom, enters into relationship with creation. Expressing his goal, Barth states that "there is such a thing as a holy mutability of God," with the result that God partakes in our "alteration, so that there is something corresponding to that alteration in His own essence."[42] This is a striking statement. At the same time, Barth continues in the next sentence, "His constancy consists in the fact that He is always the same in every change." And below on the same page, Barth affirms, "in biblical thinking God is certainly the immutable, but as the immutable He is the living God and He possesses a mobility and elasticity which is no less divine than His perseverance." Barth has made his point clear that God's "immutability" does not mean that God is static or immovable, as some might suppose. Rather, it means that God is the same, or constant, in every change.[43] According to Barth, God is constant in his knowing, willing, and acting. And God responds to humanity, while remaining constant—reliable and true to God's living being—as God repents[44] and responds to prayers.[45]

The constancy of God in God's relationships *ad extra* is grounded in the eternal triune relationality of God. Barth proposes that since God is eternally constant, "all multiplicity and movement have their prototype and pre-existence in himself."[46] The result is that God can change in relationship to creation, but without any change in the divine nature. As Kevin Hector explains, Barth presents "God's acts *ad extra* as repetitions of God's triune life," and therefore "God need not change in order to be with us."[47]

---

40. Price, *Letters of the Divine Word*, 69.
41. Barth, *CD* II/1, 495. Cf. 312, 315, 494, 515, and 562.
42. Ibid., 496.
43. Ibid.
44. Ibid.
45. Ibid., 511.
46. Ibid., 612.
47. Kevin Hector, "Immutability, Necessity and Triunity: Towards a Resolution of the Trinity and Election Controversy," *Scottish Journal of Theology* 65, no. 1 (2012): 69.

Barth finds divine constancy exhibited in Jesus Christ, whom God has elected from all eternity.[48] In Christ, God is one with the creature and God reveals the constancy of God's love. Barth explains, "God is constant, he does not alter, when he becomes and is one with the creature in Jesus Christ. . . . The incarnation as such confirms and explains the fact that God has befriended and continually befriends fallen creation, and will lead it on to a full redemption."[49] Barth confirms again in *CD* IV/1 that the incarnation does not change God, but "corresponds to His divine nature" in as much as God is—forever—the one who loves in freedom.[50]

Barth is suspicious of the term immutability because he is concerned that it does not adequately reflect the living God who enters into relationship with creation. Likewise, Pentecostals emphasize that God is relational. They proclaim that God longs for relationship with humanity as their Father and "calls people into a dynamic learning journey with himself that is experiential in its fullest sense." This, Keith Warrington proposes, implies that for Pentecostals "God is not immutable but interactive, not impassable [sic] but permeating their lives, not immoveable but capable of being moved by those he has created."[51]

While having some reason to reject the notion of divine immutability, the Pentecostal emphasis on "the full gospel" supports the doctrine of God's constancy. In this theological narrative, Pentecostals emphasize that Jesus Christ is the savior, healer, baptizer (with the Spirit), sanctifier, and coming King.[52] And Pentecostals are specifically concerned with affirming that Christ *remains* this way to affirm their present experiences of the Spirit. When affirming that Christ *still* baptizes people in the Spirit, Pentecostals remind believers that this is a promise for all generations or "for all who are far off" (Acts 2:39). And when preaching that Jesus Christ *still* heals today, Pentecostals will remind those in need that God does not change for "Jesus Christ is the same yesterday and today and forever" (Heb. 13:8).[53] These affirmations of the unchanging nature of Christ serve as means of affirming divine constancy or divine immutability.

Shifting from Christology, pneumatology can also support what Barth refers to as the divine constancy. The Spirit is the presence of God that constantly sustains

---

48. *CD* II/I, 505. The question of how God's electing to be God-with-us does not change God is a significant debate in recent Barth scholarship. The debate concerns itself with the extent to which Barth's theological ontology changes after he developed his doctrine of election in *CD* II/2 and how to correctly interpret later sections of the *Church Dogmatics*. But the debate is just as much about Bruce McCormack's proposal that God's act of election is logically prior to the triunity of God. See Molnar, *Faith, Freedom and the Spirit*, 149–86.

49. *CD* II/1, 515.

50. Barth, *CD* IV/1, 187. Cf. *CD* IV/2, 84–7.

51. Keith Warrington, *Pentecostal Theology: A Theology of Encounter* (London: T&T Clark, 2008), 33.

52. Vondey, *Pentecostal Theology*, 6.

53. Steven Jack Land, *Pentecostal Spirituality: A Passion for the Kingdom* (Cleveland: CPT Press, 2010, first published in 1993), 60–1.

creation (Ps. 104:29-30; cf. Job 33:4), and the Spirit is the Giver of Life, who is faithful to liberate creation from its groaning (Rom. 8:20-26). At the same time, the Spirit is immutably constant in change in as much as the Spirit's presence changes as it intensifies in relation to creation.

The theological intuitions of Barth's doctrine of omnipresence provide a good starting point for developing a pneumatological understanding of the mutable presence of God. Barth affirms that God is omnipresent but he also offers three somewhat unique insights regarding the doctrine: God is not nonspatial (he possesses place);[54] the general (omni)presence of God is recognized in light of the special presence of God; and, most importantly for the discussion at hand, God can be present in different and special ways.[55] With respect to the last point, he argues, if God were "so to speak, an *immovable omnipresence*, excluding a divine here and there and its relationships and distances, it is inevitable that He would again be lifeless and loveless and therefore fundamentally unfree."[56] Barth finds a basis for a differentiation of divine presence within the triune life where the divine persons are free to be present to one another. This is God's "differentiated presence within Himself." Similarly, God is free to be present in all of creation "with a presence which is not uniform but distinct and differentiated."[57] For example, God was present in a *special way* on Mount Sinai with Moses (Exod. 24:16), and also in the tabernacle (Exod. 25:8), but especially in Jesus Christ (Col. 2:9).[58] These instances of the "special presence of God" are, Barth explains, "concrete cases of God being here or there, which rise like mountain peaks from the plain of God's general presence with His creation."[59]

Other than a brief note that the Spirit is present in a distinct way in Christians,[60] Barth's reflections on the presence of God take place with little reference to pneumatology, even though the Holy Spirit is frequently associated with the presence of God. And yet, from Barth's conclusions one can begin with the premise that the Spirit can be present in a special way and, therefore, be present in different places in changing ways. Barth himself does not relate the idea of the special and differentiated presence of God to his doctrine of immutability. Nevertheless, such a relation is apparent.

The sending of the Spirit at Pentecostal marks one significant change in the presence of the Spirit. Jesus is reported to have said "I *will send* [the Holy Spirit] to you from the Father" (Jn 15:26, cf. 16:7). Thomas Torrance rightly attests that Pentecost brought about a "radical change in the nature and mode of his [God's] presence in the world." Furthermore, he maintains that the events of incarnation

---

54. *CD* II/1, 467–76.
55. Ibid., 470–3.
56. Ibid., 473 (emphasis added).
57. Ibid., 473. On the presence of God "in himself," see 462–3, 472–4, and 487.
58. *CD* II/1, 479 and 483.
59. Ibid., 477.
60. Ibid., 483.

and Pentecost "tell us that far from being a static or inertial Deity like some 'unmoved mover,' the mighty living God who reveals himself to us through his Son and in his Spirit is absolutely free to do what he had never done before, and free to be other than he was eternally."[61] That is, from the perspective of the coming of the Holy Spirit on the Day of Pentecost (and the incarnation), we see that God is free to change and does change in how God is present so as to remain faithful, or constant, to who God is.

Jesus continues to pour out the Spirit on the church. And the church continues to call for the presence of the Spirit to come, especially in Orthodox and Catholic traditions. One epicletic prayer implores God, "May your Holy Spirit fall on these gifts and on your people."[62] Yves Congar also speaks of "the life of the Church as one long epiclesis."[63] Such invocations of the Spirit are calls for the Spirit to come and be present in the church in a special and differentiated way, to use Barth's terminology.

The Holy Spirit's presence also changes as the Spirit intensifies in the life of believers. The Spirit is present to all people giving them life and breath (Job 34:14; Ps. 104:29-30). And yet the Spirit's presence intensifies in people when they "receive the Spirit . . . by believing" the gospel (Gal. 3:2, cf. Rom. 8:15). The result is that God lives in believers by the Spirit in a new way (1 Jn 4:13). And Pentecostal theology emphasizes that, subsequent to conversion, a believer can continue to be filled with the Spirit, especially as Jesus Christ baptizes them with the Holy Spirit. As a result, like the apostle Paul, Pentecostals continue to exhort one another to "be filled with the Spirit" (Eph. 5:18).[64]

Spirit baptism will not be complete until the final consummation of God's plans and purposes take place. The church receives "the promised Holy Spirit, who is a deposit guaranteeing" *what is to come* (Eph. 1:13-14, cf. 2 Cor. 1:22 and 5:5). Therefore, one might say that Spirit baptism continues and will eventually be completed at the final consummation of all things. Matthew Thompson explains, "the Second Coming of Son and Spirit [in resurrection] means a cosmic Pentecost and a full presence of the Triune God in the world in glory" with the result that the whole world is transfigured as God is "all in all" (1 Cor. 15:28, cf. Rev. 21:3-5).[65] Likewise, Paul describes the ascension of Christ and the outpouring of the Spirit at

---

61. Thomas F. Torrance, *The Christian Doctrine of God: One Being Three Persons* (Edinburgh: T&T Clark, 1996), 208.

62. Paul Evdokimov, *l'Esprit Saint dans la tradition orthodoxe*, Bibliothèque Œcuménique, 10 (Paris: Cerf, 1969), 101.

63. Yves M. J. Congar, *I Believe in the Holy* Spirit, trans. David Smith, vol. 3 (New York: Seabury, 1983), 267.

64. Andrew K. Gabriel, "The Intensity of the Spirit in a Spirit-Filled World: Spirit Baptism, Subsequence, and the Spirit of Creation," *Pneuma* 34 (2012): 372-81.

65. Matthew K. Thompson, *Kingdom Come: Revisioning Pentecostal Eschatology*, JPTSup, 37 (Blandford Forum: Deo, 2010), 124. On his eschatological and cosmic view of Spirit baptism, see further 129-37. Similarly, see Macchia, *Baptized in the Spirit*, 101-7.

Pentecost as having the goal that God would "fill the whole universe" (Eph. 4:10). In this expectation, there is a latent understanding that the presence of the Spirit changes.

As Barth states, since God is omnipresent, "there is no place where He is less present than in all others." Yet, "in virtue of the freedom of His love He is this in continually differing and special ways."[66] And, in the Spirit, God is and will be present in special and changing ways in the church, individuals, and even the whole cosmos. This conclusion supports the idea that God immutably changes as God is constant in relation to creation.

Challenges for Pentecostal and Barthian Doctrines of God

Barth's theology and Pentecostal theology both challenge and reformulate the doctrines of divine impassibility and immutability, but from different angles. Barth's trinitarian approach to the divine attributes challenges Pentecostals to continue to develop their doctrine of God in a thoroughly trinitarian way. No doubt many of Barth's followers would echo Bruce McCormack's exhortation that "it is time for evangelicals to take more seriously their affirmation of the deity of Jesus Christ and begin to think about God on a thoroughly christological basis."[67] Pentecostal emphases should lead Pentecostal theologians to agree with this sentiment. At the same time, Pentecostals would add that it is time for Barth's followers to take more seriously their affirmation of the deity of Holy Spirit and begin to think about God on a thoroughly pneumatological basis and, therefore, a more thoroughly trinitarian basis. While Barth's doctrine of the divine perfections includes much christological reflection, one has to search hard to find pneumatological reflection in his doctrine of God. Certainly, Barth makes numerous blanket statements that in speaking of the being of God one *must* always be speaking of Father, Son, and Holy Spirit.[68] However, Barth seems not to follow this fully in practice.

In many respects, we may excuse Barth for the pneumatological deficit within his doctrine of the divine perfections given that he was, in part, overreacting to Friedrich Schleiermacher in his theology.[69] Barth himself admitted, "I wanted to place a strong emphasis on the objective side of revelation: Jesus Christ. If I had made much of the Holy Spirit, I am afraid it would have led back to subjectivism, which is what I wanted to overcome."[70] Those who follow Barth's theology today no longer have the same excuse as Barth for neglecting pneumatology in the

---

66. *CD* II/1, 470.
67. McCormack, "The Actuality of God," 242.
68. *CD* II/1, 261, 659.
69. Price, *Letters of the Divine Word*, 125.
70. Karl Barth in *Karl Barth's Table Talk*, ed. John D. Godsey, Scottish Journal of Theology Occasional Papers, 10 (Edinburgh: Oliver and Boyd, 1963), 27. Here Barth was referring specifically to his doctrine of the Word of God in *CD* I/1.

doctrine of God. This is even more so true given the explosion of contemporary pneumatology in recent decades, in part due to the growth of the global Pentecostal movement.

Aside from Schleiermacher's impact on Barth, Barth's doctrine revelation, where he articulates his doctrine of the Trinity, also contributed to the pneumatological deficit in his doctrine of the divine perfections. In *CD* I/1 and throughout the *Church Dogmatics*, Barth's pneumatology has a decidedly noetic function.[71] Barth refers to the Holy Spirit as the "Revealedness" that helps people grasp the "Revelation," who is Jesus Christ. In other words, the Holy Spirit enables each believers' affirmation (Barth's, "Yes") of the person and work of Jesus Christ. The Holy Spirit is, for Barth, the "subjective reality of revelation" and the "subjective possibility of revelation."[72] The result, Robert Jenson suggests, is that Barth's "doctrine of Trinity, when thus *used*, often seems rather to be a doctrine of binity," ignoring the various activities of the Holy Spirit.[73] Whether or not Jenson's claim may be fairly applied to the whole of Barth's theology, it seems to be legitimate with respect to Barth's doctrine of the divine attributes. One wonders, then, if theologians who follow Barth will need to revise their doctrine of revelation so that they present the Holy Spirit as more than the "revealedness" of God, with the result that they will regard both Christ and the Holy Spirit as the "revelation" of God, and of the divine perfections specifically.[74]

As theologians continue to integrate pneumatological insights into their doctrine of God alongside christological ones, they will not only follow the intuitions of Pentecostal theology and spirituality, but they will also take Barth's mature theology more seriously, specifically his dream of developing a theology of the third article. Barth himself wondered if he "was too cautious" of speaking of the Spirit in his theology. Moreover, Barth remarked, "Today I would speak more of the Holy Spirit."[75]

Overall, christological and pneumatological reflections from Pentecostal theology and Barth's doctrine of God together support the development of a thoroughly trinitarian doctrine of divine (im)passibility and (im)mutability. These doctrines witness to God's mercy, which impels God to reach out to save humanity through the power of the cross and regeneration. In this, God enters into relationship with humanity and shares in our distress as Jesus suffers on the cross and as the Spirit suffers and groans with humanity on account of our sin. Moreover, the kingdom of God continues to come as Jesus is constant in saving,

---

71. Philip J. Rosato, *The Spirit as Lord: The Pneumatology of Karl Barth* (Edinburgh: T&T Clark, 1981), 133, 161, 172, 182.

72. Barth, *CD* I/1, 295, 449 and *CD* I/2, 203, 242.

73. Robert W. Jenson, *Systematic Theology*, vol. 1 (Oxford: Oxford University Press, 1997), 154.

74. Barth seems to have thought that this was not possible. See *Karl Barth's Table Talk*, 28 and *CD* I/1, 162.

75. Barth in *Karl Barth's Table Talk*, 27.

healing, and baptizing in the Spirit. God is constant as God continues to respond to people's prayers and repentance. And the presence of the Spirit continues to intensify throughout creation until the day when "there will be no more death or mourning or crying or pain" and "the old order of things has passed away" (Rev. 21:4). This is the God who suffers impassibly and is immutably constant in every change. This is the triune God who loves in freedom.

Chapter 6

BARTH, ELECTION, AND THE SPIRIT

William Atkinson

Introduction

Pentecostalism, with its Wesleyan roots,[1] tends to focus on human responsibility rather than on divine sovereignty.[2] Thus, Pentecostals may be tempted to avoid consideration of election. However, reading Barth's work on this doctrine proves worthwhile. This is partly because Barth's doctrine of election is widely regarded as of great importance: according to Daniel W. Hardy, "Barth's redevelopment of Calvin's notion of predestination is sometimes called his greatest achievement."[3] It is also because Barth's writing on the subject suggests to Pentecostal sensitivities that there might be more for Pentecostals to say. Before offering a Pentecostal response to Barth's teaching, a brief synopsis of his position is appropriate.[4]

---

1. Donald W. Dayton, *Theological Roots of Pentecostalism* (Peabody: Hendrickson, 1987); Laurence W. Wood, *The Meaning of Pentecost in Early Methodism* (Lanham: Scarecrow Press, 2002).

2. This tendency is marked. Keith Warrington, *Pentecostal Theology: A Theology of Encounter* (London: T&T Clark, 2008), 38–40.

3. Daniel W. Hardy, "Karl Barth," 21–42 in David F. Ford with Rachel Muers, eds., *The Modern Theologians* (Oxford: Blackwell, 2005), 32.

4. For detailed discussion of Barth's election doctrine, including its developments over time, see Matthias Gockel, *Barth & Schleiermacher on the Doctrine of Election* (Oxford: Oxford University Press, 2006). For summaries of Barth's doctrine, see, for example, Monica Brands, "Vessels of Mercy: Aquinas and Barth on Election and Romans Chapters 9–11," *Journal of Theta Kappa Alpha* 37, no. 1 (2013): 23–39; Sven Ensminger, *Karl Barth's Theology as a Resource for a Christian Theology of Religions* (London: Bloomsbury, 2014), 113–29; Matthias Grebe, *Election, Atonement, and the Holy Spirit: Through and Beyond Barth's Theological Interpretation of Scripture* (Eugene: Pickwick, 2014), 10–48; Clifford Green, "Introduction: Karl Barth's Life and Theology," 11–45 in *Karl Barth: Theologian of Freedom*, ed. Clifford Green (Edinburgh: T&T Clark, 1991 [1989]), 31–2; Adrian Langdon, "Jesus Christ, Election and Nature: Revising Barth during the Ecological Crisis," *Scottish Journal of Theology* 68, no. 4 (2015): 455–7; Frank D. Macchia, *Justified in the Spirit: Creation, Redemption, and the Triune God* (Grand Rapids: Eerdmans, 2010), 137–42;

Synopsis of Barth's Position

Theologically, Barth's doctrine of election rests upon his understanding of divine freedom. This freedom is, according to Clifford Green, the "center of Barth's theology."[5] As Barth put it while expounding Romans, God "is neither bound to any independent, relative, human peculiarity, nor bounded by any second, other, contrasted thing." Rather, "only as free, regal, sovereign, unbounded and incomprehensible, can we comprehend God and do Him honour."[6] In line with this emphasis, Barth began chapter VII of *Church Dogmatics*, "The Election of God," with these words: "The doctrine of election is the sum of the Gospel because of all words that can be said or heard it is the best: that God elects man; that God is for man too the One who loves in freedom."[7]

Barth started discussion of election with the matter of God's decision regarding divine attitudes and actions: "God in His love elects another to fellowship with Himself. First and foremost this means that God makes a self-election in favour of this other."[8] "Again, God elects that He will be the covenant-God."[9] In this self-election, God elects none other than Jesus: "He elects the man of Nazareth, that He should be essentially one with Himself in His Son."[10] And God elects to send the Son: "We must take as our starting point the fact that this divine choice or election is the decision of the divine will which was fulfilled in Jesus Christ, and which has as its goal the sending of the Son of God."[11]

However, Barth did not only see Jesus as the *human object* of divine election, but as the *divine subject* of it: Christ was and is the electing God, not just the elected man.[12] The divine Christ, the eternal Word of God, chose to obey God the Father, to establish a covenant with humanity, and to become human in

---

Timothy Scheuers, "An Evaluation of Some Aspects of Karl Barth's Doctrine of Election," *Mid-American Journal of Theology* 22 (2011): 161–73.

    5. Green, "Introduction," 11.

    6. Karl Barth, *The Epistle to the Romans*, 6th ed., trans. Edwyn C. Hoskyns (London: Oxford University Press, 1933), 346, 347.

    7. Ibid., 3.

    8. Ibid., 10; see also 155.

    9. Ibid., 11.

    10. Ibid.; cf. 43, 94.

    11. Ibid., 25.

    12. *CD* II/2 repeatedly, for example, 145: "the whole dogma of predestination is contained in these two statements.... The statements belong together in a unity which is indissoluble, for both of them speak of the one Jesus Christ, and God and man in Jesus Christ are both Elector and Elect." In fact, the combinations in Christ of electing and elected, of divinity and humanity, are more complex than this "mere" duality of divine elector and human elected: Christ also in his humanity elected God—to obey God as Father; furthermore, in his divinity Christ also is the Son chosen by the Father (*CD* II/2, 103).

this pursuit.¹³ Barth's twofold doctrine of election—Christ as divine elector and human elected—is thus highly christocentric.¹⁴ In this respect, Barth claimed that he parted "company with all previous interpretations of the doctrine."¹⁵ It is, he claimed, less *mysterious* than preceding versions, for whereas in them God chooses certain people for salvation inscrutably, and the identity of the elect cannot be known, in Barth's rendition God's electing will to choose Christ *is* known, as is the recipient of this election, who is Jesus himself.¹⁶ Barth criticized the hermeneutical method of his predecessors: inexplicably, to his mind, while they championed the centrality of Christ in all things, when it came to their development of doctrines of election, they "went behind Christ" to consider some "prior" decision-making in the mind of God.¹⁷ One might suggest on Barth's behalf that they thus located election only in God the Father and ignored Christology at this point.¹⁸ However, his own version of the criticism, as expressed in his early work, was that previous renditions of the doctrine of election had been too *anthropological*. In contrast to that focus, "For Paul, the statement *God chooses!* Is primarily a statement about God"; for Barth, Paul's "outstretched finger points above, not below."¹⁹

In his exposition of election, Barth engaged with the debate between supralapsarians and infralapsarians in detail.²⁰ In this case, predictably, he regarded both sides of the debate as having "missed the decisive insight into the heart of the matter."²¹ While part of Barth's criticism was that both sides allowed themselves to become unduly speculative or rational (however biblical their starting points),²² his main concern was to show that arguments over the object of divine election—

---

13. *CD* II/2, 105.

14. For example, Ensminger, *Karl Barth's Theology*, 143; Grebe, *Election, Atonement, and the Holy Spirit*, 42; Scheuers, "Evaluation of Some Aspects of Karl Barth's Doctrine of Election," 161. Gockel indicates that Barth's doctrine became more christological over time (*Barth & Schleiermacher on the Doctrine of Election*, for example, 202–3).

15. *CD* II/2, 146. Barth's reading of previous doctrines is challenged: Scheuers, "Evaluation of Some Aspects of Karl Barth's Doctrine of Election," 172.

16. *CD* II/2, 146–8.

17. Ibid., 150–3, 156–8.

18. This is Macchia's reading of Barth's critique (*Justified in the Spirit*, 138). For the centrality of Christology in Barth's theology: Green, "Introduction," 29–32.

19. Karl Barth, *The Epistle to the Ephesians*, trans. Ross M. Wright (Grand Rapids: Baker, 2017 [2009]), 95. Barth gave this lecture series in 1921–2. He defended Ephesians' Pauline authorship, while not regarding it as important. Francis Watson, "Barth, Ephesians, and the Practice of Theological Exegesis," introductory essay in Barth, *Epistle to the Ephesians*, 13–30.

20. *CD* II/2, 127–45.

21. Ibid., 132.

22. Ibid., 135–6, 143.

creatable and fallible humanity or created and fallen humanity—miss the point that God's primary object of election was actually the man Jesus Christ.[23]

This christocentric divine election has soteriological consequence, for there is innate within the election of Christ the capacity for others in turn to be elect "in Him." Barth naturally referred at this point to Ephesians 1:4. This innate capacity arises from the worthiness of Christ, due to the fact that Christ is not only elect Man but also electing God.[24] The resultant election is "the choice of God which, preceding all His other choices, is fulfilled in His eternal willing of the existence of the man Jesus and of the people represented in Him."[25] "Through Him and in Him He elects His people."[26] This election of others is free, gracious, righteous, and demanding of a positive response, such that it is an election to be obeyed or disobeyed.[27] It is good news, for it sets free from despair and from condemnation.[28] It has both community and individual aspects, which Barth discussed in this order.[29]

Barth's reinterpretation of some traditional doctrines of election was not only to be found in its christocentrism.[30] He also reinterpreted the idea of double predestination to "election and reprobation" so that "in the election of Jesus Christ ... God has ascribed to man the former, election, salvation, and life; and to Himself He has ascribed the latter, reprobation, perdition and death."[31] This might suggest that Barth was universalist: that God suffered all reprobation in the crucified Christ so that all humanity, without exception, might receive salvation. Such is certainly the hint in Green's summary of Barth's doctrine: "Jesus Christ is the *elect human being*, not only as an individual person but above all as the representative, the head, the personification of all humanity. That is to say, *all* humanity—and precisely all *sinful* humanity—is chosen, elect, predestined by God in Jesus Christ."[32] Green points out that Barth was criticized for apparent universalism

---

23. Ibid., for example, 143.
24. Ibid., 116–17.
25. Ibid., 25.
26. Ibid., 11.
27. Ibid., 11–12, 25, 30.
28. Ibid., 12, 29.
29. See table of contents, *CD* II/2, xi.
30. For review of "weak" and "strong" readings of Barth's understanding of the relationship between election and Trinity, with pneumatological implications: Paul T. Nimmo, "Barth and the Election-Trinity Debate: A Pneumatological View," in *Trinity and Election in Contemporary Theology*, ed. Michael T. Dempsey (Grand Rapids: Eerdmans, 2011), 162–81.
31. *CD* II/2, 162–3. Grebe describes this aspect as "radically new" (*Election, Atonement, and the Holy Spirit*, 39).
32. Green, "Introduction," 31, italics original. Further discussion of Barth and universalism: Ensminger, *Karl Barth's Theology*, 130–43; Scheuers, "Evaluation of Some Aspects of Karl Barth's Doctrine of Election," 167–72.

and that he responded to such criticisms.³³ While Green seems to take Barth's responses—and Barth's lifestyle—as a clear affirmation of universalism,³⁴ Grebe, in contrast, reads Barth as someone who explicitly denied universalism.³⁵

In contrast to these confident scholarly diagnoses, Barth himself wrote that his comments about universalism "present a point of view which cannot be interpreted as for or against" the position.³⁶ He preferred to call for a reverent agnosticism on the subject:

> If we are to respect the freedom of divine grace, we cannot venture the statement that it must and will finally be coincident with the world of man as such (as in the doctrine of the so-called *apokatastasis*). No such right or necessity can legitimately be deduced. Just as the gracious God does not need to elect or call any single man, so He does not need to elect or call all mankind. . . . But, again, in grateful recognition of the grace of divine freedom we cannot venture the opposite statement that there cannot and will not be this final opening up and enlargement of the circle of election and calling.³⁷

It is thus perhaps surprising that Barth's interpreters have tried to categorize Barth's doctrine as universalist or non-universalist, but unsurprising that they have not reached consensus!³⁸

At this point, if Barth saw double predestination such that "God has ascribed to man . . . salvation, and life; and to Himself . . . perdition and death,"³⁹ one would be forgiven for imagining that Barth saw the mystery of election "solved" by positing perdition squarely in Christ and salvation in created humanity. However, this would be to miss the subtleties of Barth's position. In his exposition of Romans, Barth indicated that, mysteriously, both election *and* rejection are found in the church and in saved individuals. As far as the church is concerned, it "is related to

---

33. For Barth's response, in broader terms of God's triumph over evil, *CD* IV/3, 173–4.

34. Green, "Introduction," 32.

35. Grebe, *Election, Atonement, and the Holy Spirit*, 203–4. Grebe discusses Barth's responses to criticisms of universalism (204–5).

36. Karl Barth, "The Humanity of God" (1956 lecture), 46–66 in *Karl Barth: Theologian of Freedom*, ed. Clifford Green (Edinburgh: T&T Clark, 1991 [1989]), 63.

37. *CD* II/2, 417–18. This agnosticism is usefully critiqued by Grebe, *Election, Atonement, and the Holy Spirit*, 214.

38. "In general, there seems to be no agreement regarding the question whether Barth's doctrine of election entails universalism" (Ensminger, *Karl Barth's Theology*, 130). Introducing his own positive assessment of Barth's doctrine, O'Neil writes that "Because Barth has not always been read carefully, a great deal of misunderstanding has occurred at this point. . . . Many authors lift Barth's universalistic statements from the context in which they are grounded" (Michael O'Neil, "Karl Barth's Doctrine of Election," *Evangelical Quarterly* 76, no. 4 [2004]: 318, 319).

39. *CD* II/2, 162–3.

the living God only when it . . . knows that, in the whole expanse of its historical manifestation, it is rejected by God, and when it, nevertheless, holds on firmly, pronouncing this terrible God . . . to be, in fact, the God who can and will elect."[40] As for individuals, the

> man that is *hardened* is the visible man, who, because of his ultimate separation from God, neither knows nor practises repentance. But who among us either knows or practises repentance? This is our hardening. The man to whom God shows mercy is the invisible man, the man who is miraculously united with God, the new-born man whose repentance is God's work.[41]

All this means, at both community and individual levels, that those who believe the gospel must concurrently and humbly acknowledge their "partnership" with those who reject it. Barth poignantly illustrated this point in his descriptions of the apostles Judas and Paul, in which he observed that

> before His death Jesus had an apostle beside Him as a witness to the divine rejection of men which He bore and bore away, just as after His resurrection He had an apostle beside Him as a witness to the divine election of men which was bestowed upon Him and which He Himself fulfilled . . . in view of Judas and Paul we have to bear in mind that the elect always occupies what was originally the place of the rejected.[42]

Unsurprisingly, Barth regarded the doctrine of election as difficult and mysterious:

> All serious conceptions of the doctrine also agree that in this free decision of God we have to do with the mystery of God, i.e., with the divine resolve and decree whose basis is hidden and inscrutable. We were not admitted to the counsel of God as He made His election, nor can we subsequently call Him to give account or to make answer in respect of it.[43]

With regard to the doctrine's difficulties, he wrote of "many hasty protests against the doctrine of predestination," as well as complaints about the apparent nature of God that it might bring to people's minds. However, in his view, "God would not be God, were He not liable to such accusations."[44] In contrast, Barth held the doctrine, as he understood it, in the highest regard: "Its function is to bear basic

---

40. Barth, *Romans*, 352.
41. Ibid., 353. Other examples: Ensminger, *Karl Barth's Theology*, 117–18.
42. *CD* II/2, 480.
43. Ibid., 20.
44. Barth, *Romans*, 349.

testimony to eternal, free and unchanging grace as the beginning of all the ways and works of God."[45]

Engagement with Barth's Position

This chapter's purpose is to offer a *Pentecostal* appraisal of Barth's doctrine of election. There is much to be said from other perspectives, but my response is selective.[46]

First, Barth's work is, as he noted, thoroughly biblical. He applied to this doctrine of election the same demand that he applied throughout his expositions: "no single item of Christian doctrine is legitimately grounded, or rightly developed or expounded, unless it can of itself be understood and explained as a part of the self-revelation of God attested in Holy Scripture."[47] Indeed, in the years before he wrote most of his famous *Church Dogmatics*, he published two important editions of a commentary on Romans and gave a lecture series on Ephesians. It was here that he set out early forms of his doctrinal stance concerning election: and he found it in Paul. Not all Pentecostals are content to label themselves as "evangelical," but it is rare to find a Pentecostal who does not want to hold up the Christian Scriptures as the final and essential word from God and authoritative source from which all true Christian doctrine flows.

Second, Barth's work on this subject is manifestly Christ centered. Barth is to be praised for placing Christ at the center of this doctrine and freeing it from the versions he criticized, which, as discussed above, suggested some "prior" decision-making in the mind of God the Father, to elect some to redemption and some to reprobation—whether this be supra- or infralapsarian—and to present Christ merely as a means to the end of that paternal electing grace.[48] Pentecostals are characteristically Christ centered. The criticism that Pentecostals focus on the Holy Spirit to the detriment of their interest in and worship of Jesus Christ may be common, but it is misplaced.[49] The very fact that summaries of the "full gospel" beloved of Pentecostals from their beginnings are statements about *Jesus* (as savior, healer, baptizer in the Spirit and coming king[50]) is evidence enough of their centeredness on Jesus.

---

45. *CD* II/2, 3.

46. For broader evaluations of Barth's election doctrine: especially Grebe, *Election, Atonement, and the Holy Spirit*, throughout.

47. *CD* II/2, 35.

48. Macchia is appreciative: "By wedding election to the Christ event . . . [Barth] restores the doctrine to its role in inspiring assurance and joyful gratitude and praise" (*Justified in the Spirit*, 141).

49. See my *Jesus before Pentecost* (Eugene: Cascade Books, 2016), 3.

50. This "foursquare" statement varies from the "fivefold" statement, that Jesus is "saviour, healer, sanctifier, baptiser in the Spirit, and coming king," of Pentecostal holiness groups.

Third, Barth was thorough. He rigorously pursued the possible implications that his doctrine of election would present. Thus, some criticisms of Barth's doctrine of election seem to falter for not having taken full account of all that Barth wrote on the subject. An example of this is to be found among Grebe's critiques. He writes: "If Christ as representative man is rejected and condemned for the sins of all, are not all of humanity who belong to Christ condemned as well?"[51] This criticism seems to take insufficient account of the way in which—mysteriously in Barth's highly dialectical rendering—rejection ever "hovers close" to the elect. Thus, "the elect and others ... belong together."[52] They share a "solidarity."[53] As I quoted earlier, the church "is related to the living God only when it ... knows that, in the whole expanse of its historical manifestation, it is rejected by God, and when it, nevertheless, holds on firmly, pronouncing this terrible God ... to be, in fact, the God who can and will elect."[54] One might, from another angle, complain that this collision of contradictory statements simply results in nonsense, but Ensminger is correct in claiming that to criticize Barth for incoherence is to indulge in a "misleading trajectory," for if "we are to take Barth's emphasis on the sovereignty of God and God as *subject* seriously, the attempt to apply human logic to God seems futile at best, if not arbitrary."[55]

Fourth—and it is here that Pentecostal insights and perspectives might be able to add something useful to Barth's contribution—his work is remarkably "binitarian."[56] The Holy Spirit received scant attention in Barth's exposition.[57] Nimmo has also noted this, writing that, "in this expansive chapter in the *Church Dogmatics* on election, as in the pursuant discussions in more recent literature, most of the attention falls on matters christological. There is little directly pneumatological material here."[58] Almost the entirety of the divine work of election was regarded by Barth as performed by the Father and the Son. There are,

---

51. Grebe, *Election, Atonement, and the Holy Spirit*, 45.
52. *CD* II/2, 346.
53. Ibid., 347–8.
54. Barth, *Romans*, 352.
55. Ensminger, *Karl Barth's Theology*, 134–5, italics original.
56. For Macchia, Barth is "largely binitarian" (*Justified in the Spirit*, 142). Discussing Barth's election doctrine in relation to his trinitarianism: Scheuers, "Evaluation of Some Aspects of Karl Barth's Doctrine of Election," 162–7; Akke van der Kooi, "Election and the Lived Life: Considerations on Gollwitzer's Reading of Karl Barth in CD II/2 as a Contribution to Actual Discussions on Trinity and Election," *Zeitschrift für Dialektische Theologie* 4 (2010): 67–82.
57. Surveying Barth's pneumatology: Grebe, *Election, Atonement, and the Holy Spirit*, 218–24; Wilson Varkey, *Role of the Holy Spirit in Protestant Systematic Theology: A Comparative Study of Karl Barth, Jürgen Moltmann, and Wolfhart Pannenberg* (Carlisle: Langham Monographs, 2011), ch. 4, esp. 148–52, where Varkey considers the pneumatology underlying Barth's election doctrine.
58. Nimmo, "Barth and the Election-Trinity Debate: A Pneumatological View," 166. Macchia regards Barth's inattention to pneumatology as a "problem" (*Justified in the Spirit*, 142).

admittedly, some contributions to this work that Barth ascribed to the Spirit. Thus, for example, in a threefold portrayal of the Trinity's involvement in

> the beginning, before time and space as we know them, before creation, before there was any reality distinct from God . . . it was the choice of the Father Himself to establish this covenant . . . it was the choice of the Son to be obedient to grace . . . it was the resolve of the Holy Spirit that the unity of God, of the Father and the Son should not be disturbed or rent by this covenant.[59]

Other than that, however, the Spirit is only involved in this divine election of Christ becoming, in turn, the election of the redeemed "in him."[60] The Spirit's action is presented as occurring *after* and *as a necessary result of* election. So, for example, Barth could write, "As a result of his election, he [the elect] is summoned by the operation of the Holy Spirit. His election as it has taken place in Jesus Christ can be declared to him."[61] Notably here the election itself "has taken place" in Christ; the Spirit is only involved in the consequent "summoning."[62] The Spirit seems largely to be a divine postscript to election itself.[63]

Developing Barth's Position

It is thus with respect to pneumatology that one might take Barth's thinking somewhat further. Could it be the case that the Spirit had and has a greater role in election than Barth noted? And if so, could this have relevance to how believers live their lives of hope in the present? I will explore these questions by taking three of Barth's points explored above: first, Christ as elected human; second, Christ as electing God; and third, God's election of the church in Christ.[64] (I will

---

59. *CD* II/2, 101.
60. Ibid., 106, 348, 410, etc.
61. Ibid., 414; cf. *CD* IV/1, 667: "the work of the Holy Spirit is merely to 'realise subjectively' the election of Jesus."
62. Nimmo discusses how, thus, the Spirit can be termed "elected": to conduct this summoning work in time (Nimmo, "Barth and the Election-Trinity Debate: A Pneumatological View," 170).
63. Ironically, Barth's relegation of the Spirit's role in election thus parallels his predecessors' relegation of Christ that he criticized. (In fairness, *Church Dogmatics* was unfinished; Barth's planned fifth volume would have focused on the Holy Spirit [Karl Barth, *Karl Barth's Table Talk*, ed. John D. Godsey (Edinburgh: Oliver and Boyd, 1962), 12]. I am grateful to Ben Evans for this observation).
64. Macchia "expand[s] Barth's understanding of election pneumatologically" in a fourth direction that interacts less directly with Barth's own logic: as "Spirit baptizer," Christ reveals "the elect creature as the one who receives the Spirit, while also revealing the electing God as the one who lavishly bestows the Spirit" (*Justified in the Spirit*, 142, 144).

not consider individual believers' election separately, but subsume this under the election of the church to which all such believers belong.) With each subject, I will consider possible roles of the Spirit, and with the last one I will press the question further to consider what impact this may have on believers attempting to live in confident assurance and hope of their election.

The election of the man Christ Jesus involved the Holy Spirit. This is not difficult to demonstrate, at least in its historical outworking as attested scripturally. According especially to Luke's gospel, the identification of Jesus as God's choice was made possible by the action of the Spirit upon Mary in Jesus' conception (Lk. 1:35; cf. Mt. 1:20-21). Furthermore, all four gospels associate the paternal affirmation of the divine choice of Jesus at the beginning of his public mission with a "dove-like" descent of the Spirit (Mt. 3:16-17; Mk 1:10-11; Lk. 3:22; Jn 1:32-34; cf. Ps. 2:7; Isa. 42:1). While the Spirit also anointed Jesus for this ministry (again especially in Luke, for example, 4:18-19), no explicit role if offered by the gospels to the Spirit in the act or process of choosing and approving the Son. Nevertheless, the association at Christ's baptism, particularly when coupled with the Lukan declaration concerning Jesus' conception, allows the idea that, at least, the Spirit conveyed to the Son an assurance of the Father's approving choice.[65] Thus, the Spirit played what appears to be an "instrumental," communicative role in God's election of Jesus.

What this moment in Jesus of Nazareth's history might have to do with eternal relations of the trinitarian persons is a matter of theological debate. My previous work seeks to minimize distinctions between the immanent Trinity and the economic Trinity.[66] On this basis, the God of truth genuinely reveals immanent trinitarian relations in the interactions between God, Jesus, and the Spirit to which the gospels attest. Furthermore, what is expressed in time is representative of what is the case in eternal relations. It follows from this premise that, as the Spirit was involved in the baptismal announcement of Christ's election as presented in the gospels, so too was the Spirit involved in the Father's eternal election of the Son. Macchia rightly observes, "the Father eternally elects the Son 'in the Spirit.'"[67] One can only tentatively suggest what the Spirit's involvement was. Insofar as the Spirit can be seen in many ways as the means of communication between the Father and the Son, one might deduce that the Father indicated and constantly assures his choice to the Son by means of the Spirit; more speculatively, as the divine Spirit

---

65. Arguably, the Spirit's involvement in Jesus' divine vindication after the cross's humiliation is also evidence in time of the Spirit's eternal involvement in the Father's enduring choice of Christ as the delightful, approved and vindicated elect one (e.g., Acts 2:33; Rom. 1:4; 1 Tim. 3:16). On this, further, Macchia, *Justified in the Spirit*, 144.

66. See my *Trinity after Pentecost* (Eugene: Pickwick, 2013), 25–8; also, similarly, Steven M. Studebaker, *From Pentecost to the Triune God: A Pentecostal Trinitarian Theology* (Grand Rapids: Eerdmans, 2012), 3–5.

67. Macchia, *Justified in the Spirit*, 143.

hovered in readiness prior to God saying, "Let there be . . . ," so too this same Spirit perhaps hovered and hovers actively over the eternal act of electing the Son.[68]

It is more difficult to demonstrate that the electing work done by the eternal divine Son involved or involves the Spirit, but it is not impossible. To repeat a point made earlier in this chapter, for Barth, Christ in his divine electing chose to obey God the Father, to establish the covenant, and to become human and suffer in obedience to this calling. The scriptural witness to these processes makes scant reference to the Spirit's role in them, but it is not entirely absent. Hebrews 9:14 offers one of these rare jewels: it was "through the eternal Spirit" that Christ "offered himself blameless to God."[69] Understandably, Barth used Revelation 13:8 in presenting as eternal the selfless choice of the Son to suffer in obedience to grace.[70] This eternal filial choice, the wording in Hebrews suggests, was "through the eternal Spirit." At the center of eternal divine choice to redeem humanity by means of gracious covenant, the Spirit is present. Only by the Spirit's means was the choice made. Again, one can only make tentative suggestions as to what this "means" was and is. Perhaps the Spirit granted resolve; perhaps too encouragement. One would then understand these qualities as flowing ultimately from the Father, but "reaching" the Son by means of the Spirit.

The church's election "in Christ" involved and involves the Spirit. This point was made by Barth, as I reported earlier in the chapter. However, I also noted that Barth merely allowed the Spirit a "postscript" role to an election that had already occurred "in Christ Jesus." Is Barth's rendition sufficient, or was the Spirit more intimately involved with the "process" of election than Barth acknowledged? This question can be tackled from two angles. The first relates to the place of the Spirit in Jesus' earthly choosing of disciples. The emphatic statement in John 15:16, "*You* did not choose me, but *I* chose you," is made without reference to the Spirit. This is perhaps unsurprising, as John's gospel makes little of the Spirit's work in Jesus' life. However, Acts 1:2 is intriguing. Its unusual word order is most naturally translated, "having given commands through the Holy Spirit to the apostles whom he had chosen." However, it might be rendered, "having given commands to the apostles whom he had chosen through the Holy Spirit."[71] As Keener observes, while the choosing of the apostles narrated in Luke 6:13 does not refer to the Spirit, "it mentions that Jesus spent the night in prayer beforehand (6:12), suggesting

---

68. For discussion of the consequences for trinitarianism of positing a minimal distinction between the immanent Trinity and the economic Trinity, see my *Trinity after Pentecost*.

69. To argue that it was only in his humanity that Christ's self-offering was "through the Spirit" is to posit an unjustified divide between humanity and divinity in the incarnate Christ.

70. *CD* II/2, 102–3.

71. This partly because of textual uncertainties: F. F. Bruce, *The Acts of the Apostles* (London: Tyndale Press, 1951), 66–7.

his dependence on divine guidance."[72] Indeed, it would be consistent with Luke's portrayal of Jesus' public mission to understand any such move on Jesus' part as being led and enabled by the Spirit. On the basis, again, that these activities reflect eternal trinitarian relations, if the Spirit had an involvement in Jesus' choosing disciples, then too the Spirit has eternal if unspecified involvement in the election of the church. One might speculate that, as the Spirit presumably conveyed to Jesus the Father's choice of disciples, so too the Spirit eternally communicates to the Son the paternal choice of the church as elect.

The other angle from which the question of the Spirit's engagement in the election of the church can be approached relates to certain New Testament epistolary texts. Unsurprisingly, Barth referred to 2 Corinthians 1:20 when discussing the divine "Yes" of election.[73] It is intriguing to see how close that divine "Yes" sat in the apostle Paul's thinking to the guaranteeing deposit of the Spirit in believers' hearts (2 Cor. 1:22). Turning from this letter to Ephesians, one again finds close proximity between election and the Spirit (Eph. 1:11-14). It must be conceded that, although Ephesians places the work of the Spirit very close to election, and 2 Corinthians places it very close to God's unalloyed "Yes," the Spirit's work occurs in both letters "further along the process" than the "Yes" of election itself. However, the connection is intimate. In both letters, the Spirit "seals"[74] God's saving work in believers (2 Cor. 1:22; Eph. 1:13). One does not need to stretch this idea to see the Spirit as "sealing" God's *election* in believers, especially as the "Yes" of God's election has appeared so recently in both letters' thought flow. As God elected the church "in Christ," so too, this suggests, God elected the church "in the Spirit."

Admittedly, one might yet see this sealing as a postscript to the "real" work of election, but that raises a question of its own: Is election of the church and its members merely, with Barth, something that occurred in "eternity past"?[75] And is election merely choice *making*, in isolation from the *implementation* and *maintenance* of this choice? Might it not be arbitrary to separate these conceptually? Thus—and turning now to the intervening words in 2 Corinthians 1—"the one setting us—with you—firm into Christ, and anointing us, is God" (2 Cor. 1:21) is a statement about election as much as a statement about its resultant "aftermath." Election would not be election if this divine choice was never worked out in practice. And this short excerpt from 2 Corinthians parallels "setting firm"

---

72. Craig S. Keener, *Acts: An Exegetical Commentary*, vol. 1 (Grand Rapids: Baker Academic, 2012), 661.

73. *CD* II/2, 14.

74. For contrasting suggestions concerning backgrounds to this language, John R. Levison, *Filled with the Spirit* (Grand Rapids: Eerdmans, 2009), 255–8.

75. Barth wrote of election as the "eternal presupposing" of God's temporal work (*CD* II/2, 149), and as "God's absolutely decisive disposing which takes place in the eternity before time was" (*CD* II/2, 151). He referred to the "sphere of predestination" as "pre-temporal eternity" (*CD* II/2, 153).

with "anointing"—in other words, with the work of the Spirit. Thus, the idea of the seal sites election not just in the "past" of eternity but in the present of believers' experience. Believers were elected; believers stand elect.

More can be said. Both these passages refer to the Spirit also as a deposit, pledge, or first installment (2 Cor. 1:22; Eph. 1:14). Those chosen in Christ, evidently, have not yet received the full inheritance which this election implies. There is more to come, of which the Spirit's arrival is a mere foretaste, though a firm guarantee. So, as the idea of the seal places election in the present as well as the past, so too the idea of the deposit sites election not just in the "eternal past" but also in the *future*.

It is in view of this that perhaps the most exciting development of Barthian (and other Christian) thought concerning election can be offered: God has not only chosen the elect; God *will* also choose the elect—and the Spirit is the thread of continuity between these two aspects. However one understands the nature of "final judgment," it will surely involve a choice, ultimately made by God. It therefore deserves to be called an "election."[76] It is a choice that will depend upon God's prior choices and actions, expressed in Christ and through the Spirit. Those chosen for eternal life in this future judgment of God are those who have already been both sealed and granted a guaranteeing deposit. Whether, in the final analysis, this divine choice is universal or limited, it will nevertheless have been one guaranteed *by the Spirit of God*.

Thus, viewed from a Pentecostal perspective, election is God's dynamic approach that is, as yet, unfinished in its outworking. It is not merely something "set in stone," so to speak, in the "past" mists of God's inscrutable eternal will. It deserves present and future tenses, too. This can be of great encouragement to Christians: God holds the eternal choice safe in believers' "now" and will choose to grant full inheritance to the elect in Christ "on that day." The Spirit is vital to both.

---

76. Gockel identifies an eschatological element in Barth's early election doctrine (*Barth & Schleiermacher on the Doctrine of Election*, 132) but sees this tied to Christ's resurrection rather than to final judgment. Macchia sees Barth's election doctrine having "an eschatological horizon" (*Justified in the Spirit*, 140).

Chapter 7

EMPOWERED BY THE SPIRIT

A PNEUMATOLOGICAL REVISION OF KARL BARTH'S THEOLOGICAL ANTHROPOLOGY

Lisa P. Stephenson

Introduction

In an essay on theological anthropology, Marc Cortez notes three principles that have guided Christian theology: "1. The *imago Dei* is central to a properly Christian understanding of the human person. 2. The *imago* can only be fully understood in light of the person and work of Jesus Christ. 3. Jesus Christ himself can only be properly and fully understood in light of the person and work of the Holy Spirit."[1] While these convictions do not exhaust the concerns of theological anthropology, they certainly get to the heart of them.

Therefore, this chapter will address these three issues with respect to Karl Barth's theological anthropology with the intent of engaging it from a Pentecostal perspective.[2] That is, it will seek to inquire first, "How does Barth conceive of the *imago Dei*?" Second, "How does Barth understand the *imago Dei* in the person and work of Jesus Christ?" And, finally, "How does Barth conceptualize the relationship between the person and work of the Spirit in relation to Jesus Christ?"

---

1. Marc Cortez, "Idols, Images, and a Spirit-ed Anthropology: A Pneumatological Account of the *Imago Dei*," in *Third Article Theology: A Pneumatological Dogmatics*, ed. Myk Habets (Minneapolis: Fortress Press, 2016), 267.

2. In this chapter I will be treating Barth's theological anthropology as a given and engaging it as such. Consequently, I will not evaluate the merits or problems with Barth's *methodology* (i.e., his christological/trinitarian approach and understanding of the *imago Dei* through the lens of dialogical personalism) per se, but will focus on aspects of his content as they stand and seek to read them through a more pneumatological lens. In other works I have exemplified a different approach to theological anthropology. See Lisa P. Stephenson, *Dismantling the Dualisms for American Pentecostal Women in Ministry: A Feminist-Pneumatological Approach* (Leiden: E. J. Brill, 2012), 89–135; Stephenson, "A Feminist Pentecostal Theological Anthropology: North America and Beyond," *Pneuma* 35, no. 1 (2013): 35–47.

The answers to the first two questions are relatively clear and straightforward in Barth's theology. However, the third is more problematic. Because Barth's Christology is inadequate at times with respect to the Spirit, this in turn means that his anthropology is too since the latter is predicated upon the former. It is my contention that it is only with the gift of the Spirit that one can properly realize the co-humanity that God created human beings for and that this is no less true for Jesus than it is for humanity in general.

Below I will present a summary of Barth's christological anthropology and highlight his pneumatological deficiencies. This chapter will primarily focus on Barth's theological anthropology as it appears in *Church Dogmatics* III/2, especially §45 "Man in His Determination as the Covenant-Partner of God."[3] Then, I will offer Spirit Christology as way to preserve better the integrity of Jesus' humanity, while also acknowledging a greater role for the Spirit. Finally, I will note the implications and correlations between the Spirit's work in Jesus' life and the Spirit's work among the rest of humanity. If the Spirit is what enlivens and enables Jesus' humanity, the same must be true for humanity at large according to Barth's methodology.

In order to ground theological speculation in the biblical texts themselves, I will focus on the narratives of Luke–Acts. Besides being the privileged Pentecostal hermeneutical approach, the narratives of Luke–Acts offer two particular benefits for this chapter. First, within Luke–Acts the work of the Spirit is a main focus for the author, and pneumatological content is more prevalent in comparison to the other Synoptic Gospels.[4] Second, Luke–Acts offers the added advantage of observing the function of the Spirit both in Jesus' life (Luke) and the broader community's life (Acts), which potentially serves to offer a prototype of the Spirit's presence within the life of Jesus that then gets carried through to the Spirit's presence within the life of the community at large.

Finally, two caveats are necessary before proceeding. On the one hand, I acknowledge that the author of Luke–Acts has no concern for dialogical personalism and I–Thou structures. These are twentieth-century constructs that one should not press into the text. But, on the other hand, the way in which the Spirit works in Jesus' and the community's midst is reminiscent of the dynamics of the I–Thou encounter that Barth purports. As such, the biblical texts inform the observations offered below, but I read them with an eye toward Barth's theological program. Accordingly, what I propose is a "theological reading" of the biblical texts, rather than a biblical exegesis per se.

---

3. Karl Barth, *The Doctrine of Creation*, ed. G. W. Bromiley and T. F. Torrance, trans. J. W. Edwards, O. Bussey, and Harold Knight, 4 vols, *Church Dogmatics*, vol. III/2 (Edinburgh: T&T Clark, 1958), 203–324.

4. Roger Stronstad, *The Charismatic Theology of St. Luke*, 2nd ed. (Grand Rapids: Baker Academic, 2012), 39.

Karl Barth's Christological Anthropology[5]

Content

Barth devotes *Church Dogmatics* III/2 to exploring the subject of the human person, and, in order to accomplish this task, he maintains Christology as the starting point. With this move, Barth clearly demarcates the methodological difference between theological anthropology and anthropology in general. Theological anthropology does not begin with *a priori* philosophy, cosmology, or speculative worldviews, but with God in God's revelation. It is from this starting point that one then moves to an understanding of the human person contained in that same revelation.[6] Barth describes this central principle as follows:

> The ontological determination of humanity is grounded in the fact that one man among all others is the man Jesus. So long as we select any other starting point for our study, we shall reach only the phenomena of the human. We are condemned to abstractions so long as our attention is riveted as it were on other men, or rather on man in general, as if we could learn about real man from a study of man in general, and in abstraction from the fact that one man among all others is the man Jesus. In this case we miss the one Archimedean point given us beyond humanity, and therefore the one possibility of discovering the ontological determination of man. Theological anthropology has no choice in this matter. It is not yet or no longer theological anthropology if it tries to pose and answer the question of the true being of man from any other angle.[7]

---

5. The English translation of the *Church Dogmatics* is problematic concerning its use of inclusive language in reference to talking about human persons. The word "man," which no longer serves as an inclusive term, is used throughout to translate *Mensch* even though *Mensch* refers to the whole of humanity. This observation is not offered in order to fault the translators (though, perhaps it is time for an updated translation precisely because of this point), but to note that while inclusive language will be used throughout this chapter, when quoting Barth the original translation will remain.

6. This is not to render superfluous insights that might be gained from other disciplines that study human beings. Daniel Price convincingly argues that Barth is not placing his anthropology beyond the reach of other sciences, but rather that he believes a dialogue between dogmatics and sciences is possible as long as each respects the other discipline's boundaries. See Daniel Price, *Karl Barth's Anthropology in Light of Modern Thought* (Grand Rapids: Eerdmans, 2002).

7. Barth, *CD* III/2, 132. Barth's christological methodology can clearly be observed in looking at the way in which he structures his theological anthropology in *CD* III/2. In this volume, Barth expounds on his anthropology in four paragraphs (§44–7) and in each of these paragraphs he begins with a section on Jesus, the archetype of humanity, who then informs what can be said about humanity in general concerning these issues: §44 Man as the Creature of God: Jesus, Man for God; §45 Man in His Determination as the Covenant-

Therefore, one should understand Barth's theological anthropology as a christological anthropology. It is in the person of Jesus Christ that true human nature is revealed. Even though Jesus does have a divine nature, he is not lacking a genuine human nature; it has not been replaced or subsumed by his divinity. Jesus is "true" God and "true" human. Barth is, thus, careful to maintain a Chalcedonian Christology.[8]

So, what can we discover about humanity at large on the basis of Jesus' humanity? One of the things we learn is that the nature of humanity is intrinsically a relational one. Barth says,

> If the divinity of the man Jesus is to be described comprehensively in the statement that he is man for God, His humanity can and must be described no less succinctly in the proposition that He is man for man, for other men, His fellows . . . in His existence He is referred to man, to other men, His fellows, and this not merely partially, incidentally or subsequently, but originally, exclusively and totally. When we think of the humanity of Jesus, humanity is to be described unequivocally as fellow-humanity. In the light of the man Jesus, man is the cosmic being which exists absolutely for its fellows.[9]

As such, the incarnate Jesus was from the very beginning directed toward fellow-humanity—to them, with them, and for them. Consequently, the existence of the rest of humanity is determined by this element as well. This is not a mere optional choice, but rather predicates humanity's very essence and sets it apart from the rest of creation. Humanity is co-humanity; being is being-in-fellowship. There is an intrinsic relational nature created within humanity such that to exist is to exist *together*.[10] Barth utilizes the "I–Thou" language of dialogical personalism to describe this reality, both in relation to Jesus and the rest of humanity.

Despite this correlation between Christology and anthropology, Barth well acknowledges that the two cannot be conflated. That is, there is no direct equation of Jesus' human nature with everyone else's human nature. There is continuity, but there is also discontinuity on at least three levels: Jesus' human nature is the original and everyone else's a copy; Jesus' human nature is not distorted by sin

---

Partner of God: Jesus, Man for Other Men; §46 Man as Soul and Body: Jesus, Whole Man; §47 Man in His Time: Jesus, Lord of Time.

8. Barth, *CD* III/2, 207–8. George Hunsinger describes Barth's Christology as "one of the most fully elaborated Chalcedonian Christologies ever to have appeared in Christian doctrine." See George Hunsinger, "Karl Barth's Christology: Its Basic Chalcedonian Character," in *The Cambridge Companion to Karl Barth*, ed. John Webster (Cambridge: Cambridge University Press, 2000), 129.

9. Barth, *CD* III/2, 208.

10. Ibid., 222–50. Barth pointedly says, "In the Christian Church we have no option but to interpret humanity as fellow-humanity. And *si quis dixerit hominem esse solitarium, anathema sit*" (Barth, *CD* III/2, 319).

whereas everyone else's is;[11] consequently, Jesus' human nature is not concealed but revealed in its original and basic form, unlike everyone else's which is ruined by sin. Therefore, while one can maintain that Jesus' human nature is the same in "constitution," it is different in "status."[12] The particular way in which this discontinuity emerges when discussing the fellow-humanity of Jesus is that only in Jesus is found the

> being of an I which is wholly from and to the fellow-human Thou, and therefore a genuine I. . . . For of no other man can we say that from the very outset and in virtue of his existence he is for others. Of no other Man can we say that he is the Word of God to men, and therefore that he is directly and inwardly affected by them, or sent, commissioned and empowered to be an act in their place and as their representative, interposing and giving himself for all others, making their life possible and an actual in and with his own, and thus being for them, their guarantor, in this radical and universal sense. . . . Man generally may mean and give a great deal to His fellows, but he cannot be their Deliverer or Saviour.[13]

Another way to state this is to say that while being "for" the other is reciprocal among humanity in general, this is not the case with Jesus. The "for" is irreversible in respect to him. In this way Jesus is the "supreme" or "genuine" "I."[14]

While Christology is the linchpin of Barth's anthropology, it is connected to and thus informed by his trinitarian theology. The incarnate Jesus reflects the inner being of God. The I–Thou as lived out in Jesus of Nazareth is none other than the I–Thou of the Trinity. The humanity of Jesus is the *imago Dei*. Barth says,

> To be sure, God is One in Himself. But He is not alone. There is in Him a co-existence, co-inherence and reciprocity. God in Himself is not just simple, but in the simplicity of his essence he is threefold—the Father, the Son and the Holy Ghost . . . in this triunity He is the original and source of every I and Thou. . . . And it is this relationship in the inner divine being which is repeated and reflected in God's eternal covenant with man as revealed and operative in time in the humanity of Jesus.[15]

---

11. Christ's solidarity with humanity is not just vicarious for Barth. Christ took on fallen flesh; he took on humanity's sin and guilt, but he did so without sin. Barth says, "He made our human essence His own even in its corruption, but He did not repeat or affirm its inward contradiction. He opposed to it a superior contradiction. He overcame it in His own person when He became man." See Karl Barth, *The Doctrine of Reconciliation*, ed. G. W. Bromiley and T. F. Torrance, trans. G. W. Bromiley, 4 vols, *Church Dogmatics*, vol. IV/2 (Edinburgh: T&T Clark, 1958), 92.
12. Barth, *CD* III/2, 47–54.
13. Ibid., 222.
14. Ibid., 216, 218, 222, 243.
15. Ibid., 218–19.

Barth refers to this correspondence and similarity as an *analogia relationis*.[16] Human persons' I–Thou relationship with one another is ultimately to exist analogously to the christological I–Thou and, thus, to the trinitarian I–Thou.[17]

Barth's understanding here is underscored in his exegesis of the creation narratives found in Genesis. Genesis 1:26 contains the programmatic statement that humanity is made in the image of God. For Barth, the textual indicators of "let *us*" and "in *our* image" point to the decidedly trinitarian imprint in the creation of humanity. To be created in God's image and likeness means "to be created as a being which has its ground and possibility in the fact that in 'us,' i.e., in God's own sphere and being, there exists a divine and therefore self-grounded prototype to which this being can correspond."[18] God is the original and humanity the copy. It is for this reason that in Genesis 2 woman is created. As the image and likeness of God, humanity cannot exist in solitude. As God exists as an "I" and "Thou" in confrontation, so too must humanity. Prior to Eve's existence, Adam had not yet found his true partner and helpmeet, his "Thou" whom he could confront as an "I." With her existence the creation of humankind was complete.[19] "Personhood," divine and human, is thus constituted by communion. Moreover, for Barth, the Fall does not eradicate the *imago Dei*, it only frustrates it. "After the Fall man still retains his being as man and still is directed toward God and other men, but he is unable to obtain his goal, unable to reach either God or man."[20]

Barth maintains that humanity as "being in encounter" involves four aspects that ultimately build upon each other. First, being in encounter requires one person to look the other in the eye and, conversely, to allow the other person to look back. What Barth means by this is that the "I" and "Thou" must be open to one another. There is vulnerability in this openness, but also genuine interest

---

16. Ibid., 220. Barth cites John 17 as a plain reference to the *analogia relationis* (220–1).

17. For an extended explication of this *analogia relationis*, see Gary W. Deddo, *Karl Barth's Theology of Relations* (New York: Peter Lang Publishing, Inc., 1999).

18. Barth, *CD* III/1, 183.

19. Ibid., 185, 289–91. Fundamental to Barth's I–Thou construction of humanity is his understanding that in order for humanity's I–Thou to exist analogously to God's, it is necessary for there to be *differentiation* in relationship. It is for this reason that humanity is created male *and* female, which constitutes a foundational duality in creation. The inner logic of Barth's anthropological I–Thou is ultimately dependent upon sexuality, rather than sociality. However, an anthropology characterized by dialogical personalism is not necessarily dependent upon this principle and the constructive proposals in this chapter are not dependent upon this assumption. Moreover, the way in which Barth insists on a relational ordering in his male–female I–Thou construct is problematic and inconsistent with other portions of his anthropology. See Lisa P. Stephenson, "Directed, Ordered, and Related: The Male and Female Interpersonal Relation in Karl Barth's *Church Dogmatics*," *Scottish Journal of Theology* 61, no. 4 (2008): 435–49.

20. Karl Barth, *Karl Barth's Table Talk*, ed. John D. Godsey (Edinburgh: Oliver and Boyd, 1963), 41.

in the existence of the other. This element is the most basic and essential for the rest. Second, being in encounter consists of mutual speech and hearing. It is in this act that one has the opportunity to contribute to making oneself known. Whereas seeing only permits the other person to form a perspective based on his own resources, mutual speech and hearing allows for the individual to put herself forward, declare who and what she is according to her own understanding, and invite him to compare the picture of her with what he himself has contributed. Third, being in encounter depends upon mutual assistance provided (i.e., giving and receiving). This means that persons are there for the other, ready to be summoned to action. Self-sufficiency is inhumanity. Fourth, being in encounter means that gladness characterizes the prior three elements on both sides of the I–Thou. Whereas the first three elements were external, this is internal. This is not an imposition from without, but offered in freedom. Only then will being in encounter avoid tyranny and slavery and constitute the I–Thou as "companions, associates, comrades, fellows and helpmates."[21]

Assessment

To ground one's anthropology in Christology inevitably means that the particular Christology one purports will influence and shape the corresponding anthropology. And this is no less true with Barth. Yet, herein lies the problem. In *Church Dogmatics* III/2 Barth tends to interpret Jesus primarily through Johannine lenses, which results in a strong Logos Christology. One of the shortcomings of this approach is that the christological depictions presented in the Synoptics are marginalized, frequently resulting in a Christology that is deficient of pneumatology. And, because for Barth Christology and anthropology are connected, this hermeneutical move results in an anthropology that is deficient of pneumatology too.

Various scholars have critiqued Barth for his strong christological focus, labeling him more of a binatarian than a trinitarian at times. For example, Eugene Rogers, Jr., claims that between volumes I/2 and IV/3 Barth's christological statements render pneumatological ones superfluous. In addition, Robert Jenson maintains that because Barth's trinitarian fellowship is described as two-sided—since the Spirit is the fellowship itself joining the I–Thou of the Father and Son—and this model stands as the archetype within Barth's *analogia relationis*, the two-sidedness gets reproduced at every ontological level.[22]

---

21. Barth, *CD* III/2, 250–74. Curiously, these four features do not seem to follow the christological method he wants to uphold with his anthropology. When listing these four defining features he fails to ground any of them in Christology or the biblical texts.

22. Eugene F. Rogers, Jr., "The Eclipse of the Spirit in Karl Barth," in *Conversing with Barth*, ed. John C. McDowell and Mike Higton (Burlington: Ashgate, 2004), 175; see also his *After the Spirit: A Constructive Pneumatology from Resources Outside the Modern West* (Grand Rapids: Eerdmans, 2005), 19–32; Robert W. Jenson, "You Wonder Where the Spirit

This is not to suggest that there is no pneumatology in Barth's Christology or anthropology, but to note that in *Church Dogmatics* III/2 it largely remains in the shadows offering very little substance to his theological construction with respect to these two loci, especially within his dialogical personalism paradigm. In III/2, one finds a theological anthropology whose christological underpinnings are clear, but whose pneumatological ones are less so. Admittedly, at other points in the *Church Dogmatics* Barth does exhibit more of a Spirit Christology and touches on its implications for humanity at large, particularly in IV/2. However, what Barth develops in IV/2 does not interface Spirit Christology and anthropology in an extended and pervasive way such that it is evident how the dialogical personalism exemplified in Christ's life is pneumatologically informed and empowered, as well as embodied then in the rest of humanity.

Spirit Christology = Spirit Anthropology

Spirit Christology

So, what can be done to strengthen the role of the Spirit in Barth's Christology and, thus, his anthropology? Barth needs to allow his christological model to be more influenced by a Spirit Christology rather than an incarnational Christology. Whereas Barth tends to favor the latter, the former intentionally situates the work and mission of Christ as an aspect of the Spirit's work and mission.[23] In the Synoptic Gospels, the story of Jesus does not begin with his preexistence or birth, but rather with the overshadowing of the Spirit upon Mary (Mt. 1:18-20; Lk. 1:35). Jesus' growth and development is related to the presence of the Spirit, as he is described as becoming strong in Spirit (Lk. 2:40). In Jesus' baptism, the Spirit is also at work descending on him in the form of a dove, thus signifying his anointing

---

Went," *Pro Ecclesia* 2, no. 3 (Summer 1993): 300-1. It is not just individual scholars making such claims, but in fact the Karl Barth Society of North America that has noticed this glaring lacuna in his work too! See Jenson, "You Wonder Where the Spirit Went," 296-8. Consequently, Philip Rosato's work on Barth's pneumatology in *The Spirit as Lord: The Pneumatology of Karl Barth* (Edinburgh: T&T Clark, 1981), though seminal, presents an overly optimistic depiction of Barth as a pneumatic theologian.

23. It is important to recognize that there are at least two very different types of Spirit Christology maintained among scholars today. On the one hand, there are those who seek to *replace* the Logos Christology with a Spirit Christology and have been labeled as post-trinitarian. On the other hand, there are those who seek to *complement* Logos Christology with a Spirit Christology by preserving the trinitarian distinctions as they have classically been understood, but advancing a more robust pneumatology than has traditionally been the case. It is this latter form of Spirit Christology that I am deploying in this essay. See Myk Habets, "Spirit Christology: Seeing in Stereo," *Journal of Pentecostal Theology* 11, no. 2 (2003): 199-234.

as the Christ and the power by which he will minister to others (Mt. 3:16; Mk 1:10; Lk. 3:22; Jn 1:32-33). Jesus is led by the Spirit (Mt. 4:1; Mk 1:12; Lk. 2:27; 4:1, 14). Jesus describes his own ministry in terms of the Spirit's empowerment (Mt. 12:28; Lk. 4:18; Jn 3:34). And Jesus is resurrected by the vivifying power and presence of the Spirit (Rom. 8:11; 1 Pet. 3:18).[24] From beginning to end, the missions of the Spirit and of Jesus are intertwined.

Ian McFarland maintains that a Spirit Christology—which he terms a "pneumatic Chalcedonianism"—not only grants a more significant role to the Spirit in the life of Christ, but also is more advantageous to preserving a Chalcedonian Christology (which Barth himself wants to uphold).[25] McFarland suggests that within the incarnation it is the Spirit, rather than the Logos, that is the causative agent of Jesus' human operations. While the Word is still the subject of Jesus' thoughts and actions, it cannot be the cause. For if it is the cause, then one ruins the integrity of Christ's human nature "since to attribute any of Christ's capacities or behaviors to the power of the Word in him would be to make Jesus' virtues—his love, righteousness, obedience, compassion and so forth—different from ours at their very root and consequently of no value as the ground or goal of a redeemed *human* existence."[26] Jesus *is who he is* by virtue of the hypostatic union of the Word with a human nature, but Jesus *does what he does* by virtue of the power of the Holy Spirit.

Gerald Hawthorne, similar to McFarland, posits Jesus' dependence upon the Spirit as "unimpeachable" proof that Jesus was genuinely a human being. Just like the Spirit came upon persons in the Old Testament in order to empower them to the tasks to which God had called them, so also the Spirit came upon Jesus in the New Testament. It is through the empowerment of the Spirit that Jesus overcomes his human limitations and this is the significance of the Spirit in Jesus' life.[27] Bruce

---

24. For a fuller treatment of the ways in which the Spirit is essential to understanding Jesus' identity and mission, see Myk Habets, *The Anointed Son: A Trinitarian Spirit Christology* (Eugene: Pickwick Publications, 2010), 118–87.

25. While McFarland actually eschews the title "Spirit Christology" because he associates it with current post-trinitarian theologies—and, thus, presumably only identifies Spirit Christology with adoptionistic models—what he maintains with his pneumatic Chalcedonianism is essentially a Spirit Christology as developed by others who are not seeking to replace Logos Christology, but complement it. Therefore, I will use "Spirit Christology" to describe his model, even if he does not. See Ian McFarland, "Spirit and Incarnation: Toward a Pneumatic Chalcedonianism," *International Journal of Systematic Theology* 16, no. 2 (April 2014): 143.

26. McFarland, "Spirit and Incarnation," 153. This echoes precisely Barth's concern in his own Christology with respect to preserving the integrity of Jesus' human nature, though he does not attribute the significance of the Spirit with respect to Jesus' human nature like McFarland does. See Barth, *CD* III/2, 53.

27. Gerald Hawthorne, *The Presence and the Power: The Significance of the Holy Spirit in the Life and Ministry of Jesus* (Dallas: Word Publishing, 1991), 35.

Ware goes so far as to say this is the only way to make sense of the presence of the Spirit in the life of Christ. Jesus relied on the "Spirit to provide the power, grace, knowledge, wisdom, direction, and enablement he needed, moment by moment and day by day, to fulfill the mission the Father sent him to accomplish."[28]

This christological understanding is particularly exemplified in the Gospel of Luke where the author goes to great redactional lengths at the beginning to demonstrate that Jesus is dependent upon an empowering of the Spirit to fulfill his mission as the Christ. In Luke 3:21-22 the Spirit descends upon Jesus as both a divine attestation and divine empowerment. The former understanding is evident, whereas the latter becomes *clearer* as the narrative continues. In Luke 4:1, Luke adds the observation that Jesus was "fully of the Holy Spirit" (cf. Mk 1:12-13; Mt. 4:1), which should be understood as a general characterization of Jesus' relationship to the Spirit in Jesus' ministry from the Jordan onward. Also, in Luke 4:1, Jesus is portrayed as being continually "led in the Spirit" during this event, which grants the Spirit a more significant and permanent role than just leading Jesus to *where* he was tested (cf. Mk 1:12-13; Mt. 4:1). In Luke 4:14, a redaction occurs again and Luke adds the phrase "in the power of the Spirit" to describe the way in which Jesus returns from his temptation episode and begins his redemptive ministry (cf. Mk 1:14-15). And, finally, in Luke 4:18-19, the Nazareth pericope is moved forward in the narrative (cf. Mk 6:1-16) in order to link Jesus' reception of the Spirit with the announcement of his messianic task. Here Jesus himself provides the clarification of the significance of his baptismal reception: the pneumatic anointing was to equip and enable Jesus to carry out his incarnational mission. This understanding is also echoed later in Acts when Peter is recounting the life and ministry of Jesus to Cornelius (Acts 10:38; cf. 2:22).[29] Thus, the significance of the descent of the Spirit for Jesus' entire ministry cannot be overstated and certainly confirms McFarland's pneumatic Chalcedonianism noted above.

---

28. Bruce A. Ware, "The Man Christ Jesus," *Journal of the Evangelical Theological Society* 53, no. 1 (March 2010): 6. The difference between Hawthorne and Ware is the former maintains that Jesus did not utilize his divine prerogatives at all, while the latter claims that there are experiences that Jesus had that are distinctive to his deity (e.g., forgive sins).

29. Robert P. Menzies, *Empowered for Witness: The Spirit in Luke-Acts* (Sheffield: Sheffield Academic Press, 1994), 132–56; James B. Shelton, *Mighty in Word and Deed: The Role of the Holy Spirit in Luke-Acts* (Peabody: Hendrickson Publishers, 1991), 46–73; Max Turner, *Power from on High: The Spirit in Israel's Restoration and Witness in Luke-Acts* (Sheffield: Sheffield Academic Press, 1996), 188–266. It should be noted that I neither understand nor am employing the phenomenon of being "filled with the Spirit" in a parochial sense. Luke–Acts is best interpreted through the lens of the Isaianic New Exodus motif, within which the Spirit is present to effect Israel's restoration and bring about the new creation. See Stephenson, *Dismantling the Dualisms for American Pentecostal Women in Ministry*, 89–114.

Spirit Anthropology

What, then, does a Spirit Christology imply for Barth's christological anthropology? Whereas Barth wants to maintain that Jesus is humanity's "fellow-man," that he is "to them and with them and for them," and that as such he is "sent and ordained by God to be their Deliverer," Spirit Christology insists that all of this is possible only by the power and presence of the Spirit in Jesus' life.[30] This is what enables Jesus to be the genuine and supreme "I." *This* is what makes Jesus the "I" wholly from and to humanity's "Thou." *This* is what empowers Jesus' humanity to be described unequivocally as fellow-humanity. Aaron Kuecker's work on the role of the Spirit in Luke–Acts, which is concerned with personal identity, confirms this understanding of the role of the Spirit in Jesus' life. Kuecker describes the Spirit's effect upon individuals as creating a transformational openness that results in a personal identity whose interest is centered in other persons rather than oneself. To put it in Barthian terms, the Spirit is responsible for helping persons exist "for" the other. And in the Gospel of Luke, Jesus is the primary example of this Spirit-formed identity.[31]

Moreover, following Barth's methodology, if the Spirit is essential in relation to Jesus' humanity, then this must also be true in regard to the rest of humanity. Specifically, humanity's existence "for" others is also only made possible by the presence of the Spirit in their lives. It is only by the power of the Spirit that humanity can be co-humanity. This, too, is exemplified in the biblical narratives in Acts. The descent of the Spirit upon Jesus (Lk. 3:22) parallels the descent of the Spirit on those gathered in Jerusalem (Acts 2:1-4). In Luke, Jesus is anointed with the Holy Spirit and power, and in Acts he in turn dispenses the Spirit and subsequent power to his disciples and followers.[32] Subsequently, Acts recounts at multiple points the way in which the Spirit then turns persons outward toward the other (e.g., the Samaritans, Ethiopian eunuch, and Gentiles).[33] While not wanting to jeopardize the integrity of the biblical texts by pressing Barth's "being in encounter" schema too far, it is worth noting that there are interesting correlations

---

30. Barth, *CD* III/2, 209.

31. Aaron Kuecker, *The Spirit and the "Other:" Social identity, Ethnicity and Intergroup Reconciliation in Luke-Acts* (New York: Bloomsbury, 2013), 18–19, 72–96.

32. It has been well recognized that an important feature of Luke–Acts is the parallels that exist between the two books. This is true both in content and sequence, and form a primary architectonic pattern in the text. Charles Talbert notes that "only Luke-Acts in early Christianity reflects the conviction that both the story of Jesus and the story of the apostolic church are incomplete without the other as complement. Hence any attempt at understanding the architecture of the Lucan writings must treat the Gospel-Acts pattern as basic." See Charles Talbert, *Literary Patterns, Theological Themes and the Genre of Luke-Acts* (Missoula: Scholars Press, 1974), 15.

33. Kuecker maintains that the Spirit empowered examples of intergroup reconciliation in Luke–Acts are largely unprecedented within the ancient world. Kuecker, *The Spirit and the "Other,"* 18–20.

in Acts with respect to the four characteristics that Barth delineates as constitutive of I–Thou encounters noted above (i.e., seeing, speaking and hearing, offering assistance, and gladness). And, especially crucial for the argument thus far, in each instance the presence of the Spirit is noted in the text.

First, in Acts 9:1-19a, one finds a description of Saul's conversion that hinges upon the loss and restoration of his *sight*. In fact, the first account of the incident in Acts intentionally limits language of sight to Saul—as the men traveling with him "hear" but do not "see" (cf. Acts 22:9)—such that the narrative focuses the reader's attention on this aspect solely in relation to Saul. Saul's encounter with Jesus literally blinds him and he only receives his sight again when Ananias lays his hands upon him. The text describes the restoration of Saul's sight as "scales falling from his eyes" (Acts 9:18). One way of understanding this feature of the account is to recognize that Saul's spiritual condition was made physical.[34] That is, prior to this event, Saul could not really "see" those whom he was persecuting; there was no openness or genuine interest in the other. But, after Ananias lays hands on him, Saul can truly see for the first time. He is now open to the others to which he was previously closed. And what is the causative power that enables Saul's sight? Nothing less than being filled with the Holy Spirit (Acts 9:17).[35]

Next, in Acts 2:1-11, the event of Pentecost is detailed wherein a miracle of *speaking* and *hearing* occurs. Many scholars understand Acts 2 as a reversal of Babel (Gen. 11:1-9). Whereas Babel recounts a confusion of language that results in division, Pentecost recounts a gift of language that overcomes barriers. Whereas Babel presents a scenario in which community with one's neighbor becomes impossible, Pentecost presents a scenario in which community with one's neighbor is made possible. At Pentecost, the Spirit enables those who were filled with the Holy Spirit to *speak* in other tongues for the purpose of those present to be able to *hear* them in their own language. It was a gift of language that fostered communication and, hence, community. Moreover, this unity does not come by flattening the distinctives between persons, but affirming and preserving them.[36] And what is the causative power that enables persons to speak in other tongues and the crowd to hear their own language being spoken? Once again, nothing less than being filled with the Holy Spirit (Acts 2:4-6).

Then, in Acts 4:32-35, the early community is described as *offering assistance* to one another as they shared everything they had and there were no needy persons

---

34. Craig S. Keener, *Acts: An Exegetical Commentary*, 4 vols (Grand Rapids: Baker Academic, 2012), 2:1640–2.

35. While the author of Acts does not explicitly narrate Saul's reception of the Spirit, the narrative clearly implicates this. Ananias' task is to facilitate Saul receiving his sight and receiving the Holy Spirit, the text indicates the former happened immediately so the reader is left to presume that the latter happened immediately too. See Kuecker, *The Spirit and the "Other,"* 172–3.

36. Keener, *Acts: An Exegetical Commentary*, 1:842–4; Kuecker, *The Spirit and the "Other,"* 115–19.

among them because they acted as if their private property belonged to all. While there is no explicit reference to the Spirit in this particular passage, Acts 4:32-35 is a summary statement that follows right after the account of a "second Pentecost" in Acts 4:31. As such, the reader would naturally assume the presence of the Spirit as the source of the community life, especially its generosity (cf. Acts 2:42-47).[37] This understanding is made all the clearer when immediately following Acts 4:32-35 the narrative continues the theme of helping others by juxtaposing the example of Barnabas—who is described as one filled with the Spirit (Acts 4:31; 11:24)—with that of Ananias and Sapphira—who are described as being filled with Satan (Acts 5:3). As one filled with the Spirit, Barnabas is depicted as turning away from himself and outward toward others because he sells his field and brings all the money to the apostles. Whereas Ananias and Sapphira, who are filled with Satan rather than the Spirit, are depicted as turning in toward themselves and away from others because they also sell a field but keep some of the money and lie about it.[38] Therefore, what is the causative power that enables persons to turn toward the other in assistance? In this instance, too, it is nothing less than being filled with the Holy Spirit (Acts 4:31–5:6).

Finally, in Acts 13:52, one finds an explicit association between being filled with the Holy Spirit and *joy* (i.e., Barth's gladness). Unlike the three previous examples, this mention does not occur specifically in an I–Thou occasion. Nonetheless, it highlights a consistent theme throughout Luke–Acts of positing the Spirit as the source of joy or rejoicing, even on Jesus himself (Lk. 10:21). Max Turner argues that while Acts 13:52 marks a particularly striking charisma of joy, the reader should expect this joy to be commonplace to those with the Spirit at less remarkable levels (cf. Lk. 1:41-42; 1:44; 1:68-79; 2:29-32; Acts 2:4-13, 15; 10:46; 19:6).[39] Hence, when it is the causative power of the Spirit that enables one to see, speak and hear, and offer assistance, this same Spirit can also enable one to do all of these things gladly rather than reluctantly. Being filled with the Holy Spirit does not just affect us externally, but internally too (Acts 13:52).

In each of the instances highlighted above, persons are filled with the Holy Spirit, which in turn directs them toward the other in some form or fashion. Therefore, there is similarity between the work of the Spirit in Jesus' humanity and in humanity at large. While Jesus had to depend upon the Holy Spirit to live out his life in faithful witness to God and service to others, so too does the rest of humanity. However, as Barth reminds us, though there is continuity between Christology and anthropology there is also discontinuity. To that extent, the Spirit

---

37. Turner, *Power from on High*, 412–15.

38. Kuecker also notes that this juxtaposition between the influence of the Spirit and the influence of Satan emerges in the temptation scene of Jesus as well. See Kuecker, *The Spirit and the "Other,"* 78–80, 136–47.

39. Turner, *Power from on High*, 411; Peter J. Cullen, "Euphoria, Praise and Thanksgiving: Rejoicing in the Spirit in Luke-Acts," *Journal of Pentecostal Theology* 6 (1995): 13–24.

is Christ's in a way that the Spirit is never the rest of humanity's. Commenting on this aspect McFarland says,

> The difference between Jesus and other people therefore does not lie in any quality or capacity of the human nature on which the Spirit acts . . . but in the peculiar circumstance that in this one case the hypostasis of the human being on whom the Spirit rests in time is the same Son on whom the Spirit has rested from eternity. . . . [The] Spirit who rests on Jesus of Nazareth is *his* Spirit, to the extent that it can be called indifferently the Spirit of God or Christ. . . . By contrast, although we, too, depend on that same Spirit to lead us in lives of faith and obedience, the Spirit is never ours. Like Christ we receive the Spirit as a gift (for created human nature can only receive the Creator Spirit as gift, even when that nature is enhypostatized by the Word) that enables us to share in God's very life; but whereas Christ receives this gift as his very own Spirit (because it is the Spirit of God, and he is God), we can receive it only in acknowledging that we have no right to it (because it is the Spirit of God, and we are not God).[40]

Conclusion

If one is going to approach anthropology from a christological perspective, then this Christology—and its concomitant anthropology—must highlight the work and mission of the Spirit as a necessary empowerment for persons to properly realize their co-humanity. Certainly, the incarnation is essential to understanding what it means to be human, but the theological burden cannot rest solely on Christology. It must be born on the shoulders of pneumatology as well, wherein the role of the Spirit for theological anthropology is more clearly recognized. Thus, for Barth, the christological moorings of his anthropology are not problematic per se, but the overshadowing incarnational Christology upon which they are built is. However, as noted above, there is provision to enrich his I–Thou construct, which ultimately is more consistent both theologically and biblically. And, as such, perhaps Barth himself would readily acknowledge that a third article theology deployed in service of Christology and anthropology is not just a possibility, but a necessity.

---

40. McFarland, "Spirit and Incarnation," 155.

Part Three

Christ and Salvation

Chapter 8

JESUS THE SPIRIT BAPTIZER

A PENTECOSTAL REVISION OF KARL BARTH'S SPIRIT CHRISTOLOGY

Frank D. Macchia

Recent studies in Karl Barth's pneumatology have shown that there is indeed the beginnings of a Spirit Christology in Barth's massive treatment of christological themes. A neglected focus of attention when it comes to implications in Barth's work for a Spirit Christology has been his dual emphasis on the exaltation of the Son of Man and the humiliation of the Son of God.[1] Of relevance here is Barth's implication, especially in the concluding fragment of his *Church Dogmatics*, that one can interpret these two distinct but inseparable christological trajectories as Christ's baptism in the Spirit (exaltation of the Son of Man) and fire (humiliation of the Son of God). The neglect of this dual trajectory in treatments of Barth's pneumatology is understandable, since Barth himself does not treat Christ's trial by fire as a pneumatological theme. But the implication that it is may be found in John the Baptist's announcement in Matthew and Luke that Christ will baptize in the Spirit and fire, both of which Christ himself undergoes for us. In what follows, I will engage Barth as a dialogue partner in working out my own Pentecostal exploration of Jesus' baptism in Spirit and fire on the way to his role as the Spirit baptizer. In the process, I plan to enhance both Barth's pneumatology and the classical Pentecostal understanding of Christ's role as the Spirit baptizer.

Pentecostal Spirit Baptism

As I have argued elsewhere, the baptism in the Holy Spirit is the major point of emphasis for the Pentecostal understanding of Christian life and mission,

---

1. None of the three major book-length treatments of Barth's pneumatology highlight the distinct but inseparable relationship between Christ's baptism in the Spirit and fire. See JinHyok Kim, *The Holy Spirit and the Christian Life: Reconstructing Karl Barth's Pneumatology* (Minneapolis: Fortress, 2014); Philip Rosato, *The Holy Spirit as Lord: The Pneumatology of Karl Barth* (New York: T&T Clark, 1981); John Thompson, *The Holy Spirit in the Theology of Karl Barth*, Princeton Theological Monograph Series (Eugene: Pickwick, 1991).

including the role of Christ's messianic mission in bringing such things to fulfillment.² David William Faupel has maintained convincingly in my view that Pentecostals in their construal of the biblical message placed their accent on Christ as the mediator of spiritual fullness in the church's life and mission.³ Faupel thus maintains that Spirit baptism at least implicitly meant more to them than merely a more powerful engagement in the life of the Spirit subsequent to regeneration. Spirit baptism culminates Christ's messianic mission as well as our union with Christ by faith. W. H. Durham is the key for Faupel's transition to this more integral and expansive development of the Pentecostal theology of Spirit baptism. As a transitional figure, Durham came to view sanctification as decisively attained at the point of union with Christ by faith (regeneration), rather than as an experience subsequent to this. He then considered the filling of the Spirit as subsequent to union with Christ by faith (regeneration) but conceived of this as still integrally connected to this union. At the climax of his book, Faupel quotes this significant statement from Durham, who maintains that the full blessing of the Spirit is mediated to us by the all-sufficient victory of Christ in the atonement: "The all-sufficient atonement of Christ, justification by faith, the gift of the Spirit with His inward witness and inspired freedom, are shown to constitute a virtual unity which determines the whole nature of the Christian religion."⁴ According to Faupel, Durham's christocentric piety, which was inherent to Pentecostalism from the beginning, caused Pentecostals to develop pneumatology under the banner of Christ as Victor. Experiences of the Spirit that were "subsequent" to one's initial faith in Christ did not exceed that faith but rather deepened it.

Most significantly, Durham was then the main source of inspiration for the Oneness Pentecostals, who went a step further to deny subsequence to the experience of Spirit baptism entirely. They elaborated on Durham's proposed integration of union with Christ by faith and Spirit baptism by correlating baptism in water (in Jesus' name) with the baptism in the Holy Spirit under the rubric of being born again of water and Spirit.⁵ Union with Christ was joined as one with the baptism in the Holy Spirit, which also involved initial sanctification and empowerment for service. Faupel concludes rightly in my view that the

---

2. See Frank D. Macchia, *Jesus the Spirit Baptizer: Christology in Light of Pentecost* (Grand Rapids: Eerdmans, 2018).

3. D. William Faupel, *The Everlasting Gospel: The Significance of Eschatology in the Development of Pentecostal Thought* (Sheffield: Sheffield Academic Press, 1996).

4. W. H. Durham, "The Experience Is Standardized," *Word and Witness* (July 1910): 202. Quoted in Faupel, *The Everlasting Gospel*, 306.

5. The Oneness Pentecostals represent up to a quarter of the world Pentecostal movement today. They are called "Oneness" due to the fact that they reject the immanent Trinity for a modalistic understanding of the Father, Son, and Spirit as "manifestations" of God in history. They also came to advocate water baptism in Jesus' Name and in many segments of the movement the necessity of speaking in tongues as the sure sign of the reception of the Spirit by faith.

Oneness Pentecostal understanding of Spirit baptism as the culminating point of Christian initiation is quintessentially Pentecostal for it brings to full expression the christocentric pneumatology always inherent in the movement. Of this christocentric view of Spirit baptism as participation in the victory of Christ in the atonement Faupel remarks, "the fact remains that it was the logical and inevitable development of Pentecostal theology."[6]

Yet, there is the eschatological dimension to take into consideration, also a point emphasized by Faupel. Spirit baptism is anchored in our initial union with Christ and participation by the Spirit in his victory over sin and death, but it also reaches for eschatological actualization in Christian experience. There is still subsequent experience to be had! In my own work I have taken Faupel's argument further to say that Spirit baptism for Pentecostals (as well as for the New Testament) is also experienced in dramatic breakthroughs in the spiritual life that bring to realization the eschatological liberty of the Spirit in the here and now, granting us foretastes of the ultimate "swallowing up" of mortal life in the immortal life of the Spirit (2 Cor. 5:4).[7]

What does this christocentric and eschatological approach to Spirit baptism have to do with our understanding of Christ's messianic mission? In his significant treatise on the baptism in the Holy Spirit, James Dunn tells us that Spirit baptism in the New Testament culminates Christ's messianic mission. He wrote, "the climax and purposed end of Jesus' ministry is not the cross and the resurrection, but the ascension and Pentecost."[8] This statement would strike many as strange, but it shouldn't. All four gospels and the book of Acts, the narrative foundation of the entire New Testament, introduce Jesus with the hope of Pentecost at the horizon of his messianic mission. Jesus is the one who will baptize all flesh in the Holy Spirit by imparting the Spirit at Pentecost. John knew that Jesus was the Chosen One when he saw the Spirit descend upon him for this very purpose (Jn 1:33-34). John the Baptist did not know that Jesus would also have to endure the baptism in fire in order, as the Spirit-baptized man, to baptize others in the Spirit. I have written a Christology with this insight as my overarching point of emphasis.[9] My interlocutors not only included James Dunn but also, especially, Karl Barth. This brief chapter is dedicated to my conversation with Barth over the possibility of using the baptism in Holy Spirit and fire as the *Schwerpunkt* (point of emphasis) for Spirit Christology. I will focus especially on the connection that Barth makes between Christ's humiliation as the Son of God (his fire baptism) and exaltation as the Son of Man (connected to his Spirit baptism). But, first, I wish to discuss three

---

6. Faupel, *The Everlasting Gospel*, 304.

7. See my development of this in Frank D. Macchia, *Baptized in the Spirit: A Global Pentecostal Theology* (Grand Rapids: Zondervan, 2006).

8. James D. G. Dunn, *Baptism in the Holy Spirit*, Studies in Biblical Theology, Second Series 15 (London: SCM Press, 1970), 44.

9. I refer to Macchia, *Jesus the Spirit Baptizer*.

preludes to Barth's Spirit Christology that set the stage for the more constructive section.

First Prelude: The Spirit Materially Constitutes Christology

Barth's use of Spirit baptism as a framework for doing Christology is tied to his conviction (perhaps surprising to some) that the Holy Spirit *materially* determines Christology. Barth supports this because he assumes a continuity between how Christ proclaims himself in the Spirit and who Christ IS in the Spirit. Note what he says: "He who *is* by the Holy Spirit is also *known* by the same Spirit. How else could He be known or expounded but in the event of His own self-exposition as it corresponds to the event of His existence?"[10] Whenever a quote contains a phrase that seems atypical or unusual, it naturally warrants special attention. In the quote given above, Karl Barth notes that Christ is "known by the Spirit." Such is exactly what we have come to expect him to say. No surprises here. In the event of revelation, the Spirit typically plays a noetic role for Barth. Christ as the Word of the Father has come to declare or proclaim himself as the event of reconciliation between God and humanity. The Spirit is the power of that self-declaration, serving the important noetic function of revealing the condescending Son of God who is also the exalted Son of Man for the sake of our redemption. The church today lives from the Son's self-proclamation in both its kerygmatic and sacramental life. The Spirit continues to turn our witness into the means by which the Son's own witness of himself and of his Father is heard and embraced.

So far, so good. But there's more in the above quote that is not so typically attributed to Barth's Christology. In the above quote, Barth also notes that the Christ who is *known* by the Spirit *IS* by the same Spirit. In other words, the Spirit in the Christ event also plays a role that could be called *ontic* or constitutive of the Christ event itself. Not only does Christ determine the direction of the Spirit's work for Barth, the Spirit also in some sense determines *materially* for Barth the Christ event itself. Bear in mind that Christ as the God-Man *is* for Barth the history of reconciliation between God and humanity. Barth allows the Spirit to play a mediating role in Christ's fulfillment of his mission as the God-Man. Hence, the Spirit is material to Christology for Barth. Christ imparts himself in the freedom and power of the Spirit. Barth says the same elsewhere in the *Church Dogmatics*. For example, of the Spirit he writes, "It is in His power that the will of the Father is fulfilled in the fact that the Son of God assumes human essence and therefore becomes the Son of Man, exalting human essence to fellowship with the Godhead."[11] In other words, what many don't fully appreciate is that Barth not only offers us a christological pneumatology; he also offers resources

---

10. Emphasis is not original. Karl Barth, *Church Dogmatics*, Vol. IV, Pt. 2, *The Doctrine of Reconciliation*, trans. G. W. Bromiley (Edinburgh: T&T Clark, 1958), 39.

11. Ibid., 125.

for a pneumatological Christology. Admittedly, the Spirit's role in materially determining the Christ event is not an overall point of emphasis for Barth. One has to look for it and then seek to develop it. As I will develop below, one can do so by tying this assumption with Barth's understanding of both Jesus' conception by the Spirit in Mary's womb and, especially, Jesus' emergence from the Jordan and at Pentecost as the Spirit baptizer.

Second Prelude: Soteriology Determines Metaphysics

To understand Barth's Christology in the light of Spirit and fire baptism, one must also talk about how soteriology takes priority to metaphysics when it comes to Christology for Barth. This prioritization frees Barth from preoccupation with abstract metaphysical problems so as to highlight instead Jesus' concrete sojourn in the power of the Spirit through the captivity of flesh and through to the possibility of its freedom for God. This is the thrust of the incarnation for Barth, a bulwark christological event for him. Indeed, one is accustomed by reading classical discussions of the incarnation to deal with metaphysical issues, such as immutability or impassibility. Specifically, one is led to consider whether or not the incarnation of the divine Son of God in mutable and passible flesh makes sense. Although Barth does not ignore such issues, he also does not make them his preoccupation or point of departure. He is not taken with Christ as the metaphysical link between immutable deity and mutable flesh. For Barth, God at the incarnation enters into the far country "not only of human creatureliness but also of human corruption and perdition."[12] Barth's all-determining question is therefore: How are we to understand the merciful turning of an infinitely holy and just God toward the sinner who fundamentally opposes the divine will? How does God reestablish the covenant, bringing humanity following the path of alienation into the divine communion? How does God bridge the gulf between the Spirit of life and the reality of death? Indeed, Barth considers the flesh assumed in the incarnation to be *fallen flesh*, flesh that all fallen humans bear in common, though Christ conquered it by living a sinless life.[13] Though this point is understandably controversial, it does serve to secure Barth's point of departure as profoundly soteriological from the very beginning. The gulf to be crossed at the incarnation is not primarily that of finitude with all of its metaphysical attributes. As the faithful Son of the Father and man of the Spirit, Christ would overcome this gulf of sin and its consequences in the alienation from life. But, as we will see, he will also do so as the one baptized in the Spirit and fire on our behalf.

Barth refuses to answer the question of how God crosses this gulf by turning to some set of abstract metaphysical or philosophical principles. He simply points to how God freely chose to exercise divine love in dealing with the sinner and lets

---

12. Ibid., 20.
13. Ibid., 92.

the metaphysical chips fall where they may. He merely rejoices over how God has determined to reveal Godself, how God has actually chosen from all eternity to be God for us. Barth seeks out those theological categories that will help him to explain the freedom of a holy and just God to fulfill all righteousness by embracing sinners who live in opposition to the divine will. Barth thus concludes that God fulfills all righteousness for humanity by going to a cross, *fulfilling justice in the freedom of self-giving love.*

This soteriological point of departure yields some surprising results. For example, a metaphysical Christology might very well look at Christ's servanthood and suffering as the human reality and Christ's glorious exaltation as the divine reality at work in the Christ event. But such is not so with Barth. Taken with soteriological categories, Barth looks at the matter in the opposite way. Informed by christological texts like Philippians 2, Barth viewed the path to servanthood and suffering as mainly the *divine* reality and the exaltation as mainly the *human* reality at work in the Christ event. God condescends so as to exalt humanity to communion and covenant faithfulness. How does one understand such free and triumphant love? The Christian tradition has pointed for insights to the cross and to Pentecost, the missions of the Son and the Spirit. It is to these missions that Barth will turn in constructing his Spirit Christology.

Third Prelude: Toward a Dynamic Spirit Christology

The first two preludes open Barth to a dynamic Christology that is actualized in flesh in the history of Jesus' yielding to the Spirit and devotion to the Father. So, the Spirit's role in mediating the incarnation is the beginning and determining factor of the christological mission for Barth. Barth turns to the biblical and creedal affirmation that Jesus Christ was conceived by the Holy Spirit to explain the significance of the incarnation for Christ's overarching mission, and he does so with Christ's soteriological mission in mind. Conceived by the Spirit, Christ's flesh borne in common with us is conceived already in victory, beginning at the time of this triumph of divine love over sin and death in the incarnation. Barth also turns quite naturally to his Augustinian and Cappadocian heritage in order to bring the Holy Spirit to bear on our understanding of the triumph of divine love at the incarnation. After all, the Holy Spirit is the principle of divine love in both traditions. This insight causes Barth to regard the Spirit as of material and ontic significance for his Christology. In his *Credo*, published in 1936, Barth therefore grants the conception of Jesus by the Holy Spirit in Mary's womb (Lk. 1:35) "a general and a special, an inner and an outer, a *material* and a significant cause" of the christological event that constitutes Christ's person and work.[14]

Christ for Barth is conceived in the freedom and power of the Spirit. That point is determinative for Barth, for it marks Christ's entire sojourn to the cross, in fact, the

---

14. Emphasis mine. Karl Barth, *Credo* (New York: Charles Scribners, 1962), 70.

cross itself, as a self-giving in the freedom and power of the Spirit. In discerning the material significance of the Spirit for the Christ event, Barth significantly points to the Spirit as the principle of divine freedom, the divine freedom to graciously love and commune with sinful humans by assuming sinful flesh to redeem them. The incarnation is God's being true to the eternal divine will but in a new way, in a way that flows out from the freedom of the Father to love the Son and the Son to love the Father and the Spirit to actively participate in this mutual love as the principle of its abundant and excessive freedom. Consequently, Barth notes that God is by nature abundantly and graciously self-imparting. The love shared in the freedom of the Spirit between the Son and the Father "overflows" so as to create union with human flesh in Christ, opening fellowship with the creature.[15] Barth thus calls the incarnation of the Word in the light of this material pneumatological cause "a divine new beginning" in which God *in the freedom of the divine Spirit* unites with sinful flesh.[16] Barth attributes great importance to the Spirit of divine love in understanding the divine turn to sinful flesh in the incarnation. He says in no uncertain terms of the Holy Spirit, "he and he alone makes the unity of God and man necessary and possible."[17]

Barth explains this fascinating remark by positing an analogy between the eternal communion in the Spirit of love between the Father and the Son and the divine freedom to extend this communion of love to creation in the incarnation of the Word made flesh. In his *Dogmatics in Outline*, Barth elaborates on this analogy. He says of Jesus' human conception by the Spirit, "this human existence starts in the freedom of God Himself, in the freedom in which the Father and Son are one in the bond of love, in the Holy Spirit."[18] Barth thus views the incarnation, God's binding himself to flesh in Jesus of Nazareth, as the lens through which to penetrate the depths of God's inner freedom to love and to commune internally as the triune God: "So when we look at the beginning of the existence of Jesus, we are meant to be looking into this ultimate depth of the Godhead, in which the Father and the Son are one. This is the freedom of the inner life of God, and in this freedom the existence of this man begins in AD 1."[19] There is for Barth an *analogia caritatis* (analogy of love) between the eternal unity of love forged in the freedom of the Spirit between the Father and the Son *and* the free hypostatic union of God and flesh in time brought about through Jesus' conception by the Spirit in the Virgin's womb. The Word at the point of incarnation is thus not without the Spirit, just like the Word was never without the Spirit in communion with the Father from all of eternity.[20]

---

15. Barth, *Church Dogmatics*, Vol. II, Pt. 2, *The Doctrine of God*, ed. G. W. Bromiley et al. (Edinburgh: T&T Clark, 1957), 121.
16. Barth, *Credo*, 70.
17. Ibid.
18. Karl Barth, *Dogmatics in Outline* (London: SCM Press, 1955), 99.
19. Ibid.
20. Barth, *Church Dogmatics*, Vol. I, Pt. 2, *The Doctrine of the Word of God*, ed. G. W. Bromiley and T. F. Torrance (Edinburgh: T&T Clark, 1956), 199.

Barth also looks at Jesus' conception by the Spirit as the principle of Jesus' human freedom for, and faithfulness to, God the Father. The Holy Spirit is not only the principle of divine freedom, exercised by the divine Son in assuming sinful flesh unto himself, the Spirit is also the freedom of the flesh to be assumed: "Through the Spirit, it becomes really possible for the creature, to be there and to be free for God. Through the Spirit flesh, human nature, is assumed into unity with the Son of God."[21] The incarnation is thus for Barth the beginning of God's freedom for communion with humanity in the Spirit of divine love *and* humanity's freedom for communion with God. The freedom of the Spirit as the freedom of divine and human love in communion explains the purpose of the incarnation for Barth and explains how and why God crosses the gulf of human opposition to reestablish the covenant and to bring humanity into the embrace of divine communion.

The Spirit as the source of the human freedom to love God means that for Barth both the humiliation of the divine Son of God to take on sinful flesh (and to journey into the dark pit of judgment as a result) *and* the consequently free exaltation of Jesus as the Son of Man in faithful communion are enabled by the Holy Spirit as the force of divine love, love exercised freely in the direction of grace and communion. Barth writes, "The Holy Spirit is God in his freedom to make His creature fit for communion with Him, capable of receiving Him, object of His revelation."[22] In Christ's case, however, flesh is not only made fit for communion so as to be the object of revelation, but also, the Spirit grants freedom for Christ to be the bearer of communion, as its very accomplishment in flesh so that we may be its recipient.[23] In Christ's case, therefore, the communion that the incarnation and exaltation by the Spirit open for him involves uniquely a hypostatic union that actually identifies *him* as this free turning of God to sinful flesh and the making of this flesh ideally "fit for communion" with God. I see here in Barth echoes of Irenaeus who stated that the Spirit rests on the Son to become accustomed to rest on the human race in him.[24] For both Irenaeus and Barth, the Spirit through the Son's atoning work makes humanity "fit for communion" so that the Spirit may be "accustomed" to rest not only on the Son but also on them too.

Barth's Spirit-Baptized Christology

Now we move from prelude to substance. The preludes discussed above provide the background for Barth's use of Spirit and fire baptism as a basic category for describing the entire redemptive history of Christ's person and work in the Holy

---

21. Ibid.
22. Barth, *CD* IV/2, 39.
23. Barth, *CD* I/2, 199.
24. Irenaeus, *Against Heresies*, 3. 17. 1., in *The Apostolic Fathers: Justin Martyr and Irenaeus*, rev. ed. A. Cleveland Cox, *Ante Nicene Fathers*, vol. 1, ed. Alexander Roberts and James Donaldson (Peabody: Hendrickson, 1994).

Spirit. Barth applies this pneumatological metaphor of Spirit baptism to his Christology most elaborately in the closing Fragment of his *Church Dogmatics*, but one can find hints of it earlier in volume four and even as early as volume one (part 2).

In the closing fragment of the *Church Dogmatics*, Barth explicitly identifies Jesus as the Spirit baptizer who was baptized in fire (the baptism of his death; the suffering of the Son of God) so that others may escape this and be baptized in the Spirit instead (the exaltation of the Son of Man). His concern from the start is to establish that Christ's history as the man of the Spirit is the foundation of our life in the Spirit: "Thus Jesus Christ, His history, became and is the foundation of Christian existence; this and this alone."[25] In making this claim, Barth is careful to avoid a Christomonism in which humanity plays no role in adding uniqueness to their experiences of the Spirit and conformity to Christ, so that "all anthropology and soteriology are thus swallowed up in Christology."[26] He also wishes, however, to avoid its opposite, namely, Christ as a mere cipher of a well-honed version of religious humanity: "Christology is now swallowed up by a self-sufficient anthropology and soteriology."[27] To avoid both extremes, Barth notes that Christ's crucifixion climaxes Christ's history as both Spirit and fire baptized. The victory of this climax is revealed in his resurrection. For Barth, the full revelation of Christ's history or sojourn in the Spirit that climaxes at the cross and is revealed at the resurrection is imparted to all in Spirit baptism, determining our own sojourn in the Spirit. But this victorious life is still uniquely present to all depending on their situations in life. Barth thus concludes concerning Christ's sojourn in the Spirit, "in the work of the Holy Spirit, the history manifested to all men in the resurrection of Jesus Christ is manifest and present to a specific man in his own salvation history."[28] Our Spirit baptism is the power by which we conform in our own unique paths of faith to the history of Jesus Christ that climaxes in the cross and is revealed in his resurrection: "We thus maintain that the power of the divine change in which the event of the foundation of the Christian life of specific men takes place is the power of the baptism in the Holy Spirit."[29]

Barth's focus on Jesus' baptism in the Spirit and fire helps to fill out and qualify pneumatologically the incarnation–atonement connection for understanding Christ's redemptive work that dominated classical Christology and Barth's Christology as its definitive triumph. As Barth notes of the history of Christ's redemptive journey, "Already in the account of the baptism of Jesus this history was connected with His quality as the original Bearer of the Holy Spirit. Later (Lk. 12:50; Mk 3:35-40) it was called His own baptism of death."[30] This pneumatological

---

25. Barth, *CD* IV/4 (Fragment), 14.
26. Ibid., 19.
27. Ibid., 20.
28. Ibid., 27.
29. Ibid., 30.
30. Ibid., 31.

qualification influences how Barth conceives of the atonement. *For Barth, Jesus' baptism in the Spirit involves his baptism in fire*, the baptism of his death, "which fulfills the judgment of God and establishes His righteousness."[31] Barth sees the cross as Jesus' descent into the judgmental fire as the humiliated Son of God so that in this same Spirit he can be accepted of the Father in the bond of communion, paradoxically right there at the cross, at the place of his ultimate despair. The cross for Barth "is the act of the humiliation of the Son of God as such which is the exaltation of the Son of Man and in him of human essence."[32]

Barth locates the set up for this climax of Jesus' baptism in the Spirit and fire on the cross at Christ's baptism under John. At the Jordan, Christ counts himself already among the sinners when he is baptized by John. Barth states eloquently,

> No one who came to the Jordan was as laden and afflicted as He. No one was as needy. No one was so utterly human, because so wholly fellow human. . . . He stands alone in this. He who was elected and ordained from all eternity to partake of the sin of all in His own person, to bear its shame and curse in the place of all, to be the man responsible for all, and, as such, wholly theirs, to live and act and suffer. This is what Jesus began to do when He had Himself baptized by John with all others.[33]

When endowed by the Spirit, the Son of God starts his journey to the cross where his baptism in the Spirit will cause him to accept the fire of judgment for all. The cross for Barth is the place where the Son of God who goes into the far country to save us also returns to the household of the Father exalted to communion.

To justify viewing the cross as Christ's baptism in fire, Barth appropriately points to Luke 12:49-50. This text reads, "I have come to bring fire on the earth, and how I wish it were already kindled! But I have a baptism to undergo, and what constraint I am under until it is completed!" As Barth notes, little did John know when he announced the Messiah's fire baptism of the unrepentant that Christ would first bear this fire himself on their behalf. Barth writes, "The divine judgment which John expected did not tarry. It came in the person of Him who according to John was to baptize with the Spirit, of Him who came to kindle a fire upon the earth (Lk. 12:49)."[34] Christ's bearing the judgment for sin on the cross for all of humanity that was signaled by his baptism under John characterizes Christ's entire sojourn to the cross. Indeed, his bearing this baptism in fire, the baptism of his death, did not preclude his eschatological role as the bearer of judgment to those who reject grace. Yet, for Barth, "there can be no Pentecost, no baptism with the Holy Ghost, unless one receives Him ὡσεὶ πυρός (Acts 2:3)" or "as with fire." Receiving Christ "as with fire" for Barth means that Christ provides passage for us

---

31. Ibid.
32. Barth, *CD* 4/2, 100.
33. Barth, *CD* 4/4, 59.
34. Ibid., 80.

through the fire to the promised life of the Spirit. As the Judge is judged for us at the cross, "His wrath could no longer be regarded as the limitation but only as the unavoidable way, the consuming fire of His love."[35] Passing through the fire with Christ to the fullness of life in the Spirit is for Barth the quintessential fulfillment of the messianic bearing of the baptism in the Spirit and fire.

As noted earlier, according to Barth, Jesus' conception by the Spirit in Mary's womb reveals that the Spirit is of material significance to Jesus' person and work. Under the rubric of Spirit baptism, Barth now adds that the Spirit descended upon Jesus at his baptism in order to anoint him as the Son of God, showing us yet again that "the Holy Spirit is the mystery of this being" the very mystery of the divine freedom to love all the way to a cross. This is the history that visibly reveals Christ's person as the very event of reconciliation between God and humanity.[36] Interestingly, Barth sees a connection between the sign under which Jesus was conceived by the Spirit, the virginal conception, and the sign connected to his baptism in the Spirit at the Jordan, John's baptism in water. Jesus' baptism in water was the outward sign that Jesus is the Son of God under the anointing of the Spirit, just as the virginal conception was the outward sign of Jesus' conception by the Spirit as the Son of God in Mary's womb.[37] As Jesus steps into sinful flesh by the Spirit under the sign of the virginal conception, so Jesus also steps into visible identification with sinners by the Spirit under the sign of John's baptism of repentance. The one who will baptize others in the Spirit must first endure this baptism himself, not only in the Spirit but also in that very fire of divine judgment experienced as well. Jesus bears this fire preliminarily at the wilderness and in the Garden, and then decisively at the cross.[38] The cross reveals the place where the baptism in fire and the Spirit are one, precisely at the place where the Son triumphs. *This is Barth's pneumatological explanation for how the humiliation of the Son of God is linked to the exaltation of the Son of Man at the cross.*

Connected to the baptism in Spirit and fire, the humiliation of the Son of God and the exaltation of the Son of Man are not two stages in the journey but rather two sides of one movement, the two aspects occurring simultaneously and defining each other. Barth notes that humiliation and exaltation, the baptism in fire and Spirit, seem in opposition but they are not. They both define each other in the victory of divine love over wrath in God's turning with mercy to the sinners at the cross. These two (humiliation and exaltation) are thus "not two different and successive states" but rather "two opposed but strictly related moments in that history which operate together and mutually interpret one another."[39] Christ is elect in the freedom of the Spirit, the freedom of divine love and grace, to be the faithful Son of the Father precisely as the one who humiliates himself so as

---

35. Ibid.
36. Barth, *CD* 1/2, 199.
37. Ibid.
38. Barth, *CD* 4/4, 80.
39. Barth, *CD* 4/2, 106.

to stand in the place of the unfaithful *and* as the one who simultaneously fulfills righteousness in order to unite humanity with God in communion.

Christ rises through the fire for Barth to be the Spirit baptizer, the one who opens up the victory of his atonement revealed in his resurrection to humanity. As the self-impartation of Jesus Christ in his unique history to humanity, the baptism in the Holy Spirit is wide ranging in meaning for Barth. Not only does it cleanse from sin, it also makes us "free, able, willing, and ready" to minister in our overall witness to the crucified Christ.[40] Spirit baptism is the new beginning for the Christian, though one that is imperfect. "It is not self-sufficient, definitive, or complete. It is a commencement which points forward to the future."[41] Baptism in the Spirit has an eschatological reach for Barth; we chase after that perfection that will come to us in the Spirit with the full coming of Jesus Christ.[42] Spirit baptism is thus the "divine preparation of man for the Christian life in its totality."[43] It involves the "totality of salvation, the full justification, sanctification and vocation of man brought about in Jesus Christ."[44]

Water baptism for Barth cannot be identified in any way with Spirit baptism. Water baptism is the outward obedient response of obedient faith. "At issue is the baptism with water which responds to baptism with the Holy Spirit and which cries out for this."[45] Baptism is not the sacrament that mediates Spirit baptism; the history of Jesus Christ does that. Rather, Barth writes that "baptism responds to a mystery, the sacrament of the history of Jesus Christ, of his resurrection, of the outpouring of the Spirit."[46] It is the crucified and risen Christ of Pentecost who pours forth the Spirit that fills the believer's life with grace. Baptism for Barth responds to this outpouring and cries out for it. It is based on it and anticipates its fulfillment. Baptism is therefore the acceptance of a divine promise and pledge by faith, a promise only fulfilled in the baptism in the Spirit.[47] Through grace, faith expressed in the one-time act of baptism is strengthened, assured, nourished, and confirmed.[48] Baptism saves only as the expression of faith, which rests in the hope that is found in Christ given to us in Spirit baptism.[49] Baptism thus participates in the crucified Christ who passed through death into life. As an act of faith, baptism allows us to pass through death into life as well. Indeed, "it is the saving, protecting and keeping act of faith and obedience, which carries them through the surging element of chaos and above the abyss of perdition to the goal of their ministry

---

40. Barth, *CD* 4/4, 30–2.
41. Ibid., 38.
42. Ibid., 40.
43. Ibid., 31.
44. Ibid., 34.
45. Ibid., 101.
46. Ibid., 102.
47. Ibid., 191.
48. Ibid., 105.
49. Ibid., 207, 212.

of witness in life and suffering."⁵⁰ It takes them to the promised land of life and witness in the Spirit, all the way to the fullness that Christ will bring at his return.

A Pentecostal Evaluation

There is much I can say in response to Barth's provocative "Pentecostal" Christology. By connecting the exaltation of the Son of Man and the humiliation of the Son of God with Jesus' baptism in the Spirit and fire, Barth provides us with a Spirit Christology that grants the Jordan–Pentecost connection an important role to play in Christ's messianic mission. The incarnation–atonement connection forged by classical Christology and fulfilled in Barth is implicitly qualified to grant Jesus' reception and impartation of the Spirit a vital role to play in the narrative of Christ's messianic mission. It is my contention, however, that Barth does not make adequate adjustments to his devotion to classical Christology in order to take full advantage of his developing Spirit Christology, his accent on Jesus as the Spirit baptizer.

Barth ends up falling short of saying with Dunn unequivocally that Pentecost culminates the messianic mission. Barth was fearful of blurring the line between the objective revelation of Christ in history and the experiential realization of this revelation in the church. He believed he had Catholics to contend with, on the one hand, who in his view viewed the church as the *Christus prolongatus* (prolonged Christ) in which Christology is fundamentally determined by ecclesiology.⁵¹ And he wished also to contend with Schleiermacher, on the other hand, who in Barth's view made the fundamental question of Christology what Christ has to *be* in order to be who he is *for us* in the church. By drawing Christ's significance from what he is to the church's shared life, Schleiermacher in Barth's estimation implied that the objective revelation of the Word in Christ is dissolved into our subjective experience of the Spirit in the church.⁵² Both ways of connecting Christ to the Spirit were problematic for Barth, causing him to avoid a Christology that culminates at Pentecost.

To preserve the objectivity of Christ's self-revelation, Barth favors culminating the christological mission at the cross; it is then manifested in the resurrection and Pentecost. Our experience of Christ by faith is dependent on the history of Christ's sojourn to the cross. Barth even went so far as to speak of the cross as the place where both the Son of God's journey into suffering and the Son of Man's exaltation as a consequence occur. The cross "is the act of the humiliation of the Son of God as such which is the exaltation of the Son of Man and in him

---

50. Ibid., 213.
51. See, for example, Barth, *CD*, Vol. IV, Pt. 3 (Second Half), *The Doctrine of Reconciliation*, ed. G. W. Bromiley (Edinburgh: T&T Clark, 1962), 729.
52. See, for example, Karl Barth, *Protestant Theology in the Nineteenth Century* (Valley Forge: Judson Press, 1973), 471.

of human essence."⁵³ This exaltation is "accomplished in his death and revealed in his resurrection."⁵⁴ The resurrection is the revelation or manifestation of Christ's exaltation accomplished at the cross. The resurrection and ascension of Christ function merely as "the event of His Self-declaration" as the Christ exalted at the cross. The resurrection simply represents a "lifting of the veil," the "communication and proclamation of the perfect act of redemption once and for all accomplished in his previous existence and history."⁵⁵ It is then at Pentecost that the risen Christ in his self-revelation as risen is given to all flesh and is received by faith.⁵⁶ Barth even connects Easter to Pentecost as jointly the "manifestation" of the victory of the cross: "He is the history completed in His death, in which all righteousness was fulfilled by Him; He is the manifestation of this history in His resurrection and in the outpouring and imparting of His Holy Spirit."⁵⁷ Notice how Christ *is* this history in his person as the God-Man for Barth. As the God-Man Christ takes on this history of reconciliation between the gracious God and faithful humanity, a history that manifests who he is as the God-Man and is constitutive of his very being. Barth thus fulfills the project of classical Christology, namely, to adequately connect the incarnation and the atonement as adequate to deal with what may be said ontologically about Christ. In doing so, he tends to reduce the resurrection and Pentecost to a revelatory status.

Less than clear in Barth's "incarnation to atonement" Christology is the fact that the resurrection as Christ's rising in the fullness of the Spirit is a redemptive event in its own right, needed to fulfill the cross. After all, Paul wrote that without the resurrection we are still in our sin (1 Cor. 15:17). Not granting the resurrection proper weight as the culmination of Christ's redemptive victory tends to shortchange the role of the Spirit in that victory. The resurrection tends to be reduced to a juridical act of verification or declaration of something already fully accomplished rather than the establishment of Christ as victor "according to the Spirit of holiness" (Rom. 1:4). The narrative arc of Christ's messianic mission as a victory in the Spirit is disrupted. That Christ rises as the "life-giving Spirit" isn't granted due weight (1 Cor. 15:45). Christ's victory in the fullness of the Spirit at resurrection is indeed meant to overflow onto others. In short, Jesus' role as Spirit baptizer is eclipsed somewhat by the weight that Barth grants to the cross, thus leaving unfulfilled the moves that he makes elsewhere in support of Christ as the Spirit baptizer who passes through his baptism in fire so as to baptize us in the Spirit.

---

53. Barth, *Church Dogmatics*, Vol. IV, Pt. 2, *The Doctrine of Reconciliation*, ed. G. W. Bromiley (Edinburgh: T&T Clark, 1978), 100.

54. Ibid., 112.

55. Ibid., 133.

56. Ibid., 129.

57. Barth, *CD*, Vol. IV, Pt. 4 (Fragment), *Baptism as the Foundation of the Christian Life*, ed. G. W. Bromiley (Edinburgh: T&T Clark, 1969), 90.

To Barth's credit, he does conceive of the connection between the incarnation and the cross pneumatologically. This statement from Barth sums things up in terms of his major approach to Spirit Christology:

> It is not for nothing that . . . the New Testament calls this history (the story of the miraculous birth of Jesus, His baptism, His death according to Heb. 9:14), and its manifestation in His resurrection (Rom. 1:4; 1 Peter 3:18), the work of the Holy Spirit. It is now provisionally completed as such in the fact that the history of Jesus Christ which took place *illic et tunc* does not remain external to a man living *hic et nunc*.[58]

But, again, Barth's notion that the cross is the fulfillment of both the going out of the Son of God into the far country of human alienation *and* the return of the exalted Son of Man from the far country to the Father's household (communion with the Father) leaves little else for the resurrection and Pentecost to do than declare it. I do concede that the cross is a paradoxical event in which the Son stands with the condemned but in doing so fulfills righteousness for them. But Barth goes too far in saying the cross is the exaltation of the Son of Man or his return to the household of the Father. Even relying as Barth does on the Johannine notion that the Son's glorification begins already at the cross is not enough in my view to regard the cross as the Son of Man's exaltation to communion. One cannot load that kind of theological freight onto the cross as a redemptive event.

This is not to say that there is no value in saying that the resurrection reveals the hidden victory of the cross. The resurrection is the divine verdict concerning the cross proclaimed to us, as Barth suggests.[59] The resurrection vindicates the path to the cross as the one that fulfills righteousness. That thought deserves a great deal of attention in a Pentecostal Christology so as to avoid a pneumatological triumphalism. But the resurrection does *more* than reveal and vindicate the cross. *It fulfills it as the triumph of the Spirit in flesh.* If Jesus' entire sojourn to the cross is made in the freedom and power of the Spirit as Barth maintains, the resurrection as occurring "according to the Spirit of holiness" would also be the place where the cross attains its decisive victory as the triumph of immortal life over death. Viewing the cross as the exaltation of the Son of Man pushes Barth toward an overly juridical view of the return of the Son of Man from the far country. Clark Pinnock appropriately warns against construing the cross in exclusively juridical terms, with the result that the resurrection is reduced to a mere attestation or manifestation of a victory already completed without it. The resurrection is thereby stripped of its full significance as a salvific event.[60]

---

58. Barth, *CD* IV/4, 29.

59. Barth, *CD* IV/1, 309; Marcus Barth, *Acquittal by Resurrection* (New York: Holt, Reinhart, and Winston, 1964), 67–84.

60. Clark Pinnock, *Flame of Love: A Theology of the Holy Spirit* (Downers Grove: Intervarsity Press, 1996), 99.

Spirit Christology grants us a richer link between crucifixion and resurrection, which then helps us to grasp the full significance of Pentecost as the sharing of Christ's victory in the Spirit with us. The narrative arc of the divine Son's victory in flesh is then understood as a pneumatological victory as well. If at the cross Christ gives himself to us in the freedom and power of the Spirit, not only would the triumph of this self-giving lead to the resurrection, it would arguably lead also to Pentecost. Any victory in the fullness of the Spirit's freedom and power overflows onto others. Jesus' baptism in fire and Spirit that culminates at the resurrection overflows at Pentecost where the Son imparts himself not only for us but also to us. This overflowing is the integral link between Jesus' role as Spirit baptized and his role as Spirit baptizer. The former is distinct from the latter, but they are also inseparable and substantively one. *The cross is not only a passage to life for Christ but also to Christ's life given to us.* The Christ who rises for Paul in his "Spirit body" is thus the life-giving Spirit. So united is Christ's self-giving with the Spirit's!

> [Christ's body] is sown a natural body, it is raised a Spirit body. If there is a natural body, there is also a Spirit body. So it is written: "The first man Adam became a living being"; the last Adam, a life-giving spirit. (1 Cor. 15:44-45)

I have translated "spiritual body" in the above text as "Spirit body" in order to avoid the idea that Christ's risen body was intangible or "ghostly" and to capture the idea that the resurrection involves a body that lives from the full freedom and power of the Spirit.[61] The resurrection in the fullness of the Spirit implies the passage to the christological self-giving of Pentecost.

The cross is indeed a victory in its own right. Christ there overcomes wrath and decisively fulfills righteousness, fulfilling our debt of glory by offering up his faithful life for us out of unconditional love. In doing so, Christ breaks through the barriers of sin and alienation so as to open a path to the Spirit for humanity. Note Paul's redemptive logic: "Christ redeemed us from the curse of the law by becoming a curse for us, for it is written: 'Cursed is everyone who is hung on a pole.' He redeemed us . . . so that by faith we might receive the promise of the Spirit" (Gal. 3:13-14). Within this narrative arc of Jesus as the Spirit baptizer, the victory of the cross requires the more expansive narrative of the resurrection and Pentecost for its penultimate *telos*. Christ rises from death in the fullness of the Spirit. The resurrection is thus uncontainable and unrestrainable. It overflows at Pentecost onto all flesh. The victory of the cross fulfilled in the resurrection is thus the link to Pentecost. The risen life of Christ is unthinkable without this overflowing, or to put it more christologically, without this abundant self-impartation in the freedom and power of the Spirit. Jesus is the Spirit baptizer. Merely saying that the

---

61. I refer here to σῶμα πνευματικόν, which is typically translated as "spiritual body." The term "spiritual" has connotations today of being immaterial, ghostly, intangible, which the risen body of Christ was not. The resurrection for Paul is "according to the Spirit of holiness" (Rom. 1:4) or expressive of the full freedom and power of the Spirit.

resurrection and Pentecost manifest or declare the exaltation of the Son of Man is not adequate in my judgment to grant the resurrection and Pentecost their due in fulfilling the messianic mission, as Barth himself implies in places of his *Church Dogmatics*. I am taking a fundamentally Barthian principle and applying it in a way that might have made the grand old man from Basel frown, but maybe smile, for it would have helped him to fulfill Schleiermacher's intention without blurring the line between Christ's history and ours. *Pentecost belongs to Christ before it belongs to us.* His sojourn to the cross and the resurrection defines ours too, though we participate with all of our God-given uniqueness and diversity. The many tongues of Pentecost show that Christ gives himself in the Spirit in a way that opens his life to a global and eschatological fulfillment.[62]

---

62. I develop this chapter in my Macchia, *Jesus the Spirit Baptizer*.

Chapter 9

GIVING THE DEVIL (NO MORE THAN) HIS DUE

KARL BARTH, PENTECOSTALISM, AND THE DEMONIC

Michael J. McClymond

Whoever fights with monsters should see to it that he does not become one himself. And when you stare for a long time into an abyss, the abyss stares back into you.[1]

—Friedrich Nietzsche

Fools rush in where angels fear to tread—or where demons haunt. To discuss demons is difficult enough, yet this chapter will explore how demon-acknowledging Pentecostals might engage the learned, copious, but demon-averse theologian, Karl Barth. One of the few authors explicitly to have pondered this question is John Flett, who commented that "between Barth and . . . Pentecostalism there are areas of contest," but also "sufficient points of agreement exist to encourage a fruitful dialogue." He adds that "the two discourses agree on the most foundational point: the primacy of Jesus Christ in the New Testament depiction of the demonic."[2] As we will see in what follows, there are currents of contemporary Pentecostal–charismatic Christianity in which Christ's primacy may be implicitly compromised, though not explicitly repudiated, and in such contexts Barth's distinctive and somewhat idiosyncratic approach to Satan and the demons may function as a helpful corrective. Yet before plunging into this topic, it may be helpful to note some of the difficulties involved in discussing Barth's pertinence to Pentecostal theology.

First, there is Barth's puzzling asymmetry in approaching the spirit world, since he admits angelic agency but is reticent to speak similarly of demonic agency. Barth differs from Rudolf Bultmann, whose "demythologization" program claimed that "it is impossible to use electrical light and the wireless and to avail ourselves of modern medical and surgical discoveries, and at the same time to

---

1. Friedrich Nietzsche, *Beyond Good and Evil*, trans. Judith Norman (Cambridge: Cambridge University Press, 2002), 69 [#146].

2. John G. Flett, "Evil, Demons, and Exorcism," Unpublished Lecture, Karl Barth Conference, Princeton Theological Seminary, June 2016, 17, 20.

believe in the New Testament world of spirits and miracles."[3] Bultmann spoke simply of a "world of spirits," while Barth in his *Church Dogmatics* divided his approach to "angels" from that of "demons."[4] One must try to understand why Barth developed this twofold interpretation. *Second*, to grasp Barth on demons one must also ponder *das Nichtige* ("nothingness" or "the Nihil"), expounded over some eighty pages in *Church Dogmatics* III/3, and which was fundamental to Barth's account of evil, Satan, and the demons.[5] This hermeneutically daunting section of the *Church Dogmatics* is one area where few contemporary Christian theologians have followed Barth's lead and embraced his teaching. *Third*, Barth's account of the demonic raises paradoxes regarding belief and unbelief, since Barth states that we must admit the reality of demons yet not "believe" in them. As Wyatt Houtz comments in interpreting Barth, "believing in demons makes us demonic," and so "we do not . . . deny their existence," but concerning them "we must resolutely disbelieve."[6] *Fourth*, Barth writes in divergent ways of the demons in *Church Dogmatics*. While he is generally self-consistent, the denial in *Church Dogmatics* III/3 that demons have personal agency sits uneasily alongside passages in *Church Dogmatics* IV/1 and IV/2 where Barth's exposition of Jesus' works of exorcism might suggest the opposite view.[7]

To frame the underlying issue in Barth, we might begin with a well-known quotation from C. S. Lewis: "There are two equal and opposite errors into which our race can fall about the devil. One is to disbelieve in their existence. The other is to believe, and to feel an excessive and unhealthy interest in them. They themselves are equally pleased by both errors and hail a materialist or a magician with the

---

3. Rudolf Bultmann et al., *Kerygma and Myth: A Theological Debate* (New York: Harper and Row, 1961 [1953]), 5.

4. Barth, *CD* III/3, 369–531, covers angels and demons, yet the section on demons includes only the last dozen pages (519–31). Outside of the *Church Dogmatics*, important references to Satan and the demons are found in Barth's *Gespräche [Conversations] 1959–1962; Karl Barth Gesamtausgabe. IV. Gespräche* (Zürich: Theologischer Verlag, 1995), 108–14, 164–7; translated into English as Karl Barth, *Barth in Conversation; Volume 1, 1959–1962*, trans. Translation Fellows of the Center for Barth Studies, Princeton Theological Seminary (Louisville: Westminster John Knox, 2017), 74–7, 112–14 (cf. 179–80).

5. *CD* III/3, 289–368 contains Barth's primary discussion of "nothingness."

6. Wyatt Houtz, "Karl Barth: Believing in Demons Makes Us Demonic." https://postbarthian.com/2016/03/09/believing-in-demons-makes-you-a-little-demonic/ (accessed September 20, 2018).

7. This theme will not be further pursued in what follows, but see *CD* IV/2, 231, where Barth writes: "What we hear is that the darkness of which they [i.e., the demons] are the concretion finds itself threatened and in supreme danger, and recognizes that this is the case." The wording here implies that the demonic "concretion" is somehow conscious and so "recognizes" that it is "threatened" (cf. *CD* IV/2, 255–6).

same delight."[8] Barth himself enunciates a similar contrast in Christian approaches to the demonic:

> If we ignore demons, they deceive us by concealing their power until we are again constrained to respect and fear them as powers. If we absolutise them, respecting and fearing them as true powers, they have deceived us by concealing their character as falsehood, and it will be only a little while before we try to ignore them and are thus deceived by them again.[9]

While Lewis's statement suggests a happy medium between the two extremes, Barth's words intimate that interpreters of Satan and the demons may find themselves oscillating between the "two equal and opposite errors." Generally it would be accurate to say that Barth favored "disbelief" while Pentecostal-charismatics have inclined toward "belief." Yet, for just this reason, Pentecostals might find in Barth's "disbelief" in demons a helpful corrective against their own theological imbalances, and so learn better to give the devil his due—but not more than his due. Moreover, Barth's identification of demons with "nothingness" could help to diagnose and discern demonic activity as that which causes human beings to lose their moral and spiritual form, and to slide toward the formlessness characteristic of the demons themselves.

Pentecostal Presuppositions on the Demonic

When Bultmann launched his "demythologization" program in mid-twentieth-century Europe, he and others were convinced that "modern man" was in process of emancipating himself from belief in angels, demons, miracles, and the supernatural realm generally. In retrospect, we recognize that global culture as a whole did not trace the trajectory Bultmann had mapped out for it. Since the 1970s, Western popular culture did not undergo "demythologization" but rather a "remythologization" in the form of increased interest in angels, miracles, meditation, and paranormal phenomena. A recent cross-cultural study found that around 75 percent of the world's population accepts the reality of demons and demonic possession.[10] Researchers into Pentecostalism are well aware that an acknowledgment of the spirit world—far from being a stumbling block that keeps "modern man" from embracing the gospel message—has instead facilitated the rapid spread of Christianity in many parts of Africa, Asia, Latin America, and Oceania.

---

8. C. S. Lewis, *The Screwtape Letters* (New York: HarperCollins, 2001), ix.

9. Barth, *CD* III/3, 526–7.

10. John Dominic Crossan, *Jesus: A Revolutionary Biography* (San Francisco: HarperCollins, 1994), 85.

John Flett comments that "while [exorcism] may be distant from our own experience, something exotic and perhaps even frightful, exorcism is one of the key missionary activities found in world Christianity today." "As a practice of world Christianity," he adds, "it is common, immediate to human experience, and speaks to the power of God present in a world of uncertainty, fracture, and suffering."[11] J. Kwabena Asamoah-Gyadu states that Pentecostalism "evokes powerful responses in Africa because it affirms the 'enchanted' worldview of indigenous peoples by taking these views seriously, and presenting an interventionist theology through which the fears and insecurities of African Christians are dealt with."[12] More bluntly still, Elizabeth Amoah and Mercy Amba Oduyoye state that "the devil is a reality in Africa; witches actually operate to release life-denying forces. . . . Evil is real, and evil is embodied in persons as well as unleashed on people by spiritual forces."[13] Traditional cultures in all global regions attribute misfortune to demonic agency—illnesses, famine, family conflicts, economic hardships, harmful accidents, and temptations to sin. By interpreting the "local spirits and gods" as "Christian demons," writes Flett, Pentecostal believers "break from traditional religion though exorcism, spiritual warfare against witchcraft, and liberation from generational curses, all the while remaining in clear continuity with the basic [traditional] cosmology."[14]

Amos Yong summarizes the core assumptions in Pentecostal demonologies: "The devil and his demons are understood as personal, spiritual and malevolent beings who are responsible for the human experience of temptation, suffering and evil." This means that "humans can interact with demons even while demonic activity can influence affairs in the material world." Yet Pentecostals are fully convinced that "the life, death and resurrection of Jesus Christ has triumphed over the devil and his demons," and that "redemption has been accomplished." Thus, "this overcoming of the suffering and evil wrought by the devil and demons can be experienced in part now in anticipation of the eschatological once-for-all triumph. . . . The devil and his demons can and should be resisted and rebuked in the name of Jesus and they will have to flee." Finally, "Christians have been given divinely appointed weapons—especially a suit of spiritual armour along with the power of fasting and prayer and the sword of the Word of God—which are more

---

11. Flett, "Evil, Demons, and Exorcism," 1.

12. J. Kwabena Asamoah-Gyadu, "Mission to 'Set the Captives Free': Healing, Deliverance, and Generational Curses in Ghanaian Pentecostalism," *International Review of Mission* 93 (2009): 389–406, citing 392; cited in Flett, "Evil, Demons, and Exorcism," 11.

13. Elizabeth Amoah and Mercy Amba Oduyoye, "The Christ for African Women," in *With Passion and Compassion: Third World Women Doing Theology*, ed. Virginia Fabella and Mercy Amba Oduyoye (Maryknoll: Orbis Books, 1988), 38. Cited in Flett, "Evil, Demons, and Exorcism," 12.

14. Flett, "Evil, Demons, and Exorcism," 13.

than adequate for the task of standing against and exorcising their enemy."[15] Yong adds: "Pentecostals the world over have two interrelated strategies in dealing with [the] demonic: exorcism and spiritual warfare. Both can be and are usually applied together either at the individual or the corporate level." Generally, the concept of "spiritual warfare" applies at the corporate or social level, while "exorcism" (also called "deliverance") pertains to the individual. "Central to practice of both spiritual warfare and exorcism," writes Yong, "is the power encounter." Thus, "the power of the Holy Spirit is understood to oppose, destroy, and put to flight the powers of darkness."[16]

In what follows, we will see that this sort of "power encounter" does not occur in Barth's theology, in large part because Barth does not view creaturely agency against God as having ultimate significance or as being finally capable of negating God's purposes. Barth's writings contain statements to the effect that creaturely agents cannot oppose God, such as the following:

> We deceive ourselves if we think that we should take sin, death, and the devil seriously in the sense of ascribing to them a divine or semi-divine potentiality or the role of a real antagonist to the living God. It is when we see them as powers which are in their own peculiar way subordinate and subject to the will of God that we really take them seriously.[17]

During the 1970s and 1980s, a new literature on Satan and the demonic began to appear, much of it authored by Pentecostal or charismatic Christians, and partially in response to an upsurge of interest in and involvement with witchcraft and the occult. Since the 1990s, independent charismatics or neo-Pentecostals around the world have led in the rise of so-called strategic-level spiritual warfare. C. Peter Wagner taught that demons could dominate not only individuals but whole communities. "Warfare prayer" could break satanic "strongholds" and facilitate evangelism.[18] Such

---

15. Amos Yong, "The Demonic in Pentecostal/Charismatic Christianity and in the Religious Consciousness of Asia," in *Asian and Pentecostal: The Charismatic Face of Christianity in Asia*, ed. Allan Anderson and Edmond Tang (Oxford: Regnum Books/Baguio City, Philippines: APTS Press, 2005), 96.

16. Ibid., 100.

17. Barth, *CD* II/1, 563.

18. See C. Peter Wagner, *Warfare Prayer: How to Seek God's Power and Protection in the Battle to Build His Kingdom* (Ventura: Regal Books, 1992), Wagner, ed., *Engaging the Enemy: How to Fight and Defeat Territorial Spirits* (Ventura: Regal Books, 1991), Wagner, "Territorial Spirits," in *Supernatural Forces in Spiritual Warfare*, ed. C. Peter Wagner (Shippensburg: Destiny Image Publishers, 2012), and Wagner, *Confronting the Queen of Heaven* (n.p.: Wagner Publications, 2001). For multicultural perspectives on this theme, see Erwin Van der Meer, "Strategic Level Spiritual Warfare Theology of C. Peter Wagner and Its Implications for Christian Mission in Malawi" (ThD diss., University of South Africa, 2008); Erwin Van der Meer, "Strategic Level Spiritual Warfare and Mission in Africa,"

teachings fit well in an African context, where exorcism or deliverance ministry is often understood to be a part of conversion.[19] One step in the process was "spiritual mapping"—that is, locating the sites of false religion, violence, broken covenants, and so on, that may have given demons a "legal right" to infest a given territory. Another step was "identificational repentance," whereby believers verbally confess sins committed by other people, asking for God's forgiveness for them as well as for themselves.[20] White Christians in the United States, for example, might confess the sins of earlier, slaveholding whites that continue to poison race relations. Some of the more radical neo-Pentecostals have sought by means of prayerful, prophetic discernment to identify the hidden names of "territorial spirits" who governed particular geographical regions, on the theory that an accurate naming of these evil powers would enable believers more effectively to gain power over them and to oppose them in prayer.[21] On encountering the Gadarene demoniac, Jesus had pointedly asked the spirit(s)—"what is your name?" (Mk 5:9). In this case, it would seem that there must have been some reason for Jesus' request to know the name of the spirit(s). Critics of this practice of naming-and-binding have held that it promotes an unwholesome preoccupation with details of the demonic world that should not be a focus of attention for Christians.[22] A later section of this chapter will return to consider this question further.

Barth on Satan and the Demons

Before turning to Barth's account of demons in the *Church Dogmatics*, it may be helpful first to review his comments in interviews from 1959 to 1962.[23] An

---

Evangelical Review of Mission 34 (2010): 155–66; J. Kwabena Asamoah-Gyadu, "Pulling Down Strongholds: Evangelism, Principalities and Powers and the African Pentecostal Imagination," *International Review of Mission* 96 (2007): 306–17; and Samuel Hio-Kee Ooi, "A Study of Strategic-Level Spiritual Warfare from a Chinese Perspective," *Asian Journal of Pentecostal Studies* 9 (2006): 143–61.

19. Allan Anderson, "Exorcism and Conversion to African Pentecostalism," *Exchange* 35 (2006): 116–33.

20. Pentecostals cite Nehemiah and Daniel as biblical exemplars of this practice of "identificational repentance," since these leaders confessed before God not only their personal transgressions but also the sins of their forbears (Neh. 1:4-11; Dan. 9:4-19).

21. In the Book of Daniel, one finds brief but tantalizing references to "the prince of Persia" and "the prince of Greece" (Dan. 10:20; cf. Dan. 10:13), which in context are evidently demonic powers, since they are opposed to the holy angels Michael and Gabriel. There is thus a slender basis in Scripture for the idea of "territorial spirits."

22. Agnieszka Tennant, "Possessed or Obsessed? Many Christians Say They are in Need of Deliverance but Some May be Giving Demons More Than Their Due," *Christianity Today*, September 3, 2001. https://www.christianitytoday.com/ct/2001/september3/1.46.html

23. An outstanding secondary work on this theme is the 2017 dissertation by Patrick Carter Edwards, "Opponents of the Kingdom of Heaven: Karl Barth and the 'Fall' of the

essay published originally in French included the following: "Mademoiselle, I once taught an entire summer course of four hours per week on angels, and I only spoke for two hours on the devil and demons."[24] Barth was thus aware of the disproportionately large attention that he gave to the angels in comparison with the demons. In another passage, Barth sharply (and rather uncharacteristically) dissented from certain biblical texts: "In 2 Peter as well as in Jude, one also finds the theory of the fall of the angels and of Lucifer, a fallen angel (2 Pet. 2:4; Jude 6). I do not believe this because it is a theory that allows demons to be understood. Evil cannot be explained."[25] Here Barth appeals to a theoretical principle—that "evil cannot be explained"—to determine his interpretation of Scripture, that is, that the "fall" of the angels in at least two biblical texts cannot be taken literally.

Barth provides a fuller account of his reasoning in a 1960 exchange:

> *Question*: We have been told that the devil plays an important part in history. I should like to ask you if you think that, our own sin and disobedience apart, there can be another power that separates us from God and that we can identify with the devil? *Barth*: I must confess that I know so little of the devil that I cannot give a definition of him. I know of the effects of his existence, but I have never met him in person as Luther did. So I find it is asking too much to give some kind of a definition. Perhaps the devil is even the being who cannot be defined because of his nature, because he is the devil. He is certainly not a creature of God. He can only be, perhaps, the reason of the unreasonableness of sin. The devil is, as I like to say, the impossible possibility that cannot be defined.[26]

Some Christian thinkers prior to Barth (and especially those influenced by Platonism and neo-Platonism) aligned Satan, the demons, and evil itself with *nonbeing* and/or *irrationality*. Yet Barth was more radical in his insistence that there is something mistaken even in speaking of the devil or in seeking to define the devil or the devil's modes of operation. One gets the impression that a certain

---

Demons" (PhD diss., Southeastern Baptist Theological Seminary, 2017). See also Vernon R. Mallow, *The Demonic: A Selected Theological Study; An Examination into the Theology of Edwin Lewis, Karl Barth, and Paul Tillich* (Lanham: University Press of America, 1983), 82–6; Sung Min Jeong, *Nothingness in the Theology of Paul Tillich and Karl Barth* (Lanham: University Press of America, 2003), 81–6; and Wolf Krötke, *Sin and Nothingness in the Theology of Karl Barth*, trans. Philip Ziegler and Christina-Maria Bammel (Princeton: Princeton Theological Seminary, 2005), 52–4. Recent Barth interpreters give short shrift to the demons, so that Barth's "quick, sharp glance" toward the devil has become a mere "eye-blink." Christopher C. Green's *Doxological Theology: Karl Barth on Divine Providence, Evil, and the Angels* (London: Bloomsbury T&T Clark, 2011), 187–209 discusses evil but neglects the demons.

24. Barth, *Barth in Conversation*, 114 (Barth, *Gespräche*, 167).
25. Ibid., 165.
26. Barth, *Barth in Conversation*, 76–7 (Barth, *Gespräche*, 113).

taint or guilt accrues to one in the very act of speaking aloud the devil's name. To tell of Satan is to deflect attention from the reality of Christ's victory, and perhaps to depart from the standpoint of faith.[27]

What Barth says in opposition to the preaching of hell, as a part of the gospel message, applies equally to preaching on the devil, as a part of the teaching on Christ's victory:

> Should teaching about hell be part of the proclamation of the gospel? No! No! No! The proclamation of the gospel means the proclamation that Christ has defeated hell, that Christ has suffered hell in our place, and that we are allowed to live with him and so to have hell behind us.[28]

Barth's *dogmatic position* on the demons is at root, a *kerygmatic decision* and also a *linguistic imperative* or self-imposed verbal rule not to spend time in speaking of the devil. For Barth, one only speaks rightly of Satan in declaring that "Jesus is victor!"

In *Church Dogmatics*, Barth states that Satan and the demons are "no mere figure of speech or poetic fancy," for "nothingness has this dynamic, that it is a kingdom on the march and engaged in invasion and assault."[29] Yet he insists that "a quick, sharp glance is not only all that is necessary but all that is legitimate in their case." This must be a "glance of aversion and not in any sense of secret respect or reverence or admiration." This means that "we cannot believe in the devil and demons as we believe in angels when we believe in God."[30] He accepts the need for a "demythologization" of the demons, "but not in the superficial sense current today, in which they are grouped with the angels . . . as the figures of a world outlook which has now been superseded."[31] Premodern theologians, Barth claims, went beyond the text of Scripture in their detailed demonologies, and this ultimately brought discredit to the whole of Christian theology in the post-Enlightenment era.[32]

Barth calls the demons "indefinable concretions of indefinable chaos."[33] He writes that "their being is neither that of God nor that of the creature . . . for they are neither the one nor the other."[34] Their nothingness emerged at the "left hand" of God or as a kind of "shadow" that accompanied God's work in creating. Barth states

---

27. Consider Barth's statement that "hell can only be where there is no faith" (Barth, *Barth in Conversation*, 76 [Barth, *Gespräche*, 111]).
28. Barth, *Barth in Conversation*, 75 (Barth, *Gespräche*, 111).
29. Barth *CD* III/3, 524.
30. Ibid., 519.
31. Ibid., 521.
32. Ibid., 522.
33. Barth *CD* IV/2, 231.
34. Barth *CD* III/3, 523.

bluntly that the devil was "never a fallen angel."[35] The nothingness of the demons is not "a being which is somewhere and somehow at repose." Their "kingdom" is "not consisting anywhere, but always on the march, always invading," for "this is all [that is] to be said of demons as of nothingness. . . . They do not stand apart. They derive from it. They themselves are all always nothingness in its dynamic."[36]

Barth's account of the demons raises an issue concerning *their relation to God's will*. One might begin by noting Barth's differing ideas regarding God's will—as *effective will*, *permissive will*, and *negating will*. Barth's idea of effective will rests on his notion of divine sovereignty: "God is the free power over and in all powers. He stands over them in freedom, and is their Lord in the strict and proper sense only if they have no other power but that which He wills to give them."[37] Barth says that "the kingdom of God is the only true kingdom," and that "God alone rules."[38] Elsewhere Barth writes: "God's will is to all circumstances a *voluntas efficax*. There is no such thing as a *voluntas Dei inefficax*. God's will . . . is not conditioned from outside itself by another. In no sense is it a powerless will, an empty wish, mere volition. On the contrary, whatever God wills also comes about."[39] Because *voluntas efficax* might imply that God directly intends or wills evil, Barth sometimes qualifies his position by distinguishing God's willing from God's permitting: "In what way is it [i.e., evil] willed? The distinction between *efficere* and *permittere* provides the answer to this question." Barth identifies *efficere* with other Latin verbs (e.g., *creare*, *causare*, *producere*).[40] Here he seems to be following a well-trod path among theologians by insisting that God's will is connected to all events, but in a "permissive" rather than "efficacious" relationship to evil occurrences.

Nonetheless, Barth writes not only of *efficere* and *permittere* but also of God's negating will or "non-willing," stating that "in God Himself there is a mighty non-willing of evil."[41] In Barth's thinking this "non-willing" is in some obscure way connected with a *causing-to-be*. He writes that "the aggression of the shadow-world of Satan . . . is negated by Him [i.e., God] and . . . exists only in virtue of this negation."[42] God's "negation" thus seems to be an "affirmation" too. Linguistically speaking, the proposition that "God wills 'x' to be" has as its negation the proposition that "it is not the case that God wills 'x' to be." Obviously there are many things that God did not will (e.g., a possible world in which pigs could fly). If this is what is meant by "non-willing," then we find ourselves in the realm of the counterfactual, but not necessarily in the realm of things that God rejects as evil.

35. Ibid., 531.
36. Ibid., 523.
37. Barth *CD* II/1, 544.
38. Barth *CD* III/3, 158.
39. Barth, *CD* II/1, 596.
40. Ibid., 594.
41. Ibid., 506.
42. Barth, *CD* II/2, 124.

It seems then that the "non-willing" to which Barth refers cannot simply denote the non-actualization of possibilities, that is, to entities that God did not actualize in creating the world.

This "non-willing" is indeed puzzling, for it does not seem to be an expression of the divine will either as *efficere* or as *permittere*. Because this "non-willing" represents God's rejection of evil, one would be hard-pressed to refer to this as a form of "permission." (When someone "rejects" something, one would not ordinarily say that one also "permits" that very same thing.) Alternatively, if God's "non-willing" evil were a form of *efficere* (or what Barth calls *voluntas efficax*), then we might wonder how evil could enjoy even a shadowy existence or quasi-reality. Wouldn't the divine "No!" toward evil mean that evil would simply cease to be? Barth's account of evil in the *Church Dogmatics* thus presents a dilemma. On the one hand, Barth denies that there can be any "real antagonist to the living God," but then in effect makes *das Nichtige* into just such an "antagonist."[43] If, as Barth claims, *das Nichtige* is not created by God, then God might have not only an "antagonist" but one that stands—in dualistic fashion—beyond the scope of God's will as Creator and Lord. And if the emergence of *das Nichtige* was necessitated when God first created the world, then wouldn't *das Nichtige* continue to be necessary forever? How could it have been entailed at creation but later overcome by Christ?

One might also ask why Barth was willing to take a mere "glance" at the demons, but a long, lingering stare at evil in the form of *das Nichtige*. If the focus on evil (rather than Christ's victory over evil) is the problem, then why would nothingness deserve *so much attention*? It seems that Barth was ready to discuss evil at length, so long as evil was conceptualized in an impersonal form. Stephen Webb judges that Barth is "surely taking nothingness too far—giving it too much explanatory power." Webb notes an irony in that "Barth identifies the fall of Satan with improper metaphysical speculation, while his own account of the nothingness of evil is one of the great speculative achievements of modern theology."[44] Patrick Edwards observes: "Barth . . . wants to acknowledge evil powers while also eliminating any fear of them. . . . Barth seeks to root the Christian's confidence in Christ's victory over the shadows rejected at creation itself."[45] With his account of *das Nichtige* Barth appears to have created his own supplementary myth or narrative to stand alongside of the biblical and traditional narrative of Christ's victory over sin, death, Satan, and hell. Christina Baxter comments that Barth is usually quite good at assembling the biblical passages relevant to a given theme, and then basing his exposition on careful exegetical analysis. Yet the lengthy discussion of *das Nichtige* cites only Genesis 1:2ff., Genesis 3:22, and Romans 11:36, and so lacks the solid,

---

43. Barth, *CD* II/1, 563.

44. Stephen H. Webb, *Dome of Eden: A New Solution to the Problem of Creation and Evolution* (Eugene: Cascade Books, 2010), 207.

45. Edwards, "Opponents," 127.

exegetical foundation that supports other arguments in the *Church Dogmatics*.[46] Joseph Mangina notes that "Barth's specific concept of the Nihil has found few followers." On *das Nichtige*, recent books generally "offer summary without . . . evaluation in favor or against Barth's views."[47] The remainder of this chapter will offer suggestions for a constructive theological appropriation of Barth's position on nothingness and the demons, and then an application of Barth's views to certain contemporary charismatic teachings on combat against Satan and demonic forces.

Tornadoes, Black Holes, and Agencies-Without-Entity

One way to engage Barth's ideas regarding demons would be in terms of *meontological categories* (i.e., ideas of nonbeing) rather than ontological categories. In everyday experience, we find that certain phenomena exist tangibly in the world but only as *agencies-without-entity*. Consider the tornado (or the hurricane), which has no stable, ongoing existence as a "thing" on the surface of the earth, but arises through a rapid circular movement in the atmosphere, causing air pressure to drop at the center of the "twister." This drop in air pressure causes the tornado's destructiveness. A tornado of maximal force (termed an "EF 5" in the "enhanced Fujita" scale) can pull "well-built, well-anchored homes off their foundations and into the air before obliterating them, flinging the wreckage for miles and sweeping the foundation clean." When a "twister" of this intensity encounters "large, multi-ton steel frame vehicles and farm equipment," the vehicles or equipment may be "mangled beyond recognition and deposited miles away or reduced entirely to unrecognizable component parts." Such tornadoes are known to have stripped asphalt from roadbeds.[48] To apply the tornado metaphor, one might say that the demons represent a spiritual "funnel cloud" that effects damage wherever it travels. This mental picture offers us a way of thinking about demons that is non-substantialist and thus near in ethos to Barth's *das Nichtige*. What causes destruction in this case is not "something" but "nothing"—the void or vacuum at the core of the phenomenon in question.

An alternative mental picture is afforded by the astronomical "black hole," which draws everything near to it into its immensely powerful gravitational field and

---

46. Christina A. Baxter, "Barth—A Truly Biblical Theologian?" *Tyndale Bulletin* 38 (1987): 4–6.

47. Edwards, "Opponents," 117, n. 31; citing Joseph L. Mangina, *Karl Barth: Theologian of Christian Witness* (Louisville: Westminster John Knox, 2004), 102.

48. Wikipedia, "Tornado Intensity." https://en.wikipedia.org/wiki/Tornado_intensity. On a personal note: I have unforgettable personal impressions on this subject, having lived through the terrible tornado of May 1975 in Omaha, Nebraska, which damaged more than four thousand buildings and caused (up to that point) the greatest property damage of any tornado in US history (about $1.7 billion, in 2015 dollars). Wikipedia, "1975 Omaha Tornado Outbreak." https://en.wikipedia.org/wiki/1975_Omaha_tornado_outbreak.

then collapses it. Any entity approaching the "event horizon" (i.e., the gravitational point-of-no-return) will undergo "spaghettification." Physical objects will be pulled into the black hole so violently that they will be drawn into spaghetti-like strings and lose all trace of their original form as they are compacted in ultradense matter.[49] Essential to this process is *a transition from form to formlessness*—a loss of distinctness and individuality. Applying this analogy to spiritual realities, we might say that the demons are a destructive emptiness that causes human beings entering their gravitational field to lose their character and personhood, to cave in on themselves, and ultimately to become subhuman.

The tornado and the black hole allow us to imagine how something that does not exist as a "thing" or an "entity" in the world can nonetheless have agency in the world. A problem, however, is that these impersonal analogies do not carry the connotation of deliberation and premeditation that appears in biblical language concerning the demons. The Pauline letters speak of Satan's "schemes" (Gk. *noemata*; 2 Cor. 2:11). Ephesians summons Christian believers to stand firm "against the schemes [*methodeias*] of the devil" (Eph. 6:11). This language of "scheming" not only suggests *agency*, but *personal agency*, and even *subtle, deceit-inducing, personal agency*, like that shown in the clever conversation of the "serpent" with Eve in the Garden of Eden (Gen. 3:1-5). Much as a wicked ruler or politician might have "schemes" for subverting the rule of law or for eliminating all opponents—without appearing to have done so—so too in the Old and New Testament the enemies of souls act shrewdly and methodically to tempt people to sin, to undermine faith, to bring division into communities, to provoke hatred and violence, and so on. The Scriptures attribute various activities to Satan and the demons, and imply that these adversaries accomplish destructive effects by intentional agency.[50]

It is difficult to see how one can do justice to the New Testament texts without some conception of *deliberate, personal agency* in connection with Satan and the demons. On the other hand, Barth's interpretation of the demons as creatures of

---

49. Stephen Hawking may have been the first to present the "spaghetti" analogy. If I fell feetfirst into a black hole, then the gravity at my feet would be stronger than at my head, so that I would be stretched vertically, and so "spaghettified." See Stephen Hawking, *A Brief History of Time* (New York: Bantam Dell Publishing Group, 1988), 256.

50. In the Bible, the activities of Satan and the demons include promoting idolatry and human sacrifice (Ps. 96:4-5; 106:36-38; cf. Lev. 17:7); deceiving the nations (Rev. 20:3); influencing human governments (Mt. 4:3); preventing acceptance of gospel truth (Lk. 8:12); blinding the minds of the unbelieving (2 Cor. 4:3-4); indoctrinating into false religion (1 Tim. 4:1-3); waging war against the saints (Eph. 6:10-18); accusing and slandering (Rev. 12:10); sowing doubt (Gen. 3:1-5). Scripture attributes certain circumstances in the church to Satan's agency: lying (Acts 5:3); sexual sin (1 Cor. 7:5); reliance on human wisdom (Mt. 16:21-23); spiritual pride (1 Tim. 3:5); discouragement (1 Pet. 5:6-10); persecution of the church (Rev. 2:10); thwarted service to God (1 Thess. 2:18); false teachers in the church (1 Cor. 11:13-15); and internal division (2 Cor. 2:10-11; Jas 3:14-16).

das Nichtige might help us better to understand the demons' destructive, tornado-like vacuum that sucks creatures into its vortex, so that they become distorted by the power of the void.

Fatal Fascination? Contemporary Charismatics on the Demonic

In her book-length analysis of charismatic Christianity in Ghana, *For Freedom or Bondage?* (2014), Esther Acolatse offers a sobering assessment. She writes that the prevalent healing practices are not based on Scripture but on "beliefs acquired from African Traditional Religions, with their strong sense of the spirit world and its pervasive influence on natural phenomena." Practitioners "interpret almost all problems from a spiritual perspective," so that "hidden psychological issues are never adequately addressed."[51] She explains further:

> Ghanaians are so paranoid of spiritual attacks that they constantly live on the lookout for such occurrences. People run from church to church, from one prayer group to another, in search of security. Unfortunately, the help they receive only perpetuates the problem, because the solution operates from the same assumption . . . that there are powerful, predatory spiritual forces . . . to be reckoned with. The interpretative [*sic*] framework for understanding spiritual phenomena itself becomes a form of bondage because it completely ignores the aspects of problems that are purely psychological or spiritual.[52]

Acolatse's observations find corroboration in Opoku Onyinah's analysis of "witchdemonology" in his book, *Pentecostal Exorcism*, and ethnographer Birgit Meyer's study, *Translating the Devil*—books that all deal with Ghanaian charismatic Christians. Likewise, Erwin Van Der Meer's writings on spiritual warfare ideas and practices in Malawi converged toward very similar conclusions to those of Acolatse, Onyinah, and Meyer. Onyinah claims that "the major flaw of 'witchdemonology' . . . patterned after Akan cosmology [i.e., traditional beliefs of the Akan people]" was that it "made it appear that people were always at the mercy of the unrestrained evil powers."[53] Van Der Meer comments that involvement by charismatic Christians in so-called strategic-level spiritual warfare is "likely to reinforce rather than diminish the prevalent witchcraft fears in the Malawian society."[54] He adds that "such a pseudo-Gospel also strengthens the traditional fear

---

51. Esther Acolatse, *For Freedom or Bondage? A Critique of African Pastoral Practices* (Grand Rapids: Eerdmans, 2014), 1.

52. Ibid., 29.

53. Opoku Onyinah, *Pentecostal Exorcism: Witchcraft and Demonology in Ghana* (Blandford Forum: Deo Publishing, 2012), 287.

54. Van Der Meer, "Strategic Level Spiritual Warfare" (2008), 1.

of supernatural evil and confirms the traditional belief that witchcraft is at the root of all suffering."[55]

The late C. Peter Wagner (1930–2016) was well known for promoting what became known as "strategic-level spiritual warfare." Essentially Wagner's theory was based on an argument from analogy. Just as Christians from ancient times exorcized demons from individual persons, so too one might presume that regions dominated by evil powers that Wagner called "territorial spirits" could be liberated from destructive social patterns and from unbelief toward Christ if such spirits could somehow be identified and then expelled or neutralized. Wagner assigned more weight to supernatural factors than to natural causes in explaining why some regions were highly responsive to the Christian message (e.g., South Korea), while other regions were strongly resistant (e.g., Japan).

Wagner's *Confronting the Queen of Heaven* (2001) suggests that the ancient Greco-Roman goddess Diana (mentioned in Acts 19) is just one manifestation of an enduring and influential spirit-being who continues to dominate modern-day Turkey and to block the spread of the Christian message there. This is also Wagner's explanation for resistance to Christian preaching in Japan, in Nepal, and in parts of India. Yet he warns that "dealing with territorial spirits is major league spiritual warfare." Wagner tells of a Presbyterian missionary in Ghana who—heedless of warnings received from local residents—ordered that a tree previously dedicated by satanic priests be chopped down. He then recounts: "On the day that the last branch of the tree was lopped off, the pastor collapsed and died."[56] This story is striking because it inverts a famous account regarding the eighth-century missionary, St. Boniface, who reportedly chopped down a massive tree dedicated to the pagan god, Thor, to show German bystanders that they had nothing to fear either from Thor or from his tree. Boniface is then said to have built a chapel on the spot from wood taken from the tree.[57] Wagner thus reinforces belief in the efficacy of witchcraft, while the story regarding Boniface manifests the opposite tendency.

In his articles and books on spiritual warfare, Wagner endorses investigation into territorial spirits and what one might call occultic research. Wagner says that Rita Cabeza has "done considerable research on the names of the highest levels of the hierarchy of satan," and has found that there are six worldwide principalities, and then subordinate to these are six spirits that are assigned to each nation, which, for Costa Rica, are "Shiebo, Quiebo, Ameneo, Mephistopheles, Nostradamus, and Azazel." For the United States the six demons are named "Ralphes, Anoritho, Manchester, Apolion, Deviltook, and one who is unnamed." To these demons are

---

55. Ibid., 258. For a comparative study of witchcraft and demonological views in Africa and Melanesia, see Rio, Knut, Michelle MacCarthy [sic], and Ruy Blanes, eds., *Pentecostalism and Witchcraft: Spiritual Warfare in Africa and Melanesia* (Cham, Switzerland: Palgrave Macmillan, 2017).

56. Wagner, "Territorial Spirits," 87.

57. Wikipedia, "Donar's Oak." https://en.wikipedia.org/wiki/Donar's_Oak.

delegated different areas of evildoing—for example, lust, fornication, and sexual seduction to Anoritho, and violence and homicide to Apolion.[58] In his summary article on "territorial spirits," Wagner forbears to say how this diabolical "research" is done, how one might assess the validity of such demonic names, or how Christians might invoke (or rather revoke) these names in prayer. The underlying idea that demons must first be named in order to be neutralized might encourage Christians to study occultic literature or to consult with occultic practitioners.[59] It is difficult to see how any of this would square with the Hebrew Bible injunction never even to take upon one's lips the names of foreign gods (Exod. 23:13; Josh. 23:7; Ps. 16:4; Hos. 2:17).

One of the deeper ironies in the charismatic literature on spiritual warfare is that the explicit message that "Jesus is victor!" may be undermined by an implicit message that "witchcraft works!" Quite often, charismatic authors assert that success, wealth, and pleasure will accrue to the practitioner of witchcraft, while untold harm may fall upon the innocent and unsuspecting Christian—unless he or she takes effective countermeasures.

Yet Wagner's writings on spiritual warfare against the demons may seem tame in comparison with some of the newer charismatic literature. A prolific author, published in Lagos, Nigeria, named Prayer Madueke—with more than hundred books published under his name—writes the following in his book *Queen of Heaven, Wife of Satan* (2015):

> The Queen of Heaven is one of the wicked and daring principalities that Satan trusts very much. She is connected with virtually all evil. She is to Satan whom the Holy Spirit is to God. Her witchcraft is the most sophisticated. . . . She is the direct executive of Satan. No department of Satan's kingdom can act without her

---

58. Wagner, "Territorial Spirits," 85.

59. The influential handbook on Pentecostal deliverance ministry, *Pigs in the Parlor*, by Frank and Ida Mae Hammond, takes a stance toward the naming of demons that differs from that of Wagner. To the question, "Is it necessary to call demons by specific names?", they at first say that there had been situations in their own experience where demons resisted coming out of particular individuals unless they were first properly identified by name. Yet they added: "I am personally of the opinion that a demon's insistence upon being called by a particular designation is a delaying tactic. I have had demons balk at coming out by declaring 'But that's not my name.' In such cases I usually say, 'Well, you have to come out anyhow.' And they come out" (Frank Hammond and Ida Mae, *Pigs in the Parlor: The Practical Guide to Deliverance* [Kirkwood: Impact Christian Books, 2010 (1973)], 206). In comparison with Wagner, the Hammonds are rather nonchalant on this question of properly addressing the demons by name. The Hammonds presuppose that it is Christian exorcists, and not the demons, who are ultimately in charge of the process. Admittedly, the Hammonds's book is focused on individual deliverance ministry and not on territorial spirits, but one wonders nonetheless whether Wagner took the demons a bit too seriously—and perhaps almost as seriously as they take themselves.

knowledge. She is in possession of every sinner's file. Satan himself, in most cases [,] cannot do much without this principality. Her office is next to that of Satan. She is the inspirer of all false doctrines. She is the overseer of dead churches and all evil groups, anti-God and anti-Christ organizations. She is the character builder of all evil men. Her chief ministry is to misinterpret, oppose and fight against God and his people.... The desire of the Queen of Heaven is to capture the whole reverence or worship meant for God under heaven. She demands full worship from all creatures and where she fails to receive direct worship, she presents a false identity in the similitude of God under the auspices of religion through which men and women will eventually worship her.... The Queen of Heaven feeds on blood and she is responsible for all the secret societies in the world. She is in charge of sorcery, magic, witchcraft, divination and idolatry. She gives power to native doctors, herbalists, etc. She also gives wealth, protection, fame, health, children and life.[60]

While Madueke affirms that the Queen of Heaven confers this-worldly blessings, he adds parenthetically that "all her gifts are fake and temporary."[61] It is not clear though that such a perfunctory statement is sufficient. The official message that Jesus is Lord could easily be eclipsed by the illicit thought that evil spirits are available to exert their potent influence on one's behalf. Moved by unholy curiosity or greed for gain, some readers might be willing to make a Faustian bargain, selling their soul to the devil in exchange for passing enjoyments. In an upside-down interpretation, Madueke's book could offer encouragement to traffic with the evil spirits, not to oppose and guard against them.

In the comprehensively paranoic universe depicted in this book, some Christian pastors "secretly love evil," and "eat human flesh . . . through witchcraft," while they "commit immorality with their members."[62] Spiritually speaking, one can never be too careful—even with regard to one's own leader. Likewise, because church members may have obtained through witchcraft the things they give as offerings in church, pastors must beware that they are not spiritually contaminated and undermined by the offerings presented by their own members.[63] The book goes on to speak of other spirit-beings, called Leviathan, and the Queen of the Coast, and these—like the Queen of Heaven—are treated as effectual emanations or manifestations that particularize Satan's purpose and will. In this way Madueke's cosmology largely parallels that of Yoruba religion, in which a singular supreme deity (*Olodumare*) is effective through many smaller and localized manifestations (the *Orishas*).[64] Yet unlike the traditional Yoruba religion—where the various

---

60. Prayer M. Madueke, *Queen of Heaven, Wife of Satan* (Lagos: Prayer Publications, 2015), 9, 23, 44.
61. Ibid., 44.
62. Ibid., 145.
63. Ibid., 110–11.
64. Wikipedia, "Yoruba Religion." https://en.wikipedia.org/wiki/Yoruba_Religion.

spirit-beings are either beneficent or morally ambiguous—the system of spiritual entities sketched out by Madueke is utterly evil and hostile to human well-being. For this reason, one must first discern the particular spirit-being responsible for one's sufferings: "The day you begin to have knowledge about your Leviathan, God will begin to deal with your Leviathan."[65] *Queen of Heaven, Wife of Satan* has far more to say regarding the evil spirits, than it does concerning prayer to Christ or to the God of the Bible as a remedy against Satan. When read in the context of an African society, in which the fear of witchcraft remains potent, Madueke's teachings will likely reinforce this attitude of fear, foment interest in demons, and possibly, as noted above, encourage an unwholesome curiosity regarding occultic practices.

Conclusion—Problems and Possibilities Regarding Demons

With a sense of relief, we may now turn from the demon-haunted cosmos of C. Peter Wagner and Prayer Madueke. The writings surveyed in the section above would of course not be representative of the entire global community of more than six hundred million Pentecostal–charismatic Christians. Yet a significant swath of Christianity today has been infected by an attitude of fear and of fascination toward the devil and the demons, encompassing far more persons than some scholars of Pentecostalism might imagine. To cite just one statistic to indicate the scope of the phenomenon: the all-time best-selling book on Pentecostal exorcism or deliverance ministry is likely to be Frank and Ida Mae Hammond, *Pigs in the Parlor* (1973), and as of 2020 this book has sold some 1.5 million copies. One might therefore recall the words of Nietzsche cited in the epigraph to this chapter: "Whoever fights with monsters should see to it that he does not become one himself. And when you stare for a long time into an abyss, the abyss stares back into you."[66] Hasn't one large segment of Spirit-filled Christians fallen into just this trap, becoming monstrous by battling monsters? Hasn't the abyss stared back into those staring into it? Karl Barth said that he would give only "a quick, sharp glance" toward Satan and the demons.[67] But hasn't the momentary glance given way in our day to open-mouthed gawking?

Barth's warnings about an undue preoccupation with Satan and the demons might not have been a word in season among increasingly secularized Westerners in the mid-twentieth century. Yet among global Pentecostals in the early twenty-first century Barth's teachings may serve as a helpful corrective. If as C. S. Lewis says—and as Barth agrees—there are two different errors regarding Satan and the demons, then the message needed in one situation will not be the same as that needed in another. Wherever there is an unwholesome focus upon the demons,

---

65. Madueke, *Queen of Heaven, Wife of Satan*, 181.
66. Nietzsche, *Beyond Good and Evil*, 69 [#146].
67. Barth, *CD* III/3, 519.

these powers will compete for attention with God and Christ, and perhaps even evoke responses of faith or veneration. "Do you believe in demons?" Barth is quite right to challenge the appropriateness of the question and the practice of using the word "believe" in reference to demons as one might use it in reference to God, Christ, or the holy angels.

At the same time, we identified above a number of unresolved issues in Barth's account of Satan and the demons, as tied to his doctrine of "nothingness" (*das Nichtige*). Barth's *das Nichtige* is hard to understand as a source of evil in the world, since it is a metaphysical idea that is essentially *impersonal*. Human life is filled with instances of *personal evil*, or rather, *interpersonal evil*, that is, wrongdoing voluntarily inflicted by one person on another person. Scripture regularly depicts Satan and the demons along similar lines as embodying an invisible yet very real form of interpersonal evil. Furthermore, there is the pastoral and practical question of how to "resist the devil" (Jas 4:7; 1 Pet. 5:9), to "rebuke" the devil (Jude 9), or to tell the devil to "begone!" (Mt. 4:10; cf. Mt. 16:23). The devil can be rebuked, but how would anyone *rebuke* the "nothingness" or *resist das Nichtige*? Would this not be something like fighting against entropy or gravity? *Das Nichtige* is at such a level of abstraction and remoteness from everyday life that it renders the idea of spiritual battle equally abstract and remote. One argument against identifying Satan, demons, and evil with *das Nichtige* comes in G. C. Berkouwer's idea that when a spiritual adversary is identified with nothingness, the struggle against this adversary itself becomes hollow and void. How can there be a "real" victory over an enemy that is not itself "real"? The person opposing nothingness appears like a man boxing against his shadow and battling with empty air.[68] Moreover, the identification of *das Nichtige* as neither Creator nor creature, and the parallel idea that Satan was "never a fallen angel," leaves Barth's theology hanging in metaphysical midair. Everything that "exists" or "has reality" must seemingly be either Creator or created. What sort of tertium quid is neither of these?

Christian believers must be careful not to speak overmuch regarding the devil. The Hebrew Scripture commanded the Israelites not to let the names of foreign gods ever be on their lips. "Do not mention the name of other gods, nor let them be heard from your mouth" (Exod. 23:13, ESV; cf. Josh. 23:7; Hos. 2:17; Ps. 16:4). Barth's approach to the demonic seems to be in continuity with the ancient Hebrew attitude toward foreign gods. This long-forgotten imperative might be reconsidered today. While the secular culture of the Enlightenment was ready to pooh-pooh the devil, and this trend may have continued (in academic circles especially) up to the time of Barth and Bultmann, the secular culture of the early twentieth-first century seems instead to be permeated with the paranormal. In any major bookstore today in Chicago, London, Paris, or Moscow, one will find innumerable books on occult and esoteric themes—not to mention all the reams of new titles on vampires, zombies, and ghouls, and novels in the genre of

---

68. G. C. Berkouwer, *The Triumph of Grace in The Theology of Karl Barth*, trans. Harry R. Boer (Grand Rapids: Eerdmans, 1956), 237–9.

supernatural and young-adult fiction. Films on Netflix, Amazon, and YouTube further confirm this point.

Twenty-first-century, global, digital culture is pivoting from a denial of the devil to a new fixation on the demonic. The typical adolescent of today might be less likely to deny the devil's existence than to become fascinated with Satan—and perhaps to gather some friends and try out some magic spells to summon an unholy angel or the Dark Lord himself. At least in popular culture, the greater danger today is not the denial of the devil but rather an obsession with the devil. Pentecostal–charismatic Christians who are fixated on spiritual agencies of evil may thus unwittingly be contributing to this growing preoccupation with the devil in contemporary culture. Thus, we might consider the applicability—as in Old Testament times—of the command not to take upon our lips the names of the foreign gods. An old English saying maintains that "speak of the devil and he's sure to appear." Like many traditional proverbs, there might be something true—and not simply superstitious—in the saying.

The notion of formless, insubstantial, nonentities that are nevertheless destructive—understood on the analogy of tornadoes and black holes—might offer insights into the modes of operation or methods and strategies of demons and the demonic realm. Whatever becomes caught in the field of low-pressure air (the tornado) or ultra-intense gravity (the black hole) will begin to lose its features and form, and then enter into a degenerative and deconstructive process. Barth's *das Nichtige* might therefore engender a new practical rule for spiritual discernment of Satan's presence: *quidquid informem sub potentia diaboli*, "whatever is formless is under the devil's influence." To "resist the devil" means to preserve one's own form—and the forms of things generally—when faced by the forces of formlessness and deformation.

Chapter 10

SUBJECTS AND PREDICATES

BARTHIAN GRAMMAR AND PENTECOSTAL SOTERIOLOGY

David J. Courey

In her essay "Sentences and Verbs: Talking about God," Fleming Rutledge explains her concern for the parts of speech. Popular spirituality, she complains, has emptied religious language of divine agency, replacing it with talk of the "triumph of the human spirit." She laments that Karl Barth's call for kerygmatic preaching that puts the emphasis on God's journey to us, rather than our personal pilgrimages to him has gone largely unheeded. It's a matter of theological grammar. "All of us can develop a sense of the power of verbs. Most important, all of us can learn to make God the subject of the sentence."[1]

But, the Pentecostal might object, what about the theological power of testimony and the role of human agency?[2] Personal experience and witness are two sides of a coin for Pentecostals. Surely testimony should be christocentric, the experience Spirit mediated, but the role of the individual as subject of theologically significant predicates is essential to Pentecostal spirituality. Steven Land cites an early testimony (note the imperatives and their implied subjects): "Come! Awake! Be Ready! You can be ready if you will. Stir up the gift that is in you by prayer and fasting if needs be, and testimony and praise, until you are all aglow and overflowing with His love again."[3] As Wolfgang Vondey claims, the fullness of the gospel "engages human agency in relation to God, self and others."[4]

---

1. Fleming Rutledge, "Sentences and Verbs: Talking About God," in *Apocalyptic and the Future of Theology: With and Beyond J. Louis Martyn*, ed. Joshua B. Davis and Douglas Harink (Eugene: Cascade Books, 2012), 297–314, here 298, 300.

2. Mark J. Cartledge, *The Mediation of the Spirit: Interventions in Practical Theology* (Grand Rapids: Eerdmans, 2015), 24–5; see also Cartledge, *Testimony in the Spirit: Rescripting Ordinary Pentecostal Theology* (Farnham: Ashgate, 2010).

3. *The Evening Light and Church of God Evangel* 1, no. 1 (1916, March 1): 8, cited in Steven Jack Land, *Pentecostal Spirituality: A Passion for the Kingdom* (Sheffield: Sheffield University Press, 1993).

4. Wolfgang Vondey, *Pentecostal Theology: Living the Full Gospel* (London: T&T Clark, 2017), 176.

The question of human agency is a recurrent one in the discussion of Karl Barth.[5] On first reading, it may appear that perhaps here, more than at any other locus, Barth and Pentecostals find themselves at an impasse. For at the heart of Pentecostalism is the individual's existential response to the Spirit, while the core of Barth's system appears to be centered in a monergistic soteriology.[6] For Barth, it seems, God is the subject of all theologically significant verbs. Barth himself claimed that "Jesus Christ, is the One who accomplishes the sovereign act in which God has made true and actual in time the decree of His election by making atonement, in which He has introduced the new being of all men."[7] Indeed "the turning" and "the reconciliation of all men" has taken place in him.[8] Thus, "the grace of God triumphs over man and his sin. . . . It triumphs now—in face of human opposition—miraculously, unilaterally and autocratically—to its own self glory."[9] John Webster points to the problem this created for Barth's early notions of moral theology. In his violent response to liberalism which had displaced the divine Subject, Barth's critics claimed he had "abandoned any sense that the human

---

5. For treatments of this question, see John Webster, *Barth's Moral Theology: Human Action in Barth's Thought* (London: Bloomsbury T&T Clark, 2004); Paul T. Nimmo, *Being in Action: The Theological Shape of Barth's Ethical Vision* (London and New York: T&T Clark, 2007); William Werpehowski cites James Gustafson (*Can Ethics Be Christian?* [1975]) and Stanley Hauerwas (*Character and Christian Ethics*, [1975]) as contemporary critics who question the place of human agency in Barth's ethics, in his own treatment of moral agency, *Karl Barth and Christian Ethics: Living in Truth*, Barth Study Series (Burlington: Routledge, 2014), ch. 2. Interest in this problem goes beyond ethics, as witness Nicholas M. Healy, "The Logic of Karl Barth's Ecclesiology: Analysis, Assessment and Proposed Modifications," *Modern Theology* 10, no. 3 (1994): 253–70 who critiques lack of moral agency in Barth's ecclesiology. See also Terry L. Cross, "Christ in Us: The Hope of Glory or the Sentimentality of a 'Bohemian Private Enterprise'? Barth, Pietists, and Pentecostals," in *Karl Barth and the Future of Evangelical Theology*, ed. Christian Collins Winn and John Drury (Eugene: Cascade, 2014), 69–90, who discovers an existential heart theology in both the early and late Barth (*CD* IV/4) and Gerald McKenny, "Freed by God for God: Divine Action and Human Action in Karl Barth's *Evangelical Theology* and Other Late Works," in *Karl Barth and the Making of Evangelical Theology: A Fifty-Year Perspective*, ed. Bruce L. McCormack and Clifford B. Anderson (Grand Rapids: Eerdmans, 2015), 119–39, who finds evidence for the reality of moral agency in Barth's American lectures delivered in 1962.

6. Alister McGrath, *Iustitia Dei: A History of the Christian Doctrine of Justification*, 3rd ed. (Cambridge: Cambridge University Press, 2005), 401–3; Daniel Kirkpatrick, *Monergism or Synergism: Is Salvation Cooperative or the Work of God Alone?* (Eugene: Pickwick, 2018), 56, n. 10; Barth's monergism is related to his unique doctrine of election and raises the question of his alleged universalism, a topic beyond the focus of the present chapter.

7. *CD* IV/1, 91–2.

8. Ibid., 132.

9. Ibid., 68.

subject is an ethical agent."[10] That this is not the case, and how that is so, will be seen in the course of this chapter.

In distinction from Barth, Pentecostalism has traditionally offered an account of human agency that clearly embraces an intentional collaboration between divine and human subjects. Vondey aptly describes this cooperative relationship.

> Pentecostals hold to a strong synergistic understanding of salvation: the human being participates in the work of redemption through a joining of the Spirit of God with the human spirit, and such participation is affective and experiential because "it is that very Spirit bearing witness with our spirit that we are children of God." (Rom. 8:16)[11]

The clear denotation of these words is that both humans and God are appropriate subjects of theologically significant verbs.

This chapter asks if any rapprochement is possible between Barth and Pentecostalism on the question of human agency in soteriology. We access the question through the doctrine of reconciliation, which will for our purposes ramify into the domains of Christology, sanctification, and ethics. I propose that Barth's emerging Spirit Christology, as introduced in his doctrine of reconciliation, offers a suitable point from which to engage Pentecostal Spirit Christologies allowing for a rapprochement between Pentecostal notions of human agency and the Barthian assertion of divine agency in soteriology. While I do not imagine a full reconciliation of the two, Spirit Christology offers a grammar that makes for useful dialogue between them.

The Usefulness of "Spirit Christology" in This Context

One might question the appropriateness of Spirit Christology as an integrating concept in this chapter, especially when the term is alien to Barth. Between disparagement that his doctrine of the Spirit is swallowed up by his Christology and criticism that Barth limits the Spirit's work to noetic revelation, one might justly ask about the nexus between Barthian soteriology and Pentecostal thought.[12] As Frank Macchia has shown, Barth was sensitive to this assessment and proposed to reconsider a theology of the Third Article.[13] George Hunsinger notes that

---

10. Webster, *Barth's Moral Theology*, 11. Webster goes on to show continuities between Barth's early ethics and his account of human agency in *Church Dogmatics*, 37–8.

11. Vondey, *Pentecostal Theology*, 53–4.

12. JinHyok Kim offers a typology of various critiques of Barth's pneumatology in *The Spirit of God and the Christian Life: Reconstructing Karl Barth's Pneumatology*, Emerging Scholars (Minneapolis: Fortress Press, 2014), 2–5.

13. Frank D. Macchia, "The Spirit of God and the Spirit of Life: An Evangelical Response to Karl Barth's Pneumatology," in *Karl Barth and Evangelical Theology: Convergences and Divergences*, ed. Sung Wook Chung (Grand Rapids: Baker Academic, 2006), 149–71.

this project was to be undertaken in Volume V of *CD* under an eschatological consideration of the doctrine of redemption that would close the trinitarian loop with his treatments of revelation and reconciliation.[14] At the same time, Philip Rosato viewed pneumatology as the key to Barth's doctrine of reconciliation.[15] So while Barth at no point uses the terminology of Spirit Christology, the above considerations invite the use of this category in terms of its interaction with Pentecostal pneumatology. This section, then, observes the incipient nature of Barth's Spirit Christology in *CD* IV and proposes a few points of contact with contemporary Pentecostal thought.

While a challenging term to define, we may say that Spirit Christology refers to any number of means of explicating the christological fact in pneumatological terms.[16] As a model, Spirit Christology serves multiple purposes. On the one hand, it possesses the explanatory power to account for supernatural signs and wonders in Jesus' ministry through the ministry of the Spirit rather than as a function of divine prerogative. On the other, when employed in tandem with Logos Christology, it provides an appropriate emphasis on Jesus' humanity. While Pentecostals will affirm the value of human agency in the synergy implied by Spirit Christology, it is a useful construct in this discussion, because it also captures a facet of Barth's emerging pneumatology and can be shown to be a valuable notion in Barth's construal of soteriology. Spirit Christology also has a long pedigree among Pentecostals, with roots in the nineteenth-century ministry of Scottish Presbyterian Edward Irving. In later sections we will examine its relation to human agency.

---

14. George Hunsinger, "The Mediator of Communion: Karl Barth's Doctrine of the Holy Spirit," in *The Cambridge Companion to Karl Barth*, ed. John Webster (Cambridge; New York: Cambridge University Press, 2000), 171–94, here 178–9. Hunsinger argues in an enlarged version of this chapter that Barth refuses all "Spirit-oriented Christologies" that imply a *unio mystica* rather than a *unio hypostatica*. He states that a Barthian pneumatology claims that "[t]he Spirit who enabled Christ alone to accomplish our salvation as a finished work there and then is the very Spirit who enables us to participate in it and attest to it here and now." This is no more and no less than will be claimed here; ch. 7, *Disruptive Grace: Studies in the Theology of Karl Barth* (Grand Rapids: Eerdmans, 2000), 148–85, here 158–9.

15. Philip Rosato, *The Spirit as Lord: The Pneumatology of Karl Barth* (Edinburgh: T&T Clark, 1981); John Thompson disagreed with the prominence Rosato gave the Spirit, while still affirming a significant pneumatology in Vol. 4 of *CD* in *The Holy Spirit in the Theology of Karl Barth*, Princeton Theological Monographs (Eugene: Pickwick, 1991).

16. Ralph Del Colle admitted that Spirit Christology "is not a precisely definable christological construction"; *Christ and the Spirit: Spirit-Christology in Trinitarian Perspective* (Oxford and New York: Oxford University Press, 1994), 5. Philip Rosato claimed there are two schools, one which rejects Logos Christology altogether, and the other which seeks to integrate Spirit Christology with it; "Spirit Christology: Ambiguity and Promise," *Theological Studies* 38, no. 3 (1977, September 1): 423–49, here 423.

The elaboration of a provisional Spirit Christology appears to be Barth's project in *CD* IV/2. This part-volume concerns itself with the doxological elevation of the man, Jesus, who has endured the kenotic descent of incarnation and the cross. Useful for our discussion is the Spirit's role in this trajectory, and particularly the parallelism between his ministry in Jesus, and, because of that, his ministry in us.

> The Spirit of this man—His own Spirit, who proceeds from Him and attests Him and unites other men with Him—is the Spirit of God the Son . . . the Spirit in whom the Father and Son, eternally distinct, are also eternally united; the Spirit . . . in which He freely elects man and causes him to be free, thus associating Himself with him in a faithfulness which is no less free. . . . His Spirit—the Spirit who controls this man, and proceeds from Him, and attests Him, and unites other men with Him—is none other than the Spirit of God acting and revealing Himself in the created world among and to us men. And within all earthly and human history the history between Him and us is primarily and properly the representation, reflection and correspondence of the life of God Himself, God's own most proper self-activation and self-revelation, in which there does not take place anything that is alien to God.[17]

For Barth, Christology and soteriology, normally two distinct systematic loci, become one, and neither can be understood without some account of the Spirit's role.[18] Significantly, for our purposes, this includes both the accomplishment and application of reconciliation. The same Spirit who unites Father and Son in Trinity unites God and Man in Christ and humanity and divinity in salvation.[19] Skip Jenkins offers a nuanced critique of Barthian Spirit Christology. His discussion

---

17. *CD* IV/2, 347–8.

18. Colin Gunton finds that proper attention to the Spirit's role in the incarnation and salvation is a weakness in Barth's treatment and finds a corrective in the work of Irving, "Barth, the Trinity, and Human Freedom," *Theology Today* 43, no. 3 (1986, October 1): 316–30, here 327–9.

19. Barth expands on this with some clarity in *Credo*, Rpt. 1962 (Eugene: Wipf & Stock Pub, 2005), 70: "He [the Spirit] and He alone makes the unity of God and man necessary and possible. The Holy Spirit is God Himself in His freedom to make his creature fit for communion with Him, capable of receiving Him, the object of His revelation. . . . The flesh, what is human, becomes free to be assumed into that unity with the Son of God only through the Holy Spirit, not through its own capacity. But through the Holy Spirit it really becomes free for that, it really becomes recipient of the eternal Word." See also Karl Barth, *The Faith of the Church: A Commentary on the Apostles' Creed According to Calvin's Catechism*, trans. Gabriel Vahanian, Rpt. 1958 (Eugene: Wipf & Stock, 2006), 127–8: "The connections between human freedom and God's action might thus be represented. Man acts whenever he wants, but his action has import only if it coincides with God's action. . . . If we want to understand what God and man are together, we must always raise up our eyes towards heaven, seek what is above, look to the person of Christ."

touches on Jesus' assumption of a fallen human nature and the possibility of change, struggle, and disobedience. What most relates to this chapter is his suggestion that Barth's treatment of the Spirit fails to break from traditional subservience to the application of the atonement. Yet Jenkins also finds that Barth's pneumatology may still contribute to the construction of a Pentecostal Spirit Christology. Of particular interest here is "Barth's notion that reconciled man is originally the man Jesus."[20] Nevertheless, Jenkins concludes that for Barth, the obedience of Jesus rests not on a Logos Christology (hypostatic union), but on the work of the Spirit in the man Jesus.

Among Pentecostals, contemporary elaborations of the theme occur in the works of Frank Macchia, Amos Yong, and Steven Studebaker. Macchia applies Spirit Christology to his notion of justification in the Spirit. Borrowing Barth's "objective pneumatology," that is, a conception of the Spirit that refuses to collapse it with subjective personal experience, Macchia agrees that "the Spirit is the very substance of justification as a divine act." But at the level of application, as baptizer in the Spirit, Jesus is the source of a justification that is both based on the objective pneumatic encounter of Spirit baptism and made personal by the subjective experience of justification as salvific encounter in the believer.[21] The revolutionary nature of this connection within Protestant thought is measured by how awkward the (biblical) construction "justified by the Spirit" (1 Cor. 6:16; 1 Tim. 3:16) sounds to the Evangelical ear. Parallels between Macchia and Barth will become apparent as we consider Barth's interpretation of Spirit Baptism; however, the essential coherency between the two may be seen when Barth describes "the power of the divine change in which the event of the foundation of the Christian life of specific men takes place" as "the power of their baptism with the Holy Ghost."[22]

In distinction from Macchia, Yong develops the notion of Spirit Christology in Luke's gospel, providing an expansive view of the "full gospel." For Yong, the consequences of Spirit Christology are the entailments of a "Spirit soteriology" within disciples and a "Spirit ecclesiology" for the church.[23] "Spirit soteriology" includes "the forgiveness of sins, the deliverance from evil powers, the healing of the body, the liberation of the poor and oppressed, the establishment of the

---

20. Jenkins, *A Spirit Christology*, Ecumenical Studies 3 (New York: Peter Lang, 2018), ch. 6; 213–17, here 216.

21. Frank D. Macchia, *Justified in the Spirit: Creation, Redemption, and the Triune God* (Grand Rapids: Eerdmans, 2010), 23, 132–3. "*Jesus was the justified Son of God precisely as the Person of the Spirit, a justification that was fulfilled in the resurrection, and that we are justified in him as bearers of the Spirit, an experience that will culminate in our resurrection*" (italics original). Frank D. Macchia, "Justification and the Spirit: A Pentecostal Reflection on the Doctrine by Which the Church Stands or Falls," *Pneuma* 22, no. 1 (2000): 3–21, here 10.

22. *CD* IV/4, 30.

23. Christopher A. Stephenson, *Types of Pentecostal Theology: Method, System, Spirit* (Oxford and New York: Oxford University Press, 2013), 100.

new people of God, and the eschatological salvation of God."[24] For Yong, the soteriological initiative includes not only the transformation of the individual into the image of Christ, but also the transformation of fallen creation into the new heavens and new earth. Spirit soteriology mediates the salvific extension of the Spirit's work beyond the individual to family, church, society, and the cosmos. Evaluated from the perspective of the eschatological redemption Barth envisioned for the final volume of *CD*, such notions seem consistent with the tropes implicit in his earlier pneumatology, since both Barth and Yong position themselves within the inaugurated eschatology that ultimate redemption accomplishes.[25] Barth acknowledges that Spirit baptism is not the culmination of a completed or perfect Christian life, but claims that it is rather "a take-off for the leap towards what is not yet present. It is a start which involves looking to and stretching for a future."[26] Yong refers to this kind of encounter when he speaks of Pentecostal expectancy. We are to anticipate actualistic breakthroughs of the eschatological kingdom calling us to transcendence, and transformation through miraculous reorientation and moral reordering.[27]

Taking seriously the active role of the Spirit in the drama of reconciliation, Steve Studebaker presents his Spirit Christology within the framework of a creation–redemption narrative. Studebaker conceives of the Spirit's work as liminal (the threshold between death and life), constitutive (the "principal actor and content" in creation–redemption), and consummative (the one who fulfills the redemptive plan).[28] He then locates the Spirit's liminality in the threshold moments of resurrection and Pentecost. Furthermore, the Spirit's implied presence in the incarnation and resurrection makes the Spirit constitutive of Christology. Regarding the consummative function, he sees the Spirit as the

---

24. Amos Yong, *The Spirit Poured Out on All Flesh: Pentecostalism and the Possibility of Global Theology* (Grand Rapids: Baker, 2009). See section 2.1 for the biblical theology and section 2.2 for theological implications of Spirit soteriology.

25. I am aware that the term "inaugurated eschatology" raises issues about Barthian notions of time and eternity beyond the scope of this chapter but is used here as a useful and accessible shorthand.

26. *CD* IV/4, 37.

27. Yong, *The Spirit Poured Out on All Flesh*. While this may go farther than Barth appears willing to go, he is also capable of reflecting on the charismatic life in remarkably actualistic terms: "When [the Spirit] is poured forth, when men are baptised with Him, He exists in the fulness of the *charismata* of the one community. Through their distribution each individual Christian—independently of the particularity of his natural character or personal concerns—receives his own special spiritual power and therewith his own special task in the total life and ministry of the community. . . . This may be the same as his divine commissioning . . . but it does not have to be. There are also wholly individual, transitory and changing endowments of this kind." *CD* IV/4, 38.

28. Steven M. Studebaker, *From Pentecost to the Triune God: A Pentecostal Trinitarian Theology* (Grand Rapids: Eerdmans, 2012), 68.

active agent as the creation–redemption narrative reaches eschatological climax.[29] Studebaker's assessment of the Spirit's role from the distinctly creative–redemptive narrative seems consonant with the way Barth's proposed theme of eschatological redemption might have developed in the final volume of *CD*. Barth's conception of the Spirit's work foreshadows the constitutive function in the "there and then" of Jesus' ministry, his liminal dimension in bringing believers "here and now" into the subjective experience of Jesus' history, and the consummative task of fulfilling the believer's destiny in the "absolute future" for which he waits.[30]

Barth's emerging pneumatology is consistent with the development of Spirit Christology among Pentecostal theologians. On both sides, Spirit Christology offers a useful paradigm for correlating christological and soteriological categories. In what follows, I outline Barth's notion of reconciliation, thereby demonstrating how Spirit Christology can provide a meaningful category for mediating Barthian and Pentecostal notions of human agency in salvation.

Soteriology, Christology, and the Spirit in Barth

We broach the question of human agency through the doctrine of reconciliation. The treatment of reconciliation in *CD* IV shows a trinitarian symmetry that orders the ministry of Jesus as priest, king, and prophet.[31] *CD* IV/1 focuses on divine initiative in the priestly saving work of Christ, "The Lord as Servant," while the second part-volume concentrates on the kingly glorification of "The Servant as Lord." Here Barth contemplates the meaning of the Christ event in terms of its humanity, in keeping with the paradigm, "what is unassumed is unhealed." The prophetic portion is developed in the third part-volume and deals with the communication of the reconciliation won by the mediatorship of the God-Man.

Thus, *CD* IV/1 makes the claim for the divine Subject: God as the agent of our salvation and Christ as the mediator, the accomplisher, as salvation itself.[32] Soteriology, then, is decisively and entirely a matter of divine action, and that action takes place in the life and history of the Son. He is the Elect One and the One Who Elects, the Judge and the Judged.[33] In fact

> Jesus Christ is the atonement. . . . He is the maintaining and accomplishing and fulfilling of the divine covenant as executed by God Himself. . . . He is the One for whose sake and towards whom all men from the very beginning are

---

29. Ibid. Studebaker develops these ideas in ch. 2.
30. *CD* IV/4, 29–30, 38–40.
31. Colin Gunton, "Salvation," in *The Cambridge Companion to Karl Barth*, ed. John Webster (Cambridge and New York: Cambridge University Press, 2000), 143–58, here 146, 149, 151.
32. *CD* IV/1, 13.
33. Ibid., 231, cf. *CD* II.2/, 3; IV/1, 211.

preserved from their youth up by the longsuffering of God, notwithstanding their evil heart.[34]

Thus, the history of every human being is taken up in the history of Jesus, and each and every individual is included in his life, death, and resurrection.

While the downward motif of the Son of God's soteriological work indicates his priestly role and the humiliation of the divine, the upward movement of the Son of Man in *CD* IV/2 demonstrates his kingly aspect and the exaltation of the human. As the *Leitsatz* of paragraph 64 indicates, this dimension requires the key ministry of the Holy Spirit.

> Jesus Christ, the Son of God and Lord who humbled Himself to be a servant, is also the Son of Man exalted as this servant to be the Lord, the new and true and royal man who participates in the being and life and lordship and act of God and honours and attests Him, and as such the Head and Representative and Saviour of all other men, *the origin and content and norm of the divine direction given us in the work of the Holy Spirit*.[35]

The role of human agency is accounted for by the action of the Holy Spirit in the man, Jesus. Barth's kingly and priestly motifs open discussion of human and divine roles in reconciliation, sanctification, and ethics. To adequately grasp this potential, it will be helpful to reconceptualize this aspect of Barth's account of the human and divine in terms of Spirit Christology. It is the implicit Spirit Christology which Barth invokes in paragraph 64 that opens a fruitful dialogue between Barthian and Pentecostal pneumatologies where human responsibility and divine initiative find adequate theological emphases.

Barth's Spirit Christology is particularly important to his narrative of the exaltation of humanity through the Son of Man. Jesus performs his earthly ministry in the power of the Spirit and goes to the cross and is resurrected in the same power.[36] But in such passages, Barth goes on to draw the connection to us. "Thus the Spirit who makes Christians Christians is the power of this revelation of Jesus Christ Himself—His Spirit."[37] Furthermore, "we have to see the fact and the extent that the Spirit of Jesus Christ, by which the latter is self-attested both as humiliated and exalted, is the Holy Spirit, who as such has power and authority over us."[38]

In Barth's account, this inaugurates the third movement of reconciliation in *CD* IV/3, which is concerned with subjective vocation, a corollary of justification and sanctification. It is a common interpretation of Barth that God is the subject

---

34. *CD* IV/1, 34–5.
35. *CD* IV/2, 3, italics added.
36. Ibid., 323.
37. Ibid.
38. Ibid., 348.

of all theologically significant predicates. But in the tale of the exaltation of the Son of Man, a meaningful shift took place that has implications for the agency of humankind in the process of reconciliation. This is accomplished through the prophetic role of the God-Man who imparts the knowledge of the gospel by the impartation of the Spirit. "The ἐπίγνωσις αὐτοῦ [knowledge of him] is thus the work of the Spirit of wisdom and revelation (Eph. 1:17) for whose gifts we pray." Such knowledge, far beyond mere *gnosis*, is the basis of *metanoia*, thus, as Barth puts it, the "object becomes the Subject."[39] That this exchange is more than merely cognitive will be shown. As the *nous* of Christ is received, it is now the individual, radically transformed (Barth's word), transfigured (my word), who repents, who trusts, who hungers and thirsts for more of this revelation. The same Spirit who makes the Son of Man the subject of divine predicates is at work within those he has called to the same effect, and this provides significant space for human action in sanctification and ethics. It is to these considerations, and the mystery they entail, that we now turn.

The Human Subject in Sanctification

Early in *Dogmatics* Barth alerts us to the mystery of justification and sanctification, as well as the place of human agency. Hunsinger sees this mystery as part of an overarching theme in *CD*, which he calls the Chalcedonian pattern. It is defined by asymmetry (divine precedence over human action), intimacy (union or coinherence of divine and human action), and integrity (action without the one collapsing into or being confounded with the other).[40] It is rooted in Barth's turn from liberalism. An account of the divine–human relationship that did not reduce the divine into the anthropological was the lodestar of the younger Barth's quest. While more nuanced in the *Dogmatics*, the asymmetry of divine primacy and human response was already present in his early writings.[41] The mystery of regeneration and the subsequent moral agency of human actors hang in the balance.

In *CD* I, Barth introduces an important contrapuntal motif between the active and passive, putting off its full exposition till the appropriate moment in *CD* IV. Sanctification, we are told, is of a piece with justification and is tied with the work of the indwelling Spirit. The two are "acts of this divine Subject" who at once "makes Himself ours" as the extension of the Trinity. "Thus and not otherwise He

---

39. *CD* IV/3.1, 185.

40. The application being given here is in the context of the doctrine of reconciliation; George Hunsinger, *How to Read Karl Barth: The Shape of His Theology* (New York and Oxford: Oxford University Press, 1991), 186–7.

41. Ethan A. Worthington, *The Claim of God: Karl Barth's Doctrine of Sanctification in His Earlier Theology* (Eugene: Pickwick, 2015); see especially ch. 1, "The Divine-Human Encounter."

becomes our salvation."⁴² The work of the Spirit weaves the counterpoint between active and passive, subject and object, divine initiative and human freedom.

> In His fellowship with God, and therefore in our fellowship with Him, this One, there is achieved our fellowship with God, the movement of man from below to above, from himself to God. It is primarily and properly this human Subject, who, as the object of the free and liberating grace of God, cannot be only an object in the event of atonement, but also becomes an active Subject. In Him man is made the new man, reconciled with God. According to 1 Cor. 1:30 He is made unto us not only righteousness but also sanctification.⁴³

In this passage there appears a curious ambiguity in the question of "this human Subject," who is made no longer the "object" of the atonement, but now an "active Subject." Having so clearly established the prominence of the divine Subject, Barth now ascribes a kind of subjectivity to the human actor. Clearly in view here is Jesus as the human actor, but as the representative of all humans: "the movement of man from below to above."⁴⁴ This ambiguity in Barth's language never reduces the divine to any less than commanding Subject, but such language allows humanity, as obeying Subject, to possess its own predicates.

From conversion to ministry, from justification to sanctification, the Spirit summons and empowers human agency. Barth calls conversion or regeneration "a mystery," "problematic," a question fraught with "difficulties" and yet a fact before which one must "ultimately stand" with "helpless astonishment."⁴⁵ For Hunsinger, the appeal to mystery signals the Chalcedonian asymmetry between divine primacy and human agency.⁴⁶ This "event of the Christian life," regeneration, Barth equates

---

42. *CD* I/1, 489. In *CD* IV/2, 503 he calls them "two different aspects of the one event of salvation."

43. *CD* IV/2, 19; Barth makes this more explicit in the following paragraph: "It is from this point therefore, in the particular light of this, the human, side of the truth of the Mediator and Reconciler, that we have now to consider and present the whole event of reconciliation.... It is from this point, as it has taken place in Him, that we have to consider ... the work of the awakening power of the Holy Spirit," 20.

44. Barth makes this more explicit in the next paragraph: "It is from this point therefore, in the particular light of this, the human, side of the truth of the Mediator and Reconciler, that we have now to consider and present the whole event of reconciliation.... It is from this point, as it has taken place in Him, that we have to consider ... the work of the awakening power of the Holy Spirit. And we have to do all this in such a way that the line leads clearly and deeply into the sphere of human existence (both general and particular), and yet is never more than a repetition and confirmation of its christological starting-point." *CD* IV/2, 19–20.

45. *CD* IV/4, 3.

46. Hunsinger, *How to Read Karl Barth*, 187. In another context, Hunsinger takes a more pneumatological tone: "Divine freedom for *koinonia* is another name for the Holy

with the baptism with the Holy Spirit. Pentecostals will find much to appreciate about Barth's actualistic account of Spirit baptism. By actualism Barth refers to the objective, historical act made available subjectively by the miracle of grace. On the one hand, it is an unrepeatable event in the salvation history of humanity; on the other, it is ongoing punctiliar encounter for the Christian.[47] "In all its actions the work of the Holy Spirit is always and everywhere a wholly new thing. At each moment of its occurrence it is itself another change, a conversion, which calls for even more radical conversion."[48]

As Barth teases this out in *CD* IV/4, he demonstrates the potential of human predicates, that is, theologically significant verbs of which humans are the appropriate subjects. Spirit baptism, though a divine work, is what frees the believer to moral agency that fulfills the divine command. Barth's account of Spirit baptism is uncompromising in its assertion of divine prerogative. "Baptism with the Spirit is effective, causative, even creative action on man and in man. It is, indeed, divinely effective, divinely causative, divinely creative."[49] Nevertheless, this does not reduce man to an automaton:

> It is not that God's act on and in man makes of him a cog set in motion thereby. The free God does not act thus with man. On the contrary, what the free God in His omnipotence wills and fashions in Jesus Christ in the work of the Holy Ghost is the free man who determines himself *under this pre-determination by God*, the obedience of his heart and conscience and will and independent action. Here man is taken seriously, and finds that he is taken seriously, as the creature which is different from God, which is *for all its dependence* autonomous before Him, which is of age. Here he is empowered for his own act, and invited, *commanded and encouraged to perform it*. Here—and the more realistically we understand *that which comes upon him from God* only as grace, the better we understand this—*he is set directly before and under God's command, and claimed directly for its fulfilment*.[50]

This dialectic is precisely what Barth summarizes in *Evangelical Theology*: "The freedom of which we talk is God's freedom to disclose himself to men, to make men accessible to himself, and so to make them on their part free for him. The one who does that is the Lord God, who is the Spirit."[51]

In this interplay of command and freedom, Barth also later accounts for ongoing sin in the life of the Christian. Between de jure and de facto sanctification, Barth claims that believers are simultaneously "disturbed sinners" yet sinners who are

---

Spirit, who unites us with Christ, and through him with the eternal Trinity, in unsurpassable communion," Hunsinger, "The Mediator Communion," 170.

47. Hunsinger, *How to Read Karl Barth*, 30–2.
48. *CD* IV/4, 38.
49. Ibid., 34.
50. Ibid., 35–6.
51. Karl Barth, *Evangelical Theology: An Introduction* (Grand Rapids: Eerdmans, 1992), 53.

"limited" by sanctification.[52] Barth strives to make clear the free agency of the individual, the responsible action that is "taken seriously." But one must likewise hear, in the midst of his theme of liberty, the contrapuntal motif of divine sovereignty: the command, claim, and predetermination of God. Colin Gunton stresses that this is a "real, though *given* and determined freedom," yet never a compelled one, and that to resist it is not autonomy but "the heteronomy of the demonic."[53]

The two dimensions, divine and human, must both be given their due, but the primacy of divine is never slackened. The medium by which the two can be heard simultaneously is the Holy Spirit. This Spirit as the Sovereign God, the Spirit of Christ, and the Spirit indwelling, even filling the believer (though Barth does not use this last term in *CD* IV/4), is the means by which the divine command takes action within the Christian—not "a mechanical consequence of his being beset by God" since it must be "his very own free decision." Rather, "[i]t can only be his own walking according to the Spirit (κατὰ πνεῦμα) with whom he is baptized—a walking genuinely on his own feet *as he is thus beset by God.*" (Even here, the counterpoint!)[54]

Sanctification as the Locus of Barthian Ethics

As John Webster says, from first to last, *Dogmatics* must be moral theology if its theme is the divine-human encounter.[55] The fact that Barth's theological ethics and sanctification should find crystallization in the notion of divine command is unsurprising given Barth's emphasis on the recapitulation of the history of Christ in the Christian and his actualist ontology.[56] The election of Christ (and of humanity in Christ), as well as the revelation of God in Jesus Christ, are all historical events that must have their counterpart in the Spirit's punctiliar action. God's Word comes to us historically and personally, not only as indicative but also as divine imperative.[57] Thus, Barth reimagined baptism as a paradigm for ethical action. Rather than means of grace, he reinterpreted the sacrament as response to grace. The Spirit-baptized person's first ethical step is to respond in obedience to the command to be baptized in water.[58] This sets the agenda for the ethics of "commanding grace."

Katherine Sonderegger sees Barth's doctrine of sanctification connected to the divine command. For Barth, impartation is the essence of sanctification, according

---

52. *CD* IV/4, 524–6. The de jure/de facto distinction becomes a useful device in dealing with certain necessary ambiguities in Barth's theology.
53. Gunton, "Barth, the Trinity, and Human Freedom," 325, 329 (italics his).
54. *CD* IV/4, 36.
55. Webster, *Barth's Moral Theology*, 8.
56. Nimmo, *Being in Action*, 18.
57. *CD* III/2, 165.
58. John Webster, *Barth's Ethics of Reconciliation* (Cambridge: Cambridge University Press, 1995), 116.

to Sonderegger, and as the Spirit imparts the command, it also imparts liberty for obedience.[59] This Word comes to us as *ratio*, as noetic revelation. It is the Spirit's work to make real and present the "Incomprehensibility" of the Divine along with its comprehensible command. The work of the Spirit, she claims, is to make the divine Subject into the (secondary) Object of Spirit-engendered seeking. By extension, she suggests, in the commanding and acting paradigm, the indwelling Spirit, as gift "to us and in us" as a secondary object who is our holiness. If this model of sanctification feels too cold, and intellectual, too *noetic*, Sonderegger places impartation against the background of participation, or, perhaps better, communication as an aspect of communion. Impartation, she admits, is supremely noetic, but not exclusively so. Here, then, is a first step toward bridging Barthian and Pentecostal sanctification. Yet, in spite of an appeal to Barth's language of transcendence, Sonderegger's reading never manages to escape the domain of *ratio* to that of experience.[60]

Daniel Migliore locates the key to Barthian sanctification and ethical behavior in Calvin's *participatio Christi*, "given to man by the Holy Spirit." He sees this union in Christ as the means by which the saints in co-agency with Christ perform works that correspond to his.[61] This provides a further step to rapprochement with a Pentecostal sense of human responsibility. But union with Christ, while it retains an "active, agential, ethical sense of free and glad participation in the service of Jesus Christ and his work of reconciliation," lacks the warmth that Barth himself would give it.[62] The Spirit's role is not exhausted in the noetic communication of the divine command; he also communicates the divine passion. The Spirit, whose work *ad intra* is to bond the internal relationship of the Trinity in love, carries on an analogous ministry *ad extra* between God and the believer.[63]

What is lacking in Migliore's account of Barth's *participatio Christi* is the affective dimension captured in Pentecostalism. While Barth does reference the affective work of the Spirit, Pentecostals emphasize this dimension of the Spirit's work in an even greater measure.[64] Steven Land's classic *Pentecostal Spirituality* proposed a model of Christian life rooted in the Pentecostal tradition. Concerning ethics, Pentecostals clearly championed right practices with strong emphases on practical holiness and mission, and while some may have occasionally run short on right doctrine, they certainly grasped that properly oriented faith must lead

---

59. Katherine Sonderegger, "Sanctification as Impartation in the Doctrine of Karl Barth," *Zeitschrift für dialektische Theologie* 18, no. 3 (2002): 308–15, here 311–12.

60. Ibid., 311, 312–13.

61. Daniel L. Migliore, "Participatio Christi: The Central Theme of Barth's Doctrine of Sanctification," *Zeitschrift für dialektische Theologie* 18, no. 3 (2002): 286–307, here 295.

62. Ibid., 291.

63. *CD* I/1, 483. See the discussion in Macchia, "The Spirit of God and the Spirit of Life," 155–6.

64. For a Pentecostal treatment of the affective dimension of Barth's theology, see Cross, "Christ in Us."

to embodied doxology. But in Land's paradigm, Christian existence is predicated on right affections.[65] The role of affections in Pentecostal theology is explored more recently by Wolfgang Vondey. He contends that there is more here than random emotive experiences, but that the affections reflect "transformative manifestations of the encounter with God."[66] Such language resonates with Barth's concern for the actualism of an engaged "moral ontology." Thus, the inverted pyramid with orthodoxy and orthopraxy arising from orthopathy offers the Barthian account of ethics and sanctification not only a further depth of warmth but provides a theoretical space for the passion Barth's *oeuvre* rightly engenders.

To capture this in more Reformed terms that still speak to Pentecostals, one might consider Jonathan Edward's preoccupation with the beauty of God. True holy and gracious affections create "the sense of the heart of the supreme beauty and sweetness of the holiness or moral perfection of divine things."[67] The sense of the heart combines affective delight with dispositional action issuing in personal sanctification, or, in this context, ethical action.[68] For Edwards such true affections (as opposed to "natural" religious affections) were mediated by the internal work of the Spirit. The Spirit himself becomes "so united to the faculties of the soul, that he becomes there a principle or spring of a new nature and life."[69] In Barthian terms this equates to moment-by-moment impartation by the Spirit of God. This notion of sanctification and the ethic that results mediates well between Pentecostal orthopathy and Barthian actualism.

The heart of Barthian ethics is the command of God and the Christian's response. "God's command is a gracious command," Migliore states tautologically, "and his grace a commanding grace."[70] The same Spirit who animates Christ in this world animates his followers, and the command comes to us, as to him, as an actualistic opportunity to express the kingdom of God by that same Spirit. Thus, holiness is not conformity to code, principle, or law, rather true sanctification occurs in the freedom that grace creates.[71] In that freedom believers reproduce

---

65. Land, *Pentecostal Spirituality*.

66. Vondey, *Pentecostal Theology*, 25, but see the entire section on "Affections: The Energy of Pentecostal Theology," 24–7.

67. Jonathan Edwards, *The Works of Jonathan Edwards, Vol. 2: Religious Affections*, ed. John E. Smith (New Haven and London: Yale University Press, 2009), 272.

68. John E. Smith, "Religious Affections and the 'Sense of the Heart,'" in *The Princeton Companion to Jonathan Edwards*, ed. Sang Hyun Lee (Princeton: Princeton University Press, 2005), 105.

69. Edwards, *Religious Affections*, 203.

70. Daniel L. Migliore, "Commanding Grace: Karl Barth's Theological Ethics," in *Commanding Grace: Studies in Karl Barth's Ethics*, ed. Daniel L. Migliore (Grand Rapids: Eerdmans, 2010), 1–25, here 11.

71. Hunsinger goes this far: "Grace does not perfect and exceed human nature in its sorry plight so much as it contradicts and overrules it"; *Disruptive Grace*, 165.

the life and history of Jesus, and discover that there, in Christ, they are most truly themselves.[72]

Conclusion: Spirit Christology as Bridging Paradigm

The question may be raised at this point whether Barth proposes a proper Spirit Christology. Indeed, the last section makes no explicit mention of the term, though it advocates an ontological and affective dimension of the Spirit's work that adds a relational element to the command ethic by which Barth is generally interpreted. But such a view does not take fully into account the trinitarian symmetry of Barth's doctrine of reconciliation proposed above. While the kingly motif in Barth's discussion moves more in tropes of Logos Christology, the priestly motif is grounded in what appears to be a distinctly Spirit Christology. And the prophetic motif, which integrates the believer's vocation, trades even more clearly in actualistic breakthroughs of the life and history of Jesus in the believer by the Spirit.[73] Jenkins projects this to the communal level: the ecclesial yield of Spirit Christology is the incarnational replication of the life of the Spirit in those upon whom he is bestowed. It is this paradigm that provides a bridge between Pentecostal and Barthian notions of soteriology.

Spirit Christologies proposed by Macchia, Yong, and Studebaker can each be articulated in Barthian terms. In each case, Spirit Christology represents the pneumatological means by which soteriological realities are realized in individuals: justification for Macchia, eschatological redemption for Yong, and the recapitulation of the drama of redemption within the life of the Spirit-filled believer for Studebaker. Set against the background of a pneumatology that Barth himself admitted was underdeveloped, and one he gave intimations of expanding, the paradigm of Spirit Christology appears both malleable and relevant enough to accommodate both Barthian and Pentecostal projects. For Barth, it creates the space for meaningful human agency in reconciliation, sanctification, and ethics within a divinely determined soteriology. For Pentecostals, and especially those with a Barthian leaning, it offers a model of divine initiative in soteriology, while allowing an appropriate synergistic emphasis on human agency.

This chapter began inquiring about an adequate grammar for soteriology. Barth, it was suggested, makes God the subject of all theologically significant predicates, while Pentecostalism places an emphasis on the human as active Subject in seeking

---

72. Migliore, "Commanding Grace," 13.

73. "However true it may be that in Christ all things have been made new, it is nevertheless the case that men and women must continually 'become what they are in Christ' moment by moment through actualistic breakthroughs of the righteousness and knowledge of God into their temporal fallen existence," Bruce L. McCormack, *Karl Barth's Critically Realistic Dialectical Theology: Its Genesis and Development 1909–1936* (Oxford and New York: Oxford University Press, 1995), 164.

God. Our study has shown that divine priority and monergism seem indelibly inscribed in Barth's theology. Similarly, the human prerogative in engaging the divine initiative is a standard characteristic of Pentecostal thought. These features will remain. Yet, this chapter shows how Spirit Christology provides a bridge across the impassible chasm. Altogether, it seems that pneumatology provides a grammar that allows for a Barthian reading of Christology, sanctification, and ethics that accounts for the freedom of human agency and a Pentecostal reading that takes seriously the sovereignty of God. In such a reading, Barth finds human subjects assuming theologically significant predicates, albeit within the asymmetry that Hunsinger indicates, and Pentecostals make room for the mystery of a divine Subject predicating the human freedom that underlies significant moral agency.

Chapter 11

SLAMMING THE DOOR AND CRACKING A WINDOW?

PNEUMATOLOGICAL INVESTIGATIONS FOR POSSIBLE OPENINGS IN KARL BARTH'S GENERALLY CLOSED THEOLOGY OF RELIGIONS

Tony Richie

Barth's insistence on God's transcendence, assumption of anthropological incapacitation, argumentation for the abolition of religion(s), stringently negative assessment of natural or general theology, and consistent emphasis on God's absolutely unique and necessary revelation in Jesus Christ apparently "slam the door" on any and all possibilities of positive assessment of or engagement with the world's religions. Accordingly, Barth is often classified as an "exclusive" theologian.[1] However, later in life Barth appears to "crack the window" just a bit.[2] Barth made three somewhat surprising, and unpredictable, moves that may potentially inform, if not alter, entirely closed interpretations and/or their applications. First, Barth makes enigmatic allusions to lesser lights bearing witness to Jesus Christ as the Light of the World. Second, he suggests more explicit and sustained attention to pneumatology could serve as a basis for important clarification of the overall

---

1. Tony Richie, *Speaking by the Spirit: A Pentecostal Model for Interreligious Dialogue*, Asbury Theological Seminary Series in World Christian Revitalization Movements, gen. ed. J. Stephen Malley, Pentecostal/Charismatic Studies, ed. William F. Faupel (Lexington: Emeth, 2011), 12. However, with Barth there is a careful nuance in that his exclusivity strictly addresses the uniqueness and necessity of Jesus Christ rather than of the religion of Christianity per se, ibid., 67 (n. 48).

2. I originally intended for the main title of this chapter to begin with "Cracking a Door?" After our session on "Barth and Pentecostal Theology" at the 47th Annual Meeting Society for Pentecostal Studies (March 8–10, 2018; Pentecostal Theological Seminary; Cleveland, TN), I talked with responding scholar John Drury. I mentioned my idea that Barth later "cracked a door" that he had previously slammed shut. He quipped, "Well, I'd say it's more like he slammed the door and cracked a window!" I liked his terminology well enough to adapt my original title. That being said, I still argue that an (even slightly) open window allows fresh air and light into a stale, dark room.

theological program. Third, he calls for cautious but—at least, potentially—appreciative evaluation of Pentecostalism for the future of Christian theology.

In conversation with Barth/Barthian and Pentecostal scholarship, this chapter investigates several significant implications of these moves for a maturing Pentecostal *theologia religionum* faithfully fulfilling its vocation in a world confronted by realities of religious pluralism. It is offered in the spirit of Barth himself who says late in life:

> Theology becomes unspiritual when it lets itself be enticed or evicted from the freshly flowing air of the Spirit of the Lord, in which it alone can prosper. The Spirit departs when theology enters rooms whose stagnant air automatically prevents it from being and doing what it can, may, and must be and do.[3]

I am optimistic that the man who never quit thinking and writing about theology would in some measure be pleased that Pentecostals are now thinking and writing together with him on this part of his thought—and just maybe pressing him a bit farther on it.

Barth's Most Direct "Religions" Work

The present chapter highlights three particular sources in Barth's mammoth theological corpus for discussion of his theology of religions. First, Barth's heated debate with Emil Brunner about natural revelation is (at the least) tone setting. Second, Barth's discussion of "The Revelation of God as the Abolition of Religion" lays out critical elements of his views. Finally, Barth's later discussion of "The Glory of the Mediator" describing lesser lights bearing witness to Jesus Christ as the True Light suggests an expansive direction in his mature thought.[4] First, in 1934, Emil Brunner, Barth's former collaborator and friend, wrote an affirmation of natural revelation and theology to which Barth responded with an angry "No!"[5] It was a

---

3. Karl Barth, *Evangelical Theology: An Introduction*, trans. Grover Foley (Grand Rapids: Eerdmans, 1963), 56.

4. Agreeing with Sven Ensminger, *Karl Barth's Theology as a Resource for a Christian Theology of Religions*, ed. John Webster, Ian A. McFarland, and Ivor Davidson, T&T Clark Studies in Systematic Theology vol. 28 (London: Bloomsbury, 2014), 79, that *CD* I/2, §17 should not be the sole source of an examination of Barth's theology of religions. Amos Yong, *Hospitality & the Other: Pentecost, Christian Practices and the Neighbor* (Maryknoll: Orbis, 2008), 69, n. 9, failure to consider Barth's wider work has led to frequent misunderstanding of Barth, particularly with harsh misapplication in certain Evangelical circles.

5. For both sides, see Emil Brunner and Karl Barth, *Natural Theology Comprising "Nature and Grace" by Professor Dr. Emil Brunner and "No!" by Dr. Karl Barth* (Eugene: Wipf and Stock, 1946, 2002). Reinhold Niebuhr, *The Nature and Destiny of Man: A Christian Interpretation: Volume I and II* (Louisville: Westminster John Knox, 1996 reprint of 1964

dramatic parting of ways. At stake was the point of contact for the gospel in human consciousness as well as the nature of the theological task itself. Brunner attached a level of legitimacy to natural theology (viz., creation and human conscience and reason) while Barth insisted there can be no knowledge of God apart from divine revelation (viz., Jesus Christ). Consequently, Brunner was somewhat open to knowledge of God in other religions while Barth was utterly closed.

Second, "The Revelation of God as the Abolition of Religion" addresses the problem of religion in theology, religion as unbelief, and true religion.[6] Here Barth basically rejects the category of "religion" in favor of "revelation." For him there is no possible comparison between the two. Revelation for Barth describes God's self-offering and self-manifestation in graciously reconciling humanity to God's self. By contrast, religion (and thus religions) describes human efforts which are really at their root nothing other than unbelief.[7] They are inevitably weak and unnecessary. Accordingly, religion as such is abolished, or abrogated, by divine revelation. Nevertheless, Christianity can be considered the true religion but only in a carefully qualified sense. To be sure, the criticism of religion extends to Christianity as a religion. This contradiction is overcome in realizing that the victorious grace of God in the mystery of the truth of Christianity is found in Jesus Christ. Thus, the relationship of the name of Jesus Christ to Christianity makes Christianity unique. Christianity is the true religion not *as* religion but only *through* Jesus Christ.[8]

In "The Glory of the Mediator," Barth carefully affirms Calvin's idea of *theatrum gloriae Dei* in which the *creatura* (cosmos or nature) may be cautiously described

---

ed.), 2:64, n. 14, opines that Brunner was right and Barth wrong but Barth won the debate anyway.

6. Karl Barth, *The Doctrine of the Word of God (Prolegomena to Church Dogmatics, being Vol. I, 2)*, trans. G. T. Thomson and Harold Knight (Edinburgh: T&T Clark, 1956, 1963), §17. Clifford Green, ed., *Karl Barth: Theologian of Freedom: Making of Modern Theology*, gen. ed. John W. de Gruchy (Minneapolis: Fortress Press, 1991), argues that the translation of "The Revelation of God as the Abolition [*Aufhebung*] of Religion," although it catches the idea of unbelief, is misleading. He offers a paraphrase instead with "the revelation of God as the death and resurrection of religion," 331. He argues that in Barth "abolition/*aufhebung*" means "not only negation, dissolution, but also overcoming and transcending," 335.

7. Tom Greggs, *Theology against Religion: Constructive Dialogues with Bonhoeffer and Barth* (New York: T&T Clark, 2011), 175–81, concludes that "religion" is for Barth a theological category standing over against Christianity's absolute and sole identity in and fidelity to Jesus Christ as the revealed Word of God. Greggs, *Theology against Religion*, 177–8, argues that although Barth's main concern is not religions (plural) but religion (singular) as a universal, there are implications providing a starting point for theology of religions.

8. Ensminger, *Barth's Theology*, 81; the end result of Barth's argument is to foster Christian humility. It is equally inaccurate to assume either that Barth granted no importance to religion or that he gave unqualified support to the Christian religion, ibid., 175.

as the theater of God's glory.⁹ Barth now connects, or better, coordinates, the grace of creation and the covenant of grace. Yet God's creative grace is not inherent in nature itself but in Jesus Christ as "the Light of Life" which is "the one true light." Nevertheless, creation has its own lights (referencing Gen. 1:14), its own words and truths, although ultimately they do not, cannot, shine independently of God's revelation in Jesus Christ. Since these lights bring illumination to human intellects, they should not be despised or ignored or denied; but, created lights do not shine with the same brilliance as the uncreated light (Jesus Christ). Still, they do shine. The greatest function of creation's lights is to point to something more lasting, persistent, and constant. Thus they point—albeit indirectly—to Jesus Christ. Yet the dynamic and orderly rhythm of existence in created lights, words, and truths should never be confused with nor rival the uncreated light: Jesus Christ. Contrariety exists in created lights, which are in a sense broken, casting both illumination and shadow. They do not proclaim the Word of God; they tell us nothing about humanity's relationship with God. The most important feature of created lights is summoning human beings in the direction of the active and ordered freedom of divine revelation. Yet nature's lights are always a riddle, ever an obscure outline. There still is no comparison with the revelation of God. Nevertheless, the inevitable limits of creaturely lights do not discount their helpfulness, their genuine fruitfulness.

Barth strives strenuously to avoid, on the one hand, dualism and, on the other, monism.¹⁰ Accordingly, he argues, the Word of God challenges and relativizes the truth of the creature even while it institutes and integrates it. The Word of God uniquely binds itself to humans who hear it in an essential, eternal, and absolute manner. Further, the Word of God has full, undivided, and indivisible unity incapable of addition or emulation. Yet the Word of God is received in the event of Jesus Christ within the context of creaturely existence with its lights, words, and truths. Along with its binding force and its unity and totality the Word of God has ultimate finality. But Barth asserts the "genuinely critical, the positive relationship of the light of lights to the lights which the God whose saving action is revealed by the one light does not withhold from His creatures as such but gives them in His eternal goodness."¹¹

Nevertheless, it would be too bold to claim that Barth backed down on natural theology. Earlier in *CD* IV/3 § 69.2 Barth developed a theology of the secular parables of the kingdom. He argued that nature has parabolic qualities but has no light of its own; rather, it reflects the light of Jesus Christ. Jürgen Moltmann understands Barth as here developing his own natural theology in/for a post-Nazi

---

9. Karl Barth, *Church Dogmatics: The Doctrine of Reconciliation, IV/3*, trans. G. W. Bromiley (Edinburgh: T&T Clark, 1961, 1976), §69, 137–54.
10. *CD* IV/3, 153–64.
11. Ibid., 164–5.

world.¹² Yet Barth explicitly and, as of old, vehemently, denies any "need to appeal to the sorry hypothesis of a so-called 'natural theology.'"¹³ He adamantly insists that such "free communications" in creation never be "laid alongside Scripture as a kind of second Bible."¹⁴ Even if one were to argue that after nearly three decades Barth had changed his mind, it is too fantastic to assume that he did so within the same section of *CD*.¹⁵ Better to describe Barth's theology of secular parables and other lights not as "natural theology" per se but as a "theology of nature"—which is not necessarily the same thing.¹⁶ Yet it does open up space for progress.

If I am reading him right, what Barth accomplishes in the trajectory outlined above is astounding. First, he does not at all concede the utter and absolute uniqueness of Jesus Christ or God's revelation in Christ according to the Holy Scriptures. Actually, he further develops it and reaffirms it. Second, he not only allows but invites and enables consideration of the divinely ordained revelatory luminosity of creaturely existence. I aver that putting these two accomplishments together has potential to provide a productive framework for a theology of religions that is unapologetically *Christian* while concomitantly open to authentic conversations with *religious pluralism*. This by no means implies that Barth's

---

12. "Jurgen Moltmann on Unfinished Summas and Natural Theology," *Theological Conversations 2009 Conference: Session 2*, https://postbarthian.com/2014/07/15/jurgen-moltmann-unfinished-summas-natural-theology/. The Barmen Declaration reveals Barth's concern to reassert the Lordship of Jesus Christ involves commitment to resist Hitler's influence. See Arthur C. Cochrane, *The Church's Confession under Hitler* (Philadelphia: Westminster Press, 1962), 237–42.

13. *CD* IV/3, 117.

14. Ibid., 133. John Polkinghorne, *Science and Theology: An Introduction* (Minneapolis: Fortress Press, 1998), notes that although Barth influenced a generation of theologians "to believe that the primacy of revelation makes natural theology an exercise that is unnecessary, dangerous and illegitimate" that nevertheless "a contemporary revival of natural theology is taking place," 71. For Polkinghorne, natural theology and a theology of nature are complementary, 69–78, arising out of the doctrine of creation, 79–81. His pneumatological proposal accents "the working of the Holy Spirit on the 'inside' of creation" "with a gentle respect for the integrity of creation," 91 and 95, as key for understanding the relationship between God and nature.

15. Veli-Matti Kärkkäinen, *An Introduction to the Theology of Religions: Biblical, Historical, & Contemporary Perspectives* (Downers Grove: IVP Academic, 2003), 177–8, although Barth became "less polemical and eventually gave some credit to other religions, as a whole his theology of religions did not change considerably."

16. Ensminger, *Barth's Theology*, 242, wonders whether one of Barth's greatest contributions to Christian theology, including its theology of religions, is his challenge to look beyond "the human categories in this world to the one who has 'overcome the world'" (Jn 16:33).

theology is religiously pluralistic—only that it provides space for a Christian theology of religious pluralism.[17]

Understanding and Evaluating Barth's Theology of Religions

My tentative deduction in the preceding may be premature. Barth's theology is infamously intricate. There is certainly more to investigate before attempting anything resembling a conclusive assessment. David Mueller notes that according to Barth "Our knowledge of God not only originates in his saving work in Jesus Christ but is also fulfilled through his work as Holy Spirit."[18] My Pentecostal antennae instantly go up. However, this statement, and this section, follows an immediately preceding section exposing Barth's struggles with the pneumatic and experiential/subjective versus the noetic and intellectual/objective aspects of divine revelation and epistemology.[19] In other words, Barth sometimes struggles with the experience of the Holy Spirit. Even when he does affirm the subjective work of the Holy Spirit he inevitably subjugates it to the objective. But again, this is not the last word. We will revisit Barth on the Holy Spirit below.

Mueller describes Barth's attack on natural theology as "without parallel in modern theology."[20] Primarily, it arises out of consistent insistence that there exists no point of contact between God and humanity, between nature and grace, apart from God's self-revelation in Jesus Christ. For support, Barth appeals to the Bible, to the doctrine of original sin, and to the uniqueness of Jesus Christ. Barth insists there is no analogy of being (*analogia entis*) between God and humanity—God is wholly other—but rather an analogy of faith (*analogia fides*) in which humans may know God through divine revelation only.[21] That would indicate no inherent affinity between God and humans.

More recently, Tom Greggs argues that Barth's critique of religion moves along the same trajectory as Bonhoeffer's "religionless Christianity" (in spite of Bonhoeffer's critique of Barth).[22] Thus, both theologians are "engaged in the prophetic admonition of religion" through the "Christianization of the critique of

---

17. Barth's indefatigable insistence on the centrality of Jesus Christ is directly counter to pluralistic relativism, Ensminger, *Barth's Theology*, 210–11. Yet neither should we assume that Barth's theology *ipso facto* eliminates all possibilities for any conversations at all between Christians and those of non-Christian faiths, ibid., 241.

18. David L. Mueller, *Karl Barth: Makers of the Modern Mind*, series editor, Bob E. Patterson (Waco: Word, 1976 [4th printing]), 85–93, here 85.

19. Ibid., 76–9.

20. Ibid., 87.

21. Niebuhr, *Nature and Destiny*, 2:66–7, argues Barth's inconsistency in his rejection of analogy.

22. Greggs, *Theology against Religion*, 2, 10.

religion in the service of an anti-religious theology."[23] If so, then Barth does not so much attack the religions per se as attempt to free Christianity from existing merely as a religion. Accordingly, Greggs argues that Barth's Christian *self*-critique of its own identity vis-à-vis religion does not negate the need for understanding and relating to the world's religions; rather, it provides a particular perspective for doing so faithfully.[24] This would mean that Barth's theology functions as a resource for rather than a rebuttal of Christian theology of religions. Yet, as is often the case with Barth, it may not be so simple.

Mueller criticized Barth's "refusal to admit that God's universal revelation of himself to all men in creation in human nature itself may issue in some true knowledge of God" and Barth's "refusal to allow for the possibility of saving knowledge of God in non-Christian religions is related to and consistent with this position."[25] He advances several specific criticisms of Barth's adamancy. First, his position appears to conflict with scriptural teaching on God's universal revelation. Also, he may have interpreted advocates of general revelation/natural theology unfairly. Most would no doubt argue that wherever divine revelation is encountered it is no less God's gracious initiative and agency. Finally, there appear to be suggestions in Barth's own (later) theology that are contrary to his (earlier) conclusion.

> Furthermore, if creation is already prepared for God's grace and if Christ as the eternal logos is already active in creation as the later Barth insists, then must not the possibility be left open that there may be some positive response by man to God's approach in creation? Does not Barth point in this direction in teaching that man always remains related to God even as sinner? Even if it is true that Barth's emphasis on man's sinful propensities negates the saving value of the light of God which shines everywhere in his creation, it appears that Barth's position is more restrictive than the Scriptures.[26]

Yet might Barth have opened a door (or cracked a window!) allowing room for more positive development in theology of religions? Mueller thinks so. Barth insisted that Jesus Christ is the True Witness and the Light of the World; he also affirmed "other lights" reflecting and attesting to the Jesus Christ as the "Light of Life."[27] Obviously, Barth's overall legacy on theology of religions is complex. At this point I am inclined to think that Barth does not back off on natural theology but develops a theology of nature allowing possible openings in his generally closed theology of religions.

---

23. Ibid., 11. See Barth, *CD* I/2, 346. Cf. Kendrik Kraemer, *Religion and the Christian Faith* (London: Lutterworth Press, 1956), 182–99.
24. Greggs, *Theology against Religion*, 173–5.
25. Mueller, *Karl Barth*, 150.
26. Ibid., 150.
27. Ibid., 136–7. Cf. Barth, *CD* IV/3-I, 1–165.

A Critic's Take on Barth

A critical assessment of Barth's theology of religions enables viewing significant contrasts. An honest opponent can identify one's strengths and weaknesses about as well as anyone. Here Barth's contemporary, and more often than not, his combatant, a great theologian in his own right, Paul Tillich, is helpful. To begin, Tillich respectfully notes Barth's wide range of thought, including not only in theology but in music and philosophy.[28] He suggests that behind Barth's quest are questions such as "What is Christianity?" and "Are we still Christians?"[29] Tillich admits that Barth criticizes his own theology for starting with man rather than God. He suggests Barth follows Kierkegaard's insistence that God comes to us from above or outside.[30] This explains Barth's categorical and caustic denial of Brunner's suggestion that there must be some "point of contact" between God and man. Tillich plainly says of Barth's denial, "I do not believe that this idea can be maintained" but admits that "negatively speaking," it has "great religious power."[31] He argues that Kierkegaard's own teaching contrasting "objective uncertainty" and "subjective certainty of the leap of faith" effectively demonstrates the opposite of Barth's claim.[32] Both objective truth and subjective faith are essentially involved.[33] According to Tillich, this tension arises out of the reality that "Jesus is both the teacher and the Savior who transforms" human beings.[34]

Further, Tillich expresses concern over Barth's setting of creation and revelation against each other. He is therefore delighted at signs in the later Barth of "a new attempt to overcome the danger of setting the God of creation against the God of revelation" which Tillich thinks has more in common with his own approach (certainly an overstatement).[35] He attributes much of Barth's problem with natural theology to a common but mistaken acceptance of Kant's criticism, on epistemological grounds, of natural reason and finite anthropology—noting that even Kant eventually acknowledges a sense of the reality of the transcendent and unconditional in human beings.[36] Tillich goes so far as to compare Barthian

---

28. Paul Tillich, *A History of Christian Thought: From Its Judaic and Hellenistic Origins to Existentialism*, ed. Carl E. Braaten (New York: Simon and Schuster, 1967, 1968), 298.

29. Ibid., 302, 316.

30. Niebuhr, *Nature and Destiny of Man*, 2:38, also suggests Barth follows Kierkegaard into extremes.

31. Tillich, *History of Christian Thought*, 469.

32. Ibid., 469–70, esp. 470. Tillich seems to be focusing on the early Barth (1922) of the Roemerbrief. As Barth himself later says in the 1950s ("A Thank You and a Bow"), it is important to go through Kierkegaard, but one must move along past him.

33. Ibid., 470.

34. Ibid., 469.

35. Ibid., n. 2, 327 (Editor's Note).

36. Ibid., 360–3. Tillich may be reaching a bit with this one.

opposition between divine revelation and natural law to the ancient heresy of Marcion in rejecting God the Creator in favor of God the savior.[37]

Paul Tillich strongly disagrees with Barth's denial that Christianity is a religion per se. He argues that it is consistent with Pauline theology to set Christ as the Absolute over against all religions, including Christianity, rather than attempting to equate Christianity itself as the Absolute because of its revealed nature. Tillich warns that failure to distinguish between Christ as Absolute from Christianity, which only has whatever absoluteness it has from Christ, can lead to idolatry.[38] Against Barth he argues that the category of "religion" is necessary to theological discourse but must be constantly critiqued—and conquered. Tillich opposes either describing Christianity as a religion which is highest or absolute because it is revealed (Schleiermacher and others) or describing all other religions as merely human attempts to know God with no revelation at all (Barthians).[39] Rather, Tillich strives to avoid the relativization of Christianity which comes with ascribing it to the category of religion. He prefers "putting the Christ against every religion, or God as manifesting his judgment in the cross against every religion, but not by elevating Christianity as a particular religion."[40]

In shorthand form, Paul Tillich sums up several of his key conclusions regarding Karl Barth.[41] He suggests that Barth rightly saw the dangerous idolatry behind political nationalism but did not see so clearly the danger of social isolationism.[42] For Barth, theology is about the ongoing crisis between the temporal and the eternal and arises out of the fundamental principle of the absoluteness of God.[43] Barth therefore depicts "religion" as the human opponent of God's revelation. However, Tillich criticizes Barth's wholly passive view of revelation and his entire rejection of natural revelation. Tillich says: "the idea which he attacked was that there was something in man as man which makes it possible for God to be recognized as God by man."[44]

---

37. Ibid., 34 and 44. This extreme statement says as much or more about Tillich's take as it does Barth's position. The tiny grain of concern, however, that it may rightly raise is the question, how far can one go in denying natural revelation until it begins to undermine a robust doctrine of creation?

38. Likely Barth would agree. He would not view religion as superficial to Christianity as a historical reality; Christianity transcends this only in its witness.

39. Ibid., 403–4. Barth did occasionally use the term "religious" positively. Note, for example, *CD* I/1, 109 and 212. However, here "religious" and "religion" are not synonyms.

40. Ibid., 404.

41. Ibid., 535–9.

42. Ibid., 535–6.

43. Ibid., 536–7. Of course, this may be a debatable statement.

44. Ibid., 537.

Tillich perceives several problems. For one, Barth claims the image of God in human being is totally destroyed.[45] For another, he is thus led to attack all forms of mysticism, to negate every point of contact between God and humans, "even the doctrine of the Spirit which might be dwelling in man."[46] For Tillich, Barth ultimately leaves "unanswered" how God can appear to human beings at all.[47] Although Barth's theology is called *dialectical*, Tillich describes it as *antithetical*, simply a deliberate polemic to liberalism and mysticism or any kind of supernatural or spiritual experience.[48] Two questions arise in my mind precisely at this point. First, to what extent does the Barth–Tillich disagreement reflect Calvinist–Arminian debates regarding soteriological initiative in the context of divine sovereignty and human liberty or soteriological universality?[49] Second, how are Pentecostals appreciative of Barth's theology able to handle Barth's apparent struggles with the Holy Spirit in terms of spiritual experience? Regrettably, on the first I do not have time to delve in but will merely recommend readers follow up with my work on the place of prevenient grace in Christian theology of religions.[50] The second, I will come back to below.

Most of Tillich's take on Barth is subject to debate, and yes, disagreement. Tillich obviously opposes Barth (and vice versa). However, opposition is not the same as misunderstanding.[51] One point that is clear whether reading Tillich or Torrance (for examples): Barth's theology of religions hinges on his doctrine of revelation which is entirely christological in orientation. However, as seen above, Tillich proposes that Barth later lightened up a bit. I agree. I further suggest that Barth's move toward openness, comparatively speaking, while finally faithful to his strict Christology, opens up pneumatological potential. That is where Pentecostal theology can come into play specifically. It is also where Tillich makes a startling contribution to Pentecostal theology. Tillich argues that pneumatology is the key to reconciling apparent contradictions inherent between Barth's theology "from above" or "from the outside," which is to say, starting with God, and Tillich's own

---

45. Niebuhr, *Nature and Destiny*, 1:158, n. 14, Barth's rejection of Augustine's theology of the image of God is inconsistent (cf., 1:269).

46. Tillich, *Christian Thought*, 537. On rare occasions Barth accepted the term "mysticism" according to his own qualifications.

47. Ibid., 538.

48. Ibid. Kärkkäinen, *Introduction*, 174. Barth was reacting to liberalism, which "blurred the boundary line between God and humanity, and made religion a matter of this world." See Karl Barth, "The Humanity of God," in *Karl Barth: Theologian of Freedom*, ed. Clifford Green (London: Collins, 1979), 48. Furthermore, the dialectical component of Barth's theology appears less evident after 1925.

49. Niebuhr, *Nature and Destiny*, 2:116–17, says as much.

50. Tony Richie, *Toward a Pentecostal Theology of Religions: Encountering Cornelius Today* (Cleveland: CPT, 2013), 39–46.

51. Ensminger, *Barth's Theology*, 42–3; a comparison of Barth and Tillich on theology of religions reveals their differing emphases more than anything else.

theology "from below" or starting with humans.[52] Again, I agree. More importantly, as I suggest below, Barth, at least to an extent, may have come to agree also.

Potential Import of Rhetoric and Redaction

Stephen Webb persuasively argues that Barth's early rhetorical style of writing theology, characterized by radical usage of metaphor, hyperbole, and irony, exists in discernible contrast with his later employment of rhetorical realism.[53] Webb argues that Barth's extreme response to Emil Brunner on natural/general revelation, which has direct implications for Christian theology of religions, is a classic example of hyperbolic polemic.[54] Close consideration of Barth's rhetorical style in writing theology calls for "retreat and reconstruction" through careful "re-reading" of Karl Barth's theological writings today.[55] Webb, even with his obvious concern to critique Barth's theology in furthering his own efforts at developing a hospitable philosophy of pluralism aside, rightly challenges us to take a careful and fresh look at Barth's views toward other religions.[56]

Accordingly, it is well worth asking, "What did Barth really mean to say?" But first a significant disclaimer: I am not arguing that Barth did not say what he meant or mean what he said.[57] Rather, it is worth noting that with his employment of varying forms of speech, coupled with a perpetual propensity to state his case in the strongest possible terms, we do well to bear in mind possibilities that overstatement occurs. My approach, while informed by this possibility, nevertheless focuses more on evidence suggesting that Barth's later writings intentionally open up space for broader considerations. It may well be that Barth finally felt ready to moderate (but not necessarily modify) his earlier comments after having made his critical point. Regardless of the method or motive in his mind there is clear indication that subsequent moderation did occur and ought to be considered.

Even very sympathetic readers of Barth appear to agree. For instance, T. F. Torrance suggests that couched in Barth's volatile rhetoric against Emil Brunner is

---

52. Tillich, *Christian Thought*, 316. Tillich insists Paul was foremost a theologian of the Spirit, 317.

53. Stephen H. Webb, *Re-Figuring Theology: The Rhetoric of Karl Barth* (Albany: State University of New York Press, 1991), 1–18.

54. Ibid., 112–14.

55. Ibid., 149–78.

56. Ibid., 174–8.

57. Green, *Karl Barth: Theologian of Freedom*, insists that "Some have misread Barth's christocentric doctrine of revelation as if he meant that nowhere else in all history and all the world was God revealed except in Jesus," adding, "Rather, it sets the terms by which we can recognize God's revelation in all times and places. The christological concentration is not an exclusiveness which shuts out those who have not encountered Jesus directly; it rather defines the nature of the universal *inclusiveness* of God's grace in Christ" (24).

frequently misunderstood humor. For example, Barth described their attempt at dialogue as analogous to an impossible conversation between an elephant and a whale.[58] A rigid reading misses Barth's implicit tone even if it gets his explicit point. And that makes a difference. One factor which makes the famous disagreement between Barth and Brunner so fascinating is that they were actually so much closer to each other in their theology than leading contemporaries.[59] That being said, it is essential to understand Barth's vehement reaction to Brunner's affirmative position on nature and grace in the context of the heat of Barth's intense battle against encroaching humanism and naturalism. Barth feared Brunner was undermining his side and lending support to his antagonists.[60] Accordingly, Torrance agrees that Barth reacted rightly but argues that when that battle was more or less behind him, and as he was able to more fully develop his Christology in the *CD*, he could—and did—take a more positive and reconciling tone.[61]

There are important implications for Barth's theology of religions. Preeminent is a moral obligation to understand, as well as possible, and to represent, as faithfully as possible, Barth's mature and most settled views. Proximate is the advantage of an opportunity provided to explore potential benefits of perceived "openings" in Barth's reputedly "closed" theology of religions. I approach that process from a Pentecostal perspective.

Constructive Pentecostal Appropriation of Barth's Theology of Religions

It is time to delve more deeply into a constructive appropriation of Barth's specific contribution to contemporary Christian theology of religions from a Pentecostal perspective. As has been often hinted previously in this chapter, pneumatology is of critical import for a Pentecostal perspective on Christian theology of religions.[62] Obviously, for Barth, theology's beginning point is crucial. His logic is clear and, at times, quite compelling. Theology is about God. Theology begins with God. Everyone and everything else is excluded. However, it is not quite that simple. What is the problem? Theology is not just about God; it is about God's relationship with God's creation and creatures. Here I draw on Pentecostal theologian Steve Land: "Theological science is basically a construal of the relationships between

---

58. Thomas F. Torrance, *Karl Barth: An Introduction to His Early Theology 1910-1931* (Edinburgh: T&T Clark, 1962, 2000), 24.

59. Ibid., 71.

60. Ibid., 137-8. Of course, Barth's primary concern at the time was Nazism.

61. Ibid., 144.

62. Although an oversimplification, my previous work in Christian theology of religions emphasizes pneumatological inclusivity in a context of christological exclusivity from an intentionally Pentecostal perspective. For example, see Richie, *Speaking by the Spirit*, and *Toward a Pentecostal Theology of Religions*. Readers can understand the following treatment of Barth accordingly.

God and the world. For Pentecostals, the starting point for such an undertaking is the Holy Spirit who is 'God with us.'"[63] True to form, Land sets the trinitarian context for a pneumatological starting point.[64]

Let's offer a few salient suggestions. First, the intrapersonal trinitarian nature of Christian theology means it is intrinsically *relational*. No relationship is ever adequately understood in isolation from any of the parties involved in the relationship. Accordingly, from its beginning and throughout its course, theology is essentially about both Creator and creation, about both God and humans. Second, Pentecostal theology starting with the Holy Spirit as "God with us" focuses on the intersection of God and humanity, where God and humans meet in *personal encounter*. Not only the beginning point but the destination and journey toward arrival must all be kept in mind throughout the theological task. Theology is like a large wall map at an interstate rest area or park trailhead (or shopping mall!). It displays an arrow pointing to "You are here" while the route and destination are all visible at a glance so theologians may plot their course constantly bearing in mind the whole trip. An integrative Christian theology of religions is simultaneously a theology "from above" and "from below," a theology "from within" and "from without." This is possible only by the *Holy Spirit* as the *God* who is *with us*. And the Holy Spirit does indeed open up slammed doors and closed windows letting fresh air and bright light into dark, stale rooms.[65] Tillich's tantalizing suggestion that pneumatology is the key to reconciling with Barth's theology of religions is right on target for Pentecostal theology.

Another Pentecostal theologian, Frank Macchia, explains that Pentecost signifies pneumatic diversity and variety finding completeness and consummation in the grace of God revealed in Jesus Christ.

> At Pentecost, the legitimate reaching for God implied in the various cultures and religious expressions finds fulfillment in the grace of God revealed in the crucified and risen Christ as the one who imparts the Spirit in the latter days. Their differences and past histories are not dissolved but affirmed and granted a new loyalty and new direction. In the process all idols are forsaken and the cultures are pruned. But the critical pruning is demanded of the church as well. Though the church is the central locus of the kingdom of God in the world, the

---

63. Steven Jack Land, *Pentecostal Spirituality: A Passion for the Kingdom* (Cleveland: CPT, 1993, 2010), 21. As Greggs, *Theology against Religion*, 33–4, notes, Barth describes the Holy Spirit as God who encounters humans in relationship without lessening his divinity.

64. See also Greggs, *Theology against Religion*, 187, Barthian emphasis on God the Holy Spirit coming to us from without, from beyond our selves, is consistent with a pneumatology affirming the Holy Spirit's presence beyond religion and religions. Empirical religions may be "places where the Holy Spirit is variously and multiply intensely present," ibid., 187. See Greggs, *Theology against Religion*, 185–6 on "multiple densities" of the Holy Spirit and 188–9 on "differentiated exclusivisms" in Barth.

65. Cf. Barth, *Evangelical Theology*, 56.

church is also a loving fellow traveler with the world's religions while pointing them to the superiority of Christ.[66]

Thus, Pentecostals have a viable pneumatological starting point with Pentecost as diversity grounded in Christ for guiding dynamics in developing our Christian theology of religions. But are these faithful to lessons learned from Barth regarding a theology of religions thoroughly Christian yet authentically open to religious others? Are we reasonably loyal to the premise and promise of Barth's theology in our appropriation of his work? I answer by returning to the topic of Barth and the Holy Spirit. I have called attention to Barth's ongoing struggles with the Holy Spirit in terms of spiritual experience. This has implications for Pentecostals' appropriation of Barth. Fortunately, Pentecostals are not left without recourse. Pentecostal theologian Terry Cross provides an assist.[67] In original translation and research Cross discovered that Barth's later work, after sustained interaction with Moravians, increasingly affirmed the experiential, subjective side of *Christus in nobis* (Christ in us) while solidly grounding it in the rational, objective side of *Christ extra nos* (Christ outside us). This delicately balanced dual emphasis allows positive space for pneumatological experience while avoiding excess. Furthermore, in conversation with Mennonites, Barth cautiously but graciously affirmed possibilities latent in the Pentecostal movement's theological attention to the Holy Spirit.[68]

Indeed, Pentecostal theologian Amos Yong takes a cue from Barth's understanding of Pentecost as an extending and transforming mystery with particularity and universality "somehow conjoined by the gift of the Spirit to all flesh."[69] Yong thinks that Barth's trinitarian framework as well as concern that pneumatology can degenerate into mere anthropology has hidden or obscured his implicit pneumatology.[70] Yet he is sure that a closer look at Barth's pneumatological

---

66. Frank D. Macchia, *Baptized in the Spirit: A Global Pentecostal Theology* (Grand Rapids: Zondervan, 2006), 188.

67. Originally presented at the English-German Colloquium in New Testament/Das English-Deutsche Kolloquium für Neues Testament, Tübingen Universität, as, "*CHRISTUS PRAESENS* or *CHRISTUS OTIOSUS*? The Role of *extra nos* and *in nobis* in Relation to the *unio cum Christo* in the Theology of John Calvin, Wilhelm Herrmann, and Karl Barth," June 2, 2008. I am grateful to Terry for a copy of the original manuscript, since published as Terry L. Cross, "Christ in Us: The Hope of Glory or the 'Sentimentality of a Bohemian Private Enterprise'? Barth, Pietists, and Pentecostals," ch. 4, *Karl Barth and the Future of Evangelical Theology*, ed. Christian T. Collins Winn and John L. Drury (Eugene: Cascade, 2014).

68. Greggs, *Theology against Religion*, 32-3, notes Barth's pneumatological positioning of religion and, further, his acknowledgment of the Holy Spirit's role in revelation. See also ibid., 177.

69. Amos Yong, *The Future of Evangelical Theology: Soundings from the Asian American Diaspora* (Downers Grove: IVP Academic, 2014), 141-2.

70. Ibid., 142.

theology of humanity results in serious reconsideration of his theology of religions amid contemporary realities of religious pluralism.[71] If so, pneumatology is critical to constructive development of Barth's theology of religions.

Yes, it is feasible that pneumatological investigations into Christian theology of religions from a Pentecostal perspective find Barth's theology a faithful and valuable resource. I further posit Barth's theology for cultivating a circumspect and authentic openness which is faithfully christocentric, pneumatologically shaped and empowered, and appropriately cognizant of and engaged with the realities of religious pluralism.

More specifically, what are a few possibilities involved in a Pentecostal appropriation of Barth's theology of religions with integration of the Pentecostal pneumatological tradition? While nothing near exhaustive, I offer four brief suggestions calling for further development:

- unapologetically Christian theology of religions which staunchly maintains the centrality, exclusivity, and necessity of Jesus Christ;
- pneumatologically enhanced and empowered Christian theology of religions exploring the rich and far-reaching possibilities of the Holy Spirit's presence and power both in the church and in the world;
- prudent theology of ecclesial mission which engages in Christian evangelism and witness in religiously plural settings in a more informed and better equipped manner; and,
- holistic theology of religions which is for the sake of the witness of Christian presence and influence for the common good characterized by authentic openness to dialogue and cooperation with religious others.

I conclude this short study of Barth's theology of religions in conversation with Pentecostal theology in substantial agreement with Greggs regarding two overarching attitudes: "appropriate mystery" and "appropriate hoping."[72] It would be going too far to insist that Barth was really wide open to world religions all along. It is fitting and suitable to propose that although Barth's early work does "slam the door" on a theology of religions which is open to positive consideration of and constructive interaction with the world's religions he eventually comes back to "crack a window." That Barth's later openness was not necessarily an outright retraction or reversal of earlier views but was more likely already present in embryonic form awaiting development at an opportune time testifies to the complexity and subtlety of this great thinker. That Pentecostal theology can constructively appropriate it testifies to the breadth and depth of the richness of its pneumatology. Late in life Barth wrote,

---

71. Ibid., 143. Pentecostals can contribute to debates about Barth as always christocentric and yet pneumato-centric or with pervasive pneumatological sensibilities, ibid., n. 40 and n. 41.

72. Greggs, *Theology against Religion*, 218 and 221.

> The first and most basic act of theological work is *prayer*. . . . But theological work does not merely begin with prayer and is not merely accompanied by it; in its totality it is peculiar and characteristic of theology that it can be performed only in the act of prayer.[73]

Accordingly, this chapter is offered in that same spirit of prayer.

---

73. Barth, *Evangelical Theology*, 160.

Chapter 12

BARTH, PENTECOSTALISM, AND THE ESCHATOLOGICAL CRY FOR THE KINGDOM

Christian T. Collins Winn

Introduction

In a recent essay on Karl Barth's relationship to Pietism, Eberhard Busch describes Barth as an "inconvenient friend" of Pietism. He notes that Barth "was *inconvenient*, because he put some serious questions to this movement, the aim of which was theological self-correction. But because he asked them in a kind and helpful way, Barth's theology is especially suitable for dialogue with Pietists."[1] I would argue that the dynamic between Barth and Pentecostalism, though somewhat different, is nevertheless profoundly similar.

The dynamic is different in that Barth never engaged in direct dialogue with Pentecostalism. There is, of course, the tantalizing meeting and exchange of letters between Barth and the Pentecostal ecumenist David du Plessis.[2] But this encounter does not rise to the level of engagement that Barth gave to Pietist texts and themes, nor can one claim any kind of substantial theological influence on Barth, as one can in regard to the Pietism of Württemberg.[3]

Nevertheless, and in spite of the relative lack of direct contact, it is indeed possible to describe Barth as "critical friend or friendly critic"[4] to Pentecostalism, and vice versa, to describe Pentecostalism as a "critical friend or friendly critic" of

---

1. Eberhard Busch, "Karl Barth and Pietism," in *Karl Barth and the Future of Evangelical Theology*, ed. Christian T. Collins Winn and John L. Drury (Eugene: Cascade, 2014), 20.

2. See Karl Barth, *Gesprache, 1964–1968*, ed. Eberhard Busch (Zürich: TVZ, 1997), 430–2. For a brief discussion of this, see Frank D. Macchia, "Karl Barth Meets David Du Plessis: A New Pentecost or a Theatre of the Absurd?" *Pneuma: The Journal of the Society for Pentecostal Studies* 23, no. 1 (Spring 2001): 5–8.

3. The most exhaustive treatment of Barth's engagement with Pietism can be found in Eberhard Busch's *Karl Barth and the Pietists: The Young Karl Barth's Critique of Pietism and Its Response*, trans. Daniel W. Bloesch (Downers Grove: InterVarsity, 2004). This includes a helpful epilogue which brings the conversation forward into Barth's later theology.

4. Busch, *Karl Barth and the Pietists*, 286.

Barth. One area where such a critical but friendly relationship might be discerned is in a mutually shared emphasis on the eschatological nature of Christian existence, with a focus on the coming of the kingdom of God. My chapter explores this relationship through a comparative analysis of their different theologies of prayer. I begin first with a brief discussion of why I believe that eschatology is an especially fruitful place to bring Barth and Pentecostal theology together. I then turn to Barth's exposition of the second petition of the Lord's Prayer, "Thy Kingdom Come!" followed by a discussion of the work of Frank Macchia and his articulation of the theological meaning of Spirit baptism and speaking in tongues. I conclude with a brief outline of some of the similarities and differences between Barth and Pentecostal theology, pointing briefly to at least one place where Barth and Pentecostal conceptions could be thought together to mutual benefit. It is hoped that this comparison will prove mutually beneficial, producing useful questions for both Barthian and Pentecostal theologians, and furthermore, may also prove valuable among those concerned with understanding and further developing the respective theological visions of Barth and Pentecostalism.

Barth, Pentecostalism, and Eschatology

Before turning to discuss their respective eschatological visions of prayer, I want to offer an argument for my focus on eschatology. Why eschatology? There are at least three reasons.

First, both Pentecostal theology and Barth seek to highlight the eschatological nature of Christian existence. As Steven J. Land has argued, "Pentecostalism lived and lives in an apocalyptic existence made existentially palpable by the presence, manifestations and power of the Holy Spirit. This longing for the Lord to come, for the Holy Spirit and for the kingdom of God are part of the same thing: it is one passion."[5] In fact, for some time, Pentecostal scholars and theologians have been arguing that early Pentecostalism understood itself as an eschatologically constituted event, which means that eschatological themes and categories have primacy of place in the Pentecostal theological imagination. William Faupel called attention to this in his seminal study *The Everlasting Gospel: The Significance of Eschatology in the Development of Pentecostal Thought*, noting that "The second coming of Jesus was the central concern of the initial Pentecostal message."[6] Following in the wake of Walter Hollenweger, Robert Anderson, and Donald Dayton, among others,[7] Faupel demonstrated that the Pentecostal message was holistic and diverse, developing under the aegis of four key motifs:

---

5. Steven J. Land, *Pentecostal Spirituality: A Passion for the Kingdom* (Cleveland: CPT Press, 1993), 58.

6. William Faupel, *The Everlasting Gospel: The Significance of Eschatology in the Development of Pentecostal Thought* (Sheffield: Sheffield Academic Press, 1996), 20.

7. Walter Hollenweger, *The Pentecostals: The Charismatic Movements in the Churches* (Minneapolis: Augsburg, 1972); Robert Anderson, *Vision of the Disinherited: The Making*

1) the full gospel, which referred to the restoration of the whole vision of salvation seen in the Bible. Expressed christocentrically, Jesus was to be proclaimed as savior, sanctifier, healer, baptizer with the Spirit, and soon coming king;
2) the Latter Rain, based loosely on the weather pattern in Palestine/Israel, in which two separate rains came to water the earth so that crops might grow (e.g., Deut. 11:10-15). This motif referred especially to the movement's theology of history. History, according to the movement, was structured along the lines of a threefold trinitarian dispensation, and within each dispensation, God sent a former and a "latter rain" which together inaugurated and brought to completion the eschatological will of God. The reappearance of Pentecost-like phenomena signified that God had in fact begun to pour out the latter rain of the era of the Spirit, a portent that the end of the ages was near;
3) the apostolic faith, which referred to the restorationist impulse within the movement; and
4) the Day of Pentecost, which emphasized that the larger cosmic drama occurring in God's Latter Rain outpouring of the Spirit, to restore the church, who would then preach the full gospel, was to be experienced in the personal lives of believers.

Though further discussion among Pentecostal theologians has occurred since Faupel's 1996 monograph, this has not resulted in the decentering of eschatology; rather it has led to an even broader consensus that eschatological categories are central to Pentecostal theology, spirituality, and identity. After all, as Frank Macchia notes, "If the Spirit is anything in the Bible, it is an eschatological gift."[8]

Conversely, it is a well-worn adage that Karl Barth was one of the early leading voices in modern theology arguing for the eschatological nature of Christian thought and life. Under the influence of Franz Overbeck,[9] Johannes Weiss, and especially Johann Christoph and Christoph Friedrich Blumhardt,[10] Barth preached from the rooftops, "If Christianity be not altogether thoroughgoing eschatology, there remains in it no relationship whatever with Christ."[11] Barth's

---

of American Pentecostalism (Peabody: Hendrickson, 1979); Donald Dayton, *Theological Roots of Pentecostalism* (Metuchen: Scarecrow, 1987); Gerald Sheppard, "Pentecostals and the Hermeneutics of Dispensationalism: The Anatomy of an Uneasy Relationship," *Pneuma: The Journal of the Society of Pentecostal Studies* 6, no. 2 (Fall 1994): 5–33; and Land, *Pentecostal Spirituality*.

8. Frank D. Macchia, *Baptized in the Spirit: A Global Pentecostal Theology* (Grand Rapids: Zondervan, 2006), 48.

9. Eberhard Jüngel, *Karl Barth: A Theological Legacy*, trans. Garrett E. Paul (Philadelphia: Westminster, 1986), 53–70.

10. Christian T. Collins Winn, *"Jesus is Victor!" The Significance of the Blumhardts for the Theology of Karl Barth* (Eugene: Pickwick, 2009).

11. Karl Barth, *The Epistle to the Romans*, 6th ed., trans. Edwyn C. Hoskyns (Oxford: Oxford University Press, 1968), 314.

thought developed in rather significant ways over the course of his career, and for some, his earlier eschatological emphasis became more and more muted as the *Church Dogmatics* lengthened.[12] But this verdict cannot be sustained in the light of the intense reemergence of eschatological categories in the late volumes of the *CD*.[13] In his posthumously published lectures on the Christian life, Barth went so far as to argue that Christian existence was marked by an eschatological passion, "a great, unconquerable, permanent, and even dangerous passion."[14] Bringing Barth and Pentecostalism into dialogue through the lens of eschatology, then, provides further food for thought regarding the eschatological potential of Barth's thought, and it may also provide a moment to reflect on whether and to what extent Pentecostal eschatology itself might contribute to the further filling out of the deep intentions of Barth's eschatological vision.

The second reason to bring Barth and Pentecostalism into dialogue around eschatological issues and themes is rooted in the scholarly argument developing among Pentecostals over the past thirty years. As already mentioned, Pentecostal scholars have reached something of a consensus on the centrality of eschatology for Pentecostal theology, spirituality, and identity. By 2012, Larry McQueen had identified no less than forty-eight different interpretations produced since the 1970s that dealt substantially with eschatological issues within Pentecostal theology, history, or biblical interpretation.[15] A driving concern occupying many of these interpreters from across the various wings of Pentecostalism—whether Wesleyan, Reformed, or Oneness—has been to revitalize the prophetic and transformative dimensions of Pentecostal eschatology, primarily by calling into

---

12. This is Jürgen Moltmann's verdict. See his *The Coming of God: Christian Eschatology* (Minneapolis: Fortress, 1996), 18.

13. I concur with the editors of the posthumously published lectures on the Christian life, who note that those concluding lectures to Barth's *Church Dogmatics* "bring out more sharply the eschatological orientation of the doctrine of reconciliation than do the corresponding discussions in IV.3. The commonly expressed view that there can be no eschatology proper in the course of the *CD* is thus shown to be even more unfounded than it previously was" (Hans-Anton Drewes and Eberhard Jüngel, "Preface," in Karl Barth, *The Christian Life:* Church Dogmatics IV,4 Lecture Fragments [Grand Rapids: Eerdmans, 1981], xii).

See also Robert Jenson, *God after God: The God of the Past and the God of the Future, Seen in the Work of Karl Barth* (New York: The Bobbs-Merrill Company, Inc., 1969); Timothy Gorringe, *Karl Barth Against Hegemony* (Oxford: Oxford University Press, 1999); Gorringe, "Eschatology and Political Radicalism: The Example of Karl Barth and Jürgen Moltmann," in *God Will Be All in All: The Eschatology of Jürgen Moltmann*, ed. Richard Bauckham (Edinburgh: T&T Clark, 1999), 87–114; and John C. McDowell, *Hope in Barth's Eschatology: Interrogations and Transformations Beyond Tragedy* (Burlington: Ashgate Publishing, Ltd., 2000).

14. Barth, *The Christian Life*, 111.

15. See Larry R. McQueen, *Toward a Pentecostal Eschatology: Discerning the Way Forward* (Dorset: Deo Publishing, 2012), 5–56.

question the prominent role of premillennial dispensationalism in Pentecostal theological circles, since the 1930s.[16]

By premillennial dispensationalism I am referring to the eschatological system of thought developed by John Nelson Darby (1800–1882), which was widely disseminated in the C. I. Scofield Study Bible, and was further popularized through different authors, the most recent of which was the *Left Behind* series by Tim LaHaye and Jerry Jenkins. A species of millennialism, or belief in the thousand-year reign of Christ on earth, classical dispensational premillennialism,[17] operated with a literalistic reading of the Bible—especially John's Apocalypse—positing that history and society were supposed to devolve into a kind of living hell on earth or tribulation period, before Christ returned to establish his kingdom. Discerning the "signs of the times" was essential to this mode of thought so that one could prepare for the impending doom. The hope of the faithful was to be taken away in a secret rapture, which would spare them from the dehumanizing violence and persecution that would attend the rise of the Anti-Christ.[18]

Though admitting that early Pentecostal eschatology certainly bore a kind of "family resemblance" to dispensational forms of thought because the return of Pentecost-like phenomena was understood as a sign of the "end of the ages,"[19] many of the more recent interpreters argue that dispensational premillennialism is fundamentally incompatible with Pentecostal theology and spirituality, especially as dispensationalism makes the kingdom irrelevant to the present age. They opt instead for a "proleptic eschatology" where the kingdom of God is understood "to have been inaugurated in the resurrection of the crucified Christ, universalized in the event of Pentecost, but awaits its final consummation in the future parousia."[20] Revision in this direction is thought to offer "a more biblical and theologically credible view of Pentecostal eschatology. Spirit baptism, healing and sanctification are seen as already present in Christ and the Pentecost event but anticipations of the new creation that are not yet complete."[21] Without getting bogged down in the details, what is relevant for this discussion is that the revisionist eschatological vision, which has produced several important monographs and essays,[22] can be

---

16. See Sheppard, "Pentecostals and the Hermeneutics of Dispensationalism."

17. I am talking here about classical premillennial dispensationalism, realizing that dispensationalism has undergone some revision in recent decades.

18. Clarence B. Bass, *Backgrounds to Dispensationalism: Its Historical Genesis and Ecclesiastical Implications* (Eugene: Wipf & Stock, 1960).

19. Peter Althouse, "'Left Behind'—Fact or Fiction: Ecumenical Dilemmas of the Fundamentalist Millenarian Tensions within Pentecostalism," *Journal of Pentecostal Theology* 13, no. (2005): 187–207.

20. Ibid., 201.

21. Ibid., 202.

22. For the most important, see Land, *Pentecostal Spirituality*; Peter Althouse, *Spirit of the Last Days: Pentecostal Eschatology in Conversation with Jürgen Moltmann* (London: T&T Clark, 2003); Matthew K. Thompson, *Kingdom Come: Revisioning Pentecostal Eschatology*

more readily engaged in a constructive fashion from Barth's perspective than can dispensational premillennialism.

This leads us to my final point, which is the fact that Barth has already played an important role in the revisionist project. Though Jürgen Moltmann, John Wesley, and John Fletcher may be said to have played a more significant role, Barth has not been absent from the discussion thus far, as is especially evident in figures like Peter Althouse and Frank Macchia. Thus, the critical comparative dialogue that I am about to engage in occurs within an ongoing conversation between Barth and Pentecostals on eschatology and the kingdom of God.[23]

"Thy Kingdom Come!"—Barth on the Cry for the Kingdom

In the posthumously published lecture fragment, *The Christian Life*, Barth's discussion of the Lord's Prayer occurs under the heading of the "The Command of God the Reconciler." Already in the second edition of his groundbreaking Romans commentary, Barth had linked together prayer, ethics, and eschatology.[24] However, in that early commentary, Barth conceived of prayer as a subsidiary of repentance,[25] while in the late lectures, invocation takes center stage as the principal lens through which ethics and the Christian life are to be understood. To the question, "What shall we do?" the answer is given, "You should pray: 'Our

(Dorset: Deo, 2010); Peter Althouse and Robby Waddell, eds., *Perspectives in Pentecostal Eschatologies: World Without End* (Eugene: Pickwick, 2010); and McQueen, *Toward a Pentecostal Eschatology.*

23. Though beyond the purview of the chapter, it is worth drawing attention to the fact that the ongoing conversation has actually been a three-way discussion, since Barth has often been engaged by Pentecostals through the bridge figures of Johann Christoph and Christoph Friedrich Blumhardt. These two Lutheran Pietist pastors, who also bore certain proto-Pentecostal characteristics, were one of the most important influences on Barth's eschatology, and especially on his understanding of the kingdom of God, and their work has produced significant fruit when mined by Pentecostal theologians.

See, for example, Frank D. Macchia, *Spirituality and Social Liberation: The Message of the Blumhardts in the Light of Wuerttemberg Pietism* (Metuchen: Scarecrow Press, 1993); Frank D. Macchia, "Jesus is Victor: The Eschatology of the Blumhardts with Implications for Pentecostal Eschatologies," in *Perspectives in Pentecostal Eschatologies: World Without End*, ed. Peter Althouse and Robby Waddell (Eugene: Pickwick, 2010), 375–400; and Peter Althouse, "Eschatology from Basel to Azusa Street: The Voices of Karl Barth and Pentecostalism in Dialogue," in *Karl Barth and the Future of Evangelical Theology*, ed. Christian T. Collins Winn and John L. Drury (Eugene: Cascade, 2014), 254–80.

24. See Barth, *The Epistle to the Romans*, 430, 458.

25. Ibid., 436.

Father, who art . . ."²⁶ The ethical life, and therefore the Christian life, is a response to the divine command, the Word of God,²⁷ and the specific command to which the Christian life is a response is the injunction for humanity to call upon the Lord (Ps. 50:15). Thus, invocation becomes "the basic meaning of all human obedience. What God permits man, what he expects, wills, and requires of him, is a life of calling upon him. This life of calling upon God will be a person's Christian life: his life in freedom, conversion, faith, gratitude, and faithfulness."²⁸ Invocation, here, is not a static concept, nor the work of automatons. Rather, it is "event, history, and action"²⁹ presupposing a real, genuine, and free intercourse between God and humanity, wherein humanity, baptized by the Spirit again and again, is moved to call upon and long ever more ardently for God's appearing, and conversely, where God hears and is moved by humanity.

The "impossible possibility"³⁰ by which the human person may turn from disobedience to obedience, from faithlessness to faithfulness—in short, may actually become an interlocutor with God—is Jesus of Nazareth, the one true faithful- covenant partner: "Jesus Christ, His history, became and is the foundation of Christian existence; this and this alone."³¹ According to Barth, in God's own free and faithful determination it has become not merely possible, but actual that humanity has become a faithful friend to God.³² Jesus' faithfulness unto death³³ is the event wherein human unfaithfulness has been judged and set aside and a new history of divine–human friendship has commenced. Correspondingly, this reality and event—though occurring *extra nos* and *pro nobis* in all of its singularity and actuality—nevertheless, also occurs *in nobis*.³⁴

---

26. This formulation is adapted from Eberhard Jüngel. See his "Invocation of God as the Ethical Ground of Christian Action," in Eberhard Jüngel, *Theological Essays*, trans. and ed. by John Webster (Edinburgh: T&T Clark, 1989), 165. I am grateful to Ry O. Siggelkow for calling my attention to this reference.

27. See Barth, *The Christian Life*, 3.

28. Ibid., 44.

29. Ibid., 85.

30. "Impossible possibility" was a favored formulation of Barth's, bringing together the twin truths that human beings are incapable of reaching, prayer, or even being faithful to God, and yet God makes them capable of doing precisely that. See, for instance, "This possession of grace occurs as the impossible possibility of God which is beyond every possibility of our own: it is the freedom which God takes to Himself in us. HE takes it, and He takes it IN us" (*Romans*, 216).

31. Barth, *The Christian Life*, 14.

32. Ibid., 13, 20-1.

33. This faithfulness is both a divine and human form of faithfulness. For an account of the divine–human *concursus* enacted in the election of Jesus Christ that intersects with elements of Barth's understanding of prayer, see Paul Dafydd Jones, "Karl Barth on Gethsemane," *International Journal of Systematic Theology* 9, no. 2 (April 2007): 148-71.

34. Barth, *The Christian Life*, 20-3.

12. Barth, Pentecostalism, and the Eschatological Cry for the Kingdom 183

Attending to the eschatological character of the messianic history signified by the name of Jesus Christ, Barth avers that the life history of Jesus "was and is already the end of all God's ways, the eschaton."[35] "Jesus himself . . . at that time was in his history, on the path that he trod to the end in his time, the imminent kingdom of God."[36] With the appearance of the One Who Comes, the true telos of all things has appeared in the midst of history; the kingdom of God has come.

This gospel of God's reign presses to be heard, for "Jesus Christ is not without His own."[37] Therefore, of necessity it moves outward toward the whole cosmos; humanity is not excluded, but rather included as a free and full partner in the history of the *totus Christus*.[38] Without emptying out the eschatological meaning and character of the life history of Jesus, Barth speaks of the ongoing transition from the *there* and *then* event to our *here* and *now* existence under the concept of a threefold *parousia*.[39]

Jesus, the One Who Comes Forth, now comes again in a threefold form, making himself effectively present both prospectively and retrospectively to all of human history. The Coming One has come forth from the grave, is poured forth in the Pentecostal Spirit, and comes to meet us from his own good future. Thus, it is by his resurrection, the outpouring of the Spirit, and the final consummation (i.e., the threefold *parousia*)—constituted as a threefold perichoretically unified movement of the Living One—that Jesus Christ moves out into the world and its history, and toward God's future and the world's true end.[40] In view of our own concern, all of this clearly places life in the interim, between the first and second coming, in a profoundly eschatological context.

The resurrection for Barth functions as an initial manifestation and announcement that in Jesus, God has triumphed over the powers and principalities. Addressing all of humanity, it announces that the history of Jesus is not only universal history, but universally effective history, because it is present to all ages. The second form of the effective presence of Jesus Christ, and the de facto basis of the Christian life as lived here and now, is the baptism of the Holy Spirit. It is in and by the Spirit that specific human beings are moved from being de jure those addressed by God, to those who are such de facto. Thus, the history of invocation into which the Christian is summoned begins with and is uncontrollably carried along by the baptism with the Spirit. Barth conceives this as a divine actuality and intervention, wherein in the midst of a particular human history, marked by

---

35. Ibid., 163.
36. Ibid., 252. Barth makes it quite clear that his conception of Jesus as kingdom is a synthetic re-presentation of the central affirmation of the Blumhardts. See ibid., 256–60.
37. Karl Barth, *CD* IV/3.1, 278.
38. Ibid., 215–16.
39. Ibid., 295–6. The concept of the threefold *parousia* is one that can also be found in fragmentary form in the elder Blumhardt. See Collins Winn, "*Jesus is Victor!*", 99–101, 252–8, 276–7.
40. Ibid., 292–6.

disobedience and faithlessness, an incomprehensibly new history begins.[41] Barth rejects that the event to which baptism points is a kind of infusion of supernatural powers. Nor is it simply the realizing of inherent natural powers.[42] Rather, he is concerned to emphasize that the awakening that occurs within the Christian is a radical alteration which occurs in the midst of the old, but is also a radical alteration which really includes the Christian as an active agent.[43]

The human being is awakened to a new reality and invited into a new history of divine–human commerce, "a concrete and dynamic" relation.[44] Baptism by the Spirit does not establish a static relation between God and the faithful, but a dynamic relation that must be actualized again and again, forming a kind of life history lived in the here and now.[45] The new dynamic relation can be described as an eschatologically inflected history of invocation, conceived as both a downward movement in the interruptive form of baptism with the Spirit and an upward and outward movement of revolt in the cry for the kingdom. Barth argues that the basic form of the "whole of the Christian life"[46] is found in the second petition of the Lord's Prayer, "Thy kingdom come!", which should also be understood as another form of the cry for the Spirit to be given afresh.[47]

The Christian life as a history of invocation, or the cry for the kingdom, envisions a communal and active relation of participatory correspondence that elicits Christian action in the form of kingdom-like parables, set within an eschatologically charged horizon of waiting and hastening. Christian prayer, as the basic form of the Christian life, is a participation in the prayer of Jesus. "The first and proper suppliant is none other than Jesus Christ Himself."[48] And so, "When we pray, we can only return to that prayer which was uttered in the person of Jesus Christ."[49] To be clear, the prayer offered by Jesus is inclusive not only of his actual

---

41. "The Christian life begins with a change which cannot be understood or described radically enough, which God has the possibility of effecting in a man's life in a way which is decisive and basic for his whole being and action and which He has in fact accomplished in the life of the man who becomes a Christian" (Barth, *CD* IV/4, 9).

42. Ibid., 5.

43. That this radical alteration occurs in the heart, and therefore can really be experienced, see Terry L. Cross, "Christ in Us: The Hope of Glory or the Sentimentality of a 'Bohemian Private Enterprise'? Barth, Pietists, and Pentecostals," in *Karl Barth and the Future of Evangelical Theology*, ed. Christian T. Collins Winn and John L. Drury (Eugene: Cascade, 2014), 69–90.

44. Ibid., 23.

45. Ibid.

46. Ibid., 76.

47. Ibid., 77–8. See also Ashley Cocksworth, *Karl Barth on Prayer* (London: Bloomsbury T&T Clark, 2015), 101.

48. Barth, *CD* III/3, 274.

49. Karl Barth, *Prayer, 50th Anniversary Edition*, trans. Sara Terrien (Louisville: Westminster John Knox, 2002), 14.

prayers, but refers to his whole life, for "in *all His actions* as a man He is *only and altogether* a Suppliant."⁵⁰ As insightfully argued by Paul Jones, Jesus' humanity is itself an actualistically conceived history of correspondence to God. That is, in his life history, Jesus actualizes his humanity by choosing, again and again, to be the human being whom God calls him to be.⁵¹ It is into *this* relation, between the divine and human as concretely actualized in Jesus Christ, that Christians are invited by the baptism of the Spirit and the corresponding history of invocation.

Because he lives, *we* too will live—because he prays, *we* too will pray. To be baptized into the history of invocation is also to find oneself in communion with others, indeed with the whole of humanity. Barth makes much of the "our," "us," and, "we," which recur throughout the Lord's Prayer as indicative of the communal dimension of the Christian life.⁵² But our solidarity does not stop at the edges of the Christian world, rather it moves out into the world, such that we pray the Lord's Prayer—and live the life demanded by it—alongside, with, and for those who cannot or will not pray it themselves.⁵³

The prayer of Jesus was also life and action, in fact a history of action. Our participatory correspondence with the prayer of Jesus, therefore, necessarily involves action: human action in correspondence with human prayer, and human action in correspondence with divine action.⁵⁴ Human action in light of Christian prayer, especially the second petition, is described by Barth as a revolt against the lordless powers, which Barth is careful to make clear are those forces—whether structural, ideological, or practical—which fundamentally dehumanize and curtail human flourishing.⁵⁵ Our active revolt is in the form of "kingdom-like" parables, which include both a real longing for and a heartfelt utterance of the second petition for the coming of the kingdom, and real vital work and action for human righteousness.

Barth argues that such action for human righteousness "must in all circumstances take place with a view to people, in address to people, and with the aim of helping people."⁵⁶ What is envisioned here is something like improvisational parables that find their touchstone in Jesus, "the partisan of the poor."⁵⁷ According to Barth, Jesus possessed a "pronouncedly revolutionary" stance vis-à-vis the world around him.⁵⁸ Christians are called into this same posture. But such a revolutionary posture cannot be confused with the mere overthrow of existing

---

50. Barth, *CD* III/3, 275. Emphasis mine.
51. Paul Daffyd Jones, *The Humanity of Christ: Christology in Karl Barth's Church Dogmatics* (London: T&T Clark, 2008), 150–69.
52. Barth, *The Christian Life*, 82–5.
53. Barth, *Prayer*, 23.
54. Cocksworth, *Karl Barth on Prayer*, 113–15.
55. Barth, *The Christian Life*, 174.
56. Ibid., 266.
57. Barth, *CD* IV/2, 180.
58. Ibid., 171.

structures for other humanly contrived structures. In the context of the Lord's Prayer, revolt is first and foremost the hope for the definitive overthrow of the godless dehumanizing powers and principalities that structure our lives; thus, it is hope for the final appearing of the kingdom, an action which only God can bring about.[59] Nevertheless, it also includes a refusal in the here and now to live with the dehumanizing structures of the world, as well as willingness to imagine alternative possibilities. Thus, the prayer for the kingdom includes a movement in which Christians "go to meet the coming kingdom of God, by seeing and grasping the possibilities which are provisionally present or which offer themselves not for divine but for human righteousness and order"[60] for "the heart of the Christian ethos is that those who are freed and summoned to pray 'Thy kingdom come' are also freed and summoned to use their freedom to obey the command that is given therewith and to live for their part with a view to the coming kingdom."[61] As such, "The very act of prayer is a reorientation of human agency towards attention, fellowship and hospitality, towards welcoming strangers, the hungry, the needy, and the thirsty."[62]

In view of the difference between the ultimate and penultimate forms of the kingdom, and the responsibility placed upon Christians to hope in the former and to enact parabolic forms of the latter, the Christian life is placed in a productive tension of waiting and hastening. As Barth puts it,

> they *wait* and *hasten* toward the dawn of God's day, the appearing of his righteousness, the parousia of Jesus Christ (2 Pet. 3:12). They not only wait but also hasten. They wait by hastening. Their waiting takes place in hastening. Aiming at God's kingdom, established on its coming and not on the status quo, they do not just look toward it but run toward it as fast as their feet will carry them.[63]

Only God can bring the kingdom, and thus we wait; but in the light of its sure coming, and in correspondence with our knowledge of its basic christological outline and our firm conviction that it shall come, we hasten toward the kingdom through righteous action.

One final element needs to be mentioned here regarding the role of human longing in the coming of God's kingdom. Barth, from early on, was radically committed to removing the kingdom of God from human hands. Thus, even our penultimate actions cannot, from Barth's perspective, be fused with the coming of the kingdom.

---

59. Barth, *The Christian Life*, 262.
60. Ibid., 213.
61. Ibid., 262–3.
62. Cocksworth, *Karl Barth on Prayer*, 152.
63. Barth, *The Christian Life*, 263. Here again, with the theme of "waiting and hastening" one can see the Blumhardtian influence on Barth. See Collins Winn, *"Jesus is Victor!"*, 49–50, 272–3.

Those who know the reality of the kingdom, Christians, can never have anything to do with the arrogant and foolhardy enterprise of trying to bring in and build up by human hands a religious, cultic, moral, or political kingdom of God on earth. God's righteousness is the affair of God's own act, which has already been accomplished and is still awaited.[64]

Though a strict demarcation is placed here, such that no human action can be directly identified with the coming kingdom, God nevertheless does enfold our waiting and hastening into the drama of the kingdom. Waiting and hastening toward the kingdom does not function as a kind of lever that brings the kingdom, but as a contingent, though nevertheless, indispensable witness to the coming of the kingdom and to the penultimate irruptions of the kingdom which occur in the midst of history.[65]

For Barth, the cry for the kingdom finds its root in the life history of Jesus of Nazareth, who was himself the kingdom come in the midst of history. This history has been poured out, as it were, in the baptism with the Spirit, an action which disrupts human unfaithfulness, liberating the community of faith and individuals therein to not only have a share in the faithfulness of Jesus, but themselves to become faithful by joining a movement of waiting and hastening toward the kingdom of God, a history of invocation that is constituted as both prayer and action. The Christian life is an act of invocation, calling ever anew for the gift of the Spirit and the coming of the kingdom in an eschatological tension of waiting and hastening toward the One Who Comes.

"Sighs too deep for words"—Pentecostal Tongues and the Coming of the Kingdom

I now turn to offer a brief sketch of the theology of tongues developed recently by Frank Macchia. Over the better part of a decade, Macchia developed the most comprehensive and ecumenically engaged theology of tongues within North American Pentecostal theology.[66] Macchia's work is especially amenable for a

---

64. Ibid., 264.

65. Barth, *CD* IV/3.2, 596–602 and *CD* IV/3.1, 331–2.

66. The most relevant publications are his seminal essay, "Sighs too Deep for Words: Toward a Theology of Glossolalia," *Journal of Pentecostal Theology* 1 (1992): 47–73. This was followed by "Tongues as a Sign: Towards a Sacramental Understanding of Pentecostal Experience," *Pneuma: The Journal of the Society for Pentecostal Studies* 15, no. 1 (Spring 1993): 61–76; "The Tongues of Pentecost: A Pentecostal Perspective on the Promise and Challenge of Pentecostal/Roman Catholic Dialogue," *Journal of Ecumenical Studies* 35, no. 1 (Winter 1998): 1–18; and "Babel and the Tongues of Pentecost: Reversal or Fulfilment?—A Theological Perspective," in *Speaking in Tongues: Multi-Disciplinary Perspectives*, ed. Mark J. Cartledge (Bletchley: Paternoster, 2006), 34–51. One could also include the review essay

constructive dialogue with Barth on the issues I have taken up in this chapter—prayer, eschatology, and ethics—for at least two reasons. First, Macchia is firmly rooted in the revisionist camp in regard to Pentecostal eschatology, and therefore is well situated for a constructive engagement with Barth. Second, his revisionist account of Pentecostal eschatology and his theological account of glossolalia have been conducted in dialogue with Barth, among others.[67]

As with Barth's reflections on the Lord's Prayer, the event of speaking in tongues is rooted in a complex act of baptism with the Spirit, which brings together pneumatological, christological, and eschatological themes. Though Pentecostal theology cannot be accused of a kind of "pneumato-centrism," in which the Spirit functions separately from Christology, there is nevertheless a shift of emphasis which can be discerned. Macchia's use of Gregory of Nyssa's formulation, "Christ is the king, and the Spirit is the kingdom," signals the shift about which I am speaking.[68] This move, however, is not so much away from Christology, as it is toward a trinitarian pneumatology. As Macchia puts it, "Spirit baptism brings the reign of the Father, the reign of the crucified and risen Christ, and the reign of divine life to all of creation through the indwelling of the Spirit."[69] Eschatology, pneumatology, and Christology are all entwined in the single movement of Spirit baptism. The Spirit is understood as the reality by which the kingdom is realized more and more fully in history, beginning first in the life of Jesus, the bearer of the Spirit, now poured out on his people, and eventually poured out on all flesh, indeed the whole creation.

In regard to the content and the center of action, Jesus is key, for he is the Spirit baptizer. In fact, the ongoing history of Spirit baptism is constitutive of the identity of Jesus. "Spirit baptism is decisive for the identity of Jesus in the New Testament as the savior and bestower of life. Spirit baptism is essential to Jesus' identity as the 'man for others' obedient to the loving will of the Father for creation as the 'God for others.'"[70] Following the Augustinian insight that in the context of the divine life the Spirit is the bond of love between Father and Son, when turned outward the Spirit comes to represent the triune God's eschatological freedom to enter into empathetic relation with the other, indeed to suffer with and even

---

of Michael Welker's *God the Spirit*. See Frank D. Macchia, "Discerning the Spirit in Life: A Review of *God the Spirit* by Michael Welker," *Journal of Pentecostal Theology* 10 (1997): 3–28.

67. It is appropriate here to again call attention to Macchia's dissertation, where he engaged the theological, spiritual, and social-ethical legacy of the two Blumhardts, father and son, who were so essential to Barth's own theological, indeed, eschatological development. See his *Spirituality and Social Liberation*.

68. Macchia, *Baptized in the Spirit*, 89. One can find a similar expression in the Wesleyan wing of the Pentecostal movement. See also Land, *Pentecostal Spirituality*, 44.

69. Ibid.

70. Ibid., 90.

for that which is not God.⁷¹ In correspondence with this divine gesture, Jesus, as the one who literally "poured himself out" *for* others, now pours out the Spirit *on* others, extending God's empathetic and royal reach, which will find is final dénouement in a liberated creation. As such, neither the life and mission of Jesus, nor the bringing of the kingdom can be said to be complete. We can only speak of an "already" and a "not yet." Jesus can be said to inaugurate the fulfillment of the kingdom—which is the liberation of creation from bondage—begun in his own person, in the event of the outpouring of the Spirit on all flesh.⁷²

Baptism with the Spirit functions as another means by which to speak of God "indwelling all of creation."⁷³ The kingdom of God which comes toward us will be a kind of cosmic Pentecost in which creation will be cleansed of sin (i.e., sanctified) and energized by God's life-giving presence. Furthermore, Macchia attributes a "Christoformic" character to the goal and direction of the Spirit, such that the end of God's ways with humanity is its conformity to Jesus who stands in the bosom of the Father.⁷⁴ As Macchia notes,

> The field of the Spirit and of the kingdom is the field of the risen and ascended Christ's increasingly diverse presence. It is also the field of the crucified Christ, meaning that it is realized among us in the power of the risen Christ as we bear one another's burdens and reach out to others in solidarity with suffering victims everywhere.⁷⁵

The baptism with the Spirit thus includes a double movement: from the Father, through the Son, and by the Spirit out into the world, and conversely, from the world, by the Spirit, through the Son, and into the presence of the Father.

It is in the context of this understanding of Spirit baptism that Macchia develops his theological account of glossolalia under five headings: glossolalia as eschatological theophany, glossolalia as language *coram Deo*, glossolalia and the communion of saints, glossolalia and the theology of the cross, and glossolalia and the new creation. The images at work in the account of Pentecost in Acts 2, the key text for any discussion of glossolalia, are drawn from multiple traditions in the Hebrew Bible. Babel, Sinai, and the apocalyptic discourse of Joel are all enfolded into an event that is above all determined by the apocalyptic event of the coming of Jesus of Nazareth. A "free, spontaneous, and dramatic"⁷⁶ event of wind, fire, speech, and hearing all coincide to indicate a moment of divine self-disclosure, a theophany that both points back to God's triumph in Jesus Christ and toward the mysterious

---

71. Ibid., 116–17, 125–9.
72. Ibid., 91–107.
73. Ibid., 103.
74. "The kingdom of God comes through the divine presence in the transformation of all things by the Spirit into the image of Christ" (Ibid., 104).
75. Ibid., 106–7.
76. Macchia, "Sighs too Deep for Words," 55.

and incomprehensible future of the final revelation of God's glory. "Pentecost was viewed there as an eschatological event that referred back to previous theophanies (which were fulfilled in Christ) and pointed ahead to the final parousia."[77] In the midst of this stands the phenomenon of tongues, functioning not so much as a sign of personal ecstatic experience, but as a public sign, or impression, of both the experience of transcendence that occurs in the presence of the living God and as a manifestation of a "liberating historical future."[78] That future will now include all nations, a fact which becomes manifest in the flow of the text of Acts as three thousand people join the messianic community.[79]

Macchia notes that most Pentecostals have correctly understood the experience of glossolalia as practiced in the community of faith as the "'sighs (groaning) too deep for words' in Rom. 8.26." Rooted in the divine disclosure, rather than any human religious potential, glossolalic groaning and sighing is a conjoined expression of both the limitations of human language and the deep longing for God's redemption of the whole creation. As such, glossolalia reveals "something very profound about human existence *coram Deo* (before God)."[80] In the worshipful presence of God, human life is revealed as fundamentally ecstatic or eccentric,[81] oriented and moving beyond itself toward the triune God. "Glossolalia is an unclassifiable, free speech in response to an unclassifiable, free God. It is the language of the *imago Dei*. It is, according to Käsemann, 'the cry for freedom.'"[82] Glossolalia arises in the midst of the tension between our need to respond to God, and our limited human ability to do so. In the outpouring of the Spirit, the mysterious and profound event wherein the "God for others" freely encounters the other, humanity is gifted a reciprocal or corresponding mysterious yet free utterance.[83]

Tongues, however, is but one gift that comes in the event of baptism in the Spirit, and even among Pentecostals it is not the most important.[84] From the very

---

77. Ibid., 57.
78. Ibid., 59.
79. Macchia, "Babel and the Tongues of Pentecost," 35. See also Daniela C. Augustine, *Pentecost, Hospitality, and Transfiguration: Toward a Spirit-Inspired Vision of Social Transformation* (Cleveland: CPT Press, 2012), 38. Augustine's description of the events of Acts 2 is apropos: "The monotone superiority of imperial culture is challenged by the polyphony of human speech as the inaugural address of a multicultural human reality" (ibid., 31).
80. Macchia, "Sighs too Deep for Words," 61.
81. For an interesting discussion in the realm of theological anthropology which brings together eccentricity, pneumatology, eschatology, and prayer, see David H. Kelsey, *Eccentric Existence: A Theological Anthropology*, vol. 2 (Louisville: Westminster John Knox, 2009), 761–4.
82. Macchia, "Sighs too Deep for Words," 61.
83. Thompson, *Kingdom Come*, 130–1.
84. Macchia, *Baptized in the Spirit*, 35.

beginning there was some measure of unease regarding the prominent place afforded to tongues in the Pentecostal movement.[85] William Seymour, one of the key figures in the founding of the movement, following Paul's reflections in 1 Corinthians 12–14 went on to emphasize that "Divine love, which is charity," or the upbuilding of the community, was the real gift of the Spirit.[86] In light of this history, and of the temptation for tongues to become the basis for a solipsistic culture of "signs and wonders" seeking and individualistic myopia, Macchia argues that a healthy theology of tongues is conducive of *koinonia*. This is seen in particular in glossolalia's ability to break down the walls that divide. As Macchia notes,

> Wherever glossolalia is experienced in Acts barriers are broken down between people: between rich and poor (ch. 2), between Jew and Gentile (ch. 10), and between Christians and the followers of John the Baptist (ch. 19).
>
> Glossolalia in this context is to be seen as an unclassifiable language that points to the hidden mystery of human freedom before God, a mystery that cuts through differences of gender, class, and culture to reveal a solidarity that is essential to our very being and that is revealed to us in God's own self-disclosure.[87]

The fact that the early experience of glossolalia among Pentecostals occurred in a racially diverse setting, in which men and women were both gifted and understood as commissioned to preach, is indicative of the kind of *koinonia* to which the experience of speaking in tongues contributes and points.

Pushing back against the all too easy triumphalism or quietism that could result even from a church-based *koinonia*, Macchia argues that the communion imagined and created by tongues has christological meaning and direction. It moves out into the world under the sign of the cross. "The Pentecost event was not simply one theophany of God in a succession of theophanies for us in the Old Testament."[88] Rather, the life, death, and resurrection of Jesus Christ is the decisive eschatological inbreaking of God's kingdom, which is now manifested within creation through the outpouring of the Spirit. As with Barth, Macchia argues that

---

85. See Cecil M. Robeck, Jr.'s classic discussion of this in his "William J. Seymour and the 'Bible Evidence,'" in *Initial Evidence: Historical and Biblical Perspectives on the Pentecostal Doctrine of Spirit Baptism*, ed. Gary B. McGee (Peabody: Hendrickson, 1991), 72–95. See also Renea Brathwaite, "Tongues and Ethics: William J. Seymour and the 'Bible Evidence': A Response to Cecil M. Robeck, Jr.," *Pneuma: The Journal of the Society for Pentecostal Studies* 32 (2010): 203–22.

86. William J. Seymour, "Questions Answered," in Gastón Espinosa, *William J. Seymour and the Origins of Global Pentecostalism: A Biography and Documentary History* (Durham: Duke University Press, 2014), 195.

87. Macchia, "Sighs too Deep for Words," 65–6.

88. Ibid., 68–9.

the prayer of tongues is also an act of correspondence. In a provocative reading of Acts 2:26-27 (Peter's quote of Psalm 16), Macchia argues that glossolalia is a participation in the "glad tongue" of Jesus, the cry Jesus uttered from both the cross and from the depths of hades on behalf of the whole creation. As such, "the praise of glossolalia is not a praise isolated from the suffering of the world. It is also a word of yearning for the deliverance of the suffering creation."[89] For Macchia, the freedom for *koinonia* which tongues envisions and fosters is meant to lead the community out into the world in suffering solidarity, so that our ecstatic freedom becomes "the ecstasy of service, not of enthusiasm."[90]

At the same time, glossolalia is evidence that the Spirit has a hold of us, and that, therefore, God's work of reclaiming the world is not only underway but will be victorious in the end. As such, glossolalia is a sign of the new creation. Macchia argues that it actually takes on a kind of sacramental character, in which God's gratuitous resurrection power is seen to be already at work in the here and now in the production of the embodied gifts and fruit of the Spirit. The event of tongues holds together the physical and embodied dimension of human-creaturely existence, with the ineffable freedom of the Spirit.

> Set in an eschatological context, tongues signifies the radically free power "of the age to come" (Heb. 6.4), liberating us to respond to God in new and unforeseen ways. But the radically free Spirit is not hidden nor without present, visible fulfillment. Tongues signify the new relationships and communities transformed and empowered to witness of the Gospel to the world.[91]

Placed in the context of the other gifts of the Spirit, particularly the gift of healing, tongues point to the final and full manifestation of God's kingdom, the recreation of heaven and earth in a final outpouring of the Spirit on *all flesh*.

Barth, Pentecostalism, and the Ecstasy of Revolt

There are a number of possible avenues that this analysis might take from here. For instance, we could point to the striking similarity between Barth and Pentecostal theology in regard to taking seriously the biblical theme of Spirit baptism. Conceived as an actualistic event of divine disruption by Barth and divine self-disclosure by Macchia, both figures share in the idea that Spirit baptism does not point to a realization of a human or religious potentiality, but to a divine decision to break into the world in the here and now to set free the captives. Corresponding to the free and spontaneous act of Spirit baptism, both authors also share an affinity for emphasizing

---

89. Ibid., 69.
90. Hans Urs von Balthasar, *Prayer* (New York: Sheed & Ward, 1961), 64, as quoted in Macchia, "Sighs too Deep for Words," 70.
91. Macchia, "Tongues as a Sign," 71.

a human response that is free and spontaneous, and that, through the longing of prayer, reaches beyond itself for the eschatological liberation that only God can bring.

We could point to the important role that the category of correspondence plays in Barth's theology and how echoes of that notion are also present in Macchia's reading of Acts 2:26-27. For Barth, the Christian life, as a history of invocation, is a life lived in participatory correspondence to the living Christ, the true and faithful-covenant partner and suppliant whose life and death was nothing less than a prayer offered to God. Participation in Christ's prayer and life (or life as prayer) through Spirit baptism necessarily gives rise to a Christian life which is conformed to the Crucified, the one who poured himself out for others, the servant who lives in solidarity with a suffering world. In Macchia, glossolalic utterance is also an act of correspondence, participating in the "glad tongue" of Jesus who, on behalf of all creation, cried from the cross and from the depths of hades.

We might also point to the different ways that each author holds together prayer and action, seeking to do justice to the embodied dimension of the Christian life. Or perhaps we might point to the relative importance that each gives to the communal dimension of prayer and the Christian life, such that the act of prayer not only occurs in the context of community, but does so for the sake of the upbuilding of *koinonia* within the community—a *koinonia* that stretches far beyond the boundaries of the so-called Christian world to reveal that the true posture of the community is solidarity with the world, rather than separation from it or superiority over it.

Of course, we might also point to the significant difference which remains between Barth and Pentecostal theologians regarding Barth's radical christocentrism and the Pentecostal emphasis on a trinitarian pneumatology. One place where this difference appeared in our discussion regards Macchia's suggestion that the act of Spirit baptism is constitutive of the identity of Jesus, such that the ongoing outpouring of the Spirit can potentially be understood as an extension and perhaps even completion of the mission of Jesus in and through the flow of history. It is unclear to what extent Macchia or other Pentecostal theologians would allow that the community on which the Spirit is poured out functions as a kind of further extension of the incarnation, or as a cooperative completion of the mission of Jesus and of the coming of the kingdom. Barth would be deeply uneasy about such an articulation.[92] It is the life of Jesus which is constitutive of the

---

92. In this vein, Barth was deeply uneasy about describing the community of faith, which is brought into being by the Spirit, as in any sense an "extension" of the incarnation, which would seem to rule out any constitutive role for the ongoing history of the body of Christ in further filling out the one history of Jesus. For example: "Even in its invisible essence it is not Christ, nor a second Christ, nor a kind of extension of the one Christ. . . . Thus to speak of a continuation or extension of the incarnation in the Church is not only out of place but even blasphemous" (*CD* IV/3.2, 729). See also *CD* IV/2, 60; *CD* IV/3.2, 543, 768; and *CD* IV/4, 118.

identity of the Spirit, and this relationship is to be understood asymmetrically.[93] Barth does not allow that the outpouring of the Spirit adds to the life history of Jesus, which is the coming of the kingdom of God in the midst of history. Rather, the outpouring of the Spirit is associated with the *manifestation* of the kingdom which has both come and is coming. In this context, the ongoing history of the people of God functions as a contingent and tentative, but indispensable witness to the life history of Jesus, which is the history of the kingdom of God. It may be that this too is what Pentecostal theologians want to emphasize, but further clarification is needed.[94]

I would, however, like to point to at least one place where one might discern a potential convergence of Barth and Pentecostal theology which would be mutually beneficial. What I am referring to here is combining Macchia's construal of glossolalia as a kind of ecstasy that pushes one out of oneself into service rather than enthusiasm, on the one hand, and on the other hand, Barth's notion of invocation as a movement of revolt or the refusal to live within the categories of the world "as it is." This is what I mean by the "ecstasy of revolt."

The phenomenon of religious ecstasy has a long and varied history, referring to persons being moved such that they are literally "outside of themselves," with connotations of frenzy, hysteria, and the like. In contrast to this, and because of the dangers and temptations of a solipsistic emotionalism within their own movement, many Pentecostal theologians describe "ecstasy" in ways that more closely resemble an existence or experience of eccentricity, or a being opened outward toward God and others.[95] They retain the word "ecstasy," rather than abandoning it altogether, because it is able to register the experiential residue that attends being oriented eccentrically, an experience which can often be overwhelming, and which is at the very least marked by passion.

For various historical and theological reasons Barth was deeply suspicious of the category of experience. Nevertheless, Barth did say that the life of prayer that

---

93. "Thus, the only content of the Holy Spirit is Jesus; His only work is His provisional revelation; His only effect the human knowledge which has Him as its object (and in Him the knowing man himself)" (*CD* IV/2, 654).

94. In this regard, a fruitful place to begin such a dialogue might be utilizing Barth's conception of the *totus Christus* or "whole Christ" which includes both the history of Jesus and his earthly-historical form of existence, the church. As Barth describes it: "In God's eternal counsel, in His epiphany, and finally in His revelation at the end of the age, He was and is and will be this *totus Christus*—Christ and Christians" (*CD* IV/2, 60). For consideration of this concept, see Kimlyn J. Bender, *Karl Bart's Christological Ecclesiology* (Eugene: Cascade Books, 2013), 202–5 and Peter Goodwin Heltzel and Christian T. Collins Winn, "Karl Bath, Reconciliation, and the Triune God," in *The Cambridge Companion to the Trinity*, ed. Peter C. Phan (Cambridge: Cambridge University Press, 2011), 173–91.

95. See also Christopher Dube, "From Ecstasy to Ecstasis: A Reflection on Prophetic and Pentecostal Ecstasy in the Light of John the Baptizer," *Journal of Pentecostal Theology* 11, no. 1 (2002): 41–52.

Christians live is an eccentric or outward moving life, which is marked by a great passion.[96] The question I want to ask is: Could the concept of "ecstasy," as carefully defined by Pentecostal scholars, also be useful within a Barthian frame? Could it help to do justice to the passionate nature of Christian existence, registering the experiential residue that comes with being turned outward toward God and others? If so, I would contend it should not be separated from Barth's notion of "revolt." For we are not talking about just any passion or "ecstasy," but the passion and ecstasy that refuses to live with the dehumanizing status quo or to make peace with the bio-politics that deforms human life. For Barth, the "theologian of permanent revolution,"[97] doesn't just imagine that the Christian life is placed in a posture of revolt; rather, he envisions a history, an actual, passionate, ecstatic movement toward revolt; a striving for human righteousness, done not as an act of self-preservation, but in solidarity with a suffering world and in protest against the powers and principalities; a movement of "charismatic action."[98]

Pentecostal theologians would also benefit from connecting "ecstasy" to "revolt," as it sharpens and brings to light the inner meaning, that phenomena like healing, tongues, and especially the barrier-breaking kingdom ethos that Pentecostal spirituality is so passionate about. Nevertheless, whether such a combination can do justice to the kind of prophetic and life-giving action that both Pentecostal and Barthian theologians might want to advocate will have to be a discussion for another time.

---

96. See Barth, *The Christian Life*, 94, 111–14.
97. Paul Lehmann, "Karl Barth, Theologian of Permanent Revolution," *Union Seminary Quarterly Review* 28 (1972): 67–81.
98. Ry Owen Siggelkow, "The Nothingness of the Church under the Cross: Mission without Colonialism," *Anabaptist Witness* 1, no. 1 (October 2014): 118–19.

Part Four

HOLY SPIRIT AND THE CHURCH

Chapter 13

SPIRIT, LOVE, AND CHARISMA

PNEUMATOLOGY IN THE THEOLOGY OF KARL
BARTH AND PENTECOSTALISM

Peter Althouse

The association of Karl Barth and Pentecostalism seems like an odd couple at first glance. What does the great theological thinker who turned from German liberal theology to forge a new path for Protestant orthodoxy have in common with an experientially based, Spirit-focused movement like Pentecostalism? Conversely, what would Pentecostals who prize ecstatic manifestations of the Spirit want from Barth's fundamentally intellectual project? Do Barth and Pentecostals have anything at all in common?

Pentecostal–charismatic Christianity is a diverse and intertwined family in contemporary Christianity that places great importance on the work and activity of the Spirit in the Christian life, especially in the experience of the manifestations of the charismatic gifts in the worship of the church and the life of prayer. Speaking in tongues, prophecy, healing, words of knowledge, and a plurality of other charismatic gifts play out in the life of the Pentecostal church. Generally, Pentecostals make a distinction between a Lucan account of speaking in tongues (glossolalia) that is a phenomenological indicator of baptism in the Spirit (often cast as evidence or sign of the baptism of the Spirit) and a Pauline account of speaking in tongues that requires interpretation. Pentecostals also tend to speak about these manifestations of the Spirit as encounters of power (*dynamis*) as separate from love, even though the Wesleyan context from which Pentecostals emerged placed great emphasis on abiding love as a second blessing experience.[1] Even in current charismatic circles the interplay between the baptism of power and the baptism of love plays important theological roles in the charismatic orientation of divine encounter.[2] The emphasis on the activity of the Spirit in Pentecostalism begs for pneumatological interrogation.

---

1. See Donald Dayton, *Roots of Pentecostalism* (Metuchen: Scarecrow Press, 1989) for a historical discussion of the shift from the Methodist and Holiness emphasis on love to the Pentecostal focus on power.

2. For instance, see Michael Wilkinson and Peter Althouse, *Catch the Fire: Soaking Prayer and Charismatic Renewal* (DeKalb: Northern Illinois University Press, 2014), 11,

Pentecostal theologians have been developing scholarship on a number of fronts over the last several decades. One area of exploration is pneumatology, especially as it relates to Pentecostal distinctives as baptism in the Spirit, glossolalia, and other charismatic gifts. Proposals have been offered that include cultivating a "pneumatological imagination" in the construction of Pentecostal theology,[3] exploring ecumenical contributions of Pentecostal pneumatology,[4] examining the relationship between pneumatology and soteriology,[5] and investigating the role of the Spirit in the church.[6] My own foray into Pentecostal pneumatology is the exploration of the relationship between the Spirit's self-giving love (kenosis) as a precondition for the manifestations of the charismata. My contention is that the expression of the charismata by believers in the church is initiated through the Spirit's prior act of kenosis as an expression of divine self-giving,[7] a position I hope to expand in the development of this chapter.

But what does Karl Barth have to offer Pentecostals? His pneumatology has been the subject of contentious debate. On the one hand, Barth's critics insist that his christocentric framework leaves little room for a healthy theology of the Spirit. On the other hand, sympathizers of Barth insist that his pneumatology is rich and complex in scope, and one needs to dig deeply in the realm of Barth's corpus in order to glean its significance. If Barth's pneumatology is so contentious though, would there be any value in appropriating it for the construction of a Pentecostal pneumatology?

53, 110, 139, for a discussion of how Catch the Fire, a charismatic movement expanding globally out of Toronto, Canada, understands these distinctions.

3. See Amos Yong, *Discerning the Spirit(s): A Pentecostal-Charismatic Contribution to Christian Theology of Religions*, JPT Sup, 20 (Sheffield: Sheffield Academic Press, 2000), 29 and throughout.

4. Veli-Matti Kärkkäinen, *Toward a Pneumatological Theology: Pentecostal and Ecumenical Perspectives on Ecclesiology, Soteriology, and Theology of Mission* (Lanham: University Press of America, 2002).

5. Vali-Matti Kärkkäinen, *Spirit and Salvation*, vol. 4 of *A Constructive Christian Theology for the Pluralistic World* (Grand Rapids: Eerdmans, 2016); Frank D. Macchia, *Justified in the Spirit: Creation, Redemption, and the Triune God* (Grand Rapids: Eerdmans, 2010).

6. Frank D. Macchia, *Baptized in the Spirit: A Global Pentecostal Theology* (Grand Rapids: Zondervan, 2006).

7. I have been developing this pneumatological proposal primarily through the lens of Moltmann's theology of Spirit kenosis though with overtures to Barth. See Peter Althouse, "Implications of the Kenosis of the Spirit for a Creational Eschatology: A Pentecostal Engagement with Jürgen Moltmann," in *Creation, Science and Spirit: Pentecostal Forays into the Science-Religion Dialogues*, ed. Amos Yong (Eugene: Pickwick Publications, 2009), 155–72. Peter Althouse, "Kenosis and the Imago Dei: Contributions of Christology to the Study of Godly Love," in *The Science and Theology of Godly Love*, ed. Amos Yong and Matthew Lee (DeKalb: Northern Illinois University Press, 2012), 56–76.

Plumbing Barth's pneumatology provides an opportunity to initiate a discussion for further constructing Pentecostal pneumatology, but reflectively, developments in Pentecostal pneumatology may offer a corrective to Barth's pneumatology. To accomplish this task, I shall first touch on the debates regarding Barth's theology of the Spirit to tease out his theology of divine love and the self-giving of the Spirit. Barth's discussion in *Church Dogmatics* IV/2, "The Holy Spirit and Christian Love," with its excursus on 1 Corinthians 13 in the Manner of Love, is particularly illuminating on the relationship between love and charisma. While prioritizing love, Barth argues that when properly of the Spirit, the gifts should not be rejected, but are distributed by the Spirit for building the community of faith. Specifically, Barth interprets the charism of speaking in tongues through the lens of the Spirit's sigh, an act which pushes beyond the limitations of creaturely finitude to express the inexpressible. Relatedly, Pentecostal theology has made connections between glossolalia and the Spirit's sigh, especially in the reflections of Frank Macchia. However, sighing is a bodily gesture, an embodied act that strains beyond the limitation of cognition when contemplating the inexplicable God. The embodied sigh is an area of theological development among Pentecostals that could be incorporated into Barth's theology.

The General Contours of Barth's Pneumatology

Near the end of his life, and in self-reflection on the theological voices that influenced him, Karl Barth makes an astonishing statement, "What I have occasionally contemplated . . . would be the possibility of a theology of the third article, in other words a theology predominantly and decisively of the Holy Spirit."[8] This giant of a figure, who wrote so prolifically on the revelation of the Word of God in Jesus Christ, thought that everything that he said and believed about the first and second articles of the creed might also be illuminated through the lens of God the Holy Spirit. Furthermore, Barth reflects on pneumatology in his opus and avers:

> In *Church Dogmatics* IV/1-3, I at least had the good instinct to place the church, and faith, love, and hope, under the sign of the Holy Spirit. But might it not even be possible and necessary to place justification, sanctification, and calling under this sign—to say nothing of creation as the *opus proprium* of God the Father? Might not even the Christology which dominates everything be illuminated on this basis (*conceptus de Spiritu Sancto!*)?[9]

The ecumenical significance of Barth's pneumatological move is that theological voices residing in different spiritual movements could be incorporated into his

---

8. Karl Barth, "Concluding Unscientific Postscript on Schleiermacher," *Studies in Religion* 7, no. 2 (1978): 134.
9. Ibid., 134.

dogmatic theology.[10] Might not the Pentecostals and charismatics, who emerged in the last century with a special emphasis on the Spirit, also be included as a voice in this dialogue?

Although a cadre of scholars complain that Barth lacks a robust pneumatology and reduces trinitarian theology to binitarianism,[11] it might be more accurate to say that Barth is better able to "show" or "display" his theology of the Holy Spirit than "state" it with theological consistency.[12] Philip J. Rosato traces the pneumatological threads that run through Barth's theological project. According to Rosato, the locus of Barth's pneumatological interest lies in his appreciation of Friedrich Schleiermacher, who was Barth's major theological dialogue partner, even though Barth would break radically from Schleiermacher's liberalism. Barth attempts to redeem Schleiermacher's valid pneumatological insights, while also rejecting his errors. "That the one aspect of Schleiermacher's thought so fascinates Barth lends credence to the daring assertion that Barth himself gradually became more properly a pneumatocentric than a Christocentric theologian."[13] Barth claims that Schleiermacher was the source for the development of both Pietism and neo-Protestantism.[14] Moreover, Barth's pneumatology was developed in the interrogation of Christian existentialism, especially that of Søren Kierkegaard and Rudolf Bultmann, which Barth connects to the subjective orientation in modern Protestantism. He saw Christian existentialism as a footnote to Schleiermacher in that both liberalism and existentialism conflate anthropology and pneumatology. Yet Barth's concern with existentialism was that while it focused on the importance of salvation, it lost its anchor in Christ as savior. The final resource in Barth's pneumatology was the mystical tradition in Roman catholic theology. Despite Barth's criticism of catholic theology on numerous fronts, he spoke approvingly of the pneumatological emphasis.[15]

---

10. Ibid., 134–5.

11. Robert W. Jenson led this charge by arguing that a full-fledged theology of the Spirit is all but missing from Barth's trinitarian theology. The near unanimity of the Karl Barth Society of North America, claims Jenson, came to a consensus that swaths of Barth's theology are more binitarian than trinitarian. Robert W. Jenson, "You Wonder Where the Spirit Went," *Pro Ecclesia* 28 (1993): 296, 300; cf. Colin E. Gunton, *The Promise of Trinitarian Theology*, 2nd ed. (Edinburgh: T&T Clark, 1997), 112; Samuel M. Powell, *The Trinity in German Thought* (Cambridge: Cambridge University Press, 2001), 225.

12. James J. Buckley, "A Field of Living Fire: Karl Barth on the Spirit and the Church," *Modern Theology* 10, no. 1 (January 1994): 81–100, here 83. Tim Hartman, "The Promise of an Actualistic Pneumatology: Beginning with the Holy Spirit in African Pentecostalism and Karl Barth," *Modern Theology* 33, no. 3 (July 2017): 333–47.

13. Philip J. Rosato, *The Spirit as Lord: The Pneumatology of Karl Barth* (Edinburgh: T&T Clark, 1981), 3.

14. Karl Barth, *The Heidelberg Catechism for Today* (Richmond: John Know Press, 1964), 84–5 as cited by Rosato, *The Spirit as Lord*, 3.

15. Rosato, *The Spirit as Lord*, 9–10.

Consequently, Rosato argues that Barth applies a pneumatological reinterpretation to Christian existentialism, to seventeenth-century Protestant spiritualist movements, to elements of Luther and Calvin, and to Roman Catholicism. "The preoccupation which Barth finds common to all of them is mysticism. As repelling as this subjective emphasis is to Barth, he can never disclaim that the personal apprehension of God's revelation on the part of the individual Christian belongs at the heart of Protestantism and of all genuine Christian theology."[16] Barth discovers this mystical element in liberal Protestantism, which blurs "the revelatory history of Jesus Christ with what the believer experiences as his personal openness to God's Spirit."[17] Rosato is critical however of Barth's failure to develop a robust pneumatology of creation.

George Hunsinger, who is the most vocal defender of Barth, argues that Barth ambitiously develops the doctrine of the Spirit's saving work as rigorously christocentric.[18] According to Hunsinger, Barth's pneumatology insists that the Spirit mediates the trinitarian communion between the Father and the Son. He articulates a christocentric pneumatology in which the Spirit mediates the presence of Christ to the individual members of the community of faith and unites each member together in Christ. There is no independent or secondary revelation that the Spirit brings to salvation other than that which is wholly and entirely wrought by Christ.[19] Barth views the Holy Spirit as the "sole effective agent" of communion between God and humanity. Faith, hope, and love do not depend on human abilities, but are awakened by the Spirit through the miracle of grace making human freedom possible.[20] The Spirit unites believers to Christ, and through him they participate in trinitarian fellowship. This *koinonia* is love that involves mutual self-giving. The mutual indwelling of the two natures of Jesus Christ, which is created by the Spirit, is the basis for uniting Christ and the church and the fellowship this unity entails, which the Spirit gathers and holds together.[21]

Like Hunsinger, Frank Macchia writes approvingly of Barth's pneumatology, but from a Pentecostal perspective. Macchia argues that Barth's pneumatology is complex, based on the Word of revelation, and directed to hearing in faith, but Barth's concern is holding together the tension between the objective and subjective sides of faith.[22] Barth's opposition to nineteenth-century anthropocentrism was held in tension with his struggle to find continuity between revelation and religious

---

16. Ibid., 5.
17. Ibid., 6.
18. George Hunsinger, "The Mediator of Communion: Karl Barth's Doctrine of the Holy Spirit," in *The Cambridge Companion to Karl Barth*, ed. John Webster (Cambridge: Cambridge University Press, 2000), 177–94, here 179.
19. Ibid., 179–81.
20. Ibid., 182–3.
21. Ibid., 188–9.
22. Frank D. Macchia, "The Spirit of God and the Spirit of Life: An Evangelical Response to Karl Barth's Pneumatology," in *Karl Barth and Evangelical Theology: Convergences and*

consciousness. Consequently, Barth increasingly realized that not only must he start from a christological stance on revelation, but this has implications of God's self-giving as Spirit.[23] The indivisibility of the triune God means, for Barth, that the Spirit cannot be separated from the Word, nor is the Spirit's power different from the Word, but found in and by the Word.[24] Moreover, the Spirit is not primarily the Spirit of the individual, but the Spirit of the community of faith. The power of the Spirit awakens the life of faith in community as the body of Christ created and renewed by the Spirit, as both Christ and the Spirit work in tandem.[25] Contra Rosato, Macchia claims that Barth saw the Spirit as the Spirit of all humanity and creation, and as the ground of creaturely existence. The Spirit is given to all so that humans have an intellectual and spiritual nature, but this should not be confused with the divine Spirit. Yet there remains an alienation between the Spirit and the creature.[26] Divine self-giving is the topic to which we now turn.

Karl Barth's Pneumatology and the Self-Giving God

Divine self-giving is an aspect of Barth's theology found in *CD* IV/2. The dogmatic statement that defines the section states that "The Holy Spirit is the quickening power in which Jesus Christ places a sinful man in His community and thus gives him the freedom, in active self-giving to God and his fellows as God's witness, to correspond to the love in which God has drawn him to Himself and raised him up, overcoming his sloth and misery."[27] In this statement Barth identifies a double movement of self-giving that through the Spirit's quickening power and the reconciling work of Jesus Christ, God empowers the sinner to surrender to God and to others. This self-giving corresponds to the movement of divine love by which God draws the sinner and bestows new life. Moreover, the Spirit actualizes self-giving in the sinner through the self-giving love of God, so that the human is placed into the Christian community to reflect God as imitation of divine love.[28]

Barth then expands this self-giving love in a threefold manner. Love stands with faith and hope in the reconciling work of God in which justification and sanctification (and eschatological hope later in *CD* IV/3) transpose conversion into discipleship.[29] The condescension of God in Christ Jesus to become the God-

---

Divergences, ed. Sung Wook Chung (Grand Rapids: Baker Academic, 2006), 149–71, here 150.

23. Ibid., 152–3.
24. Barth, *CD* I/1, 150, as referenced by Macchia, "The Spirit of God and the Spirit of Life," 157.
25. Macchia, "The Spirit of God and the Spirit of Life," 159.
26. Ibid., 167.
27. *CD* IV/2, 727.
28. Ibid., 779.
29. Ibid., 729.

Man is the power of justification by which humans are reconciled to God. The quickening power of the Holy Spirit is the power by which humans surrender in obedience to God.[30] As Barth claims, "[T]he act of a pure and total giving, offering and surrendering correspond[s] to this receiving. When we ask how are we to meet him the answer is that it is in the great self-giving which corresponds to the great reception and in which there takes place that which is pleasing to Him."[31]

Barth distinguishes the reception of faith here with the self-giving of love. Faith is awakened, people are called, justified, and gathered into Christian community. Love is the self-giving of God through which the called are quickened and sanctified in the upbuilding of the church. Barth differentiates between self-giving love and the reception of faith but sees them as the unified action of God revealed by the Spirit. Faith is worked out through love as both that which is received from God and as self-giving.[32] Moreover, Barth claims that God's love is an act rather than a state, meaning that the self-giving and life-giving God is the activity of divine reconciliation.[33] Yet what is true of God in general is also true of the Word in Christ and the Holy Spirit. The acts and works of the love of God are also the acts and work of the Spirit.[34] The Spirit is self-giving love, whose descent gives life to creation. Barth claims,

> As God is Spirit, the Spirit of the Father and the Son, as He gives Himself into human life as Spirit, and as He bears witness as Spirit to our spirit that we are His children (Rom. 8:16), God gives us to participate in the love in which as Father He loves the Son and as Son the Father, making our action a reflection of His eternal love, and ourselves those who may and will love. The fact that human action becomes the reflection, the creature similitude, of the divine can and must be described both as the work of God's love and also the work of His Spirit.[35]

To claim that God is Spirit is to claim that God is love. Just as the Spirit creates the possibility of love between the Father and the Son so too and in an analogous way, the union between God and creature.[36]

The point I want to tease out for Pentecostal pneumatology is that the Spirit is the self-giving Spirit of love, and what is gifted is faith, love, and grace by which people are brought into fellowship with God. The charismatic gifts are pneumatic in the action of the self-giving love of God. Charisma (gift) and charism (grace) are etymologically related, and this connection implies divine self-giving. Lutheran

---

30. Ibid., 728.
31. Ibid., 730.
32. Ibid., 730–1, 733.
33. Ibid., 772.
34. Ibid., 778.
35. Ibid., 778–9.
36. Rosato, *The Spirit as Lord*, 64.

theologian Ernst Käsemann argues, for instance, that the charisma of the Spirit who bestows charismatic gifts is founded in the gift of eternal life in Jesus Christ who is given by the Father (Rom. 6:23). The charismata of the Spirit flow, or to make it more Pentecostal, are poured out from God's gift of Christ Jesus, who distributes the charismatic gifts to different members of the church. The other charismata exist only because of the existence of this one charism, that is, Jesus Christ, to which all the other charismata are related and have their existence.[37] The connection of the charismata of the Spirit to Christ, who condescended to take on human flesh (Phil. 2:6-8), means that there is a condescension of the Spirit as well as a prior act to the giving of the charismatic gifts.

A Pentecostal appropriation of Barth would suggest that the manifestation of charismatic gifts is possible through the prior self-giving love and action of the Spirit, who, with the Father and the Son, give to the community of faith in order to bring believers into the life and fellowship of the triune God. In other words, every manifestation of the charismatic gifts is preceded by a prior condescension of divine self-giving in which the Father gives through Christ by the Spirit out of the abundance of love for creation.[38] For instance, the moment of glossolalic utterance, prophetic speech, or word of knowledge is predicated on the prior moment of divine self-limitation in which the Spirit accommodates creation and flows through the finitudes of human thought, voice, and bodily frailty.

Spirit, Love, Charisma, and the Pneumatic Sigh

Barth engages in an extended excursus on the relationship between love and the charismatic gifts in 1 Corinthians 13. Before evaluating Barth's discussion, it is important to note that this passage is one of profound interest to Pentecostals. The charismatic gifts outlined in the Corinthian passage and displayed in the Acts of the Apostles are the quintessential modus operandi of communal life for the Pentecostal. Speaking in tongues, prophecy, faith, healing, miracles, and the plethora of other extraordinary and ordinary gifts are expressed in Pentecostal worship, service, and prayer life. Pentecostals take the event of Pentecost depicted in Acts and argue that glossolalia, or speaking in tongues, is the quintessential phenomenological indicator of the baptism of the Holy Spirit. They distinguish the Lucan account with the Pauline view of tongues and interpretation as a

---

37. Ernst Käsemann, *Essays on New Testament Themes* (Philadelphia: Fortress Press, 1982), 64. Although not Pentecostal, Käsemann concludes that inarticulate groaning of Romans 8:26 is a reference to glossolalia, a position to be discussed below. Ernst Käsemann, *Commentary on Romans*, as cited by Jesse D. Stone, "Inward Groans and Unknown Tongues: Interpretations of Romans 8.26 in Early Pentecostalism," *Journal of Pentecostal Theology* 30 (2021): 84.

38. See Althouse, "Implications of the Kenosis of the Spirit for a Creational Eschatology," 155–72; Althouse, "Kenosis and the Imago Dei," 56–76.

spontaneous ritual act in the context of worship in the Christian community. At the risk of oversimplification, charismatic churches tend to emphasize the manifestation or impartation of the gifts, which is sometimes though not always connected to Spirit baptism.[39]

Returning to Barth, it should be noted that he takes seriously the validity of the ordinary and extraordinary charismatic gifts described by the apostle to the Corinthians. Barth does not exclude or argue that these gifts are unimportant, but declares, "Paul does not question for a moment that they were genuine gifts. . . . They are genuine, and . . . they derive from the Holy Spirit."[40] Charismata, Barth claims, are genuine gifts of the Holy Spirit that are grounded in the love of God, that point to Christ, and occur in church fellowship.[41] Although these gifts are of divine origin, argues Barth, they are not divine acts but are human acts that are given by the Spirit and under the lordship of Jesus Christ. For Barth, the charismatic gifts are not of the order of salvation. What makes these gifts genuine is whether the Christian and the Christian community are formed by the Spirit, live in the Spirit, and are expressed in the name of Jesus Christ under his discipleship.[42]

Speaking in tongues is one of the gifts of note. Barth engages in a dialectical discussion between love and speaking in tongues and locates speaking in tongues in the "sighing or groaning" of the Spirit, an important act that pushes the boundaries of human capacity and speech beyond their limits. Barth writes:

> Speaking in tongues lies on the extreme limit of Christian speaking as such. It is an attempt to express the inexpressible in which the tongue rushes past, as it were, the notions and concepts necessary to ordinary speech and utters what can be received only as a *groan* or *sigh* [my emphasis] . . . we are not to think of it as a wholly inarticulate, inhuman and bizarre stuttering and stammering. Certainly there is no question of purely "emotional eruptions" . . . otherwise Paul could hardly have described the capacity for them as pneumatic. On the other hand, it is a speech which in its decisive utterances leaves any clear coherence behind, necessarily falling apart unexpectedly in its elements, or remembering in equally unexpected equations and finally consisting only of hints or indications with very forcible marks of interrogation and exclamation. In the last resort, it may well be asked whether there is any Christian speech, any utterance of the evangelical *kerygma*, which does not finally become speaking with tongues, overleaping ordinary notions and concepts in its decisive statements, and then, of course, having to return by way of exposition to ordinary speech. . . . Human

---

39. For instance, the charismatic renewal associated with Catch the Fire, where charismatic phenomena are replete, speaks of the manifestation of tongues as a baptism of power. See Wilkinson and Althouse, *Catch the Fire*.

40. *CD* IV/2, 826.

41. Ibid., 827.

42. Ibid., 828.

speech may reach here the limit in which it becomes the hymn, but even as Christian speech it is held within this limit.[43]

The "sigh" would become the interpretative key in Barth's pneumatology in what JinHyok Kim defines as "pneumatic prayer." Through his study of Romans 8, Barth discovered the Spirit's sigh and provoked a shift in Barth's theology to see God's redemptive act of the Spirit as the leitmotif threading the contours of his theology.[44] In *The Word of God and the Word of Man*, Barth declares "there is more hope when one sighs *Veni Creator Spiritus*, than when he exults as if the spirit where already his. You have been introduced to 'my theology' if you heard this sigh."[45] For Barth, the human sigh is grasped, or more accurately gasped, in pneumatic prayer in nothing less than the Spirit's own groaning, where the Spirit of sonship transforms the supplicant into a child of God. The sigh is an invocation, but the creature is incapable of speaking with God. Yet through the Spirit's groaning in the creature, the creature is brought into communion with the divine. The Spirit prays in us by sighing through our own mouths.[46] Moreover, Barth's theology of sigh is integrally connected to eschatological glorification. Barth proclaimed, "If there were no God and if the heavenly habitation were not awaiting us, there would be no cause for groaning. But God has begun to trouble us with an anxious restlessness. He is the cause of our groaning: and therefore we must groan."[47] Needless to say, for Barth, speaking in tongues is correlated to the Spirit sighing within us.

As the lengthy quote above indicates, speaking in tongues is an utterance of a groan or sigh that reaches the limitations of human capacity, but also the prayer's sigh is "received" indicating the Spirit is sighing through the believer in prayer, advocating for what the believer is unable to grasp, comprehend, or even imagine. Barth even goes as far to suggest that speaking in tongues may be a form of kerygma. The implication, at least for Barth, is that while the groaning of tongues is contrasted with love, it is also a genuine expression of charisma as pneumatic prayer. Barth continues to say that at times there's a choice one must make between speaking in tongues and the illegitimacy of silence, the latter of which is seen by Barth as the antithesis of proclamation.[48] Yet he cautions that "it is possible to

---

43. Ibid., 829–30.

44. JinHyok Kim, *The Spirit of God and the Christian Life: Reconstructing Karl Barth's Pneumatology* (Minneapolis: Fortress Press, 2014), 38–9.

45. Karl Barth, *The Word of God and the Word of Man*, trans. Douglas Horton (n.p.: The Pilgrim Press, 1928), 134; see also Karl Barth and Eduard Thurneysen, *Come Holy Spirit*, trans. George W. Richards, Elmer G. Homrighasen, and Karl J. Ernst (Grand Rapids: Eerdmans, 1933/1978), 148, 236, 261.

46. Kim, *The Spirit of God and the Christian Life*, 39.

47. Karl Barth and Eduard Thurneysen, *God's Search for Man: Sermons*, as cited by Kim, *The Spirit of God and the Christian Life*, 39.

48. This view is somewhat different than a broadly construed Pentecostal view, which at times allows for silence as an appropriate response to God, when the inexpressibility of

speak in tongues (as enabled to do so by the Holy Ghost) and yet not to have love but to omit all self-giving to God and one's neighbour."[49] But this statement is predicated on genuine expressions of the groaning of tongues as enabled by the Spirit that is actualized with love and so produces genuine self-giving to God and neighbor. The key is that charisma and love are fused together as an expression of pneumatic self-giving.

Pentecostal scholars have made much of the relationship between glossolalia and the sighing or groaning in the Spirit, which provides a possible point of dialogue between Barth and Pentecostalism. Clark Pinnock noted the link between glossolalia and sigh as a response to the inexpressibility of the divine, "a way of crying to God from the depths and expressing the too-deep-for-words sighing" at a "deep, noncognitive level."[50] Although not explicitly linked, Pinnock also notes the work of the Spirit in the kenosis of Christ in which self-emptying is characteristic of God in self-emptying love.[51] Jean-Jacques Suurmond likewise links glossolalia to the groaning of creation as a form of solidarity with suffering in unutterable sighing before God.[52] James K. A. Smith, whose philosophical musings place glossolalia in the framework of Husserl's philosophy of language, argues that groaning as a form of tongues-speech is non-expressive speech in which God is listener, but the non-sensical vocalization of the prayer is not heard as sensical. However, Smith claims that noncognitive and non-sensical expression of glossolalia is akin to bodily gesture. Both Suurmond and Smith attempt to place the glossolalic sigh in the framework of embodiment.[53] Michael Wilkinson and Peter Althouse discover that the charismatic prayer practices of soaking prayer, in which there is high levels of glossolalia and other charismatic phenomena, are embodied in noncognitive ways and that the sighing or groaning is described as receiving the "Father's love" in a manner akin to gestation, childbirth, or the gasping of breath.[54] Sighing (and the breathing that comes with sighing) is an important bodily practice in this form of charismatic prayer.

---

glossolalic syllables also fails and only silence remains. See Greg Baer, "Quaker Silence, Catholic Liturgy, and Pentecostal Glossolalia: Some Functional Similarities," in *Perspectives on the New Pentecostalism*, ed. Russ Spittler (Grand Rapids: Baker, 1976), 150–64; also Wilkinson and Althouse, *Catch the Fire* (2014), 92, 102–5.

49. *CD* IV/2, 830.

50. Clark Pinnock, *Flame of Love: A Theology of the Holy Spirit* (Downers Grove: InterVarsity, 1996), 173.

51. Ibid., 88.

52. Jean-Jacques Suurmond, *Word and Spirit at Play: Towards a Charismatic Theology* (Grand Rapids: Eerdmans, 1994), 198.

53. For a discussion on the Pentecostal body and embodiment, see Michael Wilkinson and Peter Althouse, eds., *Pentecostals and the Body*, vol. 8 of *Annual Review of the Sociology of Religion* (Leiden: Brill, 2017), esp. chapter 2.

54. Wilkinson and Althouse, *Catch the Fire*, 103–7.

The most theologically robust contribution to ground the Pentecostal emphasis on glossolalia and baptism in the Spirit is offered by Frank Macchia. Initially, Macchia focuses on glossolalia to argue that the experience of speaking in tongues is a spontaneous, dramatic, and theophanic divine encounter. He draws on Jacques Ellul to argue that glossolalia is nonverbal prayer in an aesthetic mode that responds to the ineffable self-disclosure of God.[55] For Macchia, Pentecostals understand glossolalia as "sighs too deep for words" (Rom. 8:26), and he briefly draws on Barth to say that "only where the Spirit is sighed, cried, and prayed for does he become present and active."[56] Macchia also marshals the theology of Karl Rahner and Paul Tillich to propose that glossolalia can be developed along sacramental lines. Specifically, he employs Rahner to locate sacramental efficacy in "sign value" in the process of signification[57] and Tillich's Protestant principle that sees a connection between the revelation of God and the physical/acoustic phenomena as a sign of divine disclosure.[58] Tongues as sacramental is not causative, but glossolalia is a kind of sacrament that accents the free, dramatic, and unpredictable activity of the Spirit rather than the formal, structured, and predictable liturgies of sacramental churches.[59] However, glossolalia (and the diversity of gifts in 1 Cor. 12–14) is relativized in the context of love, where the apostle must correct the community's realized eschatology to insist that glossolalia is a paradoxical divine encounter that is already present but yearns for the yet to come of full eschatological disclosure.[60]

Macchia continues to develop his theology of tongues in *Baptized in the Spirit* with the chapter "Baptized in Love." He correlates divine love with Spirit baptism to argue that the outpouring of the Spirit is an act of divine self-giving, a gift that transcends all emotional, conceptual, and action-based categories. Love is not only the supreme gift of God but is that very essence of God.[61] The outpouring of the Spirit is the outpouring of divine love as a self-sacrificial love through Jesus Christ and the Spirit. This is the core of Spirit baptism.[62] The self-giving in Spirit baptism is the personal communication of the divine impartation of love that "bears all things, including our sin, sorrow, and death. The God of Spirit baptism is the 'crucified God.' All powerful divine love has a limitless capacity to suffer. This love cannot be overwhelmed or destroyed."[63] For Macchia, glossolalia,

---

55. Frank D. Macchia, "Sighs Too Deep for Words: Toward a Theology of Glossolalia," *Journal of Pentecostal Theology* 1 (1992): 47–73, here 1.

56. Karl Barth, *Evangelical Theology*, as cited by Macchia, "Sighs Too Deep for Words," 67.

57. Frank D. Macchia, "Tongues as a Sign: Towards a Sacramental Understanding of Pentecostal Experience," *Pneuma: The Journal of the Society for Pentecostal Studies* 18, no. 1 (Spring 1993): 61–76, here 62.

58. Ibid., 68.

59. Ibid., 63.

60. Macchia, "Sighs Too Deep for Words," 59.

61. Macchia, *Baptized in the Spirit*, 259.

62. Ibid., 258.

63. Ibid., 262–3.

which is intimately connected to and indicator of Spirit baptism, goes deeper than celebration of the divine encounter but is an expression of divine liberation from bondage through the cross and resurrection of Jesus Christ. Glossolalia cannot bypass the cross in search of an unmediated divine encounter but is a groaning for the deliverance of all creation from the suffering of bondage.[64]

If I may extend Macchia's proposals, the sigh of the Spirit expresses in the groans of broken, human utterance flows from the wounds of the cross. Jesus' cry of dereliction, when he says, "My God, my God, why hast thou forsaken me," is the groaning of utter despair. Much has been made of this moment. However, the narrative does not end there. Mark 15:37 reveals that Jesus gave up his breath, while Matthew 27:50 says that he gave up his Spirit. This is the unutterable sigh when all is lost. Jesus no longer has voice. His proclamation comes to an end. In surrendering his breath/spirit, the final sigh of the complete and total incapacitation of death, the self-giving love of God reaches its zenith. Is this not encapsulated, at least in part, in the groaning of glossolalia? Pentecostals and charismatics are quick to enjoy the celebration of praise when the gifts are expressed in worship as well as the experiences of joy and expectation, but they are also aware of the sorrow and suffering that speaking in tongues convey.[65] When hope is shattered and despair sets in, one cannot speak, the sufferer has lost her voice. The sighing of glossolalia calls out to the Spirit in lament and sorrow. A full-orbed theology of the Spirit must account for the sigh of the cross as we groan with Christ by the Spirit and as God groans with the crucified Christ in fellowship with us. This is the self-giving love of the Spirit whose gifts flow from the suffering and crucified Christ.

The sigh of the cross when Jesus gives up the spirit and no longer has voice is a kenosis event for both Christ and the Spirit. This moment is also an embodied one in which the incarnational journey abruptly ends, when the Spirit abdicates his mission in Christ's bodily death.[66] Dare we say that this is also a charismatic moment? A gift of the Spirit in inexpressible groaning? What Barth does not offer, or at least does not emphasize, is an embodiment of the Spirit in which the sigh that transverses his entire theology is kenotic self-giving, though I do not think that this is inconsistent with his theology. What Pentecostal theology has to offer, at least potentially, is a corrective to Barth in which the self-giving Spirit is also embodied, that manifests in the kenotic sigh and opens avenues for charismatic life. This is at the heart of the gospel revealed in the Word.

A Pentecostal pneumatology would do well starting from the self-giving Spirit, which is the outpouring of divine love. The Spirit takes us up in Christ so that

---

64. Macchia, "Sighs Too Deep for Words," 69.

65. See Daniel Castelo, *Pentecostalism as a Christian Mystical Tradition* (Grand Rapids: Eerdmans, 2017), 167–71.

66. See D. Lyle Dabney, "Naming the Spirit: Towards a Pneumatology of the Cross," in *Starting with the Spirit*, ed. Gordon Preece and Stephen Pickard (Australia: Australian Theological Forum, 2001), 28–58.

in fellowship with God we are given the freedom to love God and others. The diversity of gifts, including the tongues of angels, is made possible through the self-giving Spirit. Barth grasped this. The charismatic gifts, if truly of the Spirit, must be acts of love that sound the joyful notes of hope and freedom, but also the sorrowful notes of mourning and lament as prayerful sighing of the community of faith living under the shadow of the cross.

Chapter 14

LET THE CHURCH BE THE CHURCH

BARTH AND PENTECOSTALS ON ECCLESIOLOGY

Terry L. Cross

Introduction

Barth's ecclesiology has "been heavily criticized for being abstract" and therefore of no practical value for the church due to its overemphasis on *divine action*, which results in "insufficient human content."[1] Nicholas Healy has suggested that the "logic" of Barth's ecclesiology means that human action remains so muted in his theology of salvation and operation of the church that the agency of humans is rendered null and void. In particular, Healy argues that Barth's fixation on the biblical concept of the body of Christ "leads him to make a strong logical distinction between the true and concrete church, on the one hand, and the church of merely human and therefore sinful agency on the other."[2] Given the somewhat common conception that Karl Barth's ecclesiology is either too abstract with no practical value for building an ecclesiology on the one hand or too vacuous of meaningful human agency with respect to the church on the other hand, what could pragmatically minded Pentecostals learn from engaging his doctrine of the church? Given the emphasis on the missional endeavors of the church among Pentecostals, perhaps both ecclesiologies will benefit from a conversation that points to the intersection of the divine and human agencies in the life of the church.

In the last several decades, Pentecostal theologians have turned their attention to craft their own theological reflections on the doctrine of the church, although

---

1. Joseph L. Mangina, *Karl Barth: Theologian of Christian Witness* (Louisville: Westminster John Knox Press, 2004), 185.

2. Nicholas M. Healy, "The Logic of Karl Barth's Ecclesiology: Analysis, Assessment and Proposed Modifications," *Modern Theology* 10, no. 3 (July 1994): 253–70, here 258. This quote refers to the distinction in Barth's writing between *die wirkliche Kirche* ("the true church") and *die Scheinkirche* ("mere semblance of a church") in *KD* IV/2, 695–8; *CD* IV/2, 614–17.

no single approach has been greeted with embrace.[3] Some have found assistance in sacramental aspects of traditional ecclesiology;[4] others have interacted with the theological characteristics of the fivefold gospel from early Pentecostalism.[5] Some Pentecostal scholars have turned attention to the missional centerpiece for ecclesiology;[6] still others have focused the foundation of ecclesiology within the reflection of the doctrine of the Trinity.[7] While the validity of these various ecclesiological endeavors for Pentecostals remains to be fully evaluated,[8] it seems that Pentecostal ecclesiologies will need to find ways to make room for the empowering presence of God's Spirit individually and corporately as well as to engage with a central feature of Pentecost, namely, empowerment for witness and mission. It may seem that Karl Barth would be an unlikely starting place for such endeavors, but I will argue that he is a vital dialogue partner in this work.

Mission has always been at the heart of the Pentecostal movement.[9] As Frank Macchia has noted, "Mission is not just something we *do*; it is what we *are*."[10]

---

3. Wolfgang Vondey, *Pentecostal Theology: Living the Full Gospel*, Systematic Pentecostal and Charismatic Theology (London: T&T Clark, 2018), 226.

4. For example, Simon Chan, *Liturgical Theology: The Church as Worshiping Community* (Downers Grove: IVP Academic, 2006).

5. See *Toward a Pentecostal Ecclesiology: The Church and the Fivefold Gospel*, ed. John Christopher Thomas (Cleveland: CPT Press, 2010). Also, for a compilation of various views from Pentecostals on ecclesiology, see *Pentecostal Ecclesiology: A Reader*, ed. Chris E. W. Green (Leiden: Brill, 2016).

6. Gary Tyra, *A Missional Orthodoxy: Theology and Ministry in a Post-Christian Context* (Downers Grove: InterVarsity, 2013); also, Andy Lord, *Network Church: A Pentecostal Ecclesiology Shaped by Mission*, Global Pentecostal and Charismatic Studies, 11 (Leiden: Brill, 2012).

7. See especially Clark H. Pinnock, "Church in the Power of the Holy Spirit: The Promise of Pentecostal Ecclesiology," *Journal of Pentecostal Theology* 14, no. 2 (2006): 147–65; this article also appears in *Pentecostal Ecclesiology: A Reader*, 47–64. See also Peter Althouse, "Towards a Pentecostal Ecclesiology: Participation in the Missional Life of the Triune God," in *Pentecostal Ecclesiology: A Reader*, ed. Chris E. W. Green (Leiden: Brill, 2016), 88–103. This article originally appeared in the *Journal of Pentecostal Theology* 18, no. 2 (2009): 230–45.

8. Here I agree with the assessment of Veli-Matti Kärkkäinen, "'The Leaning Tower of Pentecostal Theology': Reflections on the Doctrine of the Church on the Way," in *Toward a Pentecostal Ecclesiology: The Church and the Fivefold Gospel*, ed. John Christopher Thomas (Cleveland: CPT Press, 2010), 263.

9. Illustrative of this point, the very first ecclesiology written by a Pentecostal was actually a treatise on the *mission* of the church. See Melvin L. Hodges, *Theology of the Church and Its Mission: A Pentecostal Perspective* (Springfield: Gospel Publishing House, 1977).

10. Frank D. Macchia, *The Spirit-Baptized Church: A Dogmatic Inquiry*, Systematic Pentecostal and Charismatic Theology (London: T&T Clark, 2020), 205. Cf. also the work of Lord, *Network Church: A Pentecostal Ecclesiology Shaped by Mission* and Gary Tyra, *The*

Indeed, one could argue convincingly that mission has always been at the heart of Christianity itself. The Lord of the church was *sent* on a mission from God the Father to this earth in the power of the Spirit in order to seek and save the lost.[11] This other-directed orientation of Jesus Christ was passed on to his *ekklēsia* in its structural DNA and empowerment at Pentecost. In this way, the mission of Christ continues in the mission of the church.

Somewhere in the history of Christianity, however, the church began to focus more on what happened within its walls (*intra muros*) instead of reaching those outside its walls (*extra muros*). While there were occasions in which this was not the case throughout the history of the church, much of the story of Christianity belies this inward focus. Two problems resulted from this inwardness: (1) the church became self-centered—an institution whose concern was its own growth and status; (2) the mission of the church to those outside of it became at best a secondary, add-on characteristic of its identity and at worst an incidental "take-it-or-leave-it" option of service to the world.[12] Perhaps the most important contribution of the Pentecostal movement in the twentieth century was the restoration of mission to the center of the church's identity and work.

It seems clear that this central motif of mission must be one feature that arises from the church's very essence—not an add-on feature crafted as an afterthought, but an action flowing from its very being. This is precisely what many churches have looked for in the last century. Bruce McCormack has sketched something similar in terms of the urgent need in the church today:

> Mission came to be seen as derivative of those internal practices which truly make the Church to be the Church; as a contingent activity which the Church could leave undone and still be the Church. . . . For centuries, the Church has failed to understand its true nature. . . . Given the decline of the institutions generated by the Reformation in the last two decades, there may well be no more urgent task than to re-capture a genuinely apostolic understanding of the nature of the Church. In this task, Karl Barth's later ecclesiology can be an immense help.[13]

Given the penchant of Pentecostals for the *practice* of ministry as opposed to the theoretical foundations underlying such practices, there may be hesitation

---

Holy Spirit in Mission: Prophetic Speech and Action in Christian Mission (Downers Grove: IVP Academic, 2011).

11. Christopher J. H. Wright, *The Mission of God: Unlocking the Bible's Grand Narrative* (Downers Grove: InterVarsity, 2006), 123.

12. *Missional Church: A Vision for the Sending of the Church in North America*, ed. Darrell Guder (Grand Rapids: Eerdmans, 1998), 7.

13. Bruce McCormack, "Witness to the Word: A Barthian Engagement with Reinhard Hütter's Ontology of the Church," *Zeitschrift für Dialektische Theologie*, Supplement Series 5 (2011): 59–77, here 73.

among Pentecostals to ask questions about the nature of the church in order to understand and perform its mission. However, as McCormack has suggested, Barth's ecclesiology can be immensely helpful in this regard. Where can we start? I agree with Peter Althouse's contention that a Pentecostal theology of the church (or any other ecclesiology) "must begin in Trinitarian reflection, in particular reflection on the Trinitarian activity of the *missio dei*."[14] Fortunately, such reflection has already been started for us by Karl Barth's own trinitarian reflection as couched in his doctrine of the church.

It is my contention in this chapter that Barth can help Pentecostals craft an ecclesiology of mission that is well tuned to the nature of the triune God, while at the same time, Pentecostals can assist Barth's ecclesiology by helping to clarify the necessity for an encounter with God's presence that transforms humans to continue God's mission in the world.[15] Kimlyn Bender has noted "three primary aspects" of Barth's ecclesiology: nature, task, and order.[16] I will engage these three essential aspects, presenting ways his approach to the church can assist Pentecostals in developing their own ecclesiologies. At the same time, I will interweave what I deem to be essential Pentecostal aspects that may offer some assistance to Barth's ecclesiological endeavor.

The Nature of God and the Nature of the Church

Barth's mature doctrine of the church arises within the context of his doctrine of reconciliation. After discussing the doctrine of justification, Barth engages the doctrine of the church by noting that the Holy Spirit *gathers* the Christian community;[17] in a similar fashion, after discussing the doctrine of sanctification, Barth shows that the Holy Spirit *upbuilds* the community that it has gathered;[18] in a third trek around the theme, after discussing the doctrine of vocation, Barth demonstrates that the Holy Spirit *sends* the Christian community.[19] Weaving ecclesiology and Christology within his discussion of soteriology, Barth's doctrine of the church is complex to untangle.

---

14. Althouse, "Towards a Pentecostal Ecclesiology: Participation in the Missional Life of the Triune God," 93–4. This is also one of the six themes from Clark Pinnock on the promise of Pentecostal ecclesiology. See Pinnock, "Church in the Power of the Holy Spirit," 52–4.

15. For a fuller explanation of how God's presence may be held as foundational for a Pentecostal ecclesiology, see Terry L. Cross, *The People of God's Presence: An Introduction to Ecclesiology* (Grand Rapids: Baker Academic, 2019).

16. Kimlyn Bender, *Karl Barth's Christological Ecclesiology*, Barth Studies (Burlington: Ashgate, 2005), 92.

17. *CD* IV/1.

18. *CD* IV/2.

19. *CD* IV/3.

Perhaps a starting place for this task is Barth's understanding of the being and act of God as found in this principle: *the action of God corresponds to the being of God*. Although this appears to be a statement that addresses the nature of God, it is one that has great benefit for developing a Pentecostal ecclesiology. It anchors the foundation for ecclesiology in the very nature of the triune God.

For Barth, God is a being-in-act, that is, a being whose action in revelation reflects God's nature in Godself.[20] From such an understanding, Barth "could argue that God's eternal being in and for itself could be inferred from God's being as enacted for and among us in history."[21] The being of God, then, is perfectly communicated through God's act as the One who loves in freedom.[22] Indeed, Barth calls this entire section in his *Church Dogmatics*, "The Reality of God," by which he means the "concept . . . , which holds together being and act, instead of tearing them apart like the idea of 'essence.'"[23] God's being in the act of his revelation is an "event" for humans in which God "declares His reality: not only His reality for us—certainly that—but at the same time His own, inner, proper reality, behind which and above which there is no other."[24]

As Barth moves from the doctrine of God in *CD* II/1 to the doctrine of reconciliation in *CD* IV, he maintains this definition of God as being-in-act by explicating the revelation of God in Jesus Christ.[25] Within the triune life of God, there is a teleologically oriented movement toward the human being as revealed in Jesus Christ. Reading from the fact of the revelation of Christ in human history, we can infer backward into the life of the immanent Trinity the fact that God is the One who chose from eternity to be *for humankind*—the One who loves in freedom.[26] God's life and eternal decision anticipate this movement into historical reality *for* humans. In eternity, the triune God self-determines and self-limits Godself in order to be in fellowship with humans.[27] This "primal decision" to make Godself the God of humans is a central feature of the nature of this God.[28] The being of God has determined its own act and life by a deliberate act of begetting the Son in eternity. Such begetting is not an "add-on" to the being of God; it is precisely who God is and freely chooses to be. As Eberhard Busch comments on this point, "God did not originally exist in a state of (indecisive) rest, in order then to make this choice later! God's being is in this act, and in this act God 'is' (II/1,

---

20. *CD* II/1, 257–60.
21. George Hunsinger, *How to Read Karl Barth: The Shape of His Theology* (New York: Oxford University Press, 1991), 36.
22. *CD* II/1, 272–321.
23. Ibid., 262.
24. Ibid.
25. See, for example, *CD* IV/1, 7.
26. *CD* II/1, 301.
27. *CD* II/2, 162.
28. Ibid., 50.

260)."²⁹ Hence, there is no "contradiction and rift in the being of God," but rather God remains God even in his humbling himself to become a human being.³⁰

Contained within the social life of this triune God is the *missio Dei*—the movement and orientation for the other, first within the eternal triune God as Father, Son, and Spirit, and second toward humanity as creatures standing in need of reconciliation. "As God was in Christ, far from being against Himself, or at disunity with Himself, He has put into effect the freedom of His divine love, the love in which He is divinely free."³¹ What is accomplished in the act of revelation "corresponds to His divine nature."³² Such insight into the consistency of being and acting in the divine life is vital for ecclesiology.

The point here for Barth is that God's *acting* corresponds with God's *being*— God's *mission* matches God's *nature*. Colin Gunton has noted that the consistency between God's being and acting may be seen as the "holiness" of God's character such that God's actions reflect God's being with integrity and wholeness.³³ What God does in God's acting (mission) flows directly from who God is in God's being (nature). Therefore, as John Flett has characterized this concept, "God's act in reconciling the world to himself is not a second step alongside his being in and for himself."³⁴ How may this assist us in developing an ecclesiology?

The nature of God is other-centered—eccentric.³⁵ If the church is to be the people of this God, in some sense we are meant to share in God's other-centered nature. This becomes the basis for the nature of God's people to be eccentric— other-centered. The church's *doing* must be integrally connected to its *being*. In an insightful discussion on the meaning of love, Barth notes that the one who truly loves "gives to the one he loves no more and no less than his 'heart.'"³⁶ This is precisely what God has done—God has imparted Godself to humans. Barth adds, "So seriously is love self-giving that his life is an 'eccentric' life [*ein exzentrisches Leben*], i.e., one which has its centre outside itself."³⁷ By imparting Godself to us, God demonstrates that the "center" of God's being is bent toward the radical other

---

29. Eberhard Busch, *The Great Passion: An Introduction to Karl Barth's Theology*, trans. Geoffrey Bromiley, ed. Darrell and Judy Guder (Grand Rapids: Eerdmans, 2004), 114.

30. *CD* IV/1, 180.

31. Ibid., 186–7.

32. Ibid., 187.

33. Colin E. Gunton, *Act & Being: Towards a Theology of the Divine Attributes* (Grand Rapids: Eerdmans, 2002), 117.

34. John Flett, *The Witness of God: The Trinity, missio Dei, Karl Barth, and the Nature of Christian Community* (Grand Rapids: Eerdmans, 2010), 292.

35. In English, the word "eccentric" can have two meanings: (1) off-centered, out of kilter, elliptical, not having the same center; not concentric; and (2) an oddball, someone exhibiting old-fashioned traits. It is the more mathematical term in line with the first definition that we are using here.

36. *CD* IV/2, 788; *KD* IV/2, 893.

37. Ibid.

who is unlike God, namely, human beings. Since the being of God is "eccentric," the acting of God reflects this nature. Furthermore, the people of God are meant to share this eccentric leaning toward the other, reflecting God's nature and action in their own nature and action as they extend this *missio Dei*.[38]

As John Flett has masterfully shown, any breach of an understanding between the being and acting of God can have negative ramifications for one's ecclesial theology and *praxis* in the church. How can this be? Flett argues that if there is a "breach in the being and act of God," then that rupture becomes replicated as a "breach in the being and act of his community."[39] If it is God's eternal decision to choose for Godself to be the God who is for and with humans, then we must grasp that this God is at the very core a "missionary God." Therefore, mission (witness) is not incidental to God's own life; rather, "witness is internal to the life of God."[40]

In the same way, God has chosen the people of God to reflect this bent toward the world; hence, the *being* or *nature* of the church should reflect the being or nature of its God in this core aspect of its identity. If mission is viewed as an "add-on" to the essence of being the church, then it will always be on the periphery of what the church does instead of the centerpiece of who we are. As Barth suggests, the church should be "leaping out or on the verge of leaping out to those to whom it

---

38. Wright, *The Mission of God*, 67. Wright notes that God's people participate in God's purposes for redemption. "The mission is God's. The marvel is that God invites us to join in."

39. Flett, *Witness of God*, 292–3. While many adherents to the *missio Dei* ecclesiology of the past fifty years have pointed to Karl Barth's trinitarian theology as the basis for their approach, John Flett has clearly established that Barth actually had little to do with the language or final development of the concept among missiologists. Barth's 1932 address, "Die Theologie und die Mission in der Gegenwart" [Theology and Mission in the Present] at the Brandenberg Missionary Conference (*Zwischen den Zeiten* 10, no. 3 (1932): 189–215), has provided some impetus for understanding missions differently. However, as David Bosch noted, it did not use the phrase *missio Dei* nor much of Barth's later understanding of the trinitarian missions within the Godhead (David J. Bosch, *Transforming Mission: Paradigm Shifts in Theology of Mission: Twentieth Anniversary Edition* [Maryknoll: Orbis Books, 2011], 399–400). Flett points out that there was a cognitive dissonance or breach cast by missiologists between God's being and doing that developed since 1952. Such missiology used the basic notion of Barth but then moved a very different direction in its development of *missio Dei* (Flett, *Witness of God*, esp. chapters 1–2). Barth's development of a trinitarian ecclesiology did not fully unfold until the 1950s. Unfortunately, many missiologists who claim Barth as their ancestor have missed his main point: there is no cleavage between God's being and doing, between God's nature and mission. This is the genius of Flett's argument: *missio Dei* really accomplishes what missiologists hoped to do theologically and practically when Barth's fuller trinitarian model establishes the connection between being and doing, nature and mission of the church. Only with this understanding can the church proclaim that God is a missionary God and mission is an attribute of God, not merely an activity of the church (Bosch, *Transforming Mission*, 390).

40. Flett, *Witness of God*, 179.

is sent."⁴¹ In this way, the orientation of the church in all its activities is always *ad extra* or *extra muros* ("toward the outside" or "outside the walls").⁴²

What does Barth offer nascent Pentecostal ecclesiologies? Barth can provide them with a clear foundation in the nature of the triune God that shapes the church's being, thereby avoiding the pitfall of numerous mission-oriented programs that become incidental to the life and mission of the church. Barth provides Pentecostal ecclesiology with a *raison d'etre* for mission that is anchored in the being of God, thereby securing an integrity between the church's nature (being) and mission (doing). The Pentecostal movement has experienced this integrity between its being and doing from its inception as expressed in the urgency to "go" into the world as "God's agents" for the salvation of humans.⁴³ Pentecostals felt impelled by the indwelling Spirit to share their stories and offer witness to what God had done for them. While they felt this urgency toward mission, they may not have always connected it theologically with the nature of God. Here is where Barth can be helpful in establishing the need for Pentecostal ecclesiologies to have integrity between its nature and mission, reflecting the nature and mission of God.

What can Pentecostals provide Barth's ecclesiology on this point? I shall point to two emphases: (1) an understanding of how Pentecost shapes ecclesiology and (2) a clearer grasp of how God's nature can become the nature of the people of God.

Regarding the first issue, Barth's ecclesiology speaks about the Holy Spirit, Pentecost, and power, to be sure, yet it also seems to run up against criticism precisely at this point. At times the Spirit seems entirely subsumed in the person of Christ, whose presence is brought to us by the Spirit yet it remains unclear who the Spirit is and what the Spirit does beyond making Christ present to the community. The "only content of the Holy Spirit is Jesus," Barth says.⁴⁴ Has Christology swallowed up pneumatology even here in Barth's ecclesiology?⁴⁵

While we haven't the space to engage in an extensive study regarding Barth's pneumatology, at the very least Pentecostals may provide some expansion of understanding who this triune God is by addressing the theological ramifications of Pentecost. At Pentecost we witness the birth of the church.⁴⁶ Given the diversity

---

41. *CD* IV/3.2, 780 rev.; *KD* IV/3.2, 892.

42. *CD* IV/3.2, 780.

43. Grant Wacker, *Heaven Below: Early Pentecostals and American Culture* (Cambridge, MA: Harvard University Press, 2001), 262.

44. *CD* IV/2, 654.

45. Bender, *Karl Barth's Christological Ecclesiology*, 277. Bender suggests Barth's theology does give "short shrift to the Holy Spirit," but hints that there may be more going on with the Spirit than is first understood by some of his critics. I tend to agree, but it may require some in-depth study of the German text in words like *wirken* and compounds of it (*wirken* can mean "to effect" or "to work").

46. Keith Warrington, *Pentecostal Theology: A Theology of Encounter* (London: T&T Clark, 2008), 107.

of gender, ethnicity, language, and social backgrounds on the Day of Pentecost when the church was established, some Pentecostals see important ramifications for ecclesiology. The Holy Spirit comes upon the *koinonia* of Christ and spills out into the marketplace, offering God's "hospitality" to those around.[47] Through the Holy Spirit's action at Pentecost, there is another "incarnation of Christ in the community of faith."[48] The Spirit sweeps up believers into the life of the Trinity, yet propels them back into the world for witness. The reality and ramification of this experience seems underplayed in Barth's thought.[49]

Regarding the second issue, Pentecostals speak of experiencing a *direct encounter* with God, such that they are transferred from the kingdom of darkness into the kingdom of light. What do we mean by such an encounter and how might it relate to a doctrine of the church? Elsewhere, I have proposed a Pentecostal ecclesiology based on this idea of the *direct encounter* with God for salvation, sanctification, and baptism with the Spirit. Such an encounter is not mediated (i.e., through something other than God), but rather is immediate and direct.[50] Even when God uses instruments through which to mediate God's presence to humans, I suggest that within the mediated form there is the direct presence of the Spirit engaging with the human spirit.[51] In this way, God's encounter with humans takes place at a level deeper or beyond that of sheer cognition. As a result of this direct encounter, there begins a transformation of believers that is initiated by the very presence of God's Spirit. This initial transforming moment establishes a platform on which further communal transforming moments in God's presence may occur, thereby bringing about a people who are moved to witness by the very nature of the God who encountered them. There is a cognitive engagement, to be sure, but the Spirit strikes a chord deeper than one's mind—it moves the heart, the (affective) core of one's being. This is where Barth's ecclesiology could be assisted by defining salvation in terms that provide more than a cognitive recognition that we are reconciled. In Barth's model of salvation, there is not enough of the human being that has been captured by the Spirit to produce genuine witness to the world in word and deed. Pentecostals may offer the experience of a direct encounter with God that establishes something of God's nature in our own being, thereby setting the stage for this God to work through us in ways that conform to God's

---

47. Daniela C. Augustine, "Pentecost Communal Economics and the Household of God," in *Pentecostal Ecclesiology: A Reader*, ed. Chris E. W. Green (Leiden: Brill, 2016), 65–87, here 71.

48. Daniela C. Augustine, "The Empowered Church: Ecclesiological Dimensions of the Event of Pentecost," in *Toward a Pentecostal Ecclesiology: The Church and the Fivefold Gospel*, ed. John Christopher Thomas (Cleveland: CPT Press, 2010), 157–80, here 161.

49. John Yocum, *Ecclesial Mediation in Karl Barth*, Barth Studies (Burlington: Ashgate, 2004), 133. Yocum notes that little attention is given to Acts in Barth's ecclesiological thought.

50. Cross, *The People of God's Presence*, esp. chapter 3 on "encounter."

51. Ibid., 125, deals with the concept of mediated immediacy.

own nature. In this way, the nature of the church can more closely align with the mission of the church.

Having engaged a discussion on the nature of the church as understood through the lens of the nature of the triune God, we move now to the next aspect of consideration, namely, the *task* or mission of the church. Again, we shall consider Barth's approach to mission and place it in dialogue with Pentecostal approaches so that we might provide some clarity for the missional ecclesiology in the life of the triune God.

The Task of the Church: missio ecclesiae

Correspondence Not Identity

The church as the body of Christ is the most prominent image of the church in Barth's writing. While the risen body of Christ is seated in the heavenlies, the "earthly-historical form of existence of Jesus Christ Himself" is located as the church on earth.[52] This definition of the church does not mean identity with Jesus Christ, since that would mean that the church could take the place of Christ. Hence, Barth can say, "Jesus Christ is the community," but not the community is Jesus Christ,[53] because the reverse would imply identity where only correspondence is to be understood. Christ's presence in the community is clearly brought through the work of the Spirit.[54] The Christian community, then, "exists as [Jesus Christ] exists.... He is its being as its very root."[55] Again, this does not mean that the church *is* Christ, but that the community itself lives and exists in active participation in Jesus' own mission by the power of the Spirit. The community's own being (nature) receives its quality from the one who gives it life, Jesus Christ. However, the church is not a continuation of the incarnation of Christ—such a claim would be blasphemous![56] Further, the being and activity of Jesus Christ needs no repetition; it merely needs to be pointed to by the community. Jesus Christ did not live only once; he also "lives today with us and like us."[57] Just as Christ exists for the world, the community of Jesus Christ exists for the world.[58] As the Christian community beholds God's face, it is changed—not into an *alter Christus*, but "necessarily into an image of the unrepeatable one Christ."[59] Therefore, as "Christ's earthly life corresponds to the will and character of God, so also the community in its

---

52. *CD* IV/1, 661.
53. Ibid., 655.
54. *CD* IV/2, 710.
55. *CD* IV/3.2, 788.
56. Ibid., 720; cf. *CD* IV/1, 317–18.
57. *CD* IV/3.2, 790.
58. Ibid., 786.
59. Ibid., 793.

historical life corresponds to the life of Christ."⁶⁰ The community must be faithful to Christ's life in the flesh "only in exact and honest and sober correspondence."⁶¹

Witness

The very root of the existence and service of the community is found in its *sending*—its mission.⁶² From the source and origin of its being in Jesus Christ whose presence is brought to us today by the Holy Spirit, the Christian congregation is called to "live in active participation in Jesus' own mission by the power of the Spirit."⁶³ Barth can speak on several occasions in this way: "The community is as such a missionary community, or she is not the Christian community."⁶⁴ Therefore, McCormack appropriately asserts, "The missionary character of the Church is given in the being of the Lord of the Church who is its basis."⁶⁵

What does this *mission* look like? The church's mission is essentially shaped by the stance of its Lord; the community bends in the shape of its Lord's being, making our own actions *correspond* to his actions. Thus, Barth can speak of each individual in the community as a "messenger of God," or one who is sent—an "apostle."⁶⁶ Christians are therefore *social by nature* in that they "cannot cease to testify that God in Christ has found [them]."⁶⁷ Barth's next line after this statement is crucial to understanding the being/doing relationship inherent within the nature of the church: "Therefore [the Christian's] being makes necessary a very definite doing. [Christians] simply cannot suppress or conceal or keep to themselves what they are. They are human beings found by God.... This is the irresistible summons to action. This is what they have to reveal and declare."⁶⁸ Hence, the change in status for the new creation in Christ impels the Christian forward into the world as one who lives *for the sake of the world*. In their service as heralds, they point beyond themselves to Jesus Christ.⁶⁹ For Barth, every Christian is called to testify on behalf of their Lord. The Christian community is essentially defined by the task of witness.⁷⁰ Like the finger of John the Baptist in Barth's favorite painting by Matthias Grünewald, the task of the community is to point—to direct the attention of the world to Jesus Christ. Believers are personally "liberated" in order to "be a

---

60. Bender, *Barth's Christological Ecclesiology*, 205. Cf. *CD* IV/3.2, 729, where Barth says there is correspondence but not identity.
61. *CD* IV/3.2, 725.
62. Ibid., 872; *KD* IV/3.2, 981.
63. Flett, *Witness of God*, 271.
64. *CD* III/4, 504–5; *KD* III/4, 578; also *CD* III/3, 64.
65. McCormack, "Witness to the Word," 72.
66. *CD* II/2, 415; *KD* II/2, 458.
67. *CD* I/2, 370.
68. Ibid., rev.
69. *CD* IV/1, 724; *KD* IV/1, 809.
70. Mangina, *Karl Barth*, 143.

witness of Jesus Christ."⁷¹ We are called to speak as a herald on behalf of the Living Lord, to testify to the "new reality of world history" in Christ.⁷² "The Christian existence is not an end in itself [*Selbstzweck*]. As fellowship with Christ it is in principle and essence a service [*Dienst*]. It is witness [*Zeugnis*]."⁷³ Hence, Christ's own prophetic office and work continue uninterrupted through the community: "There is no pause or vacuum in the exercise of His prophetic function. He Himself is fully present and active."⁷⁴

What has Barth provided Pentecostal ecclesiologies here? First, the concept of correspondence not identity offers us a clear connection to Jesus Christ. We are not Christ, but we may point to Christ through our witness. This allows the church to remain clear in its identity, whose basis is *in* Jesus Christ, but not *equated with* Jesus Christ. Pentecostals need such clarity because when the Spirit of God dwells in vessels, there is temptation to take God's presence as legitimation of any *human* notions we may have. Barth reminds us of who we are—and who we are not.

Second, Barth has used a most fitting word for the *missio ecclesiae*: witness. Pentecostal living has been drenched with that term, precisely because that was the promise of Jesus to his disciples ("You shall receive power . . . to be my witnesses," Acts 1:8). Just as Jesus Christ was an "anointed Herald of God's Kingdom,"⁷⁵ the church today extends that ministry of Jesus by pointing to him and his kingdom. However, Pentecostals also see Christ as bearing a "charismatic witness in word and deed,"⁷⁶ thereby giving us today a pattern for our own witness activity. Just as the ministry of Christ was led by and empowered by the Spirit through signs and wonders, the ministry of the church today is to be charismatic—led by and empowered by the Spirit. There is more to witness than mere pointing. As Clark Pinnock suggests, this type of charismatic ministry today is "the primary element in the promise of Pentecostal ecclesiology. It is a power ecclesiology, in which believers are endued with power to serve as anointed witnesses to the kingdom of God. Pentecostals experience God as empowering and commissioning them for mission."⁷⁷ Barth's concept of witness and liberation seems to provide the elementary blocks for building on the Pentecostal experience of empowerment for mission by the Spirit, but Pentecostals will want to fill out Barth's rather sketchy outline with the *power* of the Spirit.

In relation to this, Barth does offer a rather nuanced proposal for divine–human agency in the life of the church. While Barth has been criticized by some for not making justification and/or sanctification an occurrence in *this world* but rather one that is realized in the next, I have argued elsewhere (and will argue here in

---

71. *CD* IV/3.2, 663; *KD* IV/3.2, 760.
72. *CD* IV/3.2, 712.
73. Ibid., 647–8, rev.; *KD* IV/3.2, 742.
74. *CD* IV/3.1, 349–50.
75. This phrase comes from Pinnock, "Church in the Power of the Holy Spirit," 151.
76. Pinnock, "Church in the Power of the Holy Spirit," 150.
77. Ibid., 151.

this context as well) that for Barth there is a genuine effect generated by the Spirit upon the human being living in this age between the times so that humans may *respond* to God's work in them.[78] Barth does not speak clearly of transformation and deliverance as features of the Christian life here and now because these could be seized upon by humans in some type of "triumphalism," thereby bypassing the accomplished work of Christ in reconciliation. However, he does hint toward a reality of the new age impinging on the present—an "alteration" of sorts.[79] Indeed, how could his doctrine of the church as witness operate if it were not for the power of "liberation" in the Spirit, delivering us from our sin and darkness about our situation and freeing us to join with God in the effort of *witness* for him to the world? As John Drury has argued, Barth does have a grasp of how one's *testimony* or witness to Christ relies to some extent on one's *liberation*.[80]

Nevertheless, the tone of Barth's words in the doctrine of reconciliation lacks the emphatic strength of deliverance that echoes from Pentecostal experiences. Here is where we may build on Barth's thoughts by emphasizing the present transforming power of the Spirit for witness. How would this look different from Barth? Barth can address liberation (*Befreiung*) with strong words like these: a community is called to be God's witnesses so that this calling comes to humans "in such a way that they experience [*wiederfährt*] a special liberation [*eine besondere Befreiung*], namely, that it is given to them to receive it."[81] For Barth, recipients of this freeing power are "open" to receiving the content of God's reconciliation; they see it and appropriate it for themselves. God's grace in Christ is no longer unknown, nor is it "merely an external and therefore alien phenomenon; it is something known and properly understood, a part of their own experience, i.e., an element in their own life [*zu einem Element ihres eignen Lebens*]."[82] The calling from the Word of God and the revelatory knowledge and experience of the content of reconciliation mean that the recipients are "by all means, no longer the human beings they previously were" [*auf alle Fälle nicht mehr die Menschen, die sie vorher waren*].[83] It is the power of the "reality" that is disclosed and shared with them in the Word of God that "has become a factor in their own personal existence" [*ist zu einem Faktor inhrer persönlich menschlichen Existenz geworden*].[84] This is

---

78. See Terry L. Cross, "Christ in Us: The Hope of Glory or the Sentimentality of a 'Bohemian Private Enterprise'? Barth, Pietists, and Pentecostals," in *Karl Barth and the Future of Evangelical Theology*, ed. Christian T. Collins Winn and John L. Drury (Eugene: Wipf & Stock, 2014), 69–90.

79. *CD* IV/3.2, 650.

80. John L. Drury, "Barth and Testimony," in *Karl Barth and the Future of Evangelical Theology*, ed. Christian T. Collins Winn and John L. Drury (Eugene: Wipf & Stock, 2014), 110.

81. *CD* IV/3.2, 649; *KD* IV/3.2, 743.

82. *CD* IV/3.2, 649; *KD* IV/3.2, 744.

83. My translation: *KD* IV/3.2, 744; cf. *CD* IV/3.2, 649.

84. *CD* IV/3.2, 649; *KD* IV/3.2, 744.

not some merely external operation that has no impact on the present. This is liberation from the bondage of fear and sin into a freedom to respond positively to the impulse of the Spirit to become Christian witnesses of God's reconciling grace. Hence this vocation "implies and creates a distinction and alteration [*eine Auszeichnung und Veränderung*] of the being of the person who is called."[85]

What can Pentecostals add to this? My response is twofold. First, Barth's overall approach to how much humans may cooperate with God is rigidly controlled by his strong dislike of synergy. What is to be the human response to God's grace? Gratitude. "Grace and gratitude belong together like heaven and earth. Grace evokes gratitude like the voice of an echo. Gratitude follows grace like thunder lightning."[86] Even in this imagery, the divine initiative in grace *determines and controls* the human "free" response.[87] When this is examined in light of ecclesiology, the church should always *correspond* its life and work with the life and work of Jesus Christ. The church *responds* to God's grace by demonstrating their gratitude as a form of *correspondence* to Christ's life. Human work in this light is real, free, and markedly altered from before. However, this tends to mute Barth's ecclesiology in terms of mission. God accomplishes in humans what God desires, but to such a degree that God seems to be the only subject of this action and the role of the human seems relatively passive.[88] Are human *correspondence* and human *response* adequate to describe the work of the miraculously created yet definitely human church? Pentecostals have experienced the results of God's presence and power in this age in the lives of the people of God and will expect this transformation to be part of any ecclesiology. Moreover, Barth's emphasis on the *provisional* dimension of the church's nature as a representation of the "final goal of reconciliation" that will be realized only in the eschaton tends to downplay the need for deliverance and transformation here and now—something that is so central to Pentecostal life and theology.[89]

Pentecostals can offer Barth an ecclesiology that also emphasizes divine initiative (the disciples spoke in tongues as the Spirit gave them the ability, Acts 2:4) while not ignoring human cooperation. However, for Pentecostals there is more to "witness" than the Baptist's pointing finger. There is power that transforms

---

85. *CD* IV/3.2, 650, rev.; *KD* IV/3.2, 744–5.
86. *CD* IV/1, 41.
87. Ibid., 776.
88. Bender has noted the charge usually runs like this: "God everything and humanity nothing." Bender, *Karl Barth's Christological Ecclesiology*, 177. Bender thinks this charge is mistaken because it does not take into account Barth's "conception of correspondence." Mangina also argues on behalf of Barth here that the miracle of grace creates the church and "new realities." It also "empowers human beings to be responsible agents." See Mangina, *Karl Barth*, 144. My point in this chapter here is that I recognize the various ways to "rescue" Barth's downplaying of human agency, but I believe the resultant tone of this discussion mutes a vibrant ecclesial response.
89. *CD* IV/2, 620–1.

human agents into channels of God's grace with signs and wonders following them. As Jesus notes, "But if I drive out demons by the finger of God, then the kingdom of God has come upon you" (Lk. 11:20 NIV). Matthew renders this finger of God as the "Spirit of God" (Mt. 12:28). Pentecostals recognize that *our finger* points with power through the *finger of God, the Spirit*. Perhaps Barth's "tendency toward strong disjunction of the divine and human action" is overly charged on the divine aspect, rendering the human response apparently quite minimal.[90] Pentecostals can offer a robust view of sanctification that addresses concerns about the human response.

The work of the Holy Spirit is to make believers holy. Daniela Augustine notes that sanctification, whose goal is the likeness of God, "demands the synergistic collaboration between the divine and human will."[91] Augustine also engages the doctrine of the Trinity for ecclesiology by pointing to the sanctifying work of the Spirit in *theosis* in the present. Hence, the Pentecost community (both in Acts 2 and now) is an "outcome of the socio-transformative work of the Spirit" and becomes an "embodiment of God's hospitality and self-sharing with the other."[92] The community of faith becomes the household of God. "The Spirit transforms them into Christ-likeness, making them partakers of the divine nature and translating them into the life of the Trinity so that in turn they can become an incarnation of the divine communal life on earth."[93] The key point for Augustine is the transformation of humans (individuals and community) into the likeness of Christ and thus a society of transformation that continues the ministry of Christ by drawing believers up into the divine communal life on earth. Augustine's proposal requires the Trinity as the ontological basis of the Christian community, but even more so, it demands the transformation of personal desires into the desires of Christ (a *theosis* of sorts). This seems to push us toward the "promise of Pentecostal ecclesiology" that Clark Pinnock proclaimed in 2005, namely, a society that has been delivered and transformed by the power of God and shares that delivering power with the world.[94]

Second, Pentecostals view the reality of God's empowerment through the Spirit as an essential "mark" of the church.[95] The people of God receive power from the Spirit to witness to the world. This is not only about boldness to speak for Christ, but also about strength to live for Christ. For Pentecostals, there is more power for witnessing than finger pointing. Here is where discussion about the Spirit's gifts (*charismata*) could richly inform Barth's discussion of the gathering, upbuilding, and sending of the community of faith. By attaching pneumatology so closely to Christology, various aspects of the first-century church's life and practice seem

---

90. These words are from Yocum, *Ecclesial Mediation in Karl Barth*, 97.
91. Augustine, "Pentecost Communal Economics and the Household of God," 72–3.
92. Ibid., 85.
93. Ibid., 70.
94. Pinnock, "Church in the Power of the Holy Spirit," 151.
95. Vondey, *Pentecostal Theology*, 239.

ignored.[96] One of these areas is the *charismata* of the Spirit. The Spirit maintains and empowers the church to do the mission it is called to do. Without these gifts of the Spirit for the edification of the body and without the Spirit's personal indwelling and empowering of the body of Christ, all our efforts become weak, miserly constructs of human endeavors.

Having first engaged Barth and Pentecostals on the *nature* of the church as viewed from the nature of the triune God and having just considered their views on the *task* or mission of the church as the interaction of divine and human agencies, we move now to consider a third aspect of Barth's ecclesiology, namely, *order* of the church.

Institutional "Order" of the Church

Institution and Order: The Living Community of the Living Lord[97]

For all of its truly miraculous nature as the work of the Holy Spirit, the Christian community still operates with a *human* counterpart to the divine initiative. The Spirit's work does not remain in some supra-spiritual sphere, but "takes place among humans in the form of a human activity."[98] By contrast, in his work devoted to the church, Emil Brunner proposed the rather stark idea of eliminating any institutional remnant of the church and focusing instead on the more mystical fellowship of the Spirit. He argued that this was the condition of the first-century church and one to which we need return. The *ekklēsia* of the New Testament was a "*Christusgemeinde*" ["a community of Christ"] not "*eine Institution, ein Etwas*" ["an institution, a Something"].[99] At various points throughout *CD* IV, Barth takes on Brunner's proposal. In an extensive section dealing with the "order of the community" and what Barth calls "canon law," he argues that a church without law or institutional structure is not appropriate for the *communio sanctorum*.[100] While Brunner may long for a "pure fellowship of persons" (*eine Gemeinschaft von Personen*),[101] such a community abandons "its life to chance and caprice and confusion" and will be a "contradiction to the Holy Spirit of Jesus Christ" as much

---

96. Yocum, *Ecclesial Mediation in Karl Barth*, 133. "Little attention is given to the role that the New Testament seems to assign the Spirit-empowered Church in the actual accomplishment of the work of Christ."

97. This phrase comes from the title of an address by Barth, "The Church: The Living Congregation of the Living Lord Jesus Christ," in *God Here and Now*, trans. Paul van Buren (London: Routledge, 2003; 1st English ed., 1964), 75–104.

98. *CD* IV/1, 650; rev.

99. Emil Brunner, *Das Mißverständnis der Kirche* (Stuttgart: Evangelisches Verlagswerk G.M.B.H, 1951), 12.

100. *CD* IV/2, 676.

101. Brunner, *Das Mißverständnis der Kirche*, 12.

as one that is enslaved to its laws.[102] In a fashion that sounds almost Pentecostal, Barth portrays Brunner as declaring with exasperation, "What we need is the Holy Ghost!" To this cry Barth responds, "Of course we do. But . . ."[103] Without the institutional aspects of the community, we cannot remain the church but will run into a disorder that will diminish and disguise the true church. Barth reminds Pentecostals of the danger of this anti-institutional tendency.

In his challenge to Pentecostals concerning ecclesiology, Clark Pinnock raised a similar concern. He encouraged Pentecostals to include in their ecclesiologies something he called "an institutional dimension."[104] Pinnock's challenge was not to choose *one* structure, but determine which ones are "appropriate."[105] It may be that Barth can help us in this institutional dimension. Here, Barth can provide Pentecostal ecclesiology with a legitimacy for institution and order within the church as a proper, God-given counterbalance to hyper-spiritualized aspects that may creep into a Pentecostal way of being and doing church.

Another aspect where Barth may assist Pentecostals is in the area of ecclesial mediation. Kimlyn Bender notes two implications for ecclesiology that Barth's approach to Christ's presence holds: (1) Christ is present by the power of the Spirit, so the church does not stand as a "surrogate for Christ upon earth";[106] (2) Christ is present by the power of the Spirit so that the church does not mediate the "salvific effects of his past atonement through some form of sacramental action."[107] The role of the church is as *witness*, not as sacramental mediator. Hence, due to Christ's presence among us in the Spirit, the nature and mission of the church is focused on bearing witness to the ever living One, Jesus Christ. In terms of soteriology, the church is not the *mediator of salvation*, not even a *means of grace*; it cannot reconcile the world with God—only Christ can do that.[108]

The ramifications for ecclesiology in this understanding of Christ's presence are substantial. Far from being the dispensary of grace through the sacraments or any other action performed by it, the church points to the one, true sacrament—Jesus Christ.[109] Through the Spirit's work, Jesus Christ is "fully present and active" in the world today.[110] Therefore, Christ does not "need any representatives, any anointed or unanointed, great or small, sacramentally or existentially endowed vicars."[111] In line with this understanding of the non-sacramental view of the church, any of the activities the church performs cannot be "sacramental" in the sense of bringing

---

102. *CD* IV/2, 681.
103. Ibid.
104. Pinnock, "Church in the Power of the Holy Spirit," 161.
105. Ibid., 162.
106. Bender, *Karl Barth's Christological Ecclesiology*, 148.
107. Ibid.
108. *CD* IV/3.1, 349. Busch, *The Great Passion*, 263.
109. *CD* IV/2, 50, 55; Cf. also *CD* IV/2, 107 and *CD* IV/4, 102.
110. *CD* IV/3.1, 350.
111. Ibid.

grace to the human being (especially conceived as dispensed through the human hands of the church). Instead, activities like baptism and the Lord's Supper are *human actions in response to God's gracious action.*[112]

What does Barth's non-sacramental view of the church offer Pentecostals? First, Barth views the institution as nonhierarchical; essentially, it is egalitarian. In his ecclesiology, "service is not the privilege or concern of a few."[113] Each one is called to represent Christ by serving. This view works against any type of "practical clericalism" in the church.[114] The ranking or hierarchy that frequently divides the body of Christ cannot be part of Christ's *communion*. Barth clearly de-emphasizes all such "practical clericalism" [*allem praktischen Klerikalismus*] and even wants to "avoid the fatal word 'office,' [*Amt*] and replace it by 'service'" [*des Dienstes*], thereby allowing it to be a term "which can be applied to all Christians."[115]

It is my belief that this style of non-clericalism must be a feature of any Pentecostal ecclesiology because clericalism tends to make both calling and ministry into gifts and tasks reserved for a select few, whereas the Spirit of God distributes the gifts according to his own will. A Pentecostal church should be egalitarian;[116] it should be characterized by the Spirit's gifting upon all individuals within a congregation for the benefit of the local body and the world.[117] This does not mean a church should be leaderless, but it does mean that a hierarchy of authority in the local congregation is less likely to be fertile ground for the Spirit's gift to be released and used among all God's people for the common good.

Second, Barth's denial of any ecclesial mediation points Pentecostals toward non-sacramental ways of viewing the ordinances/sacraments as human *responses* to God's grace, not as means of grace. The resultant theology highlights the

---

112. Barth makes this most clear in *CD* IV/4 (*Fragment*) where baptism is a human response to God's grace, not an ecclesial action that *confers* grace. While Barth is chided by some Reformed interpreters for his shift from supporting infant baptism to denying any efficacy of baptism as a sacramental ritual (and therefore supporting credobaptism as the appropriate, NT response to God's act of grace in Christ), I see it as a long developing program in Barth's ecclesiology (since about 1943) and especially in line with his writing in the 1950s on reconciliation and the community. Baptism with water is the human response to the work of the Spirit to change and liberate humans from their bondage to sin. It is not a sacrament (*CD* IV/4, 128). "Baptism takes place in active recognition of the grace of God which justifies, sanctifies and calls. It is not itself, however, the bearer, means, or instrument of grace" (*CD* IV/4, 102).

113. *CD* IV/2, 693.

114. Ibid., 694.

115. Ibid.; *KD* IV/2, 787.

116. Vondey, *Pentecostal Theology*, 231.

117. See Terry L. Cross, *Serving the People of God's Presence: A Theology of Ministry* (Grand Rapids: Baker Academic, 2020), where I offer a strong antihierarchical view of ministry where the priesthood of believers is pointed to as the structural promise for releasing the people of God in their giftings.

sovereignty of the Spirit over and through instruments of God's choosing while not succumbing to the temptation to make the church the distributor of God's grace or gifts. It is the Spirit who gives gifts *as he determines*.

Conclusion

On December 13, 1967, Barth had a conversation with a group of Mennonites. They asked him about the Pentecostal movement. While admitting that he knew too little to respond with any depth, he said that churches should not fear this movement since the "Holy Spirit is indeed what we need."[118] If things are "aboveboard" with the movement, then we can praise God for it—yet we will have to see up close "how things are done there."[119]

It is the inspection and reflection involved in this line, "how things are done there," that can guide the beginning efforts of developing a Pentecostal ecclesiology in this century. However, as we have seen, an examination of Barth's own ecclesiology can prove fruitful when we examine "how things are done there," as well. The mutual engagement of Barth and Pentecostals can indeed show us that the Spirit is what we need.

---

118. Karl Barth, "Conversation with Mennonites (December 13, 1967)," in *Karl Barth in Conversation, Volume 3, 1964–1968*, ed. Eberhard Busch, trans. Darrell L. Guder and Matthias Gockel (Louisville: Westminster John Knox Press, 2019), 289.

119. Ibid.

Chapter 15

YOU WONDER WHERE THE REAL PRESENCE WENT

THE SACRAMENTS AND THE PENTECOSTAL EXPERIENCE OF GOD

Chris E. W. Green

Introduction

At first glance, Barth's sacramental theology as laid out in *CD* IV/4 seems to fit nicely with Pentecostal spirituality and theology. First, his emphasis on obedience in observing the water and table rites accords with Pentecostal concerns. Water baptism, for Barth, is a strictly human response to a prior divine act, "the first and exemplary step on the way of obedience."[1] Pentecostals by and large agree, identifying water baptism as a "normative practice expected of all believers as a sign of obedience to the command of Jesus," but nonetheless not in any sense necessary for salvation or a "means to regeneration."[2] Second, Pentecostals share Barth's absolute refusal of the *ex opere operato* principle.[3] Many, in fact, prefer to use the term "ordinance" precisely to avoid any magical connotations,[4] and all Pentecostals, like Barth, are quick to deny anything like "self-contained efficacy" to the sacraments.[5] In Barth's phrasing, "Christian baptism, like John's, is in no sense a self-sufficient act which is in some way divinely fulfilled or self-fulfilling within itself."[6] Third, Barth's christocentrism resonates with the Pentecostal four-/fivefold gospel. Finished-Work Pentecostals, in particular, would appreciate Barth's emphasis on the already-accomplished work of God in Jesus' death and

---

1. *CD* IV/4, 43.
2. John Bond, "What is Distinctive about Pentecostal Theology," in *What is Distinctive about Pentecostal Theology*, ed. M. S. Clark and H. I. Lederle (Pretoria: UNISA, 1989), 139.
3. See, for example, Harold D. Hunter, "Ordinances," in *New International Dictionary of Pentecostal and Charismatic Movements*, ed. Stanley M. Burgess and Eduard M. van der Maas (Grand Rapids: Zondervan, 2002), 947–9.
4. See, for example, Michael Dusing, "The New Testament Church," in *Systematic Theology*, ed. Stanley Horton (rev. ed.; Springfield: Logion Press, 1998), 558.
5. Harold D. Hunter, "Reflections by a Pentecostalist on Aspects of *BEM*," *Journal of Ecumenical Studies* 29, no. 3–4 (Summer–Fall 1992): 345.
6. *CD* IV/4, 71.

resurrection. In fact, Barth opposes the church's traditional sacramentalism precisely because it seems to suggest a "duplication" of the history of Christ,[7] which is similar to Finished-Work critiques of Wesleyan Pentecostalism.[8] Finally, and above all, Pentecostals are sure to "Amen!" Barth's claim that the living God—and not human rituals or practices—effect our salvation. But it is just there, in the claim about the present-tense work of the living God, that certain real differences begin to emerge between aspects of Barth's later dogmatics and at least some forms of Pentecostal theology/spirituality.

Barth in Dispute with the Tradition

Barth's late eucharistic theology, if we can call it that, is fairly bluntly antitraditional.[9] Barth does say that the Eucharist bears witness to the church's status as *sanctorum communio*, but it does not by any means constitute communion with Christ. Aaron Riches argues that "the Eucharist [for Barth] is not a real participation in *communio*," it merely represents "*communio*."[10] This is so, Riches contends, because of Barth's underdetermined pneumatology. "Pneumatology is accorded an ontologically minimal role, which devolves to the Eucharist an abstractly declarative function."[11]

Whatever we make of Riches's critique, *CD* IV/4 seems quite clear: Barth means his account of water baptism and the Lord's Supper to contradict the overwhelming majority of the received Christian tradition.[12] Regarding baptism, in particular,

---

7. Ibid., 102.

8. See Kimberly Ervin Alexander, "Divine Healing: Sacramental Signs of Salvation," in *The Routledge Handbook of Pentecostal Theology*, ed. Wolfgang Vondey (New York: Routledge, 2020), 257–67.

9. Arguably, this is markedly different from his earlier work. For instance, John Yocum (*Ecclesial Mediation in Karl Barth* [Aldershot: Ashgate, 2004], 136) argues that "the note of potential rivalry between the divine and human actions and between divine sovereignty and human institutions is absent from *The Knowledge of God and the Service of God*." In that volume, Barth argues that the "content" of the church service is God's work alone, while human action makes the "form." The "form . . . cannot be confounded with its content and hence cannot be made absolute, as if Jesus Christ had rendered himself superfluous through the human institution of the church," but still, "the form of the church service, cannot be detached from it content, and cannot therefore be lightly esteemed and neglected as if Jesus Christ did not wish to glorify himself expressly in the human institution of the church."

10. Aaron Riches, "Church, Eucharist, and Predestination in Barth and de Lubac: Convergence and Divergence in *Communio*," *Communio* 35 (Winter 2008): 565–98, here 587.

11. Ibid., 587.

12. So Barth (*CD* IV/4, 129–30): "According to Zwingli himself all teachers from the days of the apostles had greatly erred. . . . We for our part cannot deny that both negatively and positively Zwingli was basically right."

he opposes "in principle and *ob ovo* an ancient and overwhelmingly strong ecclesiastical and theological tradition" in all of its Roman Catholic, Lutheran, or Reformed modes.[13] In setting forth this "neo-Zwinglian" alternative,[14] Barth wants to "demythologize" the consensus view of the "so-called 'sacraments.'"[15] To that end, he insists that baptism—and, by implication, the Lord's Supper, as well—is *not* a mystery.[16] The celebration of Holy Communion is a strictly human act, although of course enabled by the Spirit, offered in response to a strictly divine one. In the same way, baptism is nothing more or less than the appropriate reaction to the sovereign act of God, accomplished otherwise.[17] He makes the point as sharp as he can: "the praise of baptism is not served but fatefully damaged if the sanctity of this action is sought, not in the true and distinctive thing which characterizes it as a human action, but in a supposedly immanent divine work."[18] What matters most is that the difference between God's work and human work is maintained. "In these rites, God does not do what human beings do, just as human beings cannot do what God does."[19]

Barth also leaves less than no room for a pietistic or mystical version of sacramentality. He warns that when the traditional view of water baptism is rejected, "the price which is blatantly paid is that the external work of water baptism, robbed of its glory as a sacrament, is replaced by an 'inner work' in the form of experiences, inspirations, illuminations, exaltations or raptures."[20] He will have none of this. Baptism and Holy Communion are not sacramental in any way—"outwardly" or "inwardly." Christ—or, better, the event of Christ's death—is

---

13. *CD* IV/4, 102.

14. It is difficult if not impossible to determine either what Barth meant exactly by "neo-Zwinglian" or for that matter what Zwingli himself held to be true Christ's presence in relation to the church's celebration of Communion. And it may be that Barth's affirmation of the Spirit's work in this context indicates that his view is not as anti-sacramental as it appears to be, especially once allowances are made for his polemical concerns.

15. *CD* IV/1, 667.

16. As is well known, Barth ended his *Church Dogmatics* before focusing his attention on the Lord's Supper as he had done on water and Spirit baptism in *CD* IV/4.

17. *CD* IV/4, 108. Adam Neder (*Participation in Christ: An Entry into Karl Barth's Church Dogmatics* [Louisville: Westminster John Knox Press, 2009], 83) concludes that "Barth accounts for the transition from de jure to de facto participation in Christ, not with a sacramental doctrine of baptism, but with a Christocentric pneumatology and a theology of the resurrection of Jesus Christ. . . . Therefore, baptism and the Lord's Supper are not divinely appointed means of grace; they do not represent or mediate salvation, and therefore they are not sacraments."

18. *CD* IV/4, 101.

19. Ibid., 105. See Anthony R. Cross, "Baptism in the Theology of John Calvin and Karl Barth," in *Calvin, Barth, and Reformed Theology*, ed. Neil B. MacDonald and Carl R. Trueman (Eugene: Wipf & Stock, 2008), 57–87.

20. *CD* IV/4, 106.

alone sacramental. The New Testament, Barth insists, never speaks of the mysteries (plural) but only the mystery (singular): "The event itself, the event of the death of man, is that of the death of Jesus Christ on Golgotha." "This is the one *mysterium*, the one sacrament, and the existential fact before and beside and after which there is no room for any other of the same rank."[21] Although the church is his body, Jesus' work stands apart from all that the church does. He does not share his glory with others, at least not in this sense.

Pentecostals in Dialogue with Barth

While Pentecostals share Barth's "Protestant" refusal of sacerdotalism and ritualism, and while they share at least something of his leeriness about the assertions of the received dogmatic tradition, they do not share his apparent distaste for "experiences, inspirations, illuminations, exaltations or raptures." Arguably, they also hold to a more pronounced and full-bodied pneumatology, which in turn allows them to celebrate human collaboration with and participation in God's work in ways Barth could not, at least in his later work.[22] For Pentecostals, therefore, what happens at the Lord's Table is indeed a mystery, accomplished in the synergy of divine and human action. French Arrington, for example, even when speaking of the Supper as a "remembrance," argues that "this word is so powerful it signifies that the death of Christ is *made effective now* and brings blessings into the present."[23] And he finds it revealing that sometimes people receive healing or are baptized in the Spirit when participating in the Communion meal.[24] Pentecostals, he concludes, come to the Table with "a sense of the profound presence of Christ and His blessing at the Supper."[25] Similarly, Frank Macchia maintains that Pentecostal spirituality can rightly be designated "sacramental," so long as the term is carefully defined.[26] He believes that even if many Pentecostals claim a Zwinglian view of the Eucharist, "their actual eucharistic devotion is more complex."[27] Despite the non- or weakly

---

21. CD IV/1, 296.
22. See Robert W. Jenson, "You Wonder Where the Spirit Went," *Pro Ecclesia* II, no. 3 (1993): 296-304. More than a few Barthians have taken issue with Jenson's reading. Thankfully, I do not have to settle the debate.
23. French L. Arrington, *Christian Doctrine Vol. 3* (Cleveland: Pathway Press, 1992), 212. Emphasis added.
24. Ibid., 214.
25. Ibid.
26. Macchia's sacramental understanding is shaped to a great degree by the works of Paul Tillich and Karl Rahner. Macchia believes Rahner and Tillich have managed to emphasize the objectivity of the sacraments without restricting divine freedom because they conceive it primarily in personalistic and not metaphysical terms.
27. Frank D. Macchia, "Eucharist: Pentecostal," in *The New Westminster Dictionary of Liturgy and Worship*, ed. Paul F. Bradshaw (Louisville: WJKP, 2002), 189-90, here 190.

sacramental theological descriptions, Pentecostals nonetheless experience baptism and the Lord's Supper as "occasions for God's redemptive presence through the power of the Spirit."[28]

Even though Veli-Matti Kärkkäinen believes that the Pentecostal movement is "loaded with anti-sacramental sentiment," he finds that the Lord's Supper nevertheless plays an important role in the churchly life of Pentecostals.[29] At least some Pentecostals affirm a "spiritual" dimension to the meal that exceeds the merely symbolic, even while they reject the classical view of real presence.[30] Kärkkäinen cites a statement by the Foursquare theologian Nathaniel van Cleave, who first repudiates the "superstition" of the classical view, but goes on to speak of the "real operation of the Spirit" for strengthening and healing those who partake of the elements in faith.[31] Dan Tomberlin argues that Pentecostals can and should recognize the sacraments—water baptism, the Lord's Supper, footwashing, and anointing with oil—as real and really effective means of grace.[32] In his own words: "The waters of the baptismal pool, the bread and cup of the Eucharist, and the anointing oil can indeed be sacraments, that is, they are means through which believers encounter the Spirit of grace."[33] As his book's subtitle makes clear, the altar serves as a focal image for Tomberlin, as does Christ's priestly ministry. He returns again and again to this image and its complex of themes to make his central point:

> Through Christ the High Priest and the Spirit of grace, sacraments are more than mere reenactments or memorials to God's redemptive acts; the baptismal water, the towel and basin, the bread and wine, and the anointing oil become mediatory gifts.[34]

Kenneth Archer, following John Christopher Thomas, argues that Pentecostals should take up the language of "sacramental ordinances," in hopes that this language will help Pentecostal hold various emphases together in dynamic tension. With Macchia, he finds it unfortunate that "some Pentecostals deny any 'real grace' being 'mediated' through the ordinances."[35] He laments such a reductionist treatment of

---

28. Frank D. Macchia, "Is Footwashing the Neglected Sacrament? A Theological Response to John Christopher Thomas," *Pneuma* 19, no. 2 (Fall 1997): 239–49, here 241.

29. Veli-Matti Kärkkäinen, "The Pentecostal View," in *The Lord's Supper: Five Views*, ed. Gordon T. Smith (Downers Grove: IVP, 2008), 118.

30. Ibid., 123.

31. Ibid., 119.

32. Dan Tomberlin, *Pentecostal Sacraments: Encountering God at the Altar* (Cleveland: Center for Pentecostal Leadership and Care, 2010), 82.

33. Ibid., 86.

34. Ibid.

35. Kenneth J. Archer, "Nourishment for our Journey: The Pentecostal Via Salutis and Sacramental Ordinances," *Journal of Pentecostal Theology* 13, no. 1 (2004): 84.

the ordinances because it truncates the "mysteries," diminishing them to "mere memorial rites" that facilitate nothing more than "cognitive reflection devoid of the Spirit's presence and power."[36] And he believes that a truly Pentecostal view of the ordinances would discern their "mystical significance," and so reveal them to be sacraments in and through which believers participate in the realities of the kingdom.[37]

Amos Yong goes even further, contending that Pentecostals can appropriate a "fully sacramental" view of both water baptism and the Lord's Supper, a view that nevertheless remains "consistent with Pentecostal intuitions regarding the Spirit's presence and activity in the worshipping community."[38] To be sure, he maintains that Pentecostals should not regard the sacraments in the "classical" sense, whereby salvation is "mediated through the priesthood, through baptism, or through the (other) sacraments."[39] Nonetheless, the "Spirit's reality" can and should be understood as in fact "mediated through the particularly embodied experiences of the community of saints." When so understood, one finds a "unique sort of pentecostal sacramentality at work" that operates with an "experiential and incarnational logic that acknowledges the Spirit's being made present and active through the materiality of personal embodiment and congregational life."[40] For example, Yong asserts that the rite of water baptism is not merely memorialistic or symbolic, but actually "enacts our participation in the death and resurrection of Christ" and serves as the "means by which we experience the life of Jesus by the Holy Spirit."[41] The baptism ritual is, in Yong's view, an act of "obedient participation in the death of Jesus." He is careful to say that the sacramentality of the rite resides not in the "materiality of consecrated water" but in the Holy Spirit's personal presence and activity.[42] Water baptism, Yong insists, is not to be regarded as "magically washing away sins," but it can and should be regarded as regenerative—insofar as it is understood to effect the Spirit's work "pneumatically and mystically," and to include the "faith response of believers."[43] As with water baptism, so with the Eucharist: the personal and intimate activity of the Holy Spirit is central and decisive. Only the Spirit's perlocutionary and illocutionary power guarantees that the Lord's Supper is indeed a genuine "remembering" of the church's memory of Christ. In the Lord's Supper, Christ is present to the celebrants and they are present to Christ, their mutual presence made possible by the Spirit-being "invited to reign over the Supper" in the epiclesis. For only the

---

36. Ibid.
37. Ibid., 96.
38. Amos Yong, *The Spirit Poured Out on All Flesh* (Grand Rapids: Baker Academic, 2005), 160.
39. Ibid., 136.
40. Yong, *The Spirit Poured Out on All Flesh*, 136.
41. Ibid., 159.
42. Ibid., 158.
43. Ibid.

Spirit's coming in response to the church's invocation "mak[es] present the living Christ in the 'membered' elements of the bread and cup and in the 'members' of the congregation as the living body of Christ."[44] Yong holds that Pentecostals and charismatics have no need for a doctrine of transubstantiation, because everything depends upon the Spirit-possibilized "intersubjective mutuality" between Christ and the believing community, a mutuality that, by the Spirit's power, "becomes a mysterious interpersonal encounter wherein Christ and his body are brought into real relationship."[45] Given that this is so, the Supper must be regarded as a "sacramental rite" that in fact "transforms the worshipping community through word and Spirit."[46]

Of course, it may be that these Pentecostal scholars are simply out of touch with the theology and practice of the movement at large. Certainly, the diversity of the movement is virtually impossible to overstate, and it would be a mistake to make essentialist assertions about Pentecostal spirituality.[47] And Terry Cross has argued that Pentecostals should be wary of the term "sacrament," following Barth's directive never to forget that these are "*human* acts, not acts of God's revelation or any conveyance of grace."[48] All such cautions notwithstanding, a great many Pentecostals in various contexts from the beginning of the movement until now have shown what Walter Hollenweger identified a generation ago as "a clear and well-developed pattern of eucharistic devotion and practice."[49] This may seem surprising to some, given that the first "wave" of Pentecostals belonged to the free-church tradition and that all Pentecostals, including Catholic charismatics, emphasize the believer's immediate experience of the Spirit. But Hollenweger's extensive study of various Pentecostal movements convinced him that the celebration of the Eucharist rite is indeed the "central point of Pentecostal worship," a veritable "holy of holies" of the worship service.[50] And Jonathan Black's recent account of the Apostolic Church (UK) affirms this conclusion. In his words, "weekly Breaking of Bread has been the practice and teaching of the Apostolic Church for the (over) 100 years of its existence,"[51] because apostolic Pentecostals believed Holy Communion holds "an absolute central place in congregational

---

44. Ibid., 162–3.
45. Ibid., 164.
46. Ibid., 163.
47. See Chris E. W. Green, "Pentecostalism," in *The Cambridge Companion to American Protestantism*, ed. Jason Vickers and Jennifer Woodruff Tait (New York: Cambridge University Press, forthcoming 2022), 461–78.
48. Terry L. Cross, *Serving the People of God's Presence: A Theology of Ministry* (Grand Rapids: Baker Academic, 2020), 195.
49. Walter Hollenweger, *The Pentecostals* (Nashville: Hendrickson, 1988), 385.
50. To underscore the point, he cites the doctrinal declaration by the Congregacao Crista that the Eucharist is a means of "intimate communion" with Christ.
51. Jonathan Black, *Apostolic Theology: A Trinitarian Evangelical Pentecostal Introduction to Christian Doctrine* (Luton: The Apostolic Church, 2016), 595.

worship."⁵² My own study of early Pentecostalism in the United States reached the same conclusion.⁵³ So, it's very hard to deny that Pentecostals—at least a great many of them—hold to a robustly sacramental view of the Lord's Supper, affirming the reality of Christ's presence for those gathered in faith.⁵⁴

It might be argued that even those Pentecostals who would disagree with Barth on the Lord's Supper would agree with him on water baptism. They tend to reject traditional theologies of baptism, although almost exclusively on pastoral grounds. They fear that treating water baptism as a sacrament leads more or less inevitably to nominal Christian practice, and they want no part of a practice that undermines the primacy of faith and the call to personal responsibility before God.⁵⁵ Insofar as Barth addresses these concerns, Pentecostals are sure to affirm his view. But significant differences remain, nonetheless. First, as their testimonies of baptism events indicate, Pentecostals expect God to act in the washing rite. The baptism rite provides "a context for experiencing the redemptive and sanctifying presence of God in great power."⁵⁶ Baptism, like footwashing and the Eucharist, is a prophetic and narratival sign bodied forth in word and deed through which the community experiences "the redemptive living presence of God in Christ through the Holy Spirit."⁵⁷ Second, while Barth does not want baptism to duplicate the history of Jesus Christ,⁵⁸ Pentecostals emphasize that baptism is a following of Christ, an entering into his story, a participation in his life. Water baptism, undertaken in faith, actually "enacts our participation in the death and resurrection of Christ." In the waters, by the Spirit, the baptized "experience the life of Jesus."⁵⁹ Third, while Barth wants to avoid at all costs a confusion of divine and human activity, a concern many Pentecostals share, Pentecostal spirituality seems to imply a "metaphysic of participation in the action of God by God's grace."⁶⁰ It is not that "at root God

---

52. Ibid., 595.
53. Chris E. W. Green, *Foretasting the Kingdom: Toward a Pentecostal Theology of the Lord's Supper* (Cleveland: CPT Press, 2012).
54. See Chris E. W. Green, "Sacraments: Rites in the Spirit for the Presence of Christ," in *The Routledge Handbook of Pentecostal Theology*, ed. Wolfgang Vondey (New York: Routledge, 2020), 311–20. See also Chris E. W. Green, "'If I Could Just Touch the Hem of His Garment': Mediation in Pentecostal Spirituality and Theology," *Journal of Pentecostal Theology* 30, no. 1 (2020): 20–9 and "The Altar and the Table: A Proposal for Wesleyan and Pentecostal Eucharistic Theologies," *Wesleyan Theological Journal* 53, no. 2 (2018): 54–61.
55. See Andrew Ray Williams, *Washed in the Spirit: Toward a Pentecostal Theology of Water Baptism* (Cleveland: CPT Press, 2021). See also *Lutherans and Pentecostals in Dialogue* (Strasbourg: Institute for Ecumenical Research, 2010), 16–17.
56. Macchia, "Is Footwashing the Neglected Sacrament," 240.
57. Archer, "Nourishment for Our Journey," 86.
58. *CD* IV/4, 102.
59. Yong, *The Spirit Poured Out on All Flesh*, 159.
60. Frank Macchia, *Baptized in the Spirit: A Global Pentecostal Theology* (Grand Rapids: Zondervan, 2006), 71.

[is] acting in the place of men and men in the place of God,"⁶¹ but that by the Spirit, Christ has made it possible for human beings genuinely to share in the one and at-one-ing activity of God. Believers are participants in and co-laborers with Christ in the Spirit. In summary, then, Pentecostal spirituality, at least in many of its forms, celebrates the washing rite as truly a sacramental act, one in which God does exactly what the signs that comprise the event promise God will do.

The Many-Splendored Heart of Pentecostal Sacramentality

Understood in this way, Pentecostal sacramentality, like Pentecostal spirituality in general, arises from and depends upon expectations of divine encounter.⁶² As Jamie Smith explains, at the heart of Pentecostal theology and spirituality is "a deep sense of expectation and an openness to surprise." Pentecostals are marked by "a position of radical openness to God, and in particular, openness to God doing something *differently* or *new*."⁶³ Hence, unlike the Barth of *CD* IV/4, Pentecostals insist on the presence—and so the present-tense activity—of Christ at the Table. As Hollenweger argues, in spite of the fact that Pentecostals come to the Eucharist out of a sense of duty—the chapter on sacraments in his book is entitled "To Them that Obey Him"—they nonetheless expect "communion with the Son of God" and in that communion "the strengthening of their inner being, strength in everyday temptations, and the healing of sickness."⁶⁴ This expectation came to the fore in Lutheran–Pentecostal dialogues. Acknowledging that sacramental practice varies in Pentecostal and charismatic communities around the world, the official statement concludes: "Because of their consistent emphasis on the real presence of God in worship, Pentecostals expect the Lord to be present in his Supper."⁶⁵

Pentecostals, like all Pietists, "wait" on the Lord, whether in silence and stillness, in penitent self-examination, or in works of mercy and justice. As Vickers rightly notes, they are committed to this waiting in whatever form it takes, "within and beyond the sacramental life of the church, through speaking and through ritual touching, in the work of the ordained and in the lives of the laity."⁶⁶ This waiting is not uncertain or insecure. Indeed, it is not a waiting *for* God to act so much as a waiting *in* the act of God. Not a waiting to see *if* God will "move," but a waiting *as* God is "moving," a way of giving time for the work of God to "sink in," to go deep.

---

61. *CD* IV/4, 106.

62. See James K. A. Smith, *Thinking in Tongues: Pentecostal Contributions to Christian Philosophy* (Grand Rapids: Eerdmans, 2010), 33.

63. Ibid.

64. Hollenweger, *The Pentecostals*, 386.

65. *Lutherans and Pentecostals in Dialogue*, 17.

66. Jason Vickers, "Holiness and Mediation: Pneumatology in Pietist Perspective," *International Journal of Systematic Theology* 16, no. 2 (April 2014): 192–206, here 204.

Hollenweger long ago recognized that Pentecostals come to the Table because of their love for Jesus. He holds that this Christ-piety is, in fact, the distinctive character of Pentecostal sacramentality, which is marked by

> a combination of the "love of Jesus," that is love for the faithful friend who is called Jesus, "blood and wounds mysticism," an absorption in the suffering and death of Jesus, and a looking forward to the coming marriage feast with Jesus, in the experience of the sacrament.[67]

The "blood and wound mysticism" focuses on Jesus' cross, as well as believers' participation in his suffering, death, and resurrection,[68] and just for that reason turns its attention to the Eucharist. In that light, D. W. Kerr's sermon in preparation for Communion service at the 1916 General Council of the Assemblies of God is seen to be exemplary.[69] As always, the emphasis lies on the present-tense effectiveness of Christ's work.

> This meal is intended not only for our spiritual, but for our physical benefit. Here is good news for the sick. You are invited to a meal for your health. As you are eating in faith you can receive healing for your body. If you cannot use the past tense and say "By His stripes ye were healed," turn it into the present tense and declare, "By His stripes I am healed." You say perhaps "I hope to be healed." What time in the future will you be healed? God brings the future down to the present tense.

Kerr is clear: the Eucharist does work as a memorial, and the emblems do in fact represent Christ's broken body and shed blood. Symbolically, the feast points both back, to Christ's death, and forward, to his return. Kerr also insists, however, that the focus must remain always on the Supper's "distinct present aspect," which is paramount: "Here is the present tense of Calvary. We have come to a place of freshness, the result of Calvary. What is it? Life and life more abundant!"[70]

---

67. Hollenweger, *The Pentecostals*, 387.
68. As the official ecumenical statement reveals, this is one of many resonances between Pentecostal and catholic spiritualities. See Wolfgang Vondey, ed., *Pentecostalism and Christian Unity Vol. Two* (Eugene: Wipf and Stock, 2013), 183. Not coincidentally, this may also be the true point of departure for Pentecostals from Barth, whose work is widely understood to be not only decidedly "Protestant" but also wholly opposed to mysticism—and not without reason! It may be, however, that Barth is denying not mysticism as such but only a particular form of spirituality, which idolizes "experience." See Austin Holmes, "Encountering Christ: Karl Barth and Mysticism," *Lumen et Vita* 8, no. 2 (2018): 27–39.
69. *Weekly Evangel* 162 (October 28, 1916), 4.
70. Ibid., 4–5.

There is nothing old or stale about this memorial feast, the fruit of the vine is not old, the shed blood is not aged, the bread is not stale, the Lord's body is not a mere thing of the past, the way is new and living. The thing most striking about the character of the feast is its presentness, not its pastness or its futureness. It has a present aspect, there is a sign of warmth, the blood is not cold and coagulated but flowing fresh from the wounded side of Jesus, "recently killed and yet living."[71]

Around the same time, in response to a reader's question about the possible benefits of taking the Supper, sometime editor and frequent contributor E. N. Bell provides a detailed explanation of his view of the Eucharist, complete with a brief overview of four historical positions. Catholics, he says, believe that the bread when it is blessed by the priest is "transmuted into the literal living body of Christ," so that "in partaking we actually eat the body of Christ and literally drink His blood, and so get eternal life by partaking of the supper." Bell rejects this teaching. He rejects the doctrine of consubstantiation, as well, which he attributes to the Episcopalians and Lutherans. The third position, proposed by "the noted theologian Zwingle" [sic], understands Communion as "simply a Memorial Feast," in which "the only good received in partaking [is] in bringing vividly to memory the truths of Christ's atoning death." In this view, as Bell understands it, neither Christ's body nor his blood are present at the Table but are only "remembered and appropriated." Bell acknowledges some truth in this position, but he finally rejects it, too: "It lowers our view of the Lord's Supper and makes it a thing too common." The fourth stance Bell attributes to Calvinists, especially Presbyterians, who maintain, he says, that the elements remain unchanged, but Christ is truly, spiritually present to the celebrants. Having provided this rough overview, Bell ventures his own view:

> there is a good deal of truth in this spiritual view. In fact there is some truth in nearly every view of it. But I do not believe the physical Christ is present in the bread nor in the cup. I believe the loaf is still real bread and the cup still only the fruit of the vine. I believe it is a memorial, for Jesus said, "This do in memory of me." But it is more than a memorial feast. Jesus is there in the Spirit to bless, quicken, uplift and heal; but what benefit the partaker will receive depends much on his spiritual discernment; his faith and his appropriation from the spiritually present living Christ.[72]

In sum, then, this is the heart of Pentecostal sacramentality: "Jesus is here in the Spirit." And where Jesus is present, his healing, delivering, sanctifying, and empowering work continues unbroken and unstinted.[73] If Barth denies *this*, then Pentecostals are bound to disagree with him.

---

71. Ibid., 5.
72. *Weekly Evangel* 146 (July 1, 1916), 8.
73. This affirmation is remarkably close to Calvin's view, which affirms that "the humanity of Christ, though absent from the bread and wine in one sense, is nevertheless

Conclusion

It is not at all clear that Barth does deny it, however, notwithstanding the fact that the passages in *CD* IV/4 seem to have that effect. It may be, as some have suggested, that Barth embraces de facto what he disallows de jure.[74]

And certainly, taken as a whole, Barth's theology is not at all anti-sacramental. Earlier, in his treatment of "the order of the community" in *CD* IV/2, explaining why and how Christians gather in Christ's name, he says that they come and go to the Lord's Supper, finding together in their shared eating and drinking "the common nourishment of them all":

> it is He, Jesus Christ, who brings them to it, who invites them, who is the Lord and Host, who is Himself, indeed, their food and drink. It is thus a question of their nourishment by Him. It takes placed in the fact that, as often as they here eat and drink together, He proffers and gives Himself to them as the One He is, as the One who is absolutely theirs, and conversely, that He continually makes them what they are, absolutely His. He strengths and upholds them in their existence as those whom He, the Crucified and Risen, accompanies in the valley of the shadow. . . . He constitutes Himself their preparation to attain this. It is to be noted how the event of his own life is reflected and repeated in the event of the Supper (as in that of confession and baptism). In remembrance of Him there takes place here and now exactly the same as took place there and then between Himself and His first disciples, immediately prior to His death and resurrection.[75]

I believe it is precisely in this description of Communion as the event in which the living Christ nourishes his community that Barth's sacramental theology is most promising for Pentecostal reflection and construction.[76] So, bearing that in mind, I offer a few proposals for the sake of the continuing conversation, proposals which I take to be appropriate to the Pentecostal spirituality that has shaped me in and for the experience of God.

First, I am convinced that we should affirm Barth's emphasis on the person and work of Christ even while we challenge his claim that Christ's death is the only sacrament or mystery.[77] We should say, instead, that Christ's life and death and life-from-death are the founding, generative mystery that in turn renders baptism

---

present in another." See David Steinmetz, *Calvin in Context*, 2nd ed. (Oxford: Oxford University Press, 2010), 177.

74. See, for example, Neder, *Participation in Christ*, 83–4.

75. *CD* IV/2, 703.

76. Thanks to Frank Macchia for pointing me to this passage and its connections to Pentecostal spirituality and theology.

77. Some of the trouble may be in the way this term itself is used. For my part, "sacrament" refers to an act, instituted by Christ, that by the Spirit accomplishes what the signs of the act promise the Father has done and will do.

and the Eucharist mysterious. These rites are sacramental only and precisely because Christ in the Spirit takes them as his own acts. In the language of the Fourth Gospel, it is because Christ has "gone to the Father" and come again in the Spirit that the church can do "greater works," works which are all-at-once the doing of both Christ and his community because they are the work of Christ in the community. Just as the Word's words are not his but the Father's, the community's words are not theirs but the Word's (Jn 14:11-13).[78]

Second, because "the divine action is never to be taken for granted in anything we do," not even in the sacramental rites, Barth is right to challenge any assumption that "the grace of God is at the church's disposal," and to maintain that personal faith is essential for the sacraments' effectiveness.[79] But, again, he seems to be assuming a radical cleavage between divine and human action when what is needed is a distinction that does not imply separation. Returning to the Johannine idiom, we can say that what the vine does and what the branches do together make one work, even if the branches cannot possibly do what the vine does. And there is no way for us to receive the gifts the vine offers except by receiving them from the branches. It is true that grace is not at anyone's disposal—that is precisely what makes it grace! But what grace would it be if it were not shared?

Third, and again in the same vein, we are also right to echo Barth's insistence on the priority of God's act. But we should go on to insist that that priority does not exclude the real participation of believers in God's ever-new work among us. Indeed, that priority is precisely what secures the integrity of what it brings about. It is precisely as God is "all in all" that creation is itself! We can, then, agree with Barth in one sense when he says, "Man's salvation is the work of God. It is therefore not the work of man."[80] But of course the God whose work saves us, the God who is our salvation, *is* human! As Barth himself says.

> It is precisely God's deity which, rightly understood, includes his humanity.... How could God's deity exclude His humanity, since it is God's freedom for love and thus His capacity to be not only in the heights but also in the depths, not only great but also small, not only in and for Himself but also with another distinct from Him, and to offer Himself to him?[81]

---

78. George Hunsinger (*The Eucharist and Ecumenism: Let Us Keep the Feast* [Cambridge: Cambridge University Press, 2008], 17) argues that T. F. Torrance, one of Barth's students, saw the truth of sacramental participation in a way his teacher never did: "'The action of the Supper', wrote Torrance, 'is not another action than that which Christ has already accomplished on our behalf, and which is proclaimed in the Gospel.' It is rather the very same action in a new and sacramental form."

79. Macchia, *Baptized in the Spirit*, 72.

80. Karl Barth, *The Knowledge of God and the Service of God According to the Teaching of the Reformation* (Eugene: Wipf & Stock, 2005), 90.

81. Barth, *The Humanity of God* (Louisville: Westminster John Knox Press, 1996), 46, 49. Strikingly, it is precisely at this point that Barth is most critical of Calvin: "It is when

So, we have to say that precisely because our salvation is solely the work of the God who is human, God can freely include our work in—and *as*—his own. God has no rivals, and just for that reason can take on the nature of his creatures and covenant himself to them as his coequal co-laborers. In other words, precisely because the saving events of Jesus' life are Spirit-grounded and not in any way dependent on the church's faithfulness, ecclesial practices can be seen for what they are promised to be: the ongoing incarnational work of the God who is grace. Here, we can take Barth at his own word: "God wants man to be His creature. Furthermore, He wants him to be His partner."[82] Nowhere is that truer than in the sacramental rites, precisely because those rites reenact the acts of Christ's own life. That, and nothing less than that, is what the Spirit of Pentecost accomplishes.

---

we look at Jesus Christ that we know decisively that God's deity does not exclude, but includes His *humanity*. Would that Calvin had energetically pushed ahead on this point in his Christology, his doctrine of God, his teaching about predestination, and then logically also in his ethics! His Geneva would then not have become such a gloomy affair. His letters would then not have contained so much bitterness." Arguably, however, Barth himself stops short of following the truth to its end. At least this is the case made by some of his students, including especially Robert Jenson. So, in his earliest work (*Alpha and Omega* [New York: Thomas Nelson, 1963], 168), Jenson acknowledges the difference between his work and Barth's, a difference that he continued to explore for the remainder of his long career: "For Barth, God's history with man is the history of God and man 'in' the person of Jesus Christ. . . . Might it not be that the history of God with man in Jesus Christ is not in the first place God's history with man-in-Christ but the history of God-in-Christ with mankind? Might it not be that the starting point is not what God does *to* Jesus but what He does *through* Jesus? Might it not be that Jesus' history indeed creates and determines all history, but less as the history which *includes* all history than as the history which *makes* all history?"

82. Barth, *The Humanity of God*, 80–1.

CONTRIBUTORS

Peter Althouse (PhD, University of St. Michael's College at the University of Toronto) is Professor of Theology and Religion and PhD Director at Oral Roberts University in Tulsa, OK, USA. His publications include *Spirit of the Last Days: Pentecostal Eschatology in Conversation with Jürgen Moltmann*, *Catch the Fire: Soaking Prayer and Charismatic Renewal*, and *Pentecostals and the Body*.

William Atkinson (PhD, the University of Edinburgh) recently retired from the London School of Theology in London, UK. His publications include *Baptism in the Spirit: Luke-Acts and the Dunn Debate* and *Trinity after Pentecost*.

David J. Courey (PhD, McMaster Divinity College) is Lecturer in Systematic Theology at Continental Theological Seminary in Brussels, Belgium. He is the author of *What Has Wittenberg to Do with Azusa? Luther's Theology of the Cross and Pentecostal Triumphalism*.

Terry L. Cross (PhD, Princeton Theological Seminary) is Distinguished Professor of Systematic Theology and Dean of the School of Theology & Ministry at Lee University in Cleveland, TN, USA. He is Translation Fellow at the Center for Barth Studies, Princeton Theological Seminary, and the author of *Dialectic in Karl Barth's Doctrine of God* as well as *The People of God's Presence: An Introduction to Ecclesiology*.

Andrew K. Gabriel (PhD, McMaster Divinity College) is Associate Professor of Theology and VP Academic at Horizon College and Seminary, an affiliated college of the University of Saskatchewan, in Saskatoon, Canada. He is the author of four books including *The Lord is the Spirit* and *Barth's Doctrine of Creation*.

Chris E. W. Green (DMin, Oral Robert University; PhD, Bangor University) is Professor of Public Theology at Southeastern University (Lakeland, FL, USA). He is the author most recently of *All Things Beautiful: An Aesthetic Christology*.

Frank D. Macchia (DTheol, University of Basel) is Professor of Theology at Vanguard University in Costa Mesa, CA, USA, and Associate Director of the Centre of Pentecostal and Charismatic Studies for Bangor University in Bangor, UK. He is a prolific writer, including the books *Jesus the Spirit Baptizer: Christology* in Light of Pentecost and Tongues of Fire: A Systematic Theology of the Christian Faith.

Michael J. McClymond (PhD, University of Chicago) is Professor of Modern Christianity at Saint Louis University in St. Louis, MI, USA. His most recent book is the two-volume The Devil's Redemption: An Interpretation of the Christian Debate over Universal Salvation.

Todd B. Pokrifka (PhD, University of St. Andrews, Scotland) is Co-director of the Institute for Community Transformation, a ministry of Frontier Ventures, in Pasadena, CA, USA. He is the author of Redescribing God: The Roles of Scripture, Tradition and Reason in Karl Barth's Doctrines of Divine Unity, Constancy and Eternity.

David A. Reed (PhD, Boston University) is Professor Emeritus of Pastoral Theology and Research Professor at Wycliffe College, an affiliated college of the University of Toronto (Toronto, Canada). He is the author of In Jesus' Name: The History and Beliefs of Oneness Pentecostals, and numerous book chapters on global Oneness Pentecostalism.

Tony Richie (DMin, Asbury Theological Seminary; PhD, London School of Theology/Middlesex University) is Associate Professor of Theology at Pentecostal Theological Seminary (Cleveland, TN, USA) as well as the co-editor of PTS Press. In addition to numerous contributions to various volumes and journals, he is the author/editor of eight books including Essentials of Pentecostal Theology and Saved, Delivered, and Healed.

Lisa P. Stephenson (PhD, Marquette University) is Professor of Systematic Theology at Lee University in Cleveland, TN, USA. She is the author of Dismantling the Dualisms for American Pentecostal Women in Ministry, which won the 2013 Pneuma Book Award, and has published various essays in other edited volumes and journals.

Gary Tyra (DMin, Fuller Seminary) is Professor of Biblical and Practical Theology at Vanguard University in Costa Mesa, CA, USA. He has also served as the senior pastor for three churches and is the author of nine books including The Holy Spirit in Mission and Introduction to Spirituality.

Christian T. Collins Winn (PhD, Drew University) is Teaching Minister and Theologian in Residence at Meetinghouse Church in Edina, MN, USA, and Adjunct Professor of Religion at Augsburg University in Minneapolis, MN, USA. He is the author or editor of eleven books, including Jesus, Jubilee, and the Politics of God's Reign.

INDEX

analogia entis 14
angels 124–5, 130–2, 141, 212
anointed, anointing 29–30, 38, 41, 44, 90, 99, 101, 117, 236
anthropocentrism, anthropocentric 14, 16, 28, 203
anthropology 91–8, 101, 103–4, 115, 190
anthropomorphism 57
apophatic 69–70
apostolic 40, 55, 57, 178, 238
Assemblies of God 48–50, 54, 59, 241
atonement 108, 115–16, 119–20, 144, 148, 150, 153
Azusa Street Revival 3, 181

baptism, baptismal, baptized 42, 49–50, 52–4, 56–8, 61, 72, 87, 98–9, 114, 117–18, 156, 184, 230, 232–7, 239, 243
    fire 4, 107, 111, 115–17, 119
    Holy Spirit 4, 26, 72, 74, 77, 86–7, 107–11, 114–22, 148, 153–5, 177, 180, 183–5, 187–90, 192–3, 200, 206–7, 210–11, 221, 235

camp meeting 49, 52, 54
Chalcedonianism 97–100, 152
charismatic, charisma 9, 22, 31, 124, 126, 128, 136, 138, 195, 199, 205–7, 209, 211, 224, 238
christocentric 24–5, 28, 31, 33–4, 49, 53, 57–8, 61, 80–1, 84, 109, 143, 174, 200–1, 203, 232, 234
community 22–3, 26, 32, 42–3, 81, 83, 92, 193, 203–5, 207, 210, 216, 219–24, 227–9, 237, 243–4
confessional attitude 12
constancy, divine 71–2
consubstantiation 242

deliverance 129, 225, 242
demons, demonic 124–8, 130–8, 140–2
discernment 36, 129
discipleship 43, 207
divine attributes, divine perfections 4, 63–8, 70, 75
divine self-giving 204–6, 209, 211
doctrine of God 64–5, 67, 75, 217, 245
dogmatics, dogma 11–13, 15, 58–9, 62–4, 66, 93, 233, 235
dogmatic theology 11, 16, 202

ecclesiology, ecclesiastical, ecclesial 5, 34, 42, 119, 174, 213–22, 224, 226–7, 229–31, 234, 245
ecstatic 21, 27, 190, 199
egalitarian 230
election, elected 4, 78–90
embodiment 59
encounter 9, 16, 19–21, 23, 25, 27, 30, 35–8, 40–1, 43–4, 56, 96–7, 102, 155, 210–11, 221, 240
eschatology, eschatological 5, 25–6, 90, 109, 116, 118, 123, 146, 148–9, 157, 177–80, 183, 188–9, 191, 193
eternity, eternal 39, 55, 59, 61, 64, 71–4, 79, 81, 84, 87–90, 95, 112–13, 116, 161, 168, 205, 217–18
ethics, ethical 145, 151–2, 157, 181, 188
eucharist 41, 235, 239–42, 244
Evangelical 12, 31, 33, 44, 49, 51–2, 54, 65, 84
existentialism 202–3
exorcism 125, 127–9, 137
experience, experiential 9, 13, 15–16, 18–22, 25–8, 30, 36, 56, 72, 194, 225

freedom   34–5, 37, 43, 70, 72, 75, 77, 79, 82, 97, 110–14, 123, 132, 153–4, 161, 182, 191–2, 212, 217, 226
Full Gospel   1, 9, 22, 72, 84, 178
fundamentalist, fundamentalism   51

glossolalia   1, 188–92, 194, 199–201, 206, 209–10
guidance, divine   89

healing, heal, healed   26, 68, 72, 180, 192, 199, 206, 242
Hearing Church   12
hell   131, 180
human agency   143–5, 150–3, 157
hypostatic union   113–14, 148

imago Dei, image of God   91, 95–6, 169, 190
immanence   63, 87
immutability   4, 63, 67, 71–3, 75–7, 111
impassibility   4, 63, 67–72, 75–7, 111
incarnation, incarnate   4, 25, 32–3, 39–40, 53, 59, 71, 73–4, 94–5, 104, 111–15, 119–21, 147, 157, 193, 211, 221, 227, 245
indwelling (of the Holy Spirit)   32–3, 53, 156, 203, 228
inerrancy   14
infallibility   14
infralapsarians   80, 84

justification   148, 152–3, 205, 216, 224

Logos Christology   97–8, 146, 148, 157
Lord's Prayer   181, 184–6
Lord's Supper   234–40, 242–3

mercy   67, 76
miracle, miraculous   16, 24, 38, 40, 56, 102, 125–6, 153, 203, 206, 226, 228
mission   214–16, 219–20, 222–3, 228–9
Modalism   59–60
mysticism, mystical   168, 203, 228, 234, 237, 241

natural theology   5, 11–12, 14, 161–6
neo-Pentecostalism   22, 128–9

neo-Protestantism   14
New Testament   22
nothingness, Nihil, *das Nichtige*   125–6, 133–6, 142

omnipresent   64, 73, 75
Oneness Pentecostalism   4, 48–52, 54–7, 59–61, 65–6, 108–9

Pentecost   1, 4, 19, 52, 69, 74–5, 102–3, 109, 111, 116, 119–23, 149, 173, 178, 189–90, 220, 227
Pentecostal Assemblies of the World   50–1
Pentecostalism, Classical   18
pentecostal theology   18, 21, 27–8, 63, 68, 71, 75–6, 108, 157, 169, 172, 177, 178, 216, 232
Pietism   51, 54, 176
pluralism   164–5, 174
pneumatological expectancy   31
pneumatological realism   3, 25, 30–5, 37, 44
prayer   38, 69, 138, 184–8, 193, 199, 208
preaching   29, 30, 32, 35–8, 40–2, 44
predestination   78–9, 81–3
pre-millennial theology, pre-millennial dispensationalism   51, 180–1
proclamation   30, 35–44, 56, 110, 208, 211
prophecy, prophetic   27, 29, 35–6, 38, 40–3, 50, 152, 195, 199, 206, 224, 239
prophetic preaching   3, 30, 35, 40, 42–4
Protestantism, liberal-modern   15

rationalism, rationality   24, 28
reason   13, 15, 18, 21, 28
reconciliation   150–3, 216–17, 225
reformation   41, 215
reformed   12, 157
resurrection   25–6, 67, 109, 118, 120–3, 127, 151, 183, 191, 211, 232, 234, 237, 239, 241
revelation   3, 5, 11, 13, 15, 25–7, 30, 32, 35–7, 48–9, 54–62, 64, 76, 115, 160–7, 169–70, 190, 194, 203–4, 210, 217–18

divine   5, 161, 166, 168
  natural   160–70
  self   15–16, 27, 32, 36–8, 40, 165
  universal   166
revival   47–8, 50

Sabellianism   59–60
sacrament, sacramental   6, 41–2, 110, 118, 210, 214, 229–30, 232–45
sacramental preaching   41–2
salvation   5, 22, 25–6, 52–3, 58, 61, 80–1, 150, 153–4, 202–3, 213, 221, 229, 232, 244–5
sanctification   19, 108, 145, 151–6, 216, 224, 227, 242
Satan, devil   5, 124–8, 130–42
scripture   13, 18–24, 28, 30, 40–1, 52, 55, 57, 60, 84
secularity   16
sermon   43–4, 49
service   39
soteriological objectivism   25
soteriology   144–5, 147–8, 151, 157, 169, 200, 216, 229
sovereignty, divine   78–9, 144, 155, 159, 230
Spirit Christology   98–9, 101, 107, 122, 146–51, 157–9

Spirit soteriology   148–9
spiritual warfare   128, 137–8
subordination   14
substitutionary atonement   51
supralapsarians   80, 84

testimony   22, 84, 143
theological realism   31–3, 37
theology of religions   160–1, 166, 170–1, 174
third article   33–4, 40, 66, 76, 145, 201
tongues   26, 69, 102, 177, 180, 187, 190–2, 199, 206–12
tradition   13, 18–21, 23, 27–8, 53, 58
transcendence   59, 63, 70, 160
transubstantiation   238
Trinity, triune, trinitarian   16, 24, 30, 32–3, 47–55, 58–60, 63–6, 68, 71, 73–6, 81, 85–8, 95–7, 99, 113, 146–7, 152, 156–7, 172–3, 188, 202–4, 214, 216–22, 227–8

universalism   81–2

Wesley, Wesleyan   78, 199, 232
Wesleyan Quadrilateral   3, 13
witness   9, 12, 16–17, 27, 40, 42, 76, 143, 160, 214, 223–7, 229

www.ingramcontent.com/pod-product-compliance
Lightning Source LLC
Chambersburg PA
CBHW050137240426
43673CB00043B/1701